The Igbo
People, History and Worldview

Adonis & Abbey Publishers Ltd
24 Old Queen Street, London SW1H 9HP United Kingdom
Website: http://www.adonis-abbey.com
E-mail Address: editor@adonis-abbey.com

Nigeria:
Plot 2560, Hassan Musa Katsina Street, Asokoro, Abuja, Nigeria
Tel: +234 (0) 7058078841/08052035034
Website: http://www.adonis-abbey.com
E-mail Address: editor@adonis-abbey.com

Copyright 2023 © Dons Eze & Chinedu Ochinanwata

British Library Cataloguing-in-Publication Data
A catalogue record for this book is available from the British Library

ISBN: 9781913976224

The moral right of the author has been asserted

All rights reserved. No part of this book may be reproduced, stored in a retrieval system or transmitted at any time or by any means without the prior permission of the publisher

The Igbo
People, History and Worldview

Dons Eze & Chinedu Ochinanwata

Table of Contents

Introduction 11

Chapter One
A Survery of The Igbo Nation 15
Who Are The Igbo? *15*
Geographical Location of the Igbo *16*
Igbo Communities Outside Core Igbo States *17*
The Igbo Languages *18*
Igbo Political And Social Organization *19*
Some Pre-Colonial Igbo Kingdoms *23*
The Nri Kinship *24*
The Onitsha Kinship system *25*
The Igbo And The Warrant Chieftaincy *26*
New Kingship System In Igboland *28*

Chapter Two
The Igbo Worldview 35
Introduction *35*
The Igbo View Of The Cosmos Or The Universe *35*
The Igbo Justice System *40*
Basic Igbo Customs And Tradition *42*
The Ọzọ Title System *42*
The Igbu Ichi Culture *44*
The Igbo Masquerade System *44*
Igbo Kola Nut (Ọjị Igbo) *45*
Iri-ji Ndịgbo (New Yam Festival) *48*
Igbo Men *49*
Igbo Women *49*
Igbo Apprenticeship System (Ịgba Bọyị) *50*
Alụsị / Arụsị *51*
Ikenga *51*
The Osu Caste System *55*
Igbo Mythology *56*
Igbo Pottery *56*
Uli *57*
Carved doors *57*
Mbari *58*
Igbo music *58*
Igbo Art *59*
Traditional Attire *59*
Modern Attire *59*
Igbo Calendar (Ịguafọ Igbo)/ Agụmafọ Igbo *60*

Naming of Children After Market Days *61*
The Igbo And Crisis Of Cultural Identity *61*
The Igbo Renaissance *65*

Chapter Three
Traditions of Igbo Origin 69
Introduction *69*
The Middle East Oriented Theory Origin of the Igbo *70*
The Claims of Jewish Ancestry *70*
The Igbo-Egyptian Connection *81*
The Ado-na-Idu Hypothesis *84*
The Aboriginal Version *92*
The Autochthonous or The Original Settlers Version *99*

Chapter Four
The Igbo Diaspora 111
Introduction *111*
Who are the Igbo Diaspora? *112*
The Transatlantic Slave Trade *113*
Life in Foreign Lands *118*
The Igbo in the Transatlantic Slave Trade *121*
Igbo Cultural Influence in the Americas *126*
Towards A Global Igbo Solidarity *130*

Chapter Five
The Igbo and Their Neighbours 139
Introduction *139*
Okrika *140*
Kalabari *141*
Ikwerre *142*
Opobo *142*
Annang *143*
Ibibio *144*
Efik *144*
Idoma *146*
Igala *147*
Indigenous Igbo People in Kogi State *149*
Bini *152*
Yoruba *154*

Chapter Six
The Igbo In Nigeria 165
Panoramic View Of Nigerian Environment *165*
Some Pre-colonial Traditional Institutions *166*

Kenem-Borno Empire *166*
The Hausa-Fulani Emirate *167*
The Yoruba States *167*
The Bini Kingdom *167*
The Nri Kingdom *168*
Akwa-Akpa *168*
The Igbo and the Delta States *169*
Contact with Europe *169*
Scramble for Africa *172*
Establishment of Military Force *174*
Making of Nigeria *175*
Unholy Wedlock *177*
Struggle for Nigerian Independence *180*
The Post-Independence Crises *185*
The January 1966 Coup and the Nigeria-Biafra War *190*
The Wonders And Miracles Of Biafra War...*194*
How Enugu Rangers Won the War for the Vanquished *199*

Chapter Seven
The Igbo in Nigerian Politics...205
The Dramatic Rise of the Igbo *205*
Inter-ethnic Rivalries *210*
The Igbo as Nigerian Guinea Pigs *212*
The Underdevelopment of Igboland *220*
The Igbo and Their Quest to Rule Nigeria *222*

- o   *Emergence of Dr. Nnamdi Azikiwe*..*223*
- o   *The 1959 Pre-Independence Election* *227*
- o   *The Politics of The Second Republic* *229*
- o   *The Fourth Republic* *230*

Chapter Eight
Quest For a United Igbo Front..233
Introduction...*233*
The Igbo State Union *234*
The Post-war Era *239*
Ohanaeze Ndigbo *240*
The World Igbo Congress *244*
Ala Development Igbo Foundation *245*
MASSOB *246*
Biafra Zionist Movement *251*
Indigenous People Of Biafra (IPOB) *253*

Chapter Nine
Way Forward For The Igbo 261
Introduction *261*
Between the New and the Old Brigades *263*
The Igbo Outside Nigeria *265*
The Igbo Inside Nigeria *268*

Chapter Ten
The Igbo Icons 273
Introduction *273*
Olaudah Equiano *273*
Henri Christophe *275*
Africanus Horton *279*
Edward Blyden *282*
Edward James Roye *285*
Jaja of Opobo *286*
Onyeama N'Eke *290*
Nneta Egbe Nwanyerxwa (1929 Aba Women Leader) *293*
Simon Ọnwụ *296*
Robert Benjamin Ageh Wellesley Cole *297*
Nnamdi Azikiwe *298*
Nwafor Orizu *303*
Dennis Osadebay *305*
Mbonu Ojike *306*
Michael Okpara *309*
Akanu Ibiam *311*
Johnson Aguiyi Ironsi *313*
Chukwuma Nzeogwu *315*
Chukwuemeka Odumegwu Ojukwu *317*
Charles Dadi Onyeama *319*
Dick Tiger *320*
Alvan Ikoku *323*
Kenneth Dike *324*
Chike Obi *325*
Chinua Achebe *327*
F.C. Ogbalu *328*
Ngozi Okonjo-Iweala *332*
Holy Nweje *333*
Cyprian Iwene Tansi *333*
Francis Cardinal Arinze *339*

Appendices
Identity Crisis In Rivers State: The 1958 Willink Commission Report *343*

How Igbo Women Used Petitions To Influence British Colonial Authorities *347*
The Igbo Firsts *349*
The Igbo Spirit *350*
Nso Ala (Abomination) In Igboland *354*
Igbo Isiagu Symbol *355*

Bibliography 363

Index 369

Introduction

The book, **The Igbo: People, History And Worldview**, is the outcome of the authors' efforts to put together, for interested readers, the various aspects of the Igbo life, including their origin, way of life, achievements, and expectations as citizens of the world as a global village.

For unknown reasons, the Igbo have become the most misunderstood ethnic group by their neighbours who see them as greedy, troublesome, restless, and overzealous in their pursuit of "money". The Igbo detractors opine that these people must be stopped before dominating the rest of the ethnic groups. This profiling of the Igbo has affected the people's psyche' with the result that, if not checked, they (the Igbo) may begin to accept that they are the "problem" of their neighbours. This situation may also have some negative effects on present and future writers who would be tempted to portray the Igbo in a way that may lend credence to the opinions of Igbo detractors, in order to please the latter or gain acceptance or readership.

The belief that the Igbo should be silenced has resulted in a dearth of some basic information on the people because some aspects of their lives and way of life have not been brought to the fore just to please some sections of Nigeria. Therefore, it has become necessary for people to come together, unearth, and champion the portrayal of the life and ways of the Igbo as they really are, at least for record-keeping purposes. Hence, this book, which we see as our own little contribution, is to remind the Igbo about who they are, their enviable living patterns, worldview, exploits, achievements etc.

The book aims at serving as a veritable instrument to document such information as the Igbo origin, the Igbo in their traditional abode, and the Igbo in the Diaspora. The Igbo as an ethnic group do not live in isolation; hence we deemed it necessary to discuss who their neighbours are and how these neighbourhoods have affected the lives of the Igbo. The Igbo traditional ways of government have been given various interpretations. Though the people are republican in nature, one observes that they never operated under an absolute republican type of governance. This is not entirely the case because one observes elements of monarchy in some parts of Igboland, such as Onitsha, Arochukwu, and some parts of Delta State.

Given what happens in the political arena, within the Igbo nation, we discussed what transpired from the onset of Igbo political awareness and development, which gave rise to their participation, in the pre- and post-independence political activities in Nigeria.

Consequently, due to the upper hand that some early Igbo participants in the political arena in Nigeria exhibited before and after independence, rival ethnic groups tried to bring them down as they (the Igbo political fathers) were profiled as mentioned earlier. The systematic profiling of the Igbo and the unwarranted antagonism against the people resulted in the formation of some Igbo ethnic organisations, as discussed in the book.

The present generation of Igbo deserve to know who they are, how their struggle for survival as a people began, and where they are expected to be heading.

This work will be extremely beneficial to both the young and the old for self-identification and recognition. It is high time the Igbo went into themselves and stopped lamenting their losses and lack of inclusion in Nigerian affairs since the Nigerian Civil War (1967–1970). They should weather the storm and move ahead. They should stop lamenting their fate in Nigeria and start reconstructing, expanding, and developing their battered psyche', economy, towns, and cities, if they want to regain their lost glory. This is time to do this, and no other group will do it for them.

The debate over where the Igbo originated from should not overshadow the fact that they are one people. Although the discussion is constructive, it does not advance it, and adds no value to the development of Igboland. Why can't the Igbo make the best of their togetherness, and make optimal use of it for the betterment of generations yet to be born? Not to do this will be regrettable. They should, individually and collectively, make Igboness their watchword.

Despite the fact that some past historians, anthropologists, philosophers, and sociologists had at various times written a lot on some of the issues raised in this book (as acknowledged inside the text and in the references), the present work does not only revisit some of the past recorded issues but also brings recent ones into the spotlight-

situations and happenings in Igboland without prejudice to what had already been documented. We recognise that it has become imperative for the Igbo story to be told and retold from time to time for emphasis and enlightenment. Both old and new facts about the Igbo must be documented for a richer account of the history of the people.

Finally, this book is a clarion call to Igbo leaders and followers to recognize who they are, sit down, and reorganize themselves for better people integration, development, peace, and progress. Taa Ka Bu Gboo! (Now is the time!).

CHAPTER ONE

A Survey of the Igbo Nation

Who are the Igbo?

The Igbo, also called Ndigbo (local parlance), Eboes (Igbo Diaspora), and Ibos (anglicized), refer to one of the most resourceful and largest ethnic groups in Africa, whose homeland is in the south-central and south-eastern parts of Nigeria, but who equally maintain a strong presence in other parts of Nigeria, in addition to virtually every corner of the globe. The Igbo, a well-traveled people, are the second largest community in every Nigerian city behind the indigenous population.

The main characteristic feature of the Igbo is that the majority of them speak the Igbo language, which is divided into numerous regional dialects that are somewhat mutually intelligible with the larger "Igboid" cluster. The Igbo language forms part of the kwa language of the "Niger-Congo" which is spoken by various Nigerian ethnic groups.

It may be necessary to stress that the ability or inability to understand or speak the Igbo language is not a sufficient criterion for determining the Igboness of a person or for distinguishing the Igbo from the non-Igbo. This is because there are many people who do not speak or understand the Igbo language but who are Igbo, while there are also other people who speak and understand the Igbo language but are not Igbo. In other words, several factors are involved in determining whether a person is Igbo or not.

Igbo people are generally resourceful and hardworking. They are forward-looking, ingenious, creative, resilient, brave, strong-willed, and willing to take risks. Indeed, there is no part of Nigeria, and no corner of the globe, where you will not find Igbo people living and doing businesses, speaking the people's languages, and marrying their people. Igbo people are friendly, hospitable, and accommodating. They do not discriminate. A 19th century former Igbo slave boy, Olaudah Equiano (2013: 355–387), in his memoir described the Igbo people of his days as "happy clean people, without unemployment, without prostitution, without drunkards, and without beggars", while G.T. Basden (1938:6), an Anglican prelate, wrote in his book "Niger Ibos", that the "Igbo are very cheery, intelligent, virile, and loveable people with a wonderfully patient persistence to attain any desired goal, a natural astuteness born of necessity together with a loyalty which, though often begotten by fear redirected along the right lines, go far to make them a great nation".

In the same vein, pioneer Catholic cleric and evangelist, Bishop Joseph Shanahan, observed that "the Ibo has a child's winsomeness. He loves fun and banter. If you show him the good side of your character, he will show you the best side of his. The people know a good man when they see one. Their own souls aspire to goodness, and they have not stifled the aspiration. It is my firm conviction that we shall meet great numbers of our Ibos, pagans, and practically all our Catholics, in heaven" (Quoted in Eze, 2011:10).

As an ethnic group, the Igbo generally encompass several people of different backgrounds who are united mostly by language - Nri, Aro and slave trade. Language, because the majority of the people speak the Igbo language; Nri, because the Nri kingship system was the first in Nigeria, while the Nri people equally introduced the Ozo title system, which many Igbo communities subscribe to; Aro, because the Aro people were the harbingers of the ugly spectacle of European slave trade that took heavy tolls on many Igbo communities.

Geographical Location of the Igbo

Specifically, the Igbo homeland, or Igboland, is located east and west of the great River Niger, stretching from the north of the Niger Delta region through the thick belt of tropical rain forest and moving gradually to the quasi-grassland vegetation belt of the north. The area is surrounded on all sides by a host of large rivers and a large number of Nigerian ethnic groups such as the Edo, the Urhobo-Isoko, the Ijaw, the Ogoni, the Tiv, the Yako, the Idoma, the Igala, the Efik, and the Ibibio, each of which, perhaps in the remote past, were related to the Igbo.

In reality, Igboland encompasses a large portion of south-eastern Nigeria, mostly on the eastern side of the River Niger, and extends westward across the River Niger to the regions of Aniọcha, Ndokwa, Ụkwụanị and Ịka in the present-day Delta State, and some small parts of

Edo State. Its eastern side is terminated by the Cross River, although there are a few small Igbo settlements on the other side of the river. Its northern-most point enters the Savannah climate around the Nsukka area.

In 1591, the Igbo region of present-day Nigeria was depicted on the Portuguese world map as being inhabited by "some vigorous people whose deep culture celebrated energy, accomplishment, and wisdom", while two years later, in 1593, the same area, later called the "Bight of Biafra", appeared on the Spanish map (Nnamani, 2001).

The Bight of Biafra, or Mafra (named after the town, Mafra, in southern Portugal), between Capes Formosa and Lopez, is the most eastern part of the Gulf of Guinea. It contains the islands of Fernando Po (Equatorial Guinea), Prince's and St Thomas's. A 1710 map indicates that the region known as "Biafra" was located in present-day Cameroon. The Bight of Biafra extends east from the River Niger Delta region until it reaches Cape Lopez in Gabon.

Other rivers that flow into the bay include the Cross River, Ndian, Wouri, Sanaga, Nyong River, Ntem, Mbia, Mbini, Muni and Komo River. The main islands in the bay are Bioko and Príncipe, while other important islands are Ilhéu Bom Bom, Ilhéu Caroço, Elobey Grande, and Elobey Chico. Countries located at the Bight of Biafra are Nigeria (eastern coast), Cameroon, Equatorial Guinea (Bioko Island and Rio Muni), and Gabon (northern coast). The internationally unrecognised self-declared state of Ambazonia, also borders the Bight of Biafra.

In the present political configuration of Nigeria, Igboland comprises roughly the five constituent states of Abia, Anambra, Ebonyi, Enugu, and Imo States, with a reasonable number in Delta and Rivers states. Some small communities in Akwa Ibom, Benue, Cross River, Edo, and Kogi states make up the rest of the area.

Igbo Communities Outside Core Igbo States

Among Igbo communities outside the core Igbo states of the South East are Etche (Rivers State), Omuma (Rivers State), Ikwerre (Rivers State), Ekpeye (Rivers State), Obigbo (Rivers State), Ogba (Rivers State), Opobo (Rivers State), Ndoni (Rivers and Delta States), Aniocha

(Delta State), Ika (Delta State), Agbor (Delta State), Oshimili (Delta State), Ndokwa (Delta State), Ukwuani (Delta State), Asaba (Delta State), (Igbanke/Igboakiri (Edo State), Osekwenike, Abuetor and Eke Okpokri (in Sagbama area of Bayelsa State), Isobo (Abi LGA, Cross River State), Umuezekaoha (numbering over 300 villages in Benue State), Ibaji and Igalamela/Odolu LGAs in Kogi State. Eke Avurugo Community, Nwajala, Ubulie-Umueze, Ozara, and Umuoye, and many other Igbo-speaking communities are also in Kogi State. At least, the Igbo comprise fifty per cent or more of the Niger Delta region.

Altogether, Igboland has an estimated area of some 40,900 to 41,400 square kilometers. With a present population of between 60 million and 70 million inhabitants and a population density of between 140 and 390 inhabitants per square kilometre. Igboland is the most densely populated area in sub-Saharan Africa. It is estimated that more than one-third of the present Igbo population lives outside their homestead, both in Nigeria and other parts of the world.

The Igboid Languages

The Igboid languages are a component of the Niger Congo Civilisation, which originated in West Africa and gave rise to the emergence of Benue Kwa languages. Other languages that belong to this Kwa group are Yoruba, Asante, Wolof, Mandinka, etc. Igbo is a Bantu language, so also is Yoruba, Tiv, and most languages spoken in West Africa. In other words, most people in West Africa originated from the same ancestral group and began expanding and claiming different language identity groups.

When we say Igboid, we mean similar or resembling. The suffix "oid" in English basically means "resembling, having the likeness of, or expressing the basic characteristics of." Used together with "Igbo", "oid" then means "having the likeness of, or resembling, or expressing the basic characteristics of what we have come to know as 'Igbo'". "Igboid," therefore means exhibiting what we know as "typical 'Igbo'" features. In laymen's terms, it means "basically sounds 'Igbo'", or that it is "recognisable as a type of 'Igbo'".

Among the variants or Igbo dialects spoken in different communities are Arochukwu, spoken by some people in Abia State;

Ngwa, spoken in the southern part of Abia State; and Wawa, spoken by most people in Enugu and parts of Ebonyi States. Within the Wawa dialect itself, there are different variants among the Agbaja, Nkanu, Nsukka, Awgu, Ikwo, Izzi, Ezza Mgbo, and Afikpo groups. Enuani is spoken in some parts of Delta State, while Awka, Onitsha, Obosi, and Ogbaru in Anambra State have their own dialects. Ndoni in Rivers State have their own dialect, and Ukwuani in Anioma, the northern part of Delta State, and in some parts of the Ogba/Egbema/Ndoni Local Government Area of Rivers State.

Qthers are Ogba (also Oba), is spoken in Ogba Rivers State; Umuezeohaka, spoken in Ado, Oju, Obi and Okpoku LGAs of Benue State; Ekpeye, spoken in Rivers State; Ikwerre spoken by the Ikwerre people in Rivers State; Ohuhu dialect is spoken by the people of Umuahia, Abia State.

Owere dialect is spoken by the people of Owere, Imo State. Agbor dialect with Bini influence is spoken by the people of Ika South, Delta state. Some people in Owere and Umuahia, both in Imo and Abia, speak the Ibeku dialect.

Ohafia dialect is spoken by the people of Bende in Abia State. Idemili dialect is spoken by the people of Idemili North and South in Anambra State. The Mbaise dialect is spoken by the people of Mbaise in Imo State. The Egbema dialect is spoken in Rivers State/Imo State. Standard Izugbe dialect is spoken generally by all Igbo groups. Isuama is no longer spoken, it only existed in the work of Koelle (1854) in his Polyglotta Africana published in Sierra Leone.

Igbo Political and Social Organisations

Before the Europeans' arrival, Igbo people lived in clusters of individual family units that constituted kindreds (*umunna*). Several of these kindreds formed an Igbo village or town. Every member of an Igbo village was related to each other in one way or another, constituting a network of beings, such that what affected one equally affected the other. Members of William Balfour Baikie's expeditionary team that visited the area in 1854 observed that, "in Igboland, each person hails, as a sailor would say, from the particular district where he was born, but when away from home are Igbos, and yet considerable differences exist between different parts of this extensive country, and the dialects spoken also vary greatly" (Isichei, 1997:25)

The Igbo practised a common political system centred on the decentralisation of power and delegation of authority exercised by heads of family units and other title holders. As Nwosu (1977:18) rightly observed, "despite the absence of centralized and consolidated political authority, the Igbo had several similarities in matters of structures, norms, and customs". Decisions were taken by way of consensus after a free debate, to which the young, the elderly, and the titled men each contributed individually. Cyril Onwumechili (2000) tells us that

> Most Igbo governed themselves without giving power to chiefs or kings. They organised themselves into many independent village governments. Village councils and assemblies met periodically and could also be summoned as the need arose to discuss both internal and external affairs of the village. The councils might be limited to certain age grades, but the assemblies were for all and sundry. Every man could and did have his say on all matters under discussion. Nobody had any special privilege because of ancestry.

Therefore, for most communities in Igboland their primordial political organisation was republicanism, where every family was represented in the village assembly by its head or the oldest man. It was this village assembly, also known as the Council of Elders, that determined what happened in every Igbo community. The Council performed all legislative and judicial functions to keep the society functioning.

However, there were some notable individuals, who on account of their personal worth, status, or merit, like celebrated, warriors, holders of the prestigious Ọzọ title, powerful medicine men, members of secret societies, etc., who equally belonged to this Council.

Young men of fairly the same age, who organised themselves into groups, known as "age grades", "Otu ọgbọ" were responsible for the executive arm of government. The "Age Grade" system was a formidable force in Igboland and gave a legitimate platform for all adult males to present themselves and participate in community administration. It was the age grades that ensured that all laws enacted by the Council of Elders were faithfully implemented. These included the carrying out of communal works such as road construction and rehabilitation, market development, provision of security services, the sanctioning of erring community members and rewarding those who excelled in their various trades or vocations, as well as rendering assistance to people in difficulties, etc.

It was this "village republicanism", the democratic nature of Igbo society, or the fact that in Igboland, power did not reside in one single person, but in a collectivity of elders, that led to the common aphorism "Igbo Enwe Eze", (the Igbo have no kings).

But the Igbo have kings, since the concept of kingship was not alien to the primordial Igbo, as evidenced by the fact that in most communities in Igboland, people bear the name or title of "Eze" or King. For instance, In Igbo's society, whoever holds the ofo – a symbol of truth and justice – is regarded as the king – Eze-ji-ofo. Some people also bear names like Eze-na-gu (I desire to be king); Eze-ewu-zie (The king has arrived); Eze-ekwu-na m (May kingship never elude me); Eze-ako-n'obi (Kingship never lacks in a homestead); etc.

However, the Igbo "monarch" is not merely a product of his birth. He grows to earn it. The Igbo king equally knows that he does not possess absolute knowledge. He rules through consultation with the village assembly.

Onwumechili however equates "Igbo kingship" to "scientific culture" which, according to him, recognises "no kings and chiefs with divine knowledge." In Igbo, as in science, he says, "promotion is by achievement." And since everybody has the right to attend and express his views in a scientific seminar, in the Igbo village assembly, everybody has the freedom to express his views, and decisions are reached by consensus.

Specifically, in Igbo village assembly, there were no government or opposition parties. Every free member of the community belonged to the assembly through his accredited representative, that is, the head of his family unit. There, all members were free to air their views, and decisions are arrived at by consensus.

Amplifying this republicanism, Ebeku Mmaduaburochukwu (2016) affirmed that traditionally, the Igbo were egalitarian and had no kings.

"The original Igbo culture is egalitarian, and the word 'Eze' does not mean 'king' in the literal sense of the word, but 'priest'. According to him,

> The idea of kings, queens, princes, and princesses was recently adopted, during Ụga Azị (slave trade), the time when the enslavers and colonisers were scrambling for Africa. The word 'Eze' most likely, originated from the Nri priesthood culture of the Igbo... The reason the Igbo do not bow down is because Igbo culture did not originate from kingships, but from egalitarianism. When we say, 'Igbo Enwe Eze', the spirit of the people refers to the fact that the word 'Eze' has been corrupted from its original meaning.

Maduaburochukwu further posited that there were five original Igbo ancestors. These, according to him, were **Agbaja, Isu, Oru, Nri and Idu**. This was why they always say "Ise-e", (this does not mean "Amen") after praying. According to him, "...the Agbaja people were into agriculture and arts; the Isu people were into iron smithery; the Oru people knew all about water; the Nri people were known for priesthood and arts; and the Idu people were known for military science".

He further posited that the Igbo were aboriginals. That is to say, the Igbo did not originate from somewhere else than Igboland. The Igbo were the first to come into existence, he says. "*Ndi Igbo bu Ndi Mbu ... Ndi so Uwa se-nite*. They did not originate from a specific kingdom created by man, like that of the Yoruba. The name Igbo, "is a name of a forest God that traces his roots back to a seed God named **Adu**. Igbo *bụ nwa Adu*, which means that Igbo people were seed people - *Ụmụ Aja Ana*".

According to Maduaburochukwu, the Igbo people were elegant nomads in ancient times. "Even today, they are still elegant nomads. Their first home is a place known today as Igboland, but they like to live everywhere in the world. The people lived together through spiritual principles that the Eze was the custodian of.

"We also had an egalitarian governmental system known as *Osu*". Because the Igbo were egalitarian, it was extremely difficult for colonisers to penetrate Igboland when they arrived. So, they did what they knew best, attack Igbo from its foundation. They did this by changing the egalitarian system of rulership. This is one of the things that created the caste system known as *Osu*. And the masses were subjugated under kingships created by the colonisers. Up till today, these colonial kingdoms are still working against the Igbo, rather than working for them. "Our culture is not the culture of *Igwe-ka-Ala*, (superior-inferior relationship). Our culture is the culture of *Enu kwudo ana kwudo*" (live and let live), he affirmed.

Under colonial authority, the Igbo people became predominantly Christian, largely unscathed by the Islamic jihad that swept through several cities in Nigeria in the nineteenth century. Igbo people were predominantly farmers, traders, and artisans, while many of them now own businesses or work in the civil service. Despite their cultural diversity, Igbo people share a common basic culture in their language, which has a cluster of mutually intelligible dialects.

However, we observe, like Maduaburochukwu, that, despite the claim of republicanism, traditional Igbo society was far from egalitarianism, since some caste groups also existed. These included the ohu (slaves) and osu (cult slaves) systems. Some people also belonged to secret societies, like the masquerade system, where only the initiates were admitted. This conferred on members of these groups, undue advantages over other people in the community.

Traditional Igbo society equally hardly allowed women to have the same say with their male counterparts. Women had limited access to the village assembly, and were similarly excluded from the masquerade cult. Thus, in traditional Igbo society, generally, women usually took a back seat, which was a serious setback.

Some Pre-Colonial Igbo Kingdoms

Notwithstanding the decentralised political and social organisation of most Igbo communities, in some parts of Igboland, in particular, Nri, Onitsha, Oguta, Ossamari, Arochukwu, and Agbọ, there existed centralised systems of administration, or kingship, before the coming of the Europeans. People in these communities appear to exhibit cultures distinct from the generality of the Igbo nation. We shall discuss only two of these kingdoms.

- ### The Nri Kingship

The Nri people, who traced their history to biblical times, through Zilpah, maidservant of Jacob's wife, Leah, who begat Gad, who in turn begat Eri, the founder of the Nri clan, claimed to have established their kingdom in 948 c.e., and thus became "the oldest kingdom in Nigeria". The first Eze Nri, (Nri king), Ìfikuánim, a priestly king, who wielded no military power over his subjects, was famous for upholding a humanistic system that was uncommon at the time (Ikime, 1980).

The Nri Kingdom provided a safe haven for all those who had been rejected in their communities and thus became a place where "slaves were set free from their bondage". It was for this reason that the Nri devised the Ọzọ title, which other communities in Igboland later embraced, to shield initiates from being taken to slavery, which was very rampant at the time.

During the slave trade era, many Igbo people were sold to the Europeans by the Aro Confederacy, which kidnapped or bought slaves from Igbo villages in the hinterland. The majority of the Igbo slaves were said to be not victims of slave-raiding wars or expeditions but sometimes debtors who committed what their communities considered to be abominations (*arụ, nsọ-ala*) or crimes.

However, everything changed when the British colonialists arrived and saw in the advanced welfare system of the Nri Kingdom and the widespread loyalty it enjoyed, a serious impediment to their parasitic and inhumane pursuits. After failing to capture the kingdom and the king, the colonial forces threatened to slaughter all the people of the kingdom, unless the king appeared before a colonial court in another town. It was then taboo for the Nri King to travel outside Nri town, his seat of power, but to save the lives of his people, Eze Nri, Obalike, who was the king at the time, agreed to travel to Awka to appear before the court.

Not content with this humiliation to which Eze Nri and his people were subjected, to completely dismantle the Nri kingdom, the British colonialists forced Eze Nri to annul all codes of taboo and abomination still binding other towns to Nri.

To finally nail the kingdom, the colonialists introduced the so-called "Warrant Chief" system, whereby many artificial kingdoms were created in various parts of Igboland, which thus rendered the Nri Kingdom almost insignificant.

Strictly speaking, Nri was not a monarchy, and Eze Nri was not a king in the monarchical sense. The Nri, which is part of the Igbo complex of five nations that includes Agbaja, Oru, Isu, Idu, and Nri, is best described as a theocracy. At the head of that theocracy was the ascetic High Priest called Eze Nri. Eze Nri, in other words, did not have the power of a king, his function was priestly rather than political. He followed the divine laws. The secular laws, *Iwu Odinani*, were operated by the Agnacy, as is constant with all the Igbo social systems.

The Eze Nri had no majesty or descendancy; an Eze Nri gave up worldly relationships, including the ritual severance with his immediate family. He was buried simply. He was not made Eze Nri by worldly selection. It was by divination. He had no power of principality. He was merely the medium between the people and their gods.

Those who propagate the mythical Kingdom of Eze Nri or Nri Kingship fail to recognize the popular saying that "Nri Enwelani" - there is no Kingdom or marked territorially. It is not a political institution. It is a spiritual institution and a theocracy, which is the closest thing that could describe the Igbo system.

- *The Onitsha Kingship System*

The Onitsha kingship system stemmed from an earlier contact the Onitsha people had with the Bini Kingdom following their migration to Bini several centuries ago. The great ancestor of Onitsha people, Eze Chima, is believed to have an Igbo origin and was said to have come from Nri or Ogidi, but migrated to Bini, where he acquired the Bini kingship system. However, some people say that Eze Chima was an Aro native doctor who, in pursuance of the role of the Aros in the Atlantic Slave Trade, left Arochukwu for Benin to set up as an agent of the Aro Long Juju, usually to collect slaves from Benin.

Umeh (1999) attested that the Onitsha people were original Igbo who migrated from the Igbo hinterland, crossed to the western bank of the River Niger, and moved into the deeper interior of the west. However, following "a quarrel with the Binis and their leaders", the

Onitsha people, which then had Eze Chima as their leader, migrated back from Benin, where they had previously led migratory lives as warriors, traders, philosophers, priests, professional artisans, carvers, blacksmiths, bronze-makers, or famers.

Similarly, Phillip Emeagwali (www.emeagwali.com) a computer scientist and an indigene of Onitsha, claimed that

> As a native of Onitsha Igbo, I trace my ancestry to Eze Chima, a prince who rebelled against the Bini Royal Dynasty and emigrated from the kingdom. Other Igbos that trace their lineage to Eze Chima include Onicha-Ukwu, Onicha-Olona, Onicha-Ugbo, Obior, Issele-Ukwu, Issele-Mkpima, Issele-Azagba, Ezi, Abeh, and Obamkpa.

Onitsha natives speak a dialect of the Igbo language with several Beni/Yoruba words such as "Obi"(of Onitsha) and "Ọba of Benin". In fact, the word Onitsha (Onicha) could have been a corruption of the word "Orisha, meaning God. The Bini name for the river is "Ohinmwin", while the Onicha Igbo call it "Orinmili."

Elizabeth Isichie (ibid), equally stated that the social, cultural, and religious practises of the Onitsha-Ado (as the Onitsha people were known), were consistent with those of the Aros, Afikpo, Bende, Okigwe (the indigenous Igbo), with other elements borrowed from the Benin. In other words, the Onitsha kingship was a borrowed system from the Bini kingdom.

A closer examination of other Igbo communities that practised the kingship system before the arrival of the colonialists would equally confirm their foreign origin.

The Igbo and the Warrant Chieftaincy

In their quest to exert political influence and control over the colonised people, the British colonial administration in Nigeria, instituted Native Courts over large parts of the country and appointed local agents to supervise over their affairs. Since the colonialists did not have enough resources, human and material, to run the territory, or did not want to spend time in a colonial territory, they decided to select some local people whom they installed as warrant chiefs, and gave them power to run the government at the local level, while the European colonial administrators sitting at the remote centres of the administration kept a watchful eye.

Known as the "Indirect Rule" system, this was imported into Nigeria by Lord Frederick Lugard, who, as Governor General of Nigeria, had experimented with it in East Africa where he once served as administrator. In both the northern and western parts of Nigeria, which already had a centralised kingship system, the indirect rule system worked perfectly well.

However, in trying to apply the system to Igboland, the British colonial administrators, without a proper understanding of the customs and traditions of the people, arbitrarily chose their preferred candidates, and gave them warrants as members of the Native Courts. Moreover, in appointing the warrant chiefs, the colonialists looked for their lackeys, those who could be referred to as stooges, or errand boys, people whose main qualification was their readiness to unquestionably obey the orders of the colonial masters.

Sometimes, people of little standing in their communities, such as slaves or slave merchants, were fished out and installed as warrant chiefs. In some other cases, persons of external origin were also installed and imposed on the people as their chief. Generally, the majority of these warrant chiefs had little or no legitimacy beyond the fact that they were being installed as kings by the colonial government. For many of these chiefs, who were not used to exercising governmental authority but who now had been called upon to do so without precedent or training, the situation was simply confusing. No wonder therefore, that many of these chiefs actually abused the system, which accounted for the many lapses and criticisms levelled against the warrant chiefs, and, by extension, the indirect rule system.

The majority of these warrant chiefs also relied heavily on forced labour, coercion, and extortion to legitimise their authority. Walter Ofonagoro (1982) explained that the main source of power for the Warrant Chiefs was the "control of Native Courts and of Labour", while Femi Adegbulu (2011) lamented that "the warrant chief institution had, in many places, become synonymous with greed, avarice, and corruption".

Despite the fact that many of the warrant chiefs were said to be corrupt, dictatorial, and rule inhumanely, some of them provided courageous and progressive leadership in the context of the time. As was generally known, the majority of the warrant chiefs did not receive formal education, nor were they taken through the rudiments of political administration before being appointed to the exalted office.

Following the "Aba Women's Riot" of 1929 over various local issues, not excluding the alleged high-handedness by the warrant chiefs, when thousands of women besieged the Native Courts and attacked warrant chiefs, it became necessary for the British to abolish the indirect rule and warrant chief systems and order the reform of the local administration in order to create a 'proper' indirect rule government.

New Kingship System in Igboland

Following the 1976 report of the committee set up by the federal government to reform the local government system and to establish a uniform standard for local government administration nationwide, which was headed by Alhaji Ibrahim Dasuki, the battle cry in many communities in Igboland, like in the Old Testament Israel, seemed to be "give us a king to rule over us, as in all the other nations," (1 Sam. 8:5).

In Nigeria, the Hausa/Fulani and the Yoruba, have established kingship systems. But there was no such system in most Igbo communities. The Dasuki Committee, in its report laid down criteria for creating local government councils, which it defined as the "third tier of government", and whose aim was to "bring government closer to the people" (Uzoigwe, 2004).

In accepting the committee's report as well as its recommendation, the federal government charged state governments with applying the same system to their constituents in creating local government councils.

In the Igbo-speaking areas of the East Central State (later split into Anambra and Imo States), the government set up a committee headed by Professor Adiele Afigbo, to advise it on the best way of implementing the committee's recommendation. The Afigbo

Committee, in its report, recommended the creation of a fourth-tier form of government, called "autonomous communities", with an officially recognised traditional ruler for each community.

Based on that recommendation, the Anambra State Government enacted Chieftaincy Edict No.8 of September 2, 1976, published in the Official Gazette No. 31, Volume 1, of November 25, 1976. According to the edict, a traditional ruler is defined as "the traditional head of an autonomous community, identified and selected by his people according to their traditions and usages". It further stated that the government would have no hand in the selection of the traditional ruler, though it reserved the right to depose any of them who misbehaved.

However, we obsereve that according to "tradition and usages" as criteria for identifying and selecting a traditional ruler, it appeared nebulous, because the people had no traditional chief or something akin to it prior to the arrival of the Europeans. Membership of the "Council of Elders" that ruled Igbo society was not hereditary, but by achievement. Were that criterion to be applied, the selection of a traditional ruler would have posed no problem. But this was left vague, which led to rancour and acrimony in many communities.

Again, in order to obtain government recognition, the traditional ruler, according to the edict, was required to prove "popular support", and then be publicly presented to the governor for recognition. This politicised the traditional institution because aspirants to the throne would have to travel around the villages canvassing for support, putting them in the same shoes as politicians. And yet, traditional rulers were supposed to be insulated from politics!

In societies with an entrenched kingship system, the searchlight for an occupant for a vacant stool is usually beamed towards the "ruling families", while in Igboland, it took a democratic process, in which every member of the community was free to contest for the seat. That put into question the "naturalness" of the Igbo kinship institution, where aspirants to the traditional stool were made to stand election with other contenders to determine the popular choice of the people. In very many cases, this naturally went to the highest bidder, to the one with a very fat pocket. Before the coming of the Europeans, membership in the Igbo ruling class, the Council of Elders, took on a natural order by virtue of one attaining a certain age, holding a particular position, or achieving a particular feat. Nobody crashed into the system by flaunting some ill-gotten wealth.

The Chieftaincy Edict further required an autonomous community to provide a written "constitution" and a "code of conduct" for the Traditional Ruler. This was necessary because it would allow for an orderly selection of occupants for chieftaincy stools, as there were no set criteria for such selection in most communities. Except in a few communities, which claimed that the institution was hereditary, many other communities, after a long tussle, produced their constitutions, which provided for the rotation of the kingship's stool among the constituent units of the area.

With criteria for the selection and recognition of traditional rulers clearly defined, a floodgate of requests for recognition of traditional rulers by the government opened in various parts of the then Anambra and Imo States. Individuals of different callings and persuasions, businessmen, contractors, and moneybags began to jostle to be recognised and crowned as traditional rulers. In almost every community in Igboland, the Chieftaincy Edict sparked off disputes and litigations, pitting brothers against brothers, which very often resulted in conflicts and confrontations. To deal with these problems, the Anambra State government, in particular, set up the Justice Agbakoba Commission, which visited various parts of the state to sort out contentious issues in the affected communities.

On December 14, 1976, the first set of 124 traditional rulers was accorded government recognition and was presented with certificates and staff of office by the then Military Governor of Anambra State, Colonel John Atom Kpera, at an impressive ceremony in Enugu. This was followed by another set of 84 Traditional Rulers who were equally accorded recognition in February and March 1977. By October 1979, when the military government handed over to the incoming civilian administration, a total of 405 traditional rulers were accorded government recognition in Anambra State (Okeke, 1994).

Interestingly, most of the people who later emerged as "traditional rulers" and received government recognition turned out to be mainly businessmen and contractors. This was not surprising since these were people who had the required cash to "purchase" the position. Even at that, as businessmen and contractors, most of these traditional rulers spent most of their time in the big cities where they had their business interests, while sparing a few weekends in their palaces to interact with their subjects. Not only that, some of the traditional rulers who were "urban brought up" were not even grounded in the customs and traditions of their people, and so remain alien to the people.

Following the return to democratic governance in the country in 1979, the "Anambra State Chieftaincy Edict" was modified in 1981 by the state house of assembly, which passed the "Anambra State of Nigeria Traditional Rulers' Law 1981". In the new law, only government recognised traditional rulers were entitled to bear the title of "Igwe" or "Obi". In Imo State, the traditional rulers were recognised as "Eze".

However, the law forbids traditional rulers, as "impartial fathers" of their communities, from engaging in partisan politics. But if they want to enter politics, they have to renounce their recognition. Traditional rulers, on the other hand, were free to bestow honorary chieftaincy titles on deserving individuals who would be known as "Chiefs".

The State Chieftaincy Edict did not provide any role for the Traditional Ruler beyond his community. This is contrary to what obtained in the First Republic, when some first-class traditional rulers were appointed members of the "House of Chiefs", and thus legislated for the entire region.

Traditional rulers are the custodians of the people's culture and traditions. However, they are to be "consulted" in all land matters. This means that the Igbo traditional ruler, unlike his counterparts in the northern and western parts of the country, has no power to alienate any community land without the consent of his subjects.

As "impartial fathers" of their people, traditional rulers are to engage in peace making within their community as well as in conflict with their neighbours. They are to promote community development and, in consultation with members of their cabinet, organise local consensus. The Anambra State Traditional Rulers' Law of 1981 further encouraged traditional rulers to "cooperate with the local government council" and assist them "in the collection of taxes".

All these functions are no easy task, which means that any genuine traditional ruler must be fully committed to his roles and responsibilities. Unfortunately, many of these traditional rulers, as businessmen and contractors, are hardly in their palaces, thereby leaving many of their functions largely unattended to.

In actuality, traditional rulers, as people at the grassroots of the administration, have the responsibility to attend to the endless streams of visitors that daily throng their palaces with one problem or another. They are to resolve local and external disputes, such as land matters and other sundry issues. They are to help mobilise their subjects for community development in accordance with the Town Union. These functions require patience, perseverance, and a good knowledge and application of human psychology.

However, many traditional rulers complain that they are not usually supported by the government. According to them, the government does not give the traditional ruler any "security votes" with which to deal with the security issues that daily confront them. This means that many of these traditional rulers have been carrying on these responsibilities with their meagre resources. It is only recently that the Enugu State government has started paying stipends to its traditional rulers; otherwise, those of them with no visible means of livelihood have been living from hand to mouth, which is very demeaning and embarrassing.

Many of today's traditional rulers, not just in Igboland, but in Nigeria as a whole, are no longer the "antiquated, archaic, and uneducated men of yesterday", who were only good at breaking kola nuts and pouring libations to the ancestors. Among these traditional rulers are retired technocrats and administrators, educationists, university lecturers, diplomats, military officers, and international businessmen. In that way, the government could tap on their wealth of experience by giving them positions of responsibility, such as membership of boards and parastatals, and by setting up a National Council of Traditional Rulers where some traditional rulers could meaningfully contribute to national development.

But unlike their counterparts in other parts of the country, the Igbo king is a mere mortal, an ordinary human being. He was not made by the gods or by the spirits, and hence, he does not wield absolute powers. The Igbo king is ceremonial. He reflects the republican character of traditional Igbo society, where the Council of Elders took charge of the political governance of the community. As such, the Igbo king rules in collaboration with members of his cabinet, which comprises some selected community's most prominent members.

But unlike the Hausa/Fulani Emir, or the Yoruba Oba, the Igbo king does not own communal land, and he is not even paid any royalty for land usage. The Igbo king may be respected, revered, and paid obeisance as the community father, but he does not possess extraordinary wisdom or intelligence. He is just like every other human being, and therefore, he cannot swing the pendulum one way or the other.

The Igbo king reigns but does not rule. It is the President General of the Town Union and members of his Executive Committee that actually rule the community. They drive all the developmental projects in the community. However, they must seek the blessing and consent of the traditional ruler for the venture to succeed. In normal circumstances, the Igbo king is normally appointed for life, but if he misbehaves, he would be deposed.

References

Adegbulu, Femi (2011) 'From Warrant Chiefs to Ezeship: A Distortion of Traditional Institution in Igboland?' *Afro Asian Journal of Social Sciences*, Volume 2, No. 2.2 Quarter II.

Anambra State of Nigeria (1981) 'Traditional Rulers Law 1981'

Anambra State Government (1976), 'Chieftaincy Edict No. 8 of Sept 2, 1976', (Awka, *Official Gazette* No. 31, Volume 1, of Nov 25

Basden, G.T. (1938) *Niger Ibos*, (London: Seeley Co.)

Ekeh, Peter et al (1989*) Nigeria Since Independence: The First Twenty-Five Years. Volume V, Politics and Constitution* (Ibadan, Heinemann Books)

Emeagwa, P. available at www.emeagwali.com

Equiano, Olaudah (2013). *The Interesting Narrative of the Life of Olaudah Equiano, or Gustavus Vassa, the African*, (New York, W.W. Norton & Company).

Eze, D (2011) *Akama Ogwugwu Ebenebe* (Enugu: Linco Press)

Ikime, O. (1980) *Ground Work of Nigerian History*, (Ibadan: Heinemann Educational Books

Isichei, E, (1997) *A History of the Igbo People* (London: Macmillan)

Maduaburochukwu, E. (2016) The Igbo Are Egalitarian (*Daily Sun* Newspapers, August 19).

New Jerusalem Bible (1985) '1 Samuel, 8:5' (Darton, Longman and Todd)

Nnamani, C. (2001) *Ndi-Igbo and The Challenge of Nation Building* (Enugu: Dawn Functions Production)

Nwosu, HN (1977) *Political Authority & The Nigerian Civil Service* (Enugu: Fourth Dimension Publishers)

Ofonagoro, Walter (1982) 'An Aspect of British Colonial Policy in Southern Nigeria: The Problems of Forced Labour and Slavery, 1895-1928' in B.I. Obiechere (ed), *Studies in Southeastern Nigerian History*, (London, Frank Cass).

Okeke, Igwebuike Romeo (1994) 'The Chieftaincy Institution and Government Recognized Traditional Rulers in Anambra State. Maiden Edition', *Media Forum* Enugu, Media Forum.

Onwumechili, CA (2000) 'Igbo Enwe Eze: The Igbo Have No Kings' (Owerri, Ahiajioku Lectures)

Umeh, J.A. (1999) *Igbo People-Their Origin and Culture Area* (Enugu, Nigeria, Gostak Printing and Publishing Co. Ltd)

Uzoigwe, G.N. (2004) 'Evolution and Relevance of Autonomous Communities in Pre-colonial Igboland', *Journal of Third World Studies*, Spring, available in

[Note: for the most recent classification of Igbo dialects, see Nwaozuzu, G.I. 2017 of Ikekeonwu, C.I. (1986)]

CHAPTER TWO

The Igbo Worldview

Introduction

There is no better way to understand or appreciate a people and how they view their universe or the world around them, particularly in a society whose ancestors left no written documents, than through their thought forms, expressed in various ways like their language, their social behaviour, and their attitude toward life. People in every society are governed by what they see in their environment or surroundings. These are things that shape or determine their attitude to life. Alexander Animalu (2001) tells us that

> Worldviews are products of experiences so pregnant with drama that such experiences give rise to symbols or totems of some sort; the symbols give rise to thought or creative intelligence, – akọ-na-uche; and creative intelligence gives rise, in turn, to the customs and codes of the society, which are so intermingled, from childhood on, that they go unquestioned as a way of life.

The Igbo View of the Cosmos or the Universe

To talk about the Igbo worldview is to go back in history, before the contact of the Igbo with their immediate neighbours as well as with the outside world, in particular, before their contact with the countries of Western Europe and the United States of America. These were the "good old days", "The Age of Innocence" (Afigbo, 1981) and "The Igbo Lost Worlds" (Ebighgbo, 2002). It was the period before "Things Fall Apart" (Achebe, 1994), before the Igbo were "destroyed" by the various winds blowing from across the four corners of the globe. It was the period when the Igbo were living in a world of their own, tucked inside the very thick forests that surrounded them, in their hamlets and villages, and interacting only among their own people.

Any encroachment on its territory was viewed with seriousness, which sometimes resulted in war. The government of each village was composed mainly of village elders and other titled men who made and interpreted laws, while the youths, who were organised into age grades, carried out communal activities and implemented laws made by the elders.

The Igbo were communalists and they expressed this in their daily activities, and in their relationships with one another. No man was an island. The people lived through others or through their relationships with the people around them. This was demonstrated in their celebration of various festivals like the festival of the gods and of various shrines, the festival of farming; the festival of harvest; the festival of marriage; the festival of childbearing; the festival of maturity of age; and even the festival of death and burial, which was a way of relieving stresses and strains and building harmonious co-existence.

The Igbo view of the cosmos or the universe was that of a harmonious and ordered existence, directed or controlled by the Supreme Deity, *Chi-ukwu*, *Chukwu Okike*, or *Chi-neke*, *Eze Chitoke* (Nsukka), the Creator of the universe and everything therein, both the visible and the invisible beings or forces, including the spirits, *muo*, the good and the bad ones. In the order of hierarchy, *Chi-ukwu*, or *Chukwu Okike*, is at the apex of the ladder. He was assisted by other divinities such as *Ani/Ala*, the Earth Goddess; *Igwe*, the Sky; *Anyanwu*, the Sun; and by other smaller deities and strange beings like the hills, streams or rivers, trees, etc., through which the Supreme Deity was honoured and worshipped.

The Igbo were very religious. Every morning they would seek the face of their Creator through the offering and breaking of kola nuts (*ikwo aka ututu*). They would ask for Divine favour, protection, and guidance in all they would set out to do. They would not do anything without first consulting the Supreme Deity through various intermediaries, such as the *dibia*, or the diviners, since it was God who gave these beings the power to foresee the future and act on His behalf. The Igbo would also not do anything that could despoil or offend the Earth Goddess (*Ani, Ala*), they would call it *Nso Ala*, abomination, since this could spell doom or bring calamity to the entire community.

The Igbo, like most traditional societies, believe in metempsychosis, or changelings, also known as *Ogbanje*. The Yoruba call it *Abiku*. The Igbo believe that each person belongs to a family of totems, which are wild animals like hyenas, snakes, deer, monkeys, etc. They both believe in reincarnation. This is not to be confused with changeling, for whereas changeling has a negative undertone, reincarnation is a good omen, which is an indication that the person who reincarnates a child is good and kind-hearted. This is called "*iyọ ụwa," ilọ ụwa*.

Reincarnation is a sign that one lived a virtuous life while on earth and has now come back and reincarnates as a child. Mbiti (1969:165) asserts that the living, the departed, and those yet to be born are ontologically related and reinforce each other. While the departed or the ancestors intervene in the affairs of their family members by bringing them good health, bountiful harvests, and a return to earth through every new birth; those living on earth, on their part, strengthen the departed or the ancestors by their prayers and sacrifices. It is a symbiotic relationship. The Igbo give their children names like *Nna-nna (ya)* (Father of his father); *Nne-nna (ya)* (Mother of her father); or *Nna-aghayo* (Father has come back), etc.

The Igbo society is one of complexity and complicated problems. As such, the traditional means of seeking solutions to these problems is through *afa*. The Yoruba call it "*ifa*". *Afa* is the instrument used by a diviner to reveal the past and foretell the future. When a child is sick, it is the diviner, through his *afa*, who will say whether the child is a changeling (*ogbanje*), who wants to torment his parents, and what should be done to restore the child to normal life. In the same vein, when a family member dies, the diviner uses his afa instrument to determine who is to blame and whether the deceased should be buried within the compound and become an ancestor, or carried away and thrown into the evil forest (*Ajo Ofia*).

Only those who led good and decent lives while on earth were, upon death, given befitting burials and thus qualified to be ancestors. The desire to have a befitting burial upon death and thus be recognised as an ancestor had helped to instill moral rectitude and social discipline in the lives of the primordial Igbo. Those who lived cruel and wicked lives while on earth were not accorded the privilege of ancestry. They were not even buried, but dumped into the evil forests for vultures to feast upon. They were malevolent spirits that swarmed the area looking for people to devour.

"These bad spirits which are mostly of two types – *Ekwensu* and *Akalogholi*, cause accidents and deviant behaviour in their lineages, respectively. Both of these bad spirits can be chained or their course changed by the environment. "They are not ancestors." (Ebighgbo ibid).

The Igbo are dualists. It is not just enough to stress only one point; there must be a need for another point of view. In other words, there was no one way to look at reality. This is exemplified in the Igbo saying, *"A nghị akwụ ofu ebe ekili mmọnwụ"* (You cannot fully view the masquerade by standing in one place. You need to change positions if you are to clearly view it.) That was the reason, following the British colonialisation of Nigeria and the 1914 amalgamation of the Northern and Southern Protectorates, the Igbo moved out in large numbers to various parts of Nigeria and beyond to seek for alternative means of livelihood.

Chinua Achebe emphasised this point in an interview with Bill Moyers. According to Achebe:

> There is no absolute anything. They (the Igbo) are opposed to excess; their world is one of duality. It is good to be brave, they say, but also remember that the coward survives.

In *Things Fall Apart,* Achebe (1958) portrayed his hero, Okonkwo, as a great wrestler, a brave warrior and a famous farmer, while on the other hand, Okonkwo's father, Unoka, was presented as a weakling and a pacifist who detested war and hated the hoe. Thus, while Okonkwo was a successful farmer, Unoka still managed to make ends meet with his flute.

The Igbo are optimists: – *Onye kwe, Chi ya ekwe* (When one says yes, his *Chi* will equally say yes). That is why the Igbo always strive for the best and try their hands on everything. At the same time, the Igbo are also fatalists. They believe that nothing happens by chance or accident. For them, everything that happened was already predetermined, or caused by one malevolent spirit or another – *"Ebe onye dara ka chi ya kwaturu ya* (Where a man falls has been destined by his *Chi*). It was extremely difficult, if not impossible, to develop a scientific thought or rational enterprise that is essential for today's technological innovation within such a mystico-religious interpretation of reality.

The Igbo also believe in the principle of reciprocity, *Tụrụ ka m tụrụ* (Live and let live); *Aka nri kwọọ Aka ekpe; Aka ekpe Akwoo Aka nri* (If the right hand washes the left hand, the left hand will equally wash the right hand). It is the principle of give-and-take. This principle is demonstrated in the celebration of the Igbo New Yam Festival, *Ifejiọkụ/Ahaiajọkụ*. Alexander Animalu (2003:3) informs that

The Igbo man gives old yam (ji akakpo) to the ground, ani, and ani 'eats it' and gives him new yam, ji ofuu: this is reciprocity, a principle of give-and-take and of dialogue, which is a principle of unity and regeneration between man and nature, man and man, as well as man and machine. A winner-takes-all situation in which ani 'eats' the yam and returns rotten yam, ji melu onwu, to the farmer is one that dooms the community, as it were, to starvation.

For the Igbo, justice is many sided, and is expressed in their various proverbs. The Igbo concept of justice is situational and depends on circumstances. It is sometimes based on the principle of reciprocity or the Mosaic law of "an eye for an eye".

For instance, the Igbo will say: *"Ogburu onye na onye ga-ala"*, or *"Ogbu mma ga ala na mma"* (He who fights with the sword, dies by the sword); *"Onye si m diri ga-adi, ma onye si m nwuo, ya buru okuko uzo lakpuo ura";* (Whoever wants me to live, will live, but whoever wants me dead, let him precede the fowl to go to bed); *"Egbe bere ugo bere, nke si ibe-ya ebena, nku kwaa ya"* (Let the kite perch and let the eagle perch, whoever does not want the other to perch, let its own wing break); *"Nke onye diri ya"* (Live and let live, or Let every person receive what is his or her due).

The Igbo also believe in the balance of justice – *"Onye kpara nku ahuhu, si ngwere kpatara ya oriri"* (He who fetched ant infested firewood, invited lizard to a feast), *"Isi kote ebu, o gbaa ya"* (The head that touches the wasp must be stung by the wasp). They equally believe in distributive justice: *"Otu aka ruta mmanu, o zuo ibe ya."* (If one finger touches oil, it affects all the other fingers).

In the opinion of Obiora Ike (2001:39) "justice is the basis and the pre-condition for peace, progress, and inter-human balance and relationship in original Igbo society".

In their appreciation and understanding of natural justice, the Igbo will say – *"Ihe onye kuru, ka o ga-aghota"* (What a man sows, so he will reap); *"Onye emeghi ihe iyi, adighi atu egbe igwe egwu"*(He who did not swear falsely before a shrine or break an oath, does not fear the sound of thunder). Similarly, the Igbo believe that "unity is strength" *(Igwe bu ike);* they are their brothers' keeper – *Onye aghana Nwanne ya.* And as communalists, the Igbo loathe a system that produces an ocean in the desert or starvation in the midst of plenty.

Chapter two | Dons Eze & Chinedu Ochinanwata

But as republicans with no kings, the contemporary Igbo can be arrogant, disrespectful, noisy, and boisterous, in the opinion of some outsiders, or those who do not understand their culture. The Igbo are independent-minded. They can look anybody in the face and say: *E si be gi eje be onye?)* (Does your house lead to anybody's house?, Where does your house lead to? In present day Nigeria, this attitude has very often brought the Igbo into misunderstandings with some of their neighbours and even their hosts.

Achebe (1983) puts it this way:

> There is a strand in contemporary Igbo behaviour which can offend by its noisy exhibitionism and disregard for humility and quietness. If you walk into the crowded waiting room at the Ikeja Airport… and you hear one man's voice high over a subdued and despondent multitude, the chances are he will be an Igbo man who 'has made it' and is desperate to be noticed and admired.

As a result of this, some other ethnic groups see the Igbo as domineering and always seeking to control or dominate their environment. This perception, rightly or wrongly, led, no doubt, to several ill-feelings and misunderstandings between the Igbo and many of their neighbours. The reason for this so-called "imperialistic" and or "domineering" attitude of the Igbo, their "noisy" and "boisterous" nature, etc., is no doubt due to the upward mobility of the Igbo and their quick adaptation to change, necessitated by European colonialism, which made many Igbo move outside their immediate environment in search of alternative means of livelihood. There is no part of the globe where you will not find the Igbo living and doing business, no matter how mean or lowly.

As a result of their hard work and industry, the Igbo always make the best out of every situation and, sometimes, squeeze water out of dry land, much to the consternation and envy of many of the people around them. That is why the Igbo are usually misunderstood by several of their neighbours, including their hosts.

The Igbo Justice System

The core ideal of the traditional Igbo justice system is founded not so much on **retribution** as on **restitution.** The Igbo justice system attempts to create balance, and to right wrongs, instead of just punishing the perpetrator of crimes. The idea was to ensure that justice also ensured compensation for the victim as well as punishment for the criminal.

There is a distinction between divine laws and laws made by humans. Breaking divine law such as murder and incest, which are taboos resulted in severe punishment, whereas transgressing man-made laws, such as theft, would result to less severe punishment. Punishment for serious offences could result in execution, banishment, or permanent compulsory exile. In this instance, restitution to the victim's family could be in the form of awarding the perpetrator's land and property to them or 'a life for a life', but punishment for lesser crimes involved the criminal being either ostracised or having to pay compensation to the victim. The criminal might also be publicly humiliated and held up for derision by the villagers.

Traditional courts comprised the elders of the village (the *egwugwu*), made up of only men, who would then consult with the gods to establish punishment once a guilty verdict had been reached. The *'audi alteram partem'* rule would be applied. Both parties would be given the opportunity to present their version of the matter. There was no formal court building or complex, and trials were conducted in the open. Both parties had to undertake an oath in which they promised before their gods that they would tell the truth.

Based on the evidence presented, the *egwugwu* would then decide on the degree of illegality (the severity of the crime) and would decide on compensation or mete out punishment after consulting with the gods. Okonkwo, in Chinua Achebe's *Things Fall Apart*, for example, was instructed to pay a fine after dishonouring "The Week of Peace" by beating his wife, Ojiugo, for not preparing him a meal. He was later banished to his mother's village, Mbanta, for seven years for accidentally shooting and killing one of Ezeudu's sons during Ezeudu's funeral.

Therefore, the Igbo had a complex justice system, that involved all members of the community. The role of judges was played by the *Egwugwu*, who were prominent citizens of the village wearing masks. The masks represented the ancestral spirits of the village, who would pass judgement on the accused.

Each person who brought a suit to the *egwugwu* received a trial in which both sides pleaded their cases, much like prosecutors and defence attorneys in modern legal courts. After hearing the case, the judges would confer together, and then decide the best course of action. Often, if the case warranted punishment, it would be a very public one, usually carried out by all members of the village.

All these things changed when the missionaries arrived. Suddenly, the Igbo became subject to laws that were not theirs, and punishments that served no purpose other than domination and humiliation. In fact, the treatment of the Igbo in the white legal system played a large role in the final events of Achebe's novel.

Some Basic Igbo Customs and Tradition

Igbo culture (*Ọmenala Ndịgbo*) is the set of customs, practices, and traditions of the Igbo people. It comprises archaic practises and new concepts added to the Igbo culture either by cultural evolution or by outside influence. These customs and traditions include the Igbo people's visual arts, music, and dance forms, as well as their attire, cuisine, and language.

1. The Ọzọ Title System

Ọzọ was a significant institution in Igboland prior to the arrival of the Europeans. It conferred honour and prestige on those who held the title, as well as opened many important doors and gates to them. They had more special privileges and recognition in society than ordinary men. As such, ambitious young men naturally aspired to join the society.

The moral authority of the society was held by Ọzọ title holders, who were men of honour and integrity. For instance, an Ọzọ must not steal. If he did, he would be immediately derobed. He must also not take part in criminal activities, or tell lies. If he did, he would be sounding his death knell. His staff (ofo) was a symbol of truth, and anybody who swore falsely by it was doomed for life.

On account of their wealth and influence, Ọzọ title holders always participated in important traditional functions and ceremonies, including village politics and administration. Their status had conferred on them the role of ambassador plenipotentiaries, or worthy ambassadors of their people. They were thus the natural leaders of the people long before the chieftaincy institution was imposed. (Eze, 2011:70).

In a male-dominated traditional Igbo society, women are disqualified from membership in the Ọzọ system. This is not just because women are flippant and could hardly keep the secrets associated with the Ọzọ institution, but also because of their biological nature, which usually makes them "unclean" and therefore could defile this sacred institution. Francis Madukasi (2018:4640-4652) explains that

> In the tradition and culture of the Igbo people, the Ọzọ as a sacred institution, is highly prized and as such, in this patriarchal tradition, there are restrictions put upon women, non-initiates and the children in-so-far as they are prohibited from becoming members or initiates

He further states that all

> Cultures across the Igbo land do not allow women's participation in such sacred rituals like that of the Ọzọ title to avoid violating the guiding rules and regulations that constitute the essence of the membership of the men's society. Women do menstruate, and a menstruating woman can defile the spiritual essence of the Ọzọ membership.

In times past, throughout Igboland, a woman in her menstrual period was considered not to be clean, and so she never entered the kitchen to prepare any meal for her husband. Such a woman would be staying in the outer part of her living room until the end of her menstrual period, which held even more for a highly spiritualised Ọzọ title holder. This explains why the Ọzọ married more than one wife, so that if one of his wives was in her menstrual period, others would be free to cook for him. The Ọzọ would never sleep with any woman in her menstrual period.

This Igbo worldview appears to have corresponded with the biblical account in Leviticus (15:19-24), where women in their menstrual period were considered "unclean" and would never come into contact with any man during the period. Perhaps, that was why some Igbo people believe that the Igbo were related to the Israelites!

2. Igbu Ichi Culture

Igbu ichi is an ancient Igbo tradition that involved both men and women. Igbu ichi is not just a tribal mark, but a mark of honour and prestige. To be initiated into the Ichi Society, one must be a brave man or woman. It is not everybody that is considered worthy to be initiated into the Ichi society. In the olden days, it was only brave men and women who could 'bear pain' and protect their communities, warriors if you like, that are initiated into the Ichi Society.

Outwardly, you could distinguish an initiated member by the marks on his or her cheeks. In the olden days, these were incisions made with 'agụba' or knife, on the person's cheeks. They distinguished him in society and drew reverence and admiration to him. Once initiated, the person became one of the trusted few who would fight for, or defend the community against external aggression. Ichi society complemented the Ọzọ society, especially in communities where they can still be found.

3. Igbo Masquerade System

According to traditional Igbo belief, masquerades are true reincarnation of the dead. They are said to originate from certain anthills, from holes, or from somewhere in the bush. Masquerades signify what they represent. Once a masquerade is designated to represent a certain deceased person or ancestor, he is regarded as representing such individual.

From time to time, the dead like to return to earth to have communion with their descendants and share in their joys and tribulations. They will bring them good wishes from the spirit world and carry back their requests to the land of the spirits. On their part, the living will approach the masked spirits, the spirits of their ancestors, friends or relations, with love and respect. They will offer them gifts and solicit their assistance in interceding on their behalf for good health, long life, and material benefits.

Masking is therefore the externalisation of that intimate relationship between the living and the dead, where the living conceives of the dead as existing in body and soul in the other world and constantly interacting with the living, albeit in a masked form. It is only a men's affair, and particularly the initiated, while women will be peeping from afar to watch them.

The reality of the masquerade is rooted in the Igbo worldview of the symbiotic relationship between the living and the dead. In a society where the living and the dead freely mingle with each other in the interpenetration of forces, it is natural that the masquerade should exist to symbolise that relationship. The Igbo cosmology does not view death as "finished", or as the end of human existence. Rather, it views the dead as existing in the other world, though in a diminished condition of life, with lessened "life forces", Tempels (1945), but nevertheless retaining their stronger fathering life force.

The principal functions of the masquerade are its roles as an agent of social control, entertainment, and mobilisation. In various Igbo societies, the masquerade plays very important roles in ensuring the healthy growth of society by providing the people with entertainment for their relaxation and mobilising them for communal works, both in peace and during periods of emergency. It also helps to maintain social discipline and cohesion. The masquerade was a powerful force for social control in traditional Igbo society, maintaining and preserving the norms and values of society.

Night masquerades would not hesitate to reveal the misdeeds of individual members of the community. An unfaithful housewife who jumped from one bed to another would have her lustful escapades exposed and warned of the unpleasant consequences if she continued in such an irresponsible behaviour. A lazy young man who is afraid to handle a hoe like Unoka, in Chinua Achebe's "Things Fall Apart", would have music composed in his name by the masquerade and be told to better change his sex and become a woman.

Night masquerades had no regard for persons or status – the rich and the poor, the young and the old, men and women – all had their secrets exposed. This is a way of instilling discipline and changing the lives of individual members of society.

4. Igbo Kola Nut (Ọjị Igbo)

The Igbo Kola nut (Ọjị Igbo) holds a unique place in Igbo people's cultural life. Ọjị is the first thing served to any visitor in an Igbo home. Ọjị is served before an important function begins, be it marriage ceremony, the settlement of family disputes, or entering into any type of agreement. Ọjị is traditionally broken into lobes by hand, and a special celebration is arranged if the kola nut breaks into three lobes.

The Igbo believe that "kola is life", and kola symbolises peace. This is why an Igbo man would welcome you with kola nuts when you visit his home, saying *"onye wetere oji, wetere udo"*, which translates to "he who brings kola, brings peace."

A kola with only one cotyledon is known as a dumb kola or Ọjị ogbu. It is called ọjị mmụọ, that is, kola of the spirits. It is not eaten. Kola with two cotyledons is equally a dumb kola and it is not eaten. This is the main reason the Igbo do not use the *gworo* or kola nitida (Oji Awusa) for rituals or in serious traditional celebrations.

Kola with three lobes is called *ọjị ike, ọjị ikenga*, that is, kola of the valiant. Only warriors or brave men and consecrated or ordained persons are permitted to eat this kola, as a matter of principle. Kola with four cotyledons is called "*ọjị udo na ngọzị*", that is, "kola of peace and blessing". This is the normal kola. The number 'four' is very sacred among the Igbo. Kola with five lobes is "*ọjị ụbara mmadụ, ọmụmụ na ụkwụọma*, which symbolizes increase in procreation, protection, and good luck.

Kola with six cotyledons indicates communion with the ancestors, that is, *"ọjị ndi mmụo na ndi mmadụ jiri gbaa ndụ"*. The smallest part, or cotyledon, is not eaten but is thrown away for the ancestors to eat.
In like manner, kola with one cotyledon is not eaten by man, which means that it is not broken during ceremonies because it belongs to the ancestors, an attitude reminiscent of the direct link between the living and the dead in Igboland. Kola with seven cotyledons is a sign of good omen, it symbolises prosperity. However, it is rarely seen or broken.

Presentation of Kola Nut

Every function or ceremony, personal or communal agreements, the welcoming of a visitor to an Igbo home, and the resolution of family disputes begin with Ọjị (kola). The Igbo welcome is incomplete without the presentation of kola nut. In the case where the host of a social gathering fails to present kola to his guests, he would have to make explanatory apology as to why kola was not provided. The kola nut is presented on a dish or saucer, or more precisely, on a wooden platter (ọkwa), prepared and kept for the sole purpose of presenting the kola nut. In the dish are one or more nuts. The owner first takes a nut and puts it to his lips, thus signifying that it is about to be offered in good faith. This symbolic gesture proves him to be free from malice. The dish is, thereupon, passed to the visitor.

The kola presentation symbolises peace and welcome, and if one makes a mistake while carrying the kola round, he is traditionally punished according to the standards of the community where he committed the error. Such an error is considered very grave and indicates that the offender is not responsible and may not be a reliable person.

Blessing of Kola

The blessing of kola is the right of the eldest person in any gathering, or it may be that of the Eze (king) whenever he is present. However, the oldest person is preferred in most cases because he is the custodian of truth and closer to the ancestors.

In the evolutionary trend of the tradition, an ordained minister or one consecrated to God now takes precedence in the blessing of the kola, but the eldest person or the king who has this right will give or transfer it to him to minister as a privilege, not as a right.

The principle behind this Igbo kola culture is that the nut cannot be broken without the saying of prayers or incantations by the eldest in the gathering. This has given rise to the proverb "He who brings kola brings life", because in the kola nut prayers, the elder, in addition to his wise sayings, normally requests for peace, prosperity, long life, happiness, and protection from all ill fortunes. Not only do the Igbo pray before the breaking of the kola nut, no traditional Igbo would drink or eat without first sharing with the ancestors.

Why Women Do Not Break Ceremonial Kola

The high degree of sanctity accorded the kola nut throughout Igboland is likened to that of the biblical "forbidden fruit of Paradise" in the sense that women are forbidden from planting, climbing, plucking, or breaking the kola nut. This does not mean that men are holier than women in Igbo society — no. It is just a question of a mentality similar to the biblical regard for women. The denial of women's right to break Igbo ceremonial kola is more of a matter of social character and organisation and does not in any way imply inferiority towards women.

Women do break the Igbo kola when they gather in their usual cultural groupings where no man has a say. On the contrary, Igbo women have their own cultural organisations that are completely independent of men.

5. Iri Ji Nd'igbo (New Yam Festival)

The New Yam Festival of the Igbo people (*Iwa ji, Iri ji or Ike ji*) is an annual cultural festival by the Igbo starting in early August. The *Iri ji* festival marks the end of a harvest season and the beginning of the next work cycle. The celebration is a very culturally-based occasion, tying individual Igbo communities together as essentially agrarian and dependent on yam, the king of crops.

The New Yam Festival is therefore a celebration depicting yam's prominence in the sociocultural life of the Igbo people. The evening before the day of the festival, all old yams (from the previous year's crop) are consumed or discarded. The next day, only dishes of yam are served at the feast, as the festival symbolises the abundance of the produce. Though the style and methods differ from one community to the next; the essential components that make up the festival remain the same.

In some communities, the celebration lasts a whole day, while in many places it may last a week or more. These festivities normally include various entertainments and ceremonies, including the performance of rites by the traditional ruler, or the eldest man, and cultural dances by men, women, and children. The festival features cultural activities in the form of contemporary shows, masquerade dances, and fashion parades.

Usually, at the beginning of the festival, the yams are offered to the gods and ancestors before being distributed to the villagers.

The ritual is performed either by the oldest man in the community/the priest of *Ala/Ani* deity or by the traditional ruler or eminent title holder, who offers the yams to God, deities, and ancestors as a way of showing gratitude to God for his protection and kindness in leading them from lean periods to the time of a bountiful harvest, without deaths resulting from hunger. After the prayer of thanksgiving to God, they eat the first yam because it is believed that their position bestows on them the privilege of being intermediaries between their communities and the gods of the land.

The rituals are meant to express the gratitude of the community to the gods for making the harvest possible. Therefore, this explains the three aspects of the Igbo worldview, that is, pragmatic, religious and appreciative. Palm oil (*mmanụ nri*) is used to eat the yam.

6. Igbo Men

Traditional Igbo men wore loin cloths wrapped around their waist, between their legs, and be fastened at their back, the type of clothing suitable for the intense heat and jobs such as farming. Men could also tie a wrapper over their loin cloth.

7. Igbo Women

Women carried their babies on their backs with a strip of clothing binding the two with a knot at the chest. Many people and groups in Africa, including the Igbo, used and still use this baby-carrying technique. This method has been modernised in the form of the child carrier. In most cases, Igbo women did not cover their chest areas. Maidens usually wore a short wrapper with beads around their waist with other ornaments such as necklaces and beads. Both men and women wore wrappers.

Children are still considered the greatest blessing of all, as reflected in popular names such as Nwakaego (a child is worth more than money) or Nwabugwu (a child is the greatest honour). In some parts of Igboland, women who successfully deliver ten children are rewarded with special celebrations and rites to honour their waists. Infertility is considered a particularly harsh misfortune. The Igbo believe that it is children who perpetuate the lineage, and to do so, children are expected to continue Igbo traditions and ways.

Women's August Meeting

The women's August meeting is an annual congress held in August by Igbo women. It is a massive home-coming whereby Igbo women in the diaspora and the cities travel back to their matrimonial villages to meet with their local counterparts to discuss matters pertaining to community development, conflict management, human development, and other socio-economic and cultural initiatives. The meeting is usually a three-day ritual and is divided into three parts: the first is held at the village level, the second within the community, and the third is held in churches where thanksgivings are held to mark the end of the meeting.

In the early years of the August meeting, the rich and influential women used the occassion of the meeting to intimidate other women by wearing expensive clothing, wrappers, and jewelry. This act caused a number of women to lose interest and discouraged them from attending, and consequently, the turnout for the meeting dropped in various communities. Many marriages also failed as wives mounted pressure on their husbands to get the latest clothing and wrapper for the August Meeting. This issue was addressed when it was decided that women should appear in pre-chosen uniforms, which put an end to the pressure and competition.

8. Igbo Apprenticeship System (Ịgba Boyi)

The Igbo have a unique form of apprenticeship in which either a male family member or a community member will spend time (usually from their teens to adulthood) with another family, while they work for them. At the end of the time spent with the family, the head of the host household, who is usually the older man who brought the apprentice into his household, will establish the apprentice by either setting up a business for him or giving him money or tools with which he makes a living.

This practise was exploited by Europeans, who used it as a way of trading in enslaved people. Olaudah Equiano although stolen from his home, was an Igbo person who was forced into service for an African family. He said that he felt like part of the family, unlike later, when he was shipped to North America and enslaved in the Thirteen Colonies (Equiano:1837).

The Igbo apprenticeship system is called *Ịmụ Ahịa* or *Igba Boyi*, which became more prominent among the Igbo. This *Ịmụ-Ahịa/Igba Boyi* model was simple. It works in such a way that business owners would take in younger boys, who could be relatives, sibling or non-relatives from the same region, house them, and have them work as apprentices in businesses, while learning how they work and the secrets of the businesses. After the allotted time for the training was reached, five and eight years, a little graduation ceremony would be held for the *Nwa Boyi* (the person that learned the trade). He would also be paid a lump sum for his services over the years, and the money would be used to start a business for the *Nwa Boyi*.

9. Alusi

Ahusi (also spelled *Arusi* or *Arunsi*) are spirits that are worshipped and served in the Igbo religion. There are many different *Alusi* and each has its own purpose and function. A wooden sculpture of the Igbo world is divided into several interconnected realms, principal among them being the realm of the living, the realm of the dead or of the ancestors, and the realm of the unborn. Individuals who led an honourable life and received a proper burial proceeded to the ancestral realm to take their place among the ancestors (*"Ndi ichie"*), who are separate from the *Alusi*. From there, they keep a watchful eye on the clan and visit their loved ones among the living, bringing blessings such as fertility, good health, longevity, and prosperity.

In gratitude, the living offer sacrifices to them at the family hearth, and seek their counsel. Each major *alusi* has a priest in every town that honours it, and the priest is assisted by a group of acolytes and devotees.

10. Ikenga

Ikenga (Igbo literal meaning "strength of movement") is a horned, carved *Alusi*. It is one of the most powerful symbols of the Igbo people and the most common cultural artifact. Ikenga is mostly maintained, kept, or owned by men, and occasionally by women of high reputation and integrity in the society. It comprises someone's *Chi* (personal god), his *Ndichie* (ancestors), aka Ikenga (righthand), and Ike (power), and spiritual activation through prayer and sacrifice.

Ikenga is the spirit of individualism, industry, progress, and self-determination or independence. In the past, the Ikenga was the personal god of most Igbo men. It was a ram-horned wooden effigy with which many Igbo men communed before they set out for the day's work. It was the spirit of Ikenga that guided the Igbo man in his decisions throughout his life. It was the Ikenga that propelled the Igbo man to move beyond his confines and out into the wide world with the sole aim of conquering and mastering anywhere he found himself. The Ikenga makes the Igbo man abhor the enslavement of his spirit. The Ikenga makes the Igbo men to detest the subjection of their spirit. The Ikenga led every Igbo man in the past. Today, the Ikenga spiritually guides every man with Igbo blood, whether or not he is aware of it.

However, some variants of Ikenga are found in the Ijaw, Ishan, Isoko, Urhobo, and Edo areas. Among the Isoko people, there are three types of personal shrine images: Oma, which represents the "spirit double" that resides in the other world; Obo, which symbolises the right hand and personal endeavour; and lvri, which stands for personal determination. In the Urhobo areas, it is also regarded as Ivri, and in the Edo areas, it is called Ikegobo.

Functions of Ikenga

- Symbol of achievement

Ikenga is a personal embodiment of human endeavour, achievement, success, and victory. Ikenga is grounded in the belief that a man's power to accomplish things is in his right hand. It also governs over industry, farming, and blacksmithing, and is celebrated every year with an annual Ikenga festival. It is believed by its owners to bring wealth and fortune as well as protection.

God of time

The concept of Ikenga is a two-faced god, with one face looking at the old year, while the other looks at the new year. This is the basis of the oldest and most ancient Igbo calendar. As a god of beginnings, it has the honorific name of *Ikenga ọwa ọta.*

- Consecration of Ikenga

Ikenga requires consecration before use. Normally, an Ikenga is consecrated in the presence of one's kinsmen or age-mates by the lineage head. Offerings of things like yam, cock, wine, kola nuts and alligator pepper are sacrificed to it. Consecrations are often more elaborate and occasionally less, depending on the financial strength of the owner. If the owner is devoted, he feeds his Ikenga on a daily basis with kola and wine; sometimes periodically, especially before an important undertaking, he offers the sacrificial blood of a cock or a ram to induce the spirit to help him succeed. Following that, the owner expresses gratitude to his Ikenga for assisting him in his success. For the Igbo, success solely depends on the personal *Chi*, represented by Ikenga, and the support of kinsmen.

- Forms of Ikenga

According to M.D.W Jeffreys (2007), there are three types of Ikenga: Ikenga mmadụ (human), Ikenga alusi (spirit), and ntu aga (divination objects). The first is a fully developed human figure with horns, seated on a stool. The second is a cylinder with horns. The divination objects are small and simple and come in different shapes.

- Warrior Ikenga

The most famous type of Ikenga is probably the "warrior," which depicts a fully-formed human figure with horns and a fierce expression. It is seated on a stool, holding objects in both hands. The right hand holds a knife with a pronounced handle and a slightly curved blade, the left hand a tusk or, more often, a severed human head with eyes, a nose, and a mouth bulging out of the concave face. The Warrior Ikenga corresponds to the stage in life when men are expected to demonstrate their military prowess. Owned by many of the younger members of the age grade, it depicts the ideal young man: robust, wearing the warrior's grass skirt, and holding a knife and a severed human head. When performing dances, warrior groups would strike this stance.

The knife is always held in the right hand, called Aka Ikenga (the Ikenga hand), and the Ikenga is also called a shrine to the right hand. In recent times, the overtly violent element of the severed head and knife has been replaced by a more metaphorical way of using them as symbols of aggression. The most characteristic of all the iconographic elements of the Ikenga, the horns (opi), also carry this connotation. The Igbo proverb says, "The ram goes into a fight head first" (*Ebune ji isi éjé ogu*); that is, one must plunge into a venture to succeed.

- Community Ikenga

A second major type of Ikenga, an elaboration of the warrior form, has a superstructure with human or animal images, or both. The seated figure often displays a tusk in the left hand and a staff in the right. In many examples, *ichi* marks are represented on the face. Some of these figures, especially the very large ones, often more than a metre high, do not belong to an individual but to an age set or a lineage segment. These community Ikenga figures represent group rather than individual achievements and prestige, and demonstrate continuity between the individual and society. They are related to the display figures known as *Ugo na-achọ mma* ("the eagle seeks out beauty") and display a great deal of artistic inventiveness.

In the simpler examples of this group, the superstructure on a disc base supports animal figures. Other large Ikenga have very intricate superstructures consisting of two horns that circle the sides of the head and continue upward to form another circle terminating in snake heads. Pointed protrusions occur on the lower part of the horns. Above the head are four ram heads and one or more leopards at the top.

The motifs on the community Ikenga tend to have complex headdresses, signifying collective ownership. The motifs also depict what the community is known for, for instance, whether they are known as warriors, hunters, traders or predominantly farmers. All males born in the previous year are brought before the community Ikenga during the annual festival and thus validated as community numbers.

- Title Holder's Ikenga

The elaborate Ikenga figures, especially those with superstructures, seem to correspond to the more advanced, title-taking stages in a man's life. The three-legged stool, known as the Awka stool (*Oche Ọka*) was reserved for one of the highest ranks of the title system, the Ọzọ title. The staff indicates authority and comes in a complex hierarchy, from a simple wooden one to a rod of forged iron with brass rings. The most common type represented in Ikenga is the *nsuagilign*, distinguished by open work on the shaft. The tusk, *Okike*, held in the left hand, is used as a trumpet, Odu. It alludes to the elephant, a wides-pread symbol of power and leadership. A stool and tusk, though not a staff, were often carried for persons of high title by a young boy or girl.

Most of the elaborate Ikenga bear the *ichi* scarification pattern, consisting of parallel vertical lines on the forehead and temples. Scarification was a specialised field of expertise. The *ichi* marks were used to distinguish the highest-ranking members of the title societies, as well as sons and daughters of the nobility. A superstructure usually also consists of references to animals. One prominent animal used on the title-holder Ikenga figures is the leopard, *odum*, the king of the animals and an emblem of the political authority of a titled man.

All Ikenga figurines feature ram or other animal horns, which represent strength and ferocity. Many elaborate examples display a whole figure of a ram, or at least, a full head. Snakes, birds, and turtles may also be included on the Ikenga.

Numerous Ikenga, both the warrior and the titled person's types, have a row of pointed projections flanking the head, usually three or another odd number on each side. Ikenga in the southern Igbo area has three knobs on a horizontal bar. Besides being associated with Ikenga, the number three is also associated with males throughout Igboland. These projections may stand for *nzu,* cone-shaped pieces of chalk used in rituals. This native chalk, suggesting purity and protection, is occasionally applied to the eyes and temples. High-ranking people need magical protection because they are often objects of envy, which is commonly expressed through witchcraft.

11. The Osu Caste System

Osu are a group of people whose ancestors were dedicated to serving in shrines and temples for the deities of the Igbo, and therefore were deemed property of the gods. Relationships and sometimes interactions with Osu were (and continue to be) prohibited in many parts of Igboland, despite the arrival of Christianity and the intervention of Christian missionaries. To this day, being called an Osu remains a stigma that prevents people's progress and life styles.

12. Igbo Mythology

While many Igbo people are Christians today, Ọdịnala is the traditional ancient Igbo religion. In the Igbo mythology, which is part of their ancient religion, the Supreme God, is called Chineke (the Creator). Chineke created the world and everything in it and is associated with all things on Earth. To the ancient Igbo, the Cosmo, or the Universe, is divided into four complex parts - Okike (Creation), Alusi/Arụsị (supernatural forces or deities), Mmụọ (Spirit), Ụwa (World).

13. Igbo Pottery

The Igbo-ukwu Archaeology dates back to the 9th century, but Isiah Anozie discovered it in 1939 while digging a cistern pit in his compound at Igbo-ukwu. Other archaeological sites in 1959 and 1964 were discovered by Thurstan Shaw – the oldest in West Africa, even older than those of Ife and Benin.

In addition to the famous bronzes, clay vessels were discovered at the Igbo-ukwu archaeological site that bear striking resemblance in terms of design to those produced during the twentieth century. The most common type in this long legacy of production is the narrow-mouth bottle design. This kind of container usually has two lug handles, one on either side, which may indicate that the objects were suspended using rope. Another possibility is that the handles could be used as anchoring points for ropes that held a stopper in place. Contemporary vessels are often decorated with various colours and motifs and used for both practical utilitarian purposes, such as carrying water or storing food, and ceremonial purposes.

Popular Western perceptions of art as works removed from daily life have resulted in a misunderstanding of the abstract meanings applied to potted vessels in the Igbo tradition. Clay objects often have physical uses but also spiritual and aesthetic uses. Decoration is often seen as superficial but has complex associations.

Unfortunately, the removal of the objects from their original context inhibits the degree to which meaning can be reconstructed. The practical and artistic qualities of the works are complementary, but display the strips clay vessels of their everyday uses. It has been argued that the process of shaping the natural material of clay is a starting point for aesthetic and metaphysical value within the Igbo culture.

Ethnographic studies have demonstrated that the production of traditional Igbo pottery has declined due to the spread of Western technologies. The heightened cross-cultural connections in the period immediately following decolonisation led to a period of peak production. However, eventually, the more widespread acceptance of modern influence coinciding with intense economic development resulted in the extinction of Igbo pottery in some areas. Despite the entrance of mass-produced containers, the traditional importance of the vessels in some locales has been cited as a driving force for continued production (Ali, 2014-07-01).

14. Uli/Uri

Uli is the name given to the traditional designs drawn by the Igbo people of Nigeria. Uli's drawings are strongly linear and lack perspective. They do, however, balance positive and negative space. Designs are frequently asymmetrical, and are often painted spontaneously. Uli, generally, is not sacred, apart from those images painted on the walls of shrines and created in conjunction with some community rituals.

The drawing of uli was once practised throughout most of Igboland, although by 1970 it had lost much of its popularity, and was being kept alive by a handful of contemporary artists. It was usually practised by women, who would decorate each other's bodies with dark dyes to prepare for village events, such as marriage, title taking, and funerals. Occasionally, designs were also created for the most major market days.

15. Carved Doors

The Igbo use carved wooden panels as entrance to doorways into the compounds of titled members of the prestigious Ọzọ title holders. Members of sufficiently high-ranking individuals have the authority to commission sculptors to carve the panels. Carved doors and panels were also apparently adopted or used in the houses of wealthy families as a means of displaying wealth. Igbo doors are delicately carved with deeply cut abstract designs in striated and hatched patterns that catch the sunlight to produce high contrasts of light and shadow (Neaher, 1981).

The carved wooden doors establish the boundary between the inner space of the structure and the area outside. The visibility of the works and their location on the boundary permit them to serve as both a warning and an invitation to the viewer. The carvings serve as visual representations of the status and privileges of the household as status markers within the Ọzọ society.

16. Mbari

Igbo art is noted for Mbarị architecture. Mbarị houses of the Owerri-Igbo are large, open-sided, square-plan shelters. They house many life-sized, painted figures (sculpted in mud to appease the *Alụsị* (deity) and *Ala, Ani*, the Earth Goddess, along with other deities of thunder and water). Other sculptures are of officials, craftsmen, foreigners (mainly Europeans), animals, legendary creatures, and ancestors (Aniakor, 1996: 214–240).

Mbarị houses take years to build in what is regarded as a sacred process. When new ones are constructed, old ones are left to decay. Everyday houses were made of mud and thatched roofs, and bare earth floors with carved design doors. Some houses had elaborate designs both in the inside and out. These designs could include Uli art designed by Igbo women.

In Mbarị houses, there is a close relationship between where material objects are placed within the domestic environment and their symbolic significance. Domains within the house reflect societal dynamics outside the house. The house delineates the private space from the public space and within the house itself, male and female spaces exist through the work performed. Accordingly, the objects within the gendered sections gain meaning through the associations with the work and activities that occur there. Mbarị houses are seen as taking on a larger societal significance beyond just being shelters. They become reflections of the cosmos and a cycle of rebirth.

17. Igbo Music

The Igbo people have a melodic and symphonic musical style, which they designed from forged iron. Among the instruments used in their music are Udu, Opi, Ogene, Ekpịlị, Ekwe, Ikoro, Ịgba, Ịchaka, and Ọja, a wind instrument similar to the flute.

Another popular musical form among Igbo people is highlife, which is a fusion of jazz and traditional music and is widely popular in West Africa. The modern Igbo highlife is seen in the works of Prince Nico Mbarga, Dr Sir Warrior, Oliver De Coque, Bright Chimezie, Celestine Ukwu, and Chief Osita Osadebe, who were some of the greatest Igbo highlife musicians of the twentieth century. There are also other notable Igbo highlife artists, like Mike Ejeagha, Paulson Kalu, Ali Chukwuma, and Ozoemena Nwa Nsugbe.

18. Igbo Art

Igbo art is known for various types of masquerades, masks, and outfits symbolising people, animals, or abstract conceptions. Igbo art is also known for its bronze castings found in the town of Igbo-ukwu, which dates back to the 9th century. Igbo culture is a form of visual art and culture.

19. Igbo Traditional Attire

Traditionally, the attire of the Igbo generally consisted of little clothing, as the purpose of clothing then was to conceal private parts, although elders were fully clothed. Children were usually naked from birth until their adolescence (the time when they were considered to have something to hide), but sometimes, ornaments such as beads (Jigida) were worn around the waist for protective reasons.

Uli body art was also used to decorate both men and women in the form of lines that formed patterns and shapes on the body. With the advent of colonialism and the Westernisation of Igbo culture, Western-style clothes such as shirts and trousers supplanted traditional clothing.

20. Modern Traditional Attire

Modern Igbo traditional attire generally comprises (for men) of the *Isiagu* top, which resembles the African Dashiki. Isiagu (or *Ishi agu*) clothing is typically embroidered with lions' heads. It can also be plain (usually black). It is worn with trousers and can be paired with either a traditional title holders' hat (a fez cap named *okpu agu* or *agwu*), or with the traditional Igbo stripped men's hat (which resembles the Bobble hat). For women, an embodied puffed sleeve blouse (influenced by

European attire) along with two wrappers (usually modern Hollandis material), or Ankara cloth and a head scarf are worn.

21. Igbo Calendar (IGUAFQ IGBQ)

In the traditional Igbo calendar, a week (*Izu Igbo*) has four days (*Ubọchị Igbo*) (*Eke, Orie, Afọ, Nkwọ*). Seven weeks make one month (*Ọnwa Igbo*). One month has 28 days, and there are 13 months in a year. An extra day is added in the last month. The names of the days have their roots in the mythology of the Kingdom of Nri. It was believed that Eri, the sky-born founder of the Nri Kingdom, had gone on a journey to discover the mystery of time. On his journey, he saluted and counted the four days by the names of the spirits that governed them, and so the names of the spirits (*Eke, Orie, Afọ and Nkwọ*) became the days of the week.

No.	Months (*Ọnwa*)	Gregorian equivalent
1	Ọnwa Mbụ	(3rd week of February)
2	Ọnwa Abụq	(March)
3	Ọnwa Ife Eke	(April)
4	Ọnwa Anọ	(May)
5	Ọnwa Agwụ	(June)
6	Ọnwa Ifejiọkụ	(July)
7	Ọnwa Alọm Chi	(August to early September)
8	Ọnwa Ịlọ Mmụọ	(Late September)
9	Ọnwa Ala	(October)
10	Ọnwa Okike	(Early November)
11	Ọnwa Ajana	(Late November)
12	Ọnwa Ede Ajana	(Late November to December)
13	Ọnwa Ụzọ Alụsị	(January to Early February)

An example of a month: Ọnwa Mbụ

Eke1	Orie2	Afọ	Nkwọ
3	4	5	6
7	8	9	10

11	12	13	14
15	16	17	18
19	20	21	22
23	24	25	26
27	28		

22. Naming Children after Market Days

Newborn babies were sometimes named after the day of the week they were born. This is no longer in fashion. Mgbeke (maiden, born on Eke day), Mgborie (maiden, born on Orie day), were popular names among the Igbo people. For males, Mgbe is replaced by Nwa or "Okoro." For example, Okoro (Nkwo), Okoro (Eke) or Okeke, Nwa (Nkwo), Nwa (Afo), Nwa (Eke), or Nweke, etc.

The Igbo and the Crisis of Cultural Identity

Many Igbo people have often been accused of being unfaithful to their culture, of literally abandoning their traditional way of life to assume or imitate other people's culture and traditions. This is due mainly to the high mobility of the Igbo, their upward movement, their ease of accommodation, and their readiness to adapt to new changes. The last of the three major ethnic groups in Nigeria to come face-to-face with an alien culture, the Igbo, as soon as they became convinced of the new system brought in by European colonialism, embraced it with all their might. In the process, they forgot about or abandoned many of their traditional practices.

Consider language culture, for instance, unlike their Hausa/Fulani and Yoruba counterparts, the majority of the Igbo prefer to communicate in English rather than their native Igbo language. Even those who could barely make one correct sentence in English would still prefer to speak with their children and wards in English, and they would proudly beat their chests to tell you that their children neither understand nor speak the Igbo language! You then begin to wonder and ask what happened to the Igbo identity, or the Igboness, in such a person who could hardly utter a word in Igbo.

Even some Igbo traditional rulers, the so-called custodians of Igbo culture and tradition, are suffering from this ailment. Take the kola nut, a symbol of Igbo hospitality, for example. Every Igbo man will tell you that the "kola nut does not understand any foreign language", yet, in the course of their breaking it, while starting the accompanying prayer in Igbo, would still end it with "... through Jesus Christ our Lord"!

The United Nations Educational, Scientific, and Cultural Organisation (UNESCO) had predicted that many indigenous languages would soon become extinct because of their neglect. We pray that the Igbo language will not be one of them.

Aside this language issue, the Anglo-Saxon culture, that is to say, the British and American culture, and by extension, the European culture in general, is now the most influential or preferred culture in the world. Critics refer to this practise as "cultural monism". Fukuda (1995) described it as the "McDonaldisation" or "Coca-Colasation" of the world, which is to say, the Americanisation or Westernisation of the world. It is also known as "the cultural domination of the world" by the United States of America and the countries of Western Europe.

European sports, European entertainment, European music, European relaxation techniques, European dress code, etc., are now the toasts of many African youths. They parrot European songs, and dance to European music. They know by heart all the football players and football clubs in Europe, and belong to each of these clubs, but they know nothing about their local football clubs.

While majority of the Yoruba and the Hausa/Fulani could be easily identified with their respective dress codes, a good number of Igbo people prefer to dress like Europeans and lead the European way of life or lifestyle. Mbonu Ojike, a former Nigerian politician, became very popular in the 1950s because of his love for and promotion of the Igbo language and culture. He was popularly called the "Boycott King" and "Boycott the Boycottable".

On inter-faith relations, African Traditional Religions (ATRs) were regarded by the Europeans as "black magic", sort of mumbo jumbo, or voodoo. These were regarded as the incarnation of the devil. African gods, always with a small 'g', were long declared dead and buried. Christianity and Islam are the only two recognised religions in Nigeria; many Igbo people prefer Christian names to their local names.

At the same time, core Igbo values like respect for elders, rendering help to those in need, being one's brother's keeper *(Onye Aghana Nwanneya)*, as well as the well-known Igbo hospitality and kindness to strangers, have equally been thrown overboard. It has become normal to see a 65-year-old man greet his 35-year-old employer, *"Oga Sir,* and carry his bag to his office, instead of the other way round.

This state of affairs started several centuries ago, during the Trans-Atlantic slave trade era, when the first European ships anchored on the coast of West Africa and carried away thousands of African youths, men, women, and children, to the United States of America and the West Indies, whom they sold into slavery. Some of the slaves who managed to survive the ordeals and torture on board the slave ships were made to forget the land of their birth, culture, language, religion and moral values, and forced to imbibe foreign cultures and foreign ways of life.

After slavery came colonialism, which included religious and cultural disorientation in addition to economic exploitation and political dominance. Generally, everything about the Igbo and Africa was considered evil and devilish, which must be rejected and thrown overboard. This made the people develop an ingrained hatred of themselves and everything about Africa, like African history, African culture, language, and religion. Frantz Fanon (1995) put it this way:

> Colonialism is not satisfied merely with holding a people in its grips and emptying the native's brain of all form and content. By a kind of perverted logic, it turns the past of the oppressed people, and distorts, disfigures and destroys it.

Michael Angulu Onwuejeogwu (1981) recalls that

> By 1700 the Igbo had reached a level of civilisation which might have developed along a different path were it not for the intervention of the Atlantic slave trade generated by Western civilisation which was devastating to the American Indians. Between 1700 and 1900 the devastating effect of the slave trade on Igbo culture and civilization was total and final...
> By 1914, the Igbo theatre of civilisation had been integrated into what we today call Nigeria. Igboland ceased to be the theatre of

civilisation; it became a periphery of a larger periphery whose capital is at Lagos and its centre in London…

Furthermore, he explained, when the British administrators "liberated" Igboland, they destroyed the moral structure and values of the people. "Crime wave, injustice, and misadministration spread all over Igboland because the backbone of Igbo morality received a mortal blow from the hands of imperialists/colonialists who built prison yards at Awka, Onitsha, Owerri, and Ngwo (Enugu) to deal with the high crimes of murder, manslaughter, felony, arson, and robbery". In the same vein, according to Chris Ebighgbo (ibid),

> Between 1914 and 1960, the Igbo spread out rapidly into all parts of Nigeria. Then a sudden change in the value system began. Some Igbo began to join secret societies of Yoruba origin. The Igbo have the mmuọnwụ cult, which was reduced to an entertainment instrument by pressure from Christian converts who were encouraged to burn or destroy all objects of traditional religion. They were stopped from singing traditional songs or even teaching traditional stories. Even traditional moral codes that were parallel to Christian moral codes were attacked.
> The Nigerian civil disturbances and war, between 1966 and 1970, had introduced a rapid change in Igboland. The Igbo from different parts of Nigeria, returned to Igboland with different ideas of community life. The war period was for criminal deeds, which further weakened the Igbo ethical code. Sexual and property crimes were on the increase. The ụmụnna moral life was severely harmed by new ideas that did not fit into the system.
> The principles of inheritance and succession to office were abused. Oral traditions were twisted to meet the ambition of reckless individuals who were power drunk and wanted to be new chiefs …
> Igboland is infested with different religious bodies preaching different dogmas of the Bible and different Gospel. They speak in tongues. They cast away demons, witches, and wizards. They claim miracles and see visions. All these change the quality and content of the Igbo value system.

This loss of the Igbo value system and cultural identity was further accentuated by the new wave of globalisation, which seeks to make all countries of the world one global family, seen only through the lenses of Western Europe and the United States of America. Under this new system, distances are drastically reduced, and events happening thousands of kilometres away are instantly brought to our doorsteps. People, races, politics, economies, cultures, and institutions now come together without difficulty. Meetings and conferences are conducted at different venues without losing a single second.

As a result of globalisation, bridges of misunderstanding and prejudice built over the years, and cultural biases that kept people apart were destroyed, in the same way that as the walls that once separated countries were pulled down. People of different races and colours now share the same worldview, the same ideology, the same religious belief, and the same cultural outlook – language, dress code, food, relaxation and entertainment spots, etc.

However, what is being shared as a result of globalisation are the dominant worldview and dominant ideology of the West, which are constantly being mirrored by the Western media. This situation, which some people call "progress", is responsible for the present social decay manifested by an increase in crime waves and different forms of deviant behaviour in many parts of Igboland, and indeed, throughout Nigeria. It is the consequence of the people's abandonment of their indigenous cultural values and the absorption of foreign life styles that are in conflict with their traditional way of life.

The Igbo Renaissance

In recent time, some appreciable efforts have been made to revive and promote the African way of life, and the Igbo language and culture. In this regard, mention must be made of the activities of the high-profile Nigerian soap opera, *Nollywood*, which has been projecting African and Igbo culture across the globe. Even though some people would criticise some aspects of the home opera as sometimes exaggerated or out of tune with reality, it somehow has helped to reconnect the Igbo with their cultural past.

The Christian missionaries, who initially were the albatross of African cultural heritage as agents used by the colonialists to destroy the African culture, are now coming out strongly to promote indigenous languages, particularly the orthodox churches that conduct most of their services in the Igbo language.

One-time military governor of old Anambra State, Sampson Emeka Omeruah, in a bid to preserve and promote the Igbo cultural heritage, once insisted that civil servants in the state come to work on certain days of the week dressed in traditional attire, just as the present Anambra State House of Assembly has mapped out one day in a week when all its deliberations must be conducted in the Igbo language.

In the same vein, the compulsory introduction of local languages as part of the school curriculum is also part of the effort to promote African languages and culture. The media, in particular, the electronic media, are equally playing significant roles in the promotion of the Igbo language and culture through their various programmes.

It is necessary to stress the need for these efforts to be sustained and for more people to be recruited to key into the scheme. As the 19th entury African educationist and writer, Edward Wilmot Blyden had posited, "Every race has a soul, and the soul of the race finds expression in its institutions, and to kill these institutions is to kill the soul. No people can profit from or be helped by institutions that are not the outcome of their own character" (Eze, 2011:112).

This is not to suggest that the Igbo or Africans should close their doors and windows and refuse to admit any wind coming from outside. On the contrary, that would be isolationism, which is anti-progress. While acculturation as a meeting of cultures is accepted, the claim of superiority of one culture over others, specifically the claim of superiority of European and American cultures, over the cultures of the rest of the world, is rejected.

Since empiricists believe that knowledge is gained through experience, through contact with the outside world, the Igbo would garner more knowledge, more information, and a better understanding of reality and the environment as a whole through contact or interaction with the people outside or around them. What is necessary is for the people to take what is good from outside and discard what is not in accord with their culture and tradition.

Thus, for the Igbo, the task is to look back at their past, take what is considered good and valuable, and discard the rest. They should, at the same time, look at what is placed before them in the form of cultural orientation, take what is considered good, and discard what is bad. This is because not everything that comes from outside is bad, and not everything from within is good.

References

Achebe, Chinua (1983) *The Trouble With Nigeria* (Enugu: Fourth Dimension Publishing Co. Ltd.)
Achebe, Chinua (1958) *Things Fall Apart* (London, Heinemman)
Afigbo A.E. (1981) *The Age of Innocence*, (Owerri, Ahiajioku Lecture)
Ali, Vincent Egwu (2014), 'A Critical Survey of the Growth, Decline, and Sustainability of Traditional Pottery Practice among the Igbo of South Eastern Nigeria', *The Journal of Modern Craft* 7 (2): 123–139.
Animalu, AOE et al (eds. 2003), *The South East Today: The way forward*, (Nsukka, Ucheakonam Foundation Ltd.)
Animalu AOE (2001) *Ucheakonam: A Way of Life in the Modern Scientific Age* (Owerri, Ahiajioku Lecture)
Aniakor, Chike C. (1996), 'Household Objects and the Philosophy of Igbo Social Space', *African Material Culture*, (Indiana, Indiana University Press) pp. 214–240.
Ebighgbo, Chris (2002), The *Igbo Lost Worlds* (Enugu: Ezu Books Ltd)
Equiano, Olaudah (1837) *The Life of Olaudah Equiano or Gustavus Vassa: The African*, (Boston, Isaac Knapp), Available at: https://docsouth.unc.edu/neh/equiano1/summary.html
Eze. D (2011) *Akama Ogwugwu Ebenebe* (Enugu: Linco Press)
Fanon, Frantz (1966) *The Wretched of the Earth* (New York, Grove Press)
Fukuda, Yuji (1995) 'Groupism', *Human Studies*, No. 15.
Ike, Obiora (2001) *Understanding Africa* (Enugu: CIDJAP Publications) p.39.
Jeffreys, MDW (2007) Ikenga: 'The Ibo Ram-headed God', African Studies, (online), January 19, available from https://www.tandfonline.com/doi/epdf/10.1080/00020185408706926
Madukasi, Francis Chuks (2018), 'Ozo Title: An Indigenous Institution In Traditional Religion That Upholds Patriarchy In Igbo Land South Eastern Nigeria', *The International Journal of Social Sciences and Humanities Invention*, 5(5):4640-4652
Mbiti, JS (1969) *African Religions and Philosophy* (London, Heinemann Educational Books Ltd.)
Moyers, Bill (1989), *A World of Ideas: Conversations with Thoughtful Men and Women about American Life Today and the Ideas Shaping Our Future* (New York, Doubleday)

Neaher, Nancy C. (1981). " 'An Interpretation of Igbo Carved Doors', *African Arts*, 15 (1) , pp . 49-55

Onwuejeogwu, MA (1981) *An Igbo Civilization: Nri Kingdom and Hegemony*, (London, Ethnographica).

Onwutalobi, Anthony-Claret (nd), 'New Yam Festival' available at. www.nnewi.info (The Official Nnewi City Portal).

Tempels, Placid (1945) *Bantu Philosophy* (Paris: Presence Africaine)

CHAPTER THREE

Traditions of Igbo Origin

Introduction

Historians have over the years formulated three different theories or versions where they try to unravel the mystery of the origin of this upwardly moving people, called the Igbo. Unlike the Yoruba, who look up to the mythical Oduduwa in Ile Ife as their ancestor, and the Hausa, who trace theirs to Bayajidda in Daura, the Igbo have no such father figure or founding home. Although some people regard Eri, the mythical ancestor of the Nri, as the founding father of the Igbo, and Nri, as their ancestral home, many scholars disagree.

In other words, the origin of the Igbo is shrouded in mystery and mired in controversy, and there are as many versions or theories of the Igbo origin as there are as many writers on the subject. This makes it difficult, if not impossible, to say which one is the most credible, or which one should be accepted.

Among these various versions of Igbo origin is the migration theory, which holds that the Igbo migrated from the Middle East, either from Israel or Egypt. This is based on the similarities between certain aspects of Igbo culture, customs, and languages and those of the Israelis or the Egyptians. In the mad rush to claim Jewish identity, this idea seems to be the most popular and, without a doubt, the most abused.

Another version is the Niger-Benue confluence theory, which is based on the linguistic affinity of a group of ethnic groups classified as the Kwa sub-family of the Niger-Congo language family. Working through glotto-chronology and lexico-statistics, the theory holds that as far back as 6,000 years ago, the Igbo, Yoruba, Edo, Idoma, Igala, Igbira, Igede, and Bassa lived together as one people and spoke one common language around the vicinity of the present Lokoja. From there, they dispersed and developed distinct dialects, which in time metamorphosed into full-blown distinct languages.

Then there is the autochthony version, which claims that the Igbo did not originate anywhere, at least, in any remembered history, but have occupied their present habitation for thousands of years. This theory is supported by the evidence of the antiquity of settlement, archaeological discoveries and excavations, as well as the study of geological fossil remains of human activities. We shall hereunder proceed to examine each of these versions.

i. The Middle East Oriented Theory Origin of the Igbo

The Igbo-Middle East theory of the origin of the Igbo has different proponents who believe that the ancestral Igbo travelled different routes to reach their present destination. These include the Jewish ancestry, the Egyptian connection, and the Ado-na-Idu hypothesis.

(a) The Claims of Jewish Ancestry

The Jewish ancestry of the Igbo is propagated by some influential writers that date back to the 18th century, like an Anglican prelate, George Thomas Basden (1938:6), and a freed Igbo slave, Olaudah Equiano **(2013: 355–387)**. These theories attract popular support. The version states that Igbo were of the Middle Eastern stock, specifically that they originated in Israel. References were made to the similarity of cultures and customs between the Igbo and the Jews to justify the claim that one evolved from the other. The Igbo were even referred to as one of the "Lost Tribes of Israel" during the Dispersion, while some parallels were drawn between the Igbo rituals and customs, and those practised by the Hebrews or Israelites.

Among these shared traditional practises were the circumcision of male children eight days after birth, refraining from eating "unclean" or taboo foods, mourning the dead for seven days, celebrating the new moon, conducting wedding ceremonies under a canopy, and using palm fronds to announce certain events.

The Jews, for instance, used palm fronds to welcome Jesus when he made a triumphant entry into Jerusalem before His crucifixion on the Cross, while the Igbo use weaved palm fronds to celebrate the New Yam festival, or the arrival of new yam, the king of all crops. Also, in Igbo, pallbearers use palm fronds to indicate that they are carrying a corpse. Anyone who sees them will give way and allow them to pass.

Mokwugo Okoye (2013: 355–387) holds that both the Igbo and the Israelites believe in "a Supreme Being, creator of heaven and earth, and in its antithesis, the Devil (*Ekwensu*); in the right of sanctuary, which enables a man to take refuge in a shrine or in his mother's natal home (*ikwunne*) after committing a serious crime like murder (Deut. iv. 41–42); and in the Igbo *Osu* or caste system". Okonkwo, in Chinua Achebe's *Things Fall Apart,* was forced to sojourn with his mother's kinsmen for seven years for committing a "female crime" by inadvertently killing a young boy during a burial ceremony.

Both the Igbo and the Israelites practise circumcision rites and purification, for example, for adultery, or after childbirth. They use intermediaries in marriage negotiations and practise the Levirate custom, which allows a man to raise children on his brother's widow or widows, etc. It is even remarkable that the old Hebrew veneration of the Ark of the Covenant reappears in the Igbo *Ofo*, a symbol of right, justice and authority, and in the ceremony of *igba ndu* (covenant) as the seal of friendship, reconciliation, and agreement.

In addition, both the Igbo and Jews have a common tradition of a lengthy funeral ceremony (Genesis 50:1-3); they have a common circumcision date, the eight-day period following the delivery of every male child; they use intermediaries in marriage negotiations; and they make a thorough family background check. Abraham did it while negotiating for Rebecca for Isaac (Genesis 24.). Similarly, in Israel, "*Ada*" means first daughter **(Gen 4 vs 19- 20),** which means the same thing in Igbo.

Just like the Israelites, the Igbo were led or ruled by elders and priests. There was no king in Israel until Samuel appointed Saul as the King of Israel, and that was why the Israelites were led by prophets like Moses, Joshua, and so many other prophets. The Igbo carry home their dead, just like the Israelites **(Gen 49 vs 29-50),** while the "Star of David" and some bronze medals were encrypted with Hebrew codes.

In addition, the Igbo-Israeli apologists examined some words/phrases and aligned them with biblical usages to further justify their claim of relationships. Among such words/phrases are: (Genesis), "*Jee na isi isi*" ("Go to the very first"), the first book in the Bible; (Deuteronomy), "*Detere nu umu*" ("written down for the children"), the fifth book in the Bible. (Sabbath), *"Asaa bu taa"*, ("today is seventh"), the day God rested after He completed creating the world; (Cherubim), *"Chere ubim"*, "guard my home," a winged angel represented in ancient Middle Eastern art as a lion or bull with eagles' wings and a human face; (Talitha cumi), *"Nta lite kuo ume"*, "Little child wake up and start breathing", etc.

In their over-zealousness, they also listed some similar sounding names of towns among the Igbo and the Israelis found in the Old Testament Bible such as Amelekite, (Amaeke); Hittite (Ihite); etc., each of which they claim, suggests previous relationship between the two groups.

There was a further claim that the word "Igbo" evolved as a corruption of the word "Hebrew". Olaudah Equiano, a slave Igbo boy who later bought his freedom, and who later bore the name, Gustavus Vessa, was among the proponents of this theory. In the "Narrative of his Life," Equiano (Ibid) said:

> The strong analogy which... appears to prevail is the manners and customs of my countrymen and those of the Jews before they reached the Land of Promise, and particularly the patriarchs while they were yet in that pastoral state which is described in Genesis, which alone would induce me to think that the one people had sprung from the other.

Interestingly, Equiano did not conclusively state that the Igbo evolved from the Jews, but that either the Igbo or the Jews evolved from the other.

We, on the other hand, believe that the so-called Igbo-Jewish relationship, which is based on the similarity of similar-sounding words and phrases between the two groups, is greatly exaggerated, because their meanings cannot be linguistically substantiated.

Nri Claims

To strengthen their claim to Jewish ancestry, the Nri people of Anambra State trace the Igbo origin back to the biblical Jacob, son of Isaac and Abraham. The story goes as follows (Jannah, 2014) "Eri, the father of all Igbos, who hailed from Israel, was the fifth son of Gad, the seventh son of Jacob (Genesis 46:15-18 and Numbers 26:16-18). He migrated from Egypt with a group of companions just before the exodus of the Israelites from Egypt many centuries ago.

> They travelled by water and finally arrived at the confluence point of the Ezu and Omambala (Anambra) Rivers, known as Agbanabo, located in present-day Aguleri, where, according to oral tradition, it was spiritually or divinely revealed to Eri that Agbanabo (i.e., the confluence point of Ezu and Omabala Rivers) was to be their final destination and settlement.
> They moved into the hinterland and settled in present-day Aguleri. But the settlement was not known as Aguleri at that time. Meanwhile, Eri lived and died at Aguleri. Agulu was the eldest son of Eri, who took over from his father after Eri's demise. As the population around Eri's compound at Aguleri increased, and in combination with other factors, some children of Eri and their descendants left Aguleri and founded various other settlements that Igbo occupy today. However, Agulu, the first son, remained in their father's home at Aguleri with his own descendants.

In December 1997, a team of Israeli archaeologists from the King Solomon Sephardic Foundation visited Aguleri, where they claimed to have discovered a memorial onyx stone engraved with "Gad", one of the twelve sons of Jacob (Daily Post, 2017).

Another account put it thus that following the Assyrian invasion of the Northern Kingdom of Israel in the eighth century BC, some ten tribes were forced into exile, among whom was Eri, who later migrated to West Africa where he founded the Igbo nation. Eri was said to be the Special Adviser on Religious Matters to the Fifth Dynasty of the Pharaohs of Egypt, who later migrated southwards and arrived at another confluence, the tributary of the River Niger and Benue, known as Ezu na Omabala. (Dotun, 2014).

The story was formulated this way: Jacob, who was the son of Isaac, son of Abraham, had twelve children namely, Ruben, Simeon, Levi, Judah, Dan, Naphtali, Gad, Asher, Issachar, Zebulun, Joseph, and Benjamin. Gad, the seventh son, had seven sons, namely: Ziphon, Haggi, Shunni, Ezbon, Eri, Arodi and Areli. Sometime in the Middle East, famine struck, and Jacob moved with his family and about 70 other relatives to Egypt (Gen. 46: 26-27). But before then, Joseph, who was the 11th son of Jacob had already been sold to Egypt by his brothers, where he was made Governor General under a King named Pharaoh.

As time progressed, when the Pharaoh who knew Joseph died, the migrants started suffering persecutions from the Egyptians. When Eri, the 5th son of Gad, foresaw the danger, the persecution, and the wickedness ahead, he decided to leave in time with his two younger brothers, Arodi and Areli, and one of his half-brothers. This happened before the arrival of Moses, who was to lead the Israelites out of Egypt.

Eri and his company travelled through Ethiopia, Sudan, and down towards West Africa through the River Nile and landed at a place known as Aguleri through the Omabala River around 1305 BC, where he established and lived close to the Omabala River. Eri was wealthy and wise like his great grandfather, called Abiama or Abraham. Agulu, Atta, Oba, Hebrew/Ibo and Menri were his five sons.

Agulu, as the first son, stayed back and established himself in a place known as Agulu-Eri (Agulu son of Eri), while Atta moved upward north and established himself in a place known as "Igala Kingdom", now in Kogi State. That was why the overall king of the Igala is known as "Atta of Igala". The third son, Oba, left and founded a place known as "Oba Kingdom" in Anambra State.

Hebrew, Hibo, or Ibo, who was a very powerful spiritual man, left and founded Igbo-Etiti, Igbo-Adagbe, and Igbo-Eze, within the Nsukka area and parts of Anambra State. At the same time, Menri left and founded a place known as "Agukwu Nri" and the Nri Kingdom; Arodi moved to a place known as "Aro-Chukwu".

It was Arodi that gave birth to Nembe, Ngwa, Abakaliki, Ogoni, Afikpo, Aro-Ikot Ekpene (Akwa Ibom State), and Aro-Echie in Rivers State. During the slave trade era, Aro people spread to many countries of the world, such as America, Cuba, and Brazil, while the "Aro-festival" was celebrated in Cuba.

Areli was a man of wisdom, who gave birth to Owerri, Umuahia, Diobu in River State, Okigwe, Orlu, Nkwerre, Elele, Mba-Ise, Mba-Ano, etc., while Eri's half-brothers moved and founded the Ijaw nationality and some parts of Edo State and many other parts of the Niger Delta.

He further claimed that in Aguleri, there was a particular house known as Obi Gad (House of Gad), which was the resting or relaxing place for Eri and his brothers. It is also called Eri Temple. Obi Gad served as a consulting place for some royal fathers from the community that had direct root in Eri. Obi Gad was the first Obi house built in Igboland, which was why every Igbo man builds an Obi or Obu in his compound.

According to him, every Igbo man had a family shrine or little oracle, which was due to the fact that the people worshipped the oracle when they were in Egypt, before God gave Moses the Ten Commandments. The first of the Ten Commandments was a warning against idol worship. ("I am the Lord your God; do not worship any other god except me"). At the burial place of Eri, there was a Trinity Tree that stood on the grave site. "They were three trees, but they were strongly united and connected by a single tap root", he claimed (Daily Sun, March 28, 2004).

- **Claims and Counter-Claims**

There are many gaps and contradictions in this migratory theory propagated by the Nri people that border on inconsistency or complete falsehood. In the first place, none of the claimants of Eri ancestry, i.e., Nri, Aguleri, and Umueri, agrees as to the order of precedence, how each of them came about their present locations, or who among them was the rightful heir or custodian of the authority of their ancestor.

For instance, while the people of Nri claim that they were the most senior clan of the Eri ancestor since they inherited the Eri kingship, the *ozo* title, and the *Ofo Igbo,* a symbol of authority, truth, and justice bestowed on them by Eri; the people of Aguleri insist that they were actually the first son of Eri; whereas the people of Umueri said that it was at their place that Eri first settled when he arrived in the Omamballa or Anambra valley, from where he began to give birth to all the other Igbo clans.

According to Nri tradition, Nri was the cradle of Igbo civilisation, with a kingship system that dated back to about AD 940, the first in Nigeria. The Nri Kingdom was said to have provided a safe haven for all those who were rejected in their communities, and thus became a place where "slaves were set free from their bondage". It was for this reason that the Nri devised the Ozo title, which other communities in Igboland later embraced. The Ozo system protected initiates from being sold into slavery, which was widespread at the time (Ikime, 1980).

On their part, the people of Umueri countered this by arguing that the Nri kingship did not come from Eri. According to them, there was no king-making when Eri arrived in Omabala Valley, implying that the Nri kingship came from somewhere else. According to them:

> Eri clan of Israel left the Israelites during their time in the wilderness (post-Egypt exile), migrated from East Jordan towards the Mediterranean Sea, and later crossed back to Egypt, from there to Ethiopia, then to Southern Sudan, from where they sailed through the rivers, and finally found themselves in Omabala or Anambra valley where they settled. They then named the place after their clan, Umu-Eri, which means "children of Eri" (Dotun, Vanguard, Sept 10, 2014).

The migration happened a very long-time ago, before Saul was made king over Isreal. At the new settlement, the culture of Hebrew worship, circumcision, burial, and other customs remained visibly the same with some modifications.

They therefore claim that the Nri kingship came from both the Igala and the Bini kingdoms, who invaded the area sometime in the past, insisting that "there was no king, or culture of king-making until the invasion of the land by the second wave of migration from the Igala descents that brought the system of priest-king along with it. The Bini Kingdom also tried introducing its kingship by imposing the $Ezes$ and $Onowus$, but with limited success".

Nwankwo Nwaezeigwe (2013) flatly denied that Eri emigrated from Israel and thus fathered the Igbo nation. According to him:

> The claim that the Nri, Umunri and Umu-Eri, whichever category one chooses to assign them, are the fountainhead of the Igbo in terms of both culture and historic origins is a mendacious fabrication. The claim that they are also the anchor of Igbo-Jewish historical connections is a sensational fallacy. Above all, their often repeated claim that the artefacts connected with the Igbo-Ukwu

archaeological excavations are of Nri origin and the land on which the excavations took place is historic Oraeri land, cannot be sustained by the circumstances of the origins, migration, and settlement of the present Oraeri town.

That Eri did not come from anywhere outside Nigeria, was also affirmed by an Aguleri born writer, M.C.M. Idigo (1955:5) who unequivocally stated that Eri was of Igala origin. According to Idigo,

> The Aguleri people originated from Igara (sic) and migrated to their present abode about three or four centuries ago. The leader, Eri, a warrior, took his people on a war expedition, and after long travel and many fights, he established his camp at Eri-aka, near the Odanduli stream, a place that lies between Ifite and Igbezunu Aguleri. Eri, with his soldiers, went out regularly from his settlement to Urada, Nnadi, and other surrounding towns on war raids and captured many of the inhabitants. These were the Ibo-speaking people, and by mixing with them and intermarrying, the immigrants adopted the language.

J.S. Boston (1960:55), a European anthropologist who carried out extensive research on the Igala kingdom, the Nsukka, and Anambra River valley communities, also stated that "the northern Umunri villages say that the clan was founded by a man named Eri who came to the Anambra area from Igala country and settled at Aguleri... Eri's son, Nri, left his father's home to found the town that bears his name, and other sons found the remaining towns in this group".

Even the celebrated Professor Michael Angulu Onwuejeogwu (1987) with all his sentimental attachment to the Nri Kingdom, emphatically stated that when Eri arrived in Aguleri, he "met an autochthonous group who had no living memory of their origins". That is to say, people who lived at the place before Eri arrived and could not remember their origin because they had been staying there for a very long time.

In other words, by Onwuejeogwu's admission, some people were already living in Aguleri long before Eri came to inhabit the place. These were the indigenes, "Umudiana" (Children of the Earth). Eri's coming from Igala and subsequent settlement at Aguleri was therefore a secondary migration, while "the migrations of the Onogu, Amanuke and Umunri groups constitute the tertiary settlement category".

Again, since there were already existing and flourishing Igbo communities by the time Eri arrived at Aguleri, it afforded Iguedo, his daughter, the opportunity to be married among their hosts, from which communities like Awkuzu, Ogbunike, Umuleri, and Umueri, sprang up.

Based on this conclusion, Umudiana were said to be the aborigines, the ancient Igbo. That is why they perform

> All the cultural vocations, rights, and privileges the Nri claim today to exercise over and above the entire Igbo, such as Ikpu-alu (cleansing of abominations), ritual roles in ozo title institution, and Igu-Aro, which were original Igbo institutions being performed by the Umudiana before the arrival of the Umunri group from Achalla and Ugbene, respectively (Nwaezeigwe, ibid).

In recognition of the Umudiana people's primacy of settlement, the Umunri bestowed on her the Igala title-name "Adama," which means "first-born" in Igala language and tradition, or "Okpala" in Igbo.

Even the institution of "Eze-Nri" (Nri King), came into existence through the institutional inspiration of the aboriginal Igbo settlers, the Umudiana, who originally used the kingship as a means of servicing their rituo-economic needs. In this respect, the Eze-Nri was initially appointed by the Umudiana to oversee the activities of the Nri ritual agents, who in turn made returns to the Umudiana (Adama). This fief relationship is manifested in the saying, *"Efesie Nri, Nri efee Adama"* (after homage has been paid to the Nri, the Nri in turn pays homage to the Adama).

The practice of Ikpu-Alu was of Igbo origin, but it was later bequeathed to the immigrant Nri group. The *Igu-Aro* ceremony, in both tradition and practice, is also the preserve of the Umudiana group. Eze-Nri himself was, in both tradition and practice, an institutional ritual pawn to the Umudiana, both living and dead, hence the saying, *"Adama na-eri Nri ekpe* (Adama the inheritor of the Nri). (Nwaezeigwe, ibid).

We observe, however, that these Eri-Jewish migratory theorists did not tell us how long or how many years it took Eri to travel all the way from the Jews' wilderness through the River Jordan, accross the Mediterranean Sea, returning to Egypt, and from there travelled to Ethiopia and Sudan, before sailing down to the Omabala Valley where he finally settled. Furthermore, because Eri might have met some people who were already living at the Omabala Valley and instilled Jewish culture in them, the implication is that he would not have been the father of the entire Igbo race, rather a group of people who came with him.

We therefore believe that the originators of Igbo migratory theory were European scholars and anthropologists who, in their bid to show that the black race had nothing to contribute to world civilisation, fabricated the lie that it was Israel that gave the Igbo existence, or that the Igbo came from Israel.

The Ooni of Ife, Oba Adeyeye Ogunwusi (Nwakanma 2019) vehemently denied this standpoint and unequivocally stated that the Igbo race had existed long before the Israelis. Speaking during the 2019 popular *Yoruba Aje Festival*, the Ooni contended that while the Igbo and the Jews were related was because the two groups were "adventurous and aggressive", the Igbo did not come from Israel but the other way around. According to him, while the Igbo and the Jews belong to the same race, the Igbo did not come from the Jews.

"People make the mistake that the Igbo came from the Jews. No. It is the other way around. The truth is that the first human race that existed were the Igbo, before the Jews. The races of the Jews and the Igbo are similar. But the Igbo are far older than the Jews. They are both commercially driven. They are both enterprise in nature. They are both driven by wealth because that is their ancestral belief. That is the race they belong to", he contended.

Similarly, when they told us about the Igbo or their forefathers travelling all the way from the Jewish wilderness, down to Egypt, Ethiopia, and Sudan before getting to the Lower Niger Valley where they allegedly founded the Igbo nation, it looked as if it was a conscious, straight-forward journey directed by God and being led by a Moses in the wilderness to a Promised Land that was already lying in wait for them to inherit.

In the same vein, we find it difficult to believe that those who started the exodus, like the mythical Eri, would have been strong enough or even alive to complete the long journey that took them several centuries to accomplish.

In any case, a deoxyribonucleic acid (DNA) test recently carried out in Anambra State by a team of Israeli experts has disproved any ancestral relationship between the Igbo and the Jews. According to the International President of Jewish Voice Ministries, Rabbi Jonatan Bernis, who led the team of experts that conducted the test, the result of saliva samples taken in Nnewi shows that the Igbo were not Jews (Ujumadu, Vanguard, August, 15, 2014).

Based on the above stated facts, it will be wrong for the Nri, Aguleri, Umueri, or whatever group that claim to come from the Eri clan to be propagating the Israeli ancestry of the Igbo or claim that they (the Nri people) fathered the Igbo nation, when in fact, they migrated to Igboland, and were not originally Igbo.

Similarities in culture and customs between the Igbo and the Israeli could have resulted from cross-cultural contacts between elements of both groups as they travelled in and out of their respective areas, rather than that one sprung from each other. Sometimes, there could be cultural domination, where an influential foreign culture will bear influence over some indigenous cultural practices, such as is currently being experienced with the Euro-American culture that is mesmerising or swallowing up several indigenous practises or traditional ways of life.

If there were migrations out of Israel during the Dispersion era, or if some people had migrated out of Igala land for one reason or another and later found themselves in Igbo land, such people would be taken as strangers (*ọbịa*), and it would be wrong for them to turn around and impose themselves or claim that they had fathered the people they met at their new sojourn.

Autochthonous Igbo society had no class distinctions, no cult, and no kingship system. These class distinctions and cult practises seem to have been imported into Igboland through those who live in riverine communities like Aguleri, Onitsha, Ossamari, Oguta, etc., which was due to the closeness between them and the Igala and Bini kingdoms.

All the same, the Jewish story of Eri should not be dismissed outright because that could be the source of the introduction of some shared traditional practises among the aboriginal Igbo on the ground, including the relatively light-skinned complexion of the Igbo relative to other Nigerians. Such practises were noted by G.T Basden in his book (Among the Igbo of Nigeria, 1921 (op cit) and Olaudah Equiano in his book (Interesting Narrative, 1789 (op cit).

There could be many reasons for this. First, a prolonged period of cross-breeding over thousands of years could lead to the loss of genetic components. Secondly, it could be that the Jewish practises observed among the Igbo in their primitive state were an external influence introduced by some Jewish-cultured migrants to the aboriginal Igbo on the ground. Hence the present Igbo are products of these Jewish-cultured migrants and the aboriginal Igbo they met. This second instance, being the most likely explanation, clearly explains the negative DNA result and affirms Igbo autochthony.

(b) The Igbo-Egyptian Connection

The theory that the Igbo were of Egyptian origin is propagated by those who believe that the Igbo never lived in the present-day Nigerian environment for more than 3,000 years. Therefore, whatever relics are said to be found in the area, such as the pottery found in the Nsukka area that dated 4,500 B.C., were either bought along with the Igbo when they came to settle in their present location or were left behind by those who originally inhabited the area.

The Negro race, to which the Igbo and the entire black race belong, is said to have originated in the Asselar-Khartoum latitude, which then had spread to Egypt, reaching as far as Asia and the southern territory of Persia. On that score, it has been suggested that if the Igbo did not originate from Lower Egypt, then they must have originated from the Near East, since that was the region where the Negro race inhabited in ancient times. As a result, the Igbo and Egyptians had a cultural affinity, which explains their relationship.

F.K. Buah (1986:147), claimed in his *"A History of West Africa States, AD 1,000, Book One: The People",* that "oral tradition of a section of Igbo people suggests that their ancestors originated from the north", probably from Egypt, while C.K. Meek **(1937:5)** similarly maintained that both the Igbo and ancient Egypt share "ancient cultural contacts such as the prevalence of sun-worship, or forms of mummification, and of dual organisation". Furthermore, the Igbo share with Egypt the "ram cult", the Igbo concept that the messenger of the gods of thunder is a white ram, as symbolised in lightning.

Another area where the Igbo were said to be related to the Egyptians was in the colour of their skin. Ancient Egyptians were said to be darker than modern Egyptians. Herodotus, a Greek historian of antiquity, was quoted as having said that "ancient Egyptians had curly hair and a black complexion" (Eluwa, 2008:73).

Although the colour of Igbo people today is either black, chocolate, copper, or reddish-yellow, traditional Igbo stories recall that in earlier times, the Igbo were of white or fair-complexion, which was similar to the complexion of ancient Egypt. Therefore, it is suggested that the difference in the colour of the skin among modern Egyptians is the result of selective marriage among them, with preference given to "persons with a light complexion, high cheekbones, and Nubian elongation of the eyes." Inter-marriages between native Egyptians and immigrant Europeans and Asians of the Caucasian race also contributed to a change in the colour of their skin.

In the same vein, the Igbo who later migrated to their present location in Africa had a fair-complexion, perhaps, much like the American Negroes. This was attested to in the people's recognition of differences in the colour of their skin, when they call or give people names like *"Nwoke ocha"*, (a fair-complexioned man), *"Nwaanyi ojii"* (black-complexioned woman), etc., to indicate that the people were conscious of differences in the colour of their skin.

Among the various tribes of present-day Nigeria, apart from some Fulani communities, the Igbo have the largest population of fair-complexioned people. Their present degree of dark skin colour might have been a result of inter-marriages between them and the people they met on their journey and in their diverse places of settlement.

It was suggested that the possible areas where the Igbo migrated from when they were in Egypt were in Lower Egypt, where the Hebrew colony of Goshen was situated; the Sinai region; or perhaps, Arabia.

To further confirm the Igbo-Egyptian relationships, similarities were also drawn between the dual organisation of the Egyptians and the Igbo, as well as in Kemitian or ancient Egyptian culture, science, and languages, with some aspects of culture found in Igbo society. A particular reference was made to the Nsude pyramids in Udi, Enugu

State, which have been in existence since time immemorial. The belief was that since the Nsude pyramids resembled the Stepp Pyramid of Saqqara in Egypt, which was constructed in 2,648 B.C, it is possible that either the Igbo or the Egyptians learned the art of constructing pyramids through their previous relationships.

The Nsude Pyramids, which are ten in number, made of clay, circular, and stepped, were replications of Nubian-like pyramids. It is not known know when or why these Nsude pyramids were built, but the idea behind them seems to have come from the same cultural, religious, and philosophical traditions that led to the building of the Egyptian Pyramid.

The first base section of the Nsude pyramids was 60 feet in circumference and three feet in height, while the next stack was 45 feet in circumference. The circular stacks kept going until they reached the top. The structures were said to be temples for the Nsude Uto God, or Deity, who was believed to reside at the top. A stick was placed at the top to represent the god's residence. The structures were laid in groups of five, parallel to each other.

The Nsude pyramids were first noticed by a European explorer named Luke Walter in 1891. But it does not seem that the man considered the pyramids to have any historical significance, which was why he did not blow any trumpet about them. It was G. I. Jones, a European anthropologist and colonial administrator, who in 1935 took pictures of the pyramids with a Roloflex camera, which he acquired and developed a system for immediate development, which produced negatives of such high quality that they continue to produce excellent prints six decades later (Ozoene, 2016, Vanguard Nov. 11).

We however observe that it was not only at Nsude that pyramids were constructed. Similar pyramids were constructed in many communities in Igboland, in particular, in some communities around the present-day Udi and Ezeagu local government areas of Enugu State.

The Igbo and the Egyptians equally share the same worship of the sun-god (Anyanwu). The Egyptians call it "Ra", while the Igbo give their child a name like Chukwu (ra). Other related cultures among the Igbo and the Egyptians include the rites of circumcision, menstrual periods among their women folk, similar hair styles, martial arts, etc.

Though, there may be some similarities between the Igbo and the Israeli and/or the Egyptian cultures, one may however confidently argue that such similarities might have been coincidental or that the Igbo might have been practising these customs on their own ever before they became acquainted with the Egyptians, the Bible, the Jewish, and the Christian missionaries. Alternatively, since it is claimed that the first man originated from Africa, is there not the possibility that the Igbo might have even existed before the Israelis and the Egyptians, who perhaps, learned these practises from the Igbo and not the other way around?

The history of the origin of a people, whose main source is tale-bearing, will not be wholly trusted or believed, particularly in the present scientific and digital age. This is because so many things could go into oral tradition, such as personal biases, fabrications, exaggerations or misrepresentations of facts, or outright falsehoods, and it would be extremely difficult, if not impossible, to authenticate or subject such stories to scientific tests.

(c) The Ado-Na-Idu Hypothesis

The Ado-na-Idu hypothesis, or the theory that a group known as Ado-na-Idu, which comprised Igbo and Edo, and their related tribes migrated from Israel, states that the people originally lived in Canaan, but later migrated to Egypt, and from there moved down to the western bank of the Lower Niger basin, where they eventually settled and established the Ado-na-Idu Empire around the 8th century B.C. (Eluwa, 2008:52-111)

That the people left Canaan was necessitated by a series of wars that started with the Hebrew invasion of the territory in the 13th century B.C. This was followed by the Egyptian, Assyrian, Babylonian, and Persian invasions, culminating in the conquest of the Hittites in 717 B.C. This forced many people to migrate to Egypt. But when Egypt itself was invaded and conquered by the Persians; another wave of migration began. P.A Talbot(1932) reported that 'many Egyptians migrated to the south and west when their country was attacked and conquered by the Persians".

The Ado-na-Idu migrants were said to have left the Middle East in the middle of the 9th century B.C., headed downward, and probably arrived in Kukawa on the bank of Lake Chad towards the end of the 9th century B.C. From there, they moved to Zaria, where they stayed for some time before arriving in the Lower Niger Basin between 800 and 750 B.C. It was during their sojourn in Egypt that the group acquired knowledge of iron works, which they imported into Nigeria.

The Ado-na-Idu Empire is said to have predated the kingdoms of Oyo, Benin, Dahomey, and the Ashanti, and was bounded on the north by Nupe land, on the east by the Niger River, on the west by Dahomey (now known as Benin Republic), and on the south by the Atlantic Ocean. The empire was not well known because neither the European nor the Arab travellers went there. Also, the area was destroyed by the slave trade for 400 years, which made it hard for people to live there.

Similarity, place names between the Ado-na-Idu group and some communities in northern Nigeria, suggest possible routes through which the migrating group passed or camped while on their way to the Lower Niger basin. For instance, along the Kukawa-Katagum-Kano-Zaria-Bida-Kabba is a town known as Nguru, found within the Katagun environs, while there are also Nguru towns in the Nsukka area of Enugu State; in Abor Mbaise and Ngor Okpala, Imo State; and in Ubakala, Abia State. Another similar place name is Ogidi, near Kabba in Kogi State, also found in Anambra State. In Zaria, Kaduna State, there is a town called Aba, while there is also Aba in Abia State; Aba(kaliki) and Aba(omega) in Ebonyi State; Aba(agana) and Aba(tete) in Anambra State; etc.

These similar place names may not be coincidence, but rather the result of previous relationships between people from these different areas. This implies that some Igbo people may be able to trace their relations in some far-flung places in Northern Nigeria, or vice versa, where some people previously thought there was no relationship.

Similar place names abound across geographical divides even within the Ado-na-Idu area. For instance, a place name like Agbaja is found in both Kogi, Imo, Anambra and Enugu States. In Kogi State, Agbaja, which constituted a whole administrative division in the Igbira area, is said to be related to the main Agbaja group in Enugu State. Other Agbaja place names are in Nnewi, Anambra State; in Ekwereazu, Obowo, Ugiri, and Osu, Imo State; and in the north-west of Ede, Oyo State. It is believed that these splinter Agbaja groups might have been those who dropped along the way or who failed to make it with the main group to their final place of settlement (Eluwa. Ibid)

Elizabeth Isichei (1973:42) identified the main Agbaja group, now in Enugu State, as occupying a land area "stretching eastwards towards the Nkanu area across Enugu Metropolis, and westwards towards the fertile Anambra valley and up to the Nsukka area", which Talbot (1926:26), quoting the 1921 census report, said had a population of 640,326 inhabitants and thus "constituted the single largest clan in Igboland".

Adiele Afigbo (1981) identified the Agbaja region, specifically the "Nsukka-Udi-Okigwe Cuesta, as the point of Igbo dispersal". It was from this area that the Igbo groups took off and began to migrate to their present locations. During the pre-colonial era, the Agbaja area was a beehive of trading activities, where both goods and slaves were traded.

Afigbo also located two principal routes into the Igbo interior, through which goods, including slaves, were exported outside Igboland. These were the Okigwe-Awgu-Udi trade routes into Nsukka, and Afikpo-Uburu-Ezza-Nkalagu trade routes, also into Nsukka, with Nike as the link between the two trade routes.

W.B. Baikie's expedition team which visited Igboland in 1864 reported the exportation of intricately woven clothing materials made in the interior clans, but exported to the North via Onitsha. They also wrote about "the famous Awka blacksmiths whose products were purchased by Elugu and Agbaja traders" (Isichei, 1977:42).

C. Nwanna (2011) believed that it was the Ezeagu people of the Agbaja clan who taught the people of Awka the art of blacksmithing. He related a popular legend of the Awka people that, following the north-south migration,

> A master smith named Nebuzu (Nebo the smith) from Agulu Umana in Ezeagu area of present-day Enugu State came and settled in Awka and took a wife from the area. He had an only son, named Agulu, who took up his father's trade and taught his own male children (eight of them) his profession.

It was Nebuzu's grandchildren who later taught the Awka people how to blacksmith.

Interestingly, it was also the Agbaja people that facilitated commercial and economic activities in Igboland and throughout West Africa with the introduction of "okpogho" currency, which was used as a medium of commodity exchange before the arrival of European colonialists, rather than the usual trade by barter.

In the language of the traditional Igbo, "okpogho" denotes money, (ego). The people would count their wealth in "okpogho," and would, for instance, say "nnali okpogho", or "nnali ona". "Nnali" means one hundred, while "okpogho" or "ona" (copper), is the denominated currency. Often, you will hear people say "o nwere okpogho" (he has money, or he is wealthy). The Abiriba people will say "gwesa okpogho" (bring money). The Whiteman called it "bracelet manilla." Another Igbo word for "okpogho" is "ego igwe" (iron-money) or "ego ayọrọ (cowries). The Igbo later migrated from "okpogho" to "ego ayọrọ."

Okpogho, in Ezeagu Local Government Area of Enugu State, could be said to be an autochthonous community in that it was the birthplace for iron smelting, or the production of "okpogho" currency. The Okpogho people had made a name for themselves in iron smelting, which effectively ended the world's barter system. The Okpogho people were the first to engage in the production of copper money. As the custodians of "okpogho" currency, they were like the Central Bank of Nigeria. Long before the coming of European colonialism, the Okpogho people had carried out monetized commerce across several cities in West Africa.

Okpoho Community had engaged in iron smelting due to the abundance of iron ore of the bauxite type in the area. The people would go from place to place in search of raw materials for iron smelting and fabrication. This accounted for why there are five different Okpogho settlements. These are Okpogho Imezi, Okpogho Ukwuagba, Okpogho Okube, Okpogho Ngbuta, and Okpogho Mbanito (Eze, 2018:27-28).

Elizabeth Isichei (op cit) reported that during the colonial era, when the colonialists used forced labour for the construction of several roads and railway projects, Okpogho people were exempted from the exercise, as the people were left to continue to ply their trade, that is, the production of "okpogho currency, which was then in very high demand. S.N. Nwabara (1977:98) also informed that it took a series of military expeditions by the British colonial administration to force the Igbo to jettison the "okpogho" or "ona" currency for the people to accept the British currency.

However, with the introduction of British paper currency, "okpogho" currency ceased to be accepted as a medium of exchange, no thanks to its cumbersomeness and the bulky nature. Because of the importance of this indigenous technology, a research group known as the "Okpogho Study Group", is currently collaborating with the Institute of African Studies of the University of Nigeria to unravel the mystery behind the currency.

Coming back to the Ado-na-Idu Empire, we were not told what led to its breakup into two separate kingdoms, Ado and Idu. While the Kingdom of Ado comprised the entire Western Nigeria, including Lagos and Kwara States, the greater part of Dahomey (now Benin Republic), the Nupe area of Niger State, Igala in Benue State, and Igbira, in present Kogi State, with Ife as its capital; the Kingdom of Idu, comprised the present-day Edo State, with Udo, as its capital.

Specifically, those who constituted the Ado Kingdom were the Igbo, Ife, Egba, Egbado, Ekiti, Ijebu, Itshekiri, Ishan, Isoko, Urhobo, Ijaw, Igala, Idoma, Ora, Nupe, and Igbira, while Edo and Iyala, made up the Idu Kingdom.

By that time, the main Yoruba group had not arrived. They were still in the Middle East. The Yoruba left Egypt soon after the Islamic Jihad of 622 A.D., and reached Zaria in 675 A.D. They waited in Zaria for some time before migrating to Ife, having been assured by the emissaries they had earlier sent out to scout the place that the people of Ado (Igbo and allied tribes), who were inhabiting the area, were peaceful by nature, but had developed an advanced knowledge of ironwork technology. Therefore, the Yoruba adopted a diplomatic approach to infiltrate the area by giving their daughters in marriage to Ado princes.

An attempt by the immigrant Yoruba to usurp power in Ife, which the Igbo had opposed, was what led to conflict between the two groups and culminated in the eastward migration of the Igbo and their kindred groups from the territory. The main issue was who should be the traditional head of Ife between Oduduwa, whom the Yoruba made into a god, and Orisa-Nla, whom the Igbo revered as the Ado god.

Upon the death of Oduduwa, the Yoruba immigrants, represented by Okanbi, his first son, sought to succeed him. This was opposed by the Igbo, on the ground that Okanbi was not a full-blooded son of the soil, his mother being an immigrant Yoruba princess, married to Oduduwa. When the crisis assumed a higher dimension, the Igbo, because they thought it is an abomination to shed human blood, particularly that of close relatives, which *Ala, Ani,* and the Earth, abhorred, decided to leave the city. They migrated first to Idu, and later moved out to settle in their present locations.

The last of the Igbo groups to leave Ife were the Onitsha people. That is why they answer "Onitsha Ado", reminiscing about their past. Onitsha people first migrated to Udo, the capital of the Idu Kingdom, where they absorbed some aspects of the Bini culture. They later moved to Aboh before crossing over the River Niger.

As proof of the Ado origin of the Igbo and the relationship between the Igbo and the Yoruba, several communities in the two areas go by the name Onitsha, Onicha, or Onisa. In Igboland, some of these communities are Onicha-Olona, Onicha-Ugbo, Onicha-Ugwu, and Onicha-Ukwuani in western Igboland. There are also Onicha-Ngwa, Onicha-Uboma, Onicha-Amiyi, Onicha-Udo, Onicha-Nkwere, Onicha-Ohazara, Onicha-Agu, Onicha-Ezza-Ama, Onicha-Enugu Enugu-Ezike, and of course, Onitsha-Ado in the east.

In Yorubaland, some communities that go by the name Onisa are to be found in South West of Oyo, North West of Ajawa, South West of Ajawa, West of Iwo, North East of Ogbomosho, SouthWest of Ogbomosho, and South West of Ijebu-Ode. There is also Onisa-Agbede in the North West of Ogbomosho.

As beautiful as this Ado-na-Idu Empire story appears to be, we have some difficulties accepting it. First, we have not been able to validate the existence of this empire in any historical record. If the empire had existed, we believe other writers on Nigerian history would not have omitted it. They would have celebrated it. But everybody seems to be silent about it.

Even renowned Yoruba historian, S.O. Biobaku, did not mention the existence of such an empire. Biobaku (1971:24) wrote that the Yoruba were preceded in their present territory "by peoples who…may be either indigenous inhabitants or more probably earlier immigrants" who were probably the ancestors of the modern Edo people and the lesser-known predecessors of the Fon or Egun, who later established themselves in the area". In other words, if the Ado Kingdom had existed, Biobaku would not have failed to mention it, particularly since its capital was said to be in Ife.

That the area was outside the orbit of Arab and European travellers and therefore was adversely affected "by the activities of the slave trade", was not enough reason why it should have escaped the eagle eye of many other historians who recorded even some lesser events that occurred in the remotest past.

Moreover, if the Ado Kingdom had existed, and the Igbo were the dominant tribe in that kingdom, why is it that the kingship system has become alien to today's majority Igbo population, only to be practised by those on the fringes through the influence of their neighbouring tribes?

Again, it seems to us very ludicrous and absurd that the Igbo could be so cowardly as to have packed their bags and baggage and deserted the town, which perhaps, was their ancestral home, simply because they were opposed to the immigrant Yoruba usurping power in Ife, but did not want to see any blood shed as a result of their opposition.

Therefore, we see the Ado-na-Idu story as a mere concoction, more or less a fable, a piece of folklore, very good for entertainment purposes, and perhaps, designed to massage the egos of some highly-placed individuals.

This is not to suggest that there is no relationship between the Igbo and the Yoruba, as well as many other tribes in Nigeria, and that these people had never lived together. On the contrary, no less a personality than the present Ooni of Ife, Oba Adeyeye Enitan Ogunwusi, has affirmed the close affinity between the Igbo and the Yoruba.

The Ooni of Ife, generally regarded as the custodian of Yoruba history, claims that the Igbo were 'ancient inhabitants of Ife" (Nwakanma, 2019), as evidenced in the traditions and oral narratives of the town. The extant lineages of the Igbo were still present in their habitations inside the Ooni's palace, while "the Igbo quarters are still present in Ife", he asserted.

Oba Ogunwusi maintained that the Igbo were the original inhabitants of Ife and had installed, and practised a culture based on their "… ancient Odinala religion of peace, of the divine rights of the individual and not of kings, of the protection and validation of the weak and infirm, of artistic and creative value rather than of war and destruction", whose values were embodied in the myth of Obatala, the sculptor and creative "demiurge" of current Yoruba mythology. The Igbo Quarters in Ile-Ife were marked by a multiplicity of settlements, known by their ancient name as "Igbo Omoku".

According to the royal father, Obatala was a high priest in the mould of the Igbo priesthood, whose aspects of his priestly function were absorbed by the Ooni, who also absorbed the monarchical order that replaced the Igbo republican order of the Obatala era. Thus, the current Ile-Ife is a hybrid system between the displaced Igbo culture, and the settler order that replaced it.

He explained that the war over Ife was fought between the Igbo and the new wave of migrants to Ife over two different ways of life: the freedom associated with the republican order and the control associated with the monarchy. The Obatala group was defeated and driven into exile, eventually dispersing as far away as Ketu, Dahomey (Benin Republic) and Togo. The republic disappeared, and the monarchy as embodied by Oduduwa, replaced it.

The Ooni further claimed that today's Yoruba festivals, such as the Egungun, Oreluere, Obameri, Moremi, and Edi, preserve and enact the wars that the Igbo had consistently waged against the new settlers (the immigrants).

However, some people dispute this Ooni's suggestion of the ancient Igbo inhabiting Ile-Ife before moving to their present location and point out that archaeological evidence has proved that a place like Igbo-Ukwu is a much older settlement than Ife. Thus, in the current Igbo historiography and assessment of their movements, Ife is a newer settlement of the Igbo, and may have been part of a wave of migration leading to a pavement of Igbo history, following an ancient catastrophe.

Notwithstanding this, there is no doubt that the Yoruba and the Igbo are close and related. Language and cultural patterns indicate points of recent contact and break-off. There is also the Nok hypothesis, which suggests a congulation that broke off at the Niger-Benue valley, with the Jukun, the Igbo, the Yoruba, the Igala, and possibly, the Idu, moving apart into their current settlements. As Adiele Afigbo (op cit) had posited:

A preliminary excursion into the glottochronology of the kwa language sub-family, of which the Igbo is a member, has yielded to the suggestion that most of the member languages of this sub-family (Igbo, Edo, Idoma, Yoruba, etc.) started diverging from their ancestral root between 5000 and 6000 years ago.

Apart from that, there is also a popular hypothesis that identifies what is known as an ancient migration and settlement pattern of the early Igbo, whereby they first occupied the plateau areas stretching from the Nsukka–Udi-Okigwe "cuesta" running in a north-south direction, including the Awka-Orlu uplands to form part of this north-south highland area.

Afigbo proposes another hypothesis in favour of this upland initial habitation by stating that the present soil condition of the northern Igbo area is such that it appears to have been over-worked and less productive for agricultural uses due to a high population density and long period of tilling and habitation, a situation that probably resulted in the development of other forms of specialisation such as smithing, medicine, the priesthood, pottery, trading, and weaving.

From the foregoing, it could be argued that the migration habit of the Igbo must have been informed by the need to seek fertile lands to feed the increasing family clans. Consequently, the migration into the surrounding plains became inevitable, giving birth to what ethnographers know today as Southern Igbo. This comprises areas made up of the people of Uratta, Ikwere, Etche, Asa, and Ndoki and so on.

(d) The Aboriginal Version

The aboriginal version of Igbo origin is the theory that the Igbo were aborigines of their present location, and that the people did not come from anywhere outside the present Igbo land. A very outstanding figure that propagates this view is Catherine Acholonu, an internationally acclaimed researcher.

Acholonu asserted in her 500-page book, "*The Gram Code of African Adam–Stone Books and Cave Libraries, R econstructing 450,000 Years of Africa's Lost Civilizations*" (2005), that the Igbo civilization was much older than any other civilisation in the world and that the Igbo had migrated from nowhere; that the people record and recall their myths and folklores, and consistently tell stories of having not come from anywhere else.

> The Igbo ancients lived by oral history and made attempts to transmit that oracular skill to justify the legacy of Igbo autochthony... The story of the Igbo is not just any other story. It is the story of the black race all over the continent for Ndi Igbo simply means the Ancients, the First People, the Aboriginals (Ndi Gboo, Ndi Mbu Uwa), she affirmed.

Acholonu further observed that the Igbo were the only single human population group to be found in every village in the world.

> They are on a mission for history making, human diversity, religiosity, cerebral and material enterprise, and solidarity... the Igbo oral tradition is consistent with scientific research into the origins of humanity.

According to her, research on the origin and meanings of symbols used in religion and sacred literatures reveal that the Hebrew Bible, the Kabbalahs of the Hebrews and the Chinese, the Hindu Vedas and Ramayana, as well as the recently discovered Egyptian Christian Bible, the Nag Hammadi, confirm the claims by geneticists that

> ...all mankind came from sub-Saharan Africa, that Eve and Adam were black Africans... that the Igbo oral traditions confirm the findings of geneticists, that by 208,000 B.C. human evolution was interrupted, and Adam, a hybrid, was created through the process of genetic engineering.

The Nag Hammadi, interpreting the first passages of Genesis, said that Adam did not initially know his wife, Eve, and that her first two conceptions, Cain and Abel, were contrived and conceived by the evil force (the Serpent in the Garden), who was created in error by a divine female called Sophia. This being, who claimed to be God, was envious of Adam, who had come forth directly from the Supreme Being.

> Intent on derailing God's creation and challenging the authority of the Supreme Being, this being, whom the Nag Hammadi equates with

Jahweh, began to recreate Adam in his own image ("let us make man in our own image and likeness"), thus causing Adam to fall from his pristine god-state. When Abel was killed and Cain was exiled, Adam then knew his wife, and she conceived and gave birth to a son whom Adam named Seth.

Seth was "the perfect son, the Word", "the Logos-Christ", existing in "three abiding entities: The Father, the Mother, and the Child". As the four luminaries of Seth and his seed represent each of the four aeons of divine time, so do the four fish-mongering market deities of Igbo cosmology represent each of the four market days of the Igbo week: *eke, olie, afọ, nkwọ*. This is the origin of the Igbo deification of the number four, Achalonu says.

According to her, the Nag Hammadi maintained that there were two gods: the God of Shem and the God of Ham and Japheth. Ham and Japheth, together with Jesus himself, are the spiritual descendants of Seth, Adam's true son from the One True God, while Shem, the ancestor of the Semitic family of nations, to which the Israelites belong, is the classical antagonist of the Sethian spiritual lineage.

The God that is known in the Hebrew Bible through the Judaic religion, is not the same God whom Jesus refers to as 'My Father'. The Jewish leaders crucified Jesus because they recognised that his teaching was in direct opposition to their religion and that He cast aspersions on their God, Jehovah, also known as Yahweh. Jesus never mentioned God by name and insisted that God had no name, and that any being with a name could only have been named by someone who existed before it.

Jesus also repudiated the Sabbath, saying that God, being infinite and incorporeal, does not need a day of rest as human beings do. This rejection was mutual because the Jewish people have rebuffed Jesus and his religion to this day and are still waiting for the "true" Messiah of the Jews to come. In fact, the biblical record of Jesus' ancestry clearly states that he was descended through David and Jesse from the unbroken lineage of a Moabite (Canaanite) woman, named Ruth.

This is the only message of The Book of Ruth. Jesus' Canaanite origin through the husbandless Moabite woman, Ruth, and the equally 'husbandless' Mary, underscores the fact that there was more Canaanite and less Hebrew blood in him. And this was a direct denial of the fierce injunction of Yahweh that Israelites must never mix their blood with that of Canaanites, either by marriage or by spoils of war.

Yahweh insisted that all Canaanite communities should be exterminated, man and beast alike, to prevent genetic, hence religious mix-ups. All of Abraham's wars and those of his descendants were fought for one reason and one reason alone: – to exterminate the Canaanites, possess their land, and, in so doing, wipe out their religion. The enmity between the Israelites and the Canaanites and the latter's brethren, which includes the Egyptians (the descendants of Ham's first son Mizraim), is therefore a direct fallout of the war of two gods – the God of Jesus, Adam, Seth, Ham, Canaan, and the Igbo, on the one hand, and the God of Noah, Shem, Abraham, Jacob, and the Israelites, on the other.

There is strong evidence to suggest that Adam and his entire lineage up to the time of Lamech, were black in colour and that Noah was the first person born white in the family tree of Adam. The Book of Enoch records that

> Lamech's wife became pregnant and brought forth a child who was to be called Noah, the flesh of whom was as white as snow and red as a rose; the hair of whose head was white as wool and long… Then, Lamech, his father, was afraid of him; and flying away, he came to his own father, Methuselah, and said, I have begotten a son unlike no other child. He is not human; but, resembling the offspring of the angels of heaven (the Nephilim), is of a different nature from ours, being altogether unlike us.

Ham, Noah's second son, was the first son in the lineage of the true God, the Great Invisible Spirit. This explains the reason why the Hamites (Canaanites/Kwa, Egyptians, etc.) undertook to migrate to Africa after the Deluge to be united with the autochthonous Igbo who still held the true light of the living God – the only people who did not experience the Fall.

According to Achalonu, the Igbo words like *Adaa m* – I have Fallen (Adam); *Nna oha* – 'Father of nations' (Noah); the Chinese name for Noah is *Nuwa*, while the Igbo equivalent is *Nna uwa* - 'Father of the whole world'; *Nshi/Eshi* Igbo equivalent of Enoch/Enshi (son of Seth) – 'Lord of mankind', 'Righteous Shepherd'; Igbo observation of leadership by primogeniture (first son) as observed from Adam and his entire lineage, all add up to link the Igbo stock directly, through Canaan and Ham to the family of Adam and Eve, and to the language they spoke – the Proto-proto-language of humanity – the one-world language of the autochthonous earthlings whose remnants still go by the name Igbo!

The creation of Adam was a downward climb on the evolutionary ladder because, Adam had lost his divine essence, he became divided, no longer whole, or wholesome. Oral and written traditions throughout Africa and in ancient Egyptian reports maintain that homo erectus people were heavenly beings with mystical powers such as telepathy, levitation, bi-location, that their words could move rocks and mountains and change the course of rivers. Adam lost all that when his right brain was shut down by those who made him.

The Father, the Mother, and the Child, "exist as perceptible speech", having within it three "aspects, three powers, and three names abiding in three 'n n n', three quadrangles, secretly in ineffable silence", which equally correspond to the Igbo cosmology.

Similarly, she claims that the Igbo language is the only language in the world in which the words for father, the mother, and the child, all begin with n – *nna, nne, nwa*, and the words for each gender begins with n – *nwoke, nwanyi, nwata* – "three powers abiding in three n n n and three quadrangles".

Seth, Adam's son, married and bore a son named Enshi. Enshi is the Sumerian equivalent of biblical Enoch. He had a son, Kenan (Cainan), who was taught "how to smelt and refine gold... ... he and his offspring". As in Igbo culture, the first human family named children according to the circumstances of their birth and according to their parents' expectations of what the child would become. Kenan or Cainan meant simply "smith." This is the origin of the name Canaan, and this connects directly with the Igbo word – *Nka*, from which is derived from the name *Qka* (Awka), master smith.

The Nri mythology records that Awka, the smith, was sent to Igbo land when Eri entreated his father to send him help to dry up the wet land he met on arrival. Eri was a sky being who came into Igbo land following the Anambra River, and on arrival, he made his home among the Igbo. Since Eri knew where he was headed and who he was looking for, when he found them after his long journey from Egypt, he made his home among them, and instituted his brand of culture and religion.

Eri also learned from the autochthonous god-men whom he found there, which was the only reason he would have made the long and hazardous journey. In the remote past, there was the coming and going between Egypt and West Africa, while the name, *Nkannu* (Royal Khennu), and *WaWa* (UaUa), Igbo clan names, were recorded in the Edfu Pyramid Texts of Egypt as the names of a West African close friend of the Egyptian god, Ra.

We however observe that "Wawa" is not the name of any clan, but an Igbo dialect spoken by the people of northern Igboland, from the Oji River through Udi, Nsukka, and Abakaliki, which means an emphatic "no."(ibid)

Achalonu further contends that the Iron Age followed the Bronze Age in the rest of the world, except in Black Africa where iron and agriculture were known as early as 9,000 B.C. By the time Africans began to colonise the world around 5,000 B.C. they took with them the knowledge of bronze working.

The impact of Black Africans in the making of the first civilisations known to man is therefore linked to the fact that Black Africans were the world's first metallurgists. That is to say, Black Africans were the first to discover metal and to work it to perfection. The world's first iron workers, bronze smiths, copper smiths, and gold smiths were black Africans, she said, while research had shown the Kwa people of West Africa as the people who fit into this mould.

Because Sub-Saharan Africa was technically isolated from the rest of the world while developing its own Metal Age at an unknown point in human history, researchers concluded that Black Africa was most likely the world's first inventors of metal-working. A dug-out canoe unearthed in Yobe State, Nigeria, by German archaeologists from the University of Frankfurt, dated 8,000 B.C., two thousand years after the Deluge during the time of Noah, points to the use of metal implements in the early Neolithic period in Sub-Saharan Africa. This supports the thesis that the Canaan metallurgists were black Africans and that the inventor of metal was first an African.

In the Old Testament, the Quenites were mentioned as inhabitants of southern Sinai, while their name literally meant 'smiths and metallurgists'". She further stated that the term, Qa-in, meant 'smith', which stemmed from the Sumerian Ki-n, meaning 'fashioner'. The Sumerian word Ki means 'to cleave', 'to cut decisively', and 'to create by cleaving apart or by division'. It shares the same meaning with the Igbo words *kie* 'to cleave apart', 'to create by cleaving asunder', 'to fashion', and *nka* - 'the art of fashioning' which has the same meaning as the Hebrew Qa-in or In-qa (read from right to left).

In-qa (*Nkwo*) is said to be the name of the father of the Igbo nation, which is why the Igbo are called Igbo-Nkwo. That this event, this myth, is also recorded in Igbo, in the etymon, *kie*, suggests that the Igbo and the Sumerian languages, may have shared the same cosmological roots. And Sumer is said to be the cradle of human civilisation!

From the foregoing according to Achalonu, it could be said that a cultural link existed between the early Sumerians and thepeople of West Africa and that these ancient Babylonians might have been Black Africans. The fact that Kwa-m implies God's creative and generative power, and Kwa-n, God's oldest son,, demonstrates that the root Kwa, is the bearer of the god-essence of the Son, the Word, the Logos – the primal sound.

This fact could be seen in the Igbo language, where Kwa, is the basic root of most words that indicate sound (the word), such as *okwu* (speech), *ukwe* (song), *akwa* (cry, wailing), *nkwa* (drum), *ekwe* (slit-drum). Its equivalent, ka, also relates to sound and to creation and creativity, for example. *ika* (to speak, to cut, to decree), *nka* (creativity), *iku* (to beat [the drum]), *iko* (to narrate), *Dioka* (carver), *Oka* (anglicised as Awka) home of master smiths and of the first known Igbo smith. The Igbo name for the creating deity is *eke*!

Similarly, the etymon Kw/Kwa is the root of the Igbo word for 'first son' or "the first male or undivided line", *O-kwa-ra*! It is also encoded within the name of the founder of the Igbo nation, Nkwo (as in Igbo Nkwo), the generic name of the Igbo nation. This tends to imply that the terms *Okwara* and *Nkwo* are definitions of the Igbo, as the bearers of the undivided bloodline of incarnate First Sons of God!

The corollary to this is the undeniable conclusion that the Khemic/Kwamic (divine) line (the lineage of Ham) could have been borne from God through Adam, through the lineage of Seth, right down to Canaan, and that through the name Kwa-in/Kan, it has been eternally imprinted in the Kwa lineage of West Africa.

Thus, there is overwhelming oral traditional, linguistic and ethnographic evidence that the migrant Kwa people and the rest of the migrants within the Niger Congo family of nations are Hamitic. The North-South Kwa/Igbo migration, which the Igbo and other West African oral traditions frequently allude to, was the same as the North-South migration of the children of Ham after the Flood, from the Middle East through North-East Africa into Sub-Saharan Africa.

Therefore, bearing in mind that the earliest inhabitants of Mesopotamia possessed customs and traditions akin to those of the Igbo, we can only conclude that a Black people who spoke the Canaanite language (a Kwa or proto-Kwa language) and bore the name prefixed by the word Akwa, could only have originated from a West African native population.

Igbo Nkwọ, the clan-name of the Igbo nation, bears the tell-tale signs that the Igbo nation is the proud carrier of the divine bloodline of the Kwa. The name Nkwọ is significant because it not only alludes to the Son of God and the Word through the –kw- stem, but it is also the Igbo word for the palm tree, *nkwụ*.

Many European and Asian languages were said to have been borrowed from the Kwa language group of the Niger-Congo family, such as the English language word: "say", which has its roots in the Igbo word "*sị*", *si-kene, nsi,* (I say), *asị-kwa m* (I say), etc. Everywhere we turn, Igbo words. Everywhere we look, Igbo words are found as root words in languages that predate 3,000 B.C., even before the Flood of Noah, 11,000 B.C., she affirmed.

In the case of the Chinese, their earliest ancestors were said to have spoken the Igbo language or an early form of it, because countless Igbo words have survived in the Chinese language vocabulary. For instance, in Chinese and Igbo: *suo* means 'shrink', 'say/to pronounce'; in Chinese and in Igbo, *ti* means 'to put forward'; *wa*, in Chinese as in Igbo, means 'to dig' 'to excavate'; *tuo*, in Chinese as in Igbo, means 'to throw off'; *mo*, in Chinese as in Igbo, means to sharpen' (knife); while *li*, in Chinese as in Igbo, means 'to stand'; *jie*, 'to take hold of, in Chinese as in Igbo; *zhi*, 'point at/ show' in Chinese as in Igbo.

Other equally obvious lexical similarities between the two languages are: Chinese *fei*, Igbo *fe* 'to fly'; Chinese: *mai* 'to bury', Igbo: *mai* 'to cast into the ground'; Chinese: *ni* 'clay/mud', Igbo: *ani* 'earth';

Chinese: *manyi* 'be pleased/satisfied', Igbo: *masi* 'to be pleasing to'. These and countless other examples of similarities in sound and meaning between the two languages indicate that there was an Igbo presence in China at the formative stages of the Chinese language, or simply that Igbo speakers birthed the Chinese language and culture.

Acholonu further stated that in Igbo culture, the Eshi/Nshi phenomenon is found in place names such as Ama-Eshi (Land of Eshi); Umu-eshi (Children of Eshi); Nwa-nshi (Child of Nshi/Eshi), the local Igbo name for dwarfs. Characteristically, the words Eshi and Nshi, combine to give Enshi, the Sumerian name of the first son of Seth! This, again, supports the thesis that the Igbo take the bearing of their bloodline from Adam through Seth, and that the Canaanite/Sumerian people of Akkad, Babylon, and Mesopotamia, had subterranean connections with the Igbo bloodline.

The dwarfs, known in Igbo as Nshi, were believed to be autochthonous and long-lived. They were holy, for the gods lived among them. It was the Nwa-Nshi - the race of dwarfs, which founded Igbo civilisation and through the Igbo cultural and genetic bloodline, maintained the divine bloodline of the sons of God. They were the ambassadors and sustainers of the Igbo nation's culture, religious practices, and cults, particularly the Ọzọ institution of title-taking and title-holding. The Nwa-Nshi were known in Igboland as wizards who commanded the elements with great ease and who were exceedingly "long lived".

Therefore, this is proof that the story of the first man and first woman started in West Africa among the Kwa, the sons of God! It is also important to note that all Kwa myths of origin insist that their ancestors were sons of God who fell from grace and from heaven and found themselves marooned on an inhospitable earth.

The Kabbalah says that Adam's fall was a breaking/smashing to pieces of the unity of the Godhead, and that the process of restoration, "repair", or "fixing" of Adam's scattered soul, or of restoring the original unity of the universe, is called *"Tikkun"*. The Igbo word for *"Tikkun"* is *tiko-onu,* which means, 'unite', 'bind', 'join separate parts together'! The universal preeminence of the *Tikkun/Tikonu* philosophy is thus expressed in the Igbo Eucharistic symbolism embedded in the ritual of the kola nut (*Oji*), a seed whose divided lobes always stick together.

Whenever the kola nut is broken and shared in Igboland, the ritual is done with the highest reverence and equanimity, with incantations intoning the spirit of unity, one life, one love, one God, and one Igbo God-race.

Oji is the embodiment of the spirit of life and love, not just the symbol, which is God. *Oji* is older than the Christian Eucharistic bread, of Hindu and Hebrew origin, which was only introduced after bread was invented. *Oji* is the remembrance of the Eternal Union and the Eternal Day when the Igbo lived in the Eternal Light of the Great Invisible God.

However, we observe that the concept of two Gods, as indicated by the Nag Hammadi: the God of Shem, and the God of Ham and Japheth, is very strange to the traditional Igbo thought, which believes in the existence of one Supreme Deity *(Chi-ukwu)*, who created everything in the universe. Though there may be some other deities, like the Earth Goddess *(Ani, Ala)*, the Sun *(Anyanwu)*, etc., they all are subordinated to the one Supreme Being.

Besides, as already discussed above, many Igbo people believe that the Igbo were descended from Israel, "The Lost Tribe of Israel". As such, the Igbo couldn't have come from another lineage different from the Israelites, as the Nag Hammadi had suggested. But as Catherine Acholonu had observed, the Igbo identification with the Jews was a result of Christianity, brought in by the missionaries, since most Igbo people were Christians. "Everybody is excited to say that they belong to the Bible, because the Bible is reigning".

- **Amnesia, Authochthony and Igbo Origin**

Before the advent of written records, many West African states in precolonial times had little or no record of events. It was not a crime to forget the time of migration or evolution. It simply meant that you were ancient or old enough to claim autochthony. Being authochthonous does not imply that you grew from the ground. It simply means that you are indigenous to the area in which you are found.

In modern times, it is difficult to calculate the age of a person who is merely 120 years old accurately; talk more about people who migrated or evolved thousands of years ago. When a people cannot remember (amnesia) the time of their migration or evolution, it implies they are autochthonous.

Igbo are an ancient people. But that does not necessarily translate to the literary meaning of the Igbo as an ancient people. The name Igbo/Eboe is derived from in vivo (from within). That was what our ancestors called themselves. Olaudah Equiano, born in 1745, referred to his kinsmen as "oye-eboe" (onye Igbo), despite being fully Igbo himself. So, we called ourselves Igbo. His father was an Nri noble, as he described the *Ichi* marks on his father, which he called, *Embrenche* (indicating nobility).

Thurstan Shaw's archaeology dated the old land surface excavations at Igbo ukwu (Igbo-jona) to 1,550 BC, which gives us an idea of how long the name "Igbo" have been in their present place. It is true that an isolated discovery of ancient archaeology does not necessarily mean it belongs to the people inhabiting the place. However, in this instance, there are some cultural transitions for the present inhabitants.

Archaeology is used to trace ancestry and the time of settlement. It can be culture-specific or non-culture-specific. Igboland has both, with culture-specific archaeology showing a transition from ancient times to the present. A cultural transition from the past to the present depicts the fact that the archaeology belongs to the aborigines of the town. For instance, the Afikpo (Ehugbo) pottery, dated 3,000 BC, which found to bear a striking resemblance in style to the pottery works of the present inhabitants or those at the time of British presence in Igboland.

The widespread use of iron and blacksmithing technologies among the itinerant Awka and Nkwere blacksmith is an attestation of a transition in the knowledge of iron smelting deposited at Opi and Lejja dating from 2,000 BC to 750 BC. It must be noted that Awka blacksmiths operated beyond the Igbo country into Igala territory and the Edo and Southern Edo areas.

Igbo Ukwu was clearly dated 800 AD to 900 AD. The bronze pendant, ritual bells, and beads represent the burial site of an Nri priest-king. The pendant and other bronzes bear the famous *Ichi* facial scarifications common among the Igbo of that time. Until the British arrived, this cultural transition had been passed down for over a thousand years.

According to research by the African Genome Variation Project (AGVP), there is evidence of widespread hunter-gatherer ancestry in African populations, including ancient (9 ky) Khoesan ancestry in the Igbo from Nigeria 1 ky (kiloyear) = 1,000. So, (9Ky) = 9,000 years. Another genetic analysis found the "Y" chromosome of Igbo genetic make-up which gives haplogroup EM2 predominance, with the time of origin being 39,300 years BP, which puts it at 37,350 BC.

With all these, we can be certain that the Igbo have lived on their land for thousands of years. The archaeological findings scattered all over Igboland, the Acheulien Handex at Ugwuele, Uturu, and the Afikpo pottery findings, all dating thousands of years, also support Igbo antiquity and evolution on their land. The discovery of this genetic make-up among Igbo and not on its neighbours all indicate that the Igbo, who were either the first to arrive in this part of the world, lived side by side with the pygmies who are said to have inhabited this part of the world, or they are their direct descendants (Anozie, 1983).

Archaeology, linguistics (glottochronology), and ethno-history have proved to be useful tools that help to explain more about the history of traditional groups, particularly those with no written history, such as the Igbo. That is not to say that they will be telling such a history with certainty or conclusive evidence, but that they will serve as guides for better speculations on the origin of a people. In the case of the Igbo, in particular, archaeologists like Thurstan Shaw, D.D. Hartle, F.N. Anozie, etc., through their works show that the Igbo occupied their present locations for a couple of millennia.

While Shaw, for instance, reported that as far back as the Acheulian period (ca. 500,000 - 200,000 years), stone artefacts were being produced in Nigeria and further held that archaeological evidence based on glotto-chronology had put "the date of the emergence of the spoken Igbo language from the proto-Niger languages at about 6,000 B.C."(Jannah 2014), D.D. Hartle (1967) claimed that "archaeology indicates that the Igbo were in occupation of parts of south eastern Nigeria by 2,000 -3,000 B.C.".

Also, archeological discoveries revealed that there was an Igbo civilisation based on stone technology that flourished around the Ugwuele-Okigwe axis between 100,000 B.C. and 30,000 B.C. Excavations showed that this technology was based on the existence of many types of lithic or stone hand axes, large quantities of stone cleavers, and large quantities of mini-flake tools used in producing various items like pots of various descriptions and usages, as well as bowls of various types. Makers of these tools ranged as far as Ikot Ekpene, Aba, Afikpo, and the Nsukka escarpment (Emeka, 1999).

The implication is that when a greater proportion of the world's population was still wanderers, or in the early stage of development, the Igbo were busy engaged in productive stone technology activities.

The Ugwuele-Okigwe Stone Technology later metamorphosed into other civilisations such as the Inyi-Achi Pottery Industry, the Nsukka-Udi-Awka Metal Technology, and the Agulu Umana Smithery (Anozie, 1979).

The Achi-Inyi axis was known for the production of various earthen wares, like pots and bowls of different types and shapes, used for domestic and religious purposes. The industry attracted patronage from both far and near.

The Nsukka-Udi-Awka Civilisation, which flourished from between 400 B.C. and 1600 A.D., led to the transformation of Igbo culture from the Stone Age to the Metal Age. The civilisation was based on furnaces and forges, which produced hunting weapons, agricultural implements, and some basic tools. Abundant in the area were iron ore and coking materials (Andah, et al 1983).

A group of archaeologists under the aegis of the African Archaeology Network (AAN) in conjunction with the Archaeology Department of the University of Nigeria, had in 2006 carried out empirical research on sample findings in Lejja town of Nsukka Local Government Area, where iron smelting technology was carried out thousands of years ago.

Findings included iron slags, furnaces still buried in the ground, tuyeres, etc., which were taken to Sweden for radiocarbon dating. The first dating, which was received in August 2007, dated 4005 years old, while the second dating, received in 2008, showed it to be 3,445 years old. The implication is that while the first dating showed the period to be 2005 B.C., the second dating showed it to be 1,445 B.C. (Afigbo, 2000).

Onwuejeogwu (1987) reported that archaeological findings had established that the "Igbo were in their present location at least between 100,000 B.C. and 5,000 B.C." This, according to him, has proved the fact that "man has started his cultural drama" in what he referred to as "the theatre of Igbo land." He explained that archaeological evidence showed that the Igbo man of today had undergone cultural evolutionary transformations from the late Stone Age to the Neolithic Age, the Metal Age, and to the Contemporary.

According to F.N. Anozie (op cit), the makers of the Ugwuele stone artefacts may have settled near the site and engaged in hunting, gathering food, and trapping animals. He distinguished three occupational layers of the people as quartz flakes or small stone tools, followed by hoe-like implements, polished stone axes, red ochre, bore stone, and pottery of the red ware type.

Onwuejeogwu (op cit) further held that the upper dates of the Ugwuele technology overlapped with the lowest dates of similar pottery industries in the Afikpo and Nsukka areas and that the same Stone Age culture had extended to the Aba, Okigwe, and Abakaliki areas, with the main factory site located at Ugwuele.

When we juxtapose these dates of Igbo civilisation with those of Egyptian civilisation or even the Egyptian pre-dynastic period of between 5,000 and 3,100 B.C., it becomes clear that the age when the Igbo began their productive activity was much older than these periods.

The Egyptian Pyramids, for instance, were said to have been built between 3,100 and 2,686 B.C., which is equally much younger than when the Igbo started their own technology. Thus, based on the period when the Igbo were said to have had contact with Egypt or Israel, it is clear that this occurred much later, as the Igbo were already trading in their current location. Adiele Afigbo (1992) put it more succinctly thus:

> The scientifically established age for the Igbo people and their culture go further back into history than the age being talked about when the reference is made to the ancient Egypt and to the Hebrews.

According to him, since the Igbo are Negro, who are known to have originated from Africa, or more specifically, south of the latitude of Arselar and Khartoum, it would "be absurd to look for the origin of the Igbo anywhere outside Africa".

Earlier, Afigbo had identified the Igbo among the larger proto-Kwa-speaking family that existed in southern Nigeria about 6,000 years ago. He proposed that this ancient group arrived in the old Sahara grasslands from the African Great Lakes and Mountains of the Moon of East and Central Africa.

According to him, it was the desertification of the Sahara that forced some of the Kwa people to migrate further down to the north of the Niger Benue confluence, where they founded the Nok culture. Some elements of these Kwa people later migrated south of the Niger Benue confluence and became the Igala, Idoma, Yoruba, Igbo, and possibly, the Tiv peoples.

> A preliminary excursion into the glotto-chronology of the kwa language sub-family of which the Igbo is a member, has yielded to the suggestion that most of the member languages of this sub-family (Igbo, Edo, Idoma, Yoruba, etc) started diverging from their ancestral root between 5,000 and 6,000 years ago.

He proposed another hypothesis in favour of this upland initial habitation by stating that the present soil condition of the northern Igbo area was such that it appeared to have been over-worked and less productive for agricultural uses due to a high population density and long period of tilling and habitation; a situation that probably resulted in the development of other forms of specialisations such as smithing, medicine, the priesthood, pottery, trading, and weaving.

Over a 5,000-year period, the Kwa people's first areas of settlement were the north central uplands of Nsukka-Udi-Afikpo-Awka-Orlu. While elements from the Orlu area migrated south, east, and north east, elements from the Awka area migrated westwards across the Niger River and became the Igbo sub-group now known as the Anịọma. The Igbo share linguistic ties with the Bini, Igala, Yoruba, and Idoma peoples.

Stories about such Igbo extractions like Onitsha and Nsukka people coming from some nearby places like Bini or Igala areas respectively, due to their similarities in culture, were equally dismissed. This was because the contacts between the people of these areas and their Igbo neighbours were relatively very late, compared to when the Igbo people found themselves in their present location.

Both Afigbo and Onwuejeogwu, basing their views on historical and anthropological research, linguistic analysis and archaeological excavations therefore, believe that the Igbo did not migrate from anywhere, at least in the recent past, but have been occupying their present location since about 6,000 B.C.

Toeing almost the same line of thought, Kay Williamson (2002) claimed that the "Igboid languages formed a cluster within the Volta-Niger phylum, most likely grouped with Yoruboid and Edoid". She further suggested that the proto-Igboid migration would have moved down the Niger from a more northern area in the savannah and settled close to the delta, with a secondary centre of Igbo proper more to the north, in the Akwa area.

Much of the Igbo population, according to him, is believed to have migrated from a smaller area in these regions, starting several independent Igbo-speaking tribes, village-groups, kingdoms, and states, with the movements generally broken into two trends in migration. While a more northerly group spreads towards the banks of the Niger and the upper quadrant of the Cross River; the other follows a southerly trail mostly rising from the Isu populations and is based nearer the axis from which the majority of southern Igbo communities were populated. Many of these groups are evidently culturally northern or southern Igbo, based on the proximity of their traditions to those of their neighbours and, many times, familial and political ties.

Be that as it may, we believe that scholars have laid the groundwork to solve the mystery of the Igbo and their origin. This is in spite of the various controversies and mysteries surrounding them. But it will still be necessary for scholars to dig in more and try to establish the real ancestor of the Igbo, or possibly to "create" a father-figure for the Igbo nation, just as the Yoruba and the Hausa had done.

Equally important is the need to ascertain whether or not all the people who now speak the Igbo language were from the same stock, children of the same parent, or whether they came from different places, and where were these places?

There is no doubt that the "Igbo" had become conscious of themselves as an ethnic group, or had developed an ethnic identity comparatively recent, particularly in the context of European colonisation and since the Nigerian-Biafran war. Before then, the various Igbo-speaking communities were historically fragmented and decentralised. Every village, every community, perceived itself to be distinct from the others. That was why there were several intercommunal wars.

So, how did the Igbo develop Igboness? What is the Igbo identity? How do we distinguish the Igbo from the non-Igbo? In other words, what makes the Igbo distinct or different from the Yoruba, the Hausa, or any other ethnic group or race? This is going to be our next focus.

References

Achebe, Chinua (1958) *Things Fall Apart* (London: Heinemann)

Acholonu, C. (2005) *The Gram Code of African Adam – Stone Books and Cave Libraries, Reconstructing 450,000 Years of Africa's Lost Civilizations* (Abuja: Afa Publications).

Adibe, Tony (2009) *Lejja, The World's Oldest Iron Smelting Site In Nigeria* (The Nation Newspapers, Lagos, April 29).

Afigbo, A.E. (1981) *Ropes of Sand: Studies in Igbo History and Culture* (Ibadan: University Press)

Afigbo, A.E. (1992) *Groundwork of Igbo History* (Lagos, Vista Books).

Afigbo, A.E. (2000) *Igbo Genesis,* (Uturu: Abia State University Press Ltd.)

Alagoa, E.J. Anozie, F.N. and Nzewunwa, Nwanna (1988), *The early history of the Niger Delta* (Port Harcourt, University of Port Harcourt)

Andah, B. W., Derefaka, A. A. (1983,) '1981 field season at the Paleolithic site of Ugwuele-Uturu, a preliminary report, (Paper presented at the *9th Congress of the Pan African Association for Prehistory and Related Studies*, Jos, Nigeria.

Anozie, F. N. (1983,) 'Preliminary analysis of the stone artifacts from Ugwuele' Paper Presented at the *9th Congress of the Pan African Association for Prehistory and Related Studies*, Jos, Nigeria

Anozie, F.N. (1979) 'Early Iron Technology in Igboland, Lejja and Umundu' (Special Book Issue of *West African Journal of Archeology*, Vol.9)

Basden, G.T. (1938) *Niger Ibos*, (London: Seeley Co.)

Biobaku, S.O. (1971) *Origin of the Yoruba* (Ibadan: University Press)

Bernis, J. (2017) No Relationship Between The Igbo and The Jews (*Daily Post Newspaper*, August 27)

Boston, J.S, (1960) 'Notes on Contact Between the Igala and the Igbo' *Journal of the Historical Society of Nigeria* (Vol.2, Vo.1,).

Buah, F.K. (1986) *A History of West Africa States AD 1000, Book One: The People* (London: Macmillan)

Dotun Ibiwoye, (2014), Controversy Over Igbo Origin (*Vanguard* newspapers, September 21)

Eluwa, B.O.N, (2008) *Ado-na-Idu, History of Igbo Origin* (Owerri: De-Bonelsons Global Ltd) p.63

Emeka, Lawrence (1999) 'The Challenges of Two Lost Industrial Civilizations in Enugu State', *Okanga Magazine*, (Enugu State Arts and Culture) April – June.

Equiano, Olaudah (2013) The Interesting Narrative of the Life of Olaudah Equiano, or Gustavus Vassa, the African, (New York, W.W. Norton & Company) .

Eze, Dons (2018) *Ezeagu Igbudu: The Land And Its People* (Enugu: Linco Press)

Hartle, D.D. (1967) 'Archeology in Eastern Nigeria' , *Nigerian Magazine* (No. 93) June

Idigo, M.C.M (1955) *The History of Aguleri* (Yaba, Lagos: Nicholas Printing and Publishing).

Ikime, O. (1980) *Ground Work of Nigerian History*, (Ibadan: Heinemann Educational Books

Isichei, Elizabeth (1977) *The Ibo Worlds*, (London: Macmillan)

Isichei, Elizabeth (1973) *The Ibo and the Europeans* (London: Faber & Faber)

Jannah, Imanuel (2014) 'History: How Igbos Came to Nigeria and Settled in the South-East', Available from: https://obindigbo.com.ng/2014/11/history-igbos-came-nigeria-settled-south-east/#:~:text=They%20traveled%20by%20water%20and,Omambala%20Rivers)%20was%20to%20be

Kenricks, John (2016), *Ancient Egypt Under the Pharaohs*, (Palala Press)

Meek, C.K. (1937) *Law and Authority in a Nigerian Tribe* (London: Oxford University Press)

Neaher, Nancy C. (1981). 'An Interpretation of Igbo Carved Doors', *African Arts*, 15 (1) , pp . 49-55

Nwabara, S.N. (1977) *Iboland: A Century of Contact With the British* (1860-1900) (London: Hodder and Stoghton)

Nwaezeigwe, N.T. (2013) *The Politics of Igbo Origin and Culture: The Igbo-*

Ukwu and Nri Factors Reconsidered (Nsukka: Institute of African Studies)

Nwanna, C. (2011), 'Awka, the Land of Metal Smiths', *Awka: Nka na Uzu*, Vol.1 No.2

Obi, Nwakanma (2019) 'Ooni of Ife and the Igbo-Yoruba relationship', *Vanguard* newspapers, August 11.

Ogbonna, CA (2002), *Nigerian Peoples & Politics* (Enugu: SNAAP Press Ltd)

Okoye, M. (1981) *Embattled Men*, (Enugu: Fourth Dimension Publishers)

Onwuejeogwu, M.A. (1987) *Ahiajoku Lecture: Evolutionary Trends in the History of the Development of the Igbo Civilization in the cultural Theatre of Igboland in Southern Nigeria* (Owerri, Culture Division Imo State Ministry of Information and Culture)

Onyeama, Dillibe (1982) *Chief Onyeama: The Story of an African God* (Enugu: Delta Publishers) p.36

Ozoene, S. (2016) 'Nsude Pyramids: Black Africa's Lost Heritage', *Vanguard* newspapers, Nov. 11.

Shaw, Thurstan (ed., 1975), *Discovering Nigeria's Past* (Ibadan OUP)

Shaw, Thurstan (1968), 'Radiocarbon dating in Nigeria', *Journal of the Historical Society of Nigeria*, Vol. 4, No. 3 (December), pp. 453-465

Talbot, Amoury (1926), *Southern Nigeria Vol. I* (Oxford: University Press)

Talbot, P. A. (1932), *The Peoples of Southern Nigeria* (London: Frank Cass & Co. Ltd.)

Uchechi Ogbonna (2021), 'Igbo History' (Igbos Since 3,000 BC). Available from https://web.facebook.com/groups/httpsyoutube.comchannelucwgna8mhaahnoxhhxlpi/posts/Uchechi-Ogbonna-posted-in-IGBO-HISTORY-(IGBOS--SINCE-3000BC)/593007770 7064114/?_rdc=1&_rdr

Ujumadu, Vincent (2014), 'Where Did The Igbo Originate From?" (*Vanguard* August 10).

CHAPTER FOUR

The Diaspora Igbo

Introduction

The Igbo are everywhere, all over the world. Edward James Roye, the fifth President of Liberia, was Igbo. Robert Wellesley Cole, whose surname was Okoroafor, was a Sierra Leonean and the first black to make the Royal College of Surgeons, had an Igbo mother. William Napoleon Barleycorn, an Igbo, wrote the first Bube Language primer. The Igbo have a strong presence on the Island of Bioko, Equatorial Guinea, which has Igbo as one of its recognised languages. Bishop Thomas Dexter (T.D) Jakes, Danny Glover, Forest Whitaker, Paul Robeson, or the descendants of Edward WilmotBlyden, were all Igbo.

In Jamaica, the Igbo occupy Montego Bay, Maroon Village, and St. Anne's Bay. There is an Igbo town there. During the period of the slave trade, Igbo people were taken in relatively high numbers to Jamaica as slaves, so it is no surprise that there is some Igbo language in the Jamaican Patois language, and Patois has such Igbo words as 'unu' and 'akara'. The "Red Ibo" or "Red Eboe" was used to refer to the Igbo slaves in Jamaica because of their light skin. Igbo slaves were distinguished physically by their fair or "yellow" skin tones, a stereotype that persists in present-day Nigeria. Today, in Jamaica, "red eboe" is used to describe people with light skin tones with African features.

Originating primarily from the Bight of Biafra in West Africa, Igbo people were taken in relatively high numbers to Jamaica as slaves between 1790 and 1809 during the Transatlantic slave trade. Besides Virginia, Jamaica was the second most common disembarkation point for slave ships arriving from Biafra. During this period, the culture and language of the Igbo diffused into Jamaican culture.

One of the major results of this diffusion is the infusion of some Igbo words into Jamaican Patois. Some of these words include: *Unu* (you people), *Ima osu* (Jamaica), *Imu oso* (Igbo), to hiss by sucking your teeth; *Akara* (Jamaica), *Akàrà (*Igbo) bean cake; *Soso* (Jamaica), *Sọsọ* (Igbo), only. Natives also allege that *Ibu* Town is named after the Ibo slaves. The Igbo also influenced the culture with actions such as "sucking-teeth" coming from the Igbo *"ima osu"* and "cutting-eye" from Igbo *"iro anya".*

The Igbo influenced the culture, music, pouring of libation, "ibo" style, idioms, language, and way of life of the Jamaicans. The Jamaicans are so akin to the ways of the Igbo that it is not uncommon to see Jamaicans watch Igbo movies (Nollywood). In Haiti, there is Radio Igbo and Igbo Beach. It is no small wonder the country recognised Biafra during the Nigeria-Biafra War. Bussa, the face on the five cents of Barbados, was an Igbo revolutionary. The Igbo spirit in America is very strong, and there is an Igbo village in Virginia, the United States.

Who are the Igbo Diaspora?

The Igbo Diaspora is of two kinds. The first were millions of people of Igbo descent who, by accident of history, are on the other side of the Atlantic Ocean as part of the Transatlantic slave trade that took place over a long period of more than four hundred years. During this long period, millions of Africans, including the Igbo, were captured and sold as slaves to work on various farm plantations in the United States of America and the West Indies.

These people were born Igbo, or their forefathers were born Igbo, and therefore had Igbo blood, Igbo DNA in them. But they now live in foreign lands as citizens. When slavery was abolished, many of these people could not come back to Africa or to Igboland, in particular, since they had long been cut off from their ancestral home. They decided to make their home in their various countries of residence as citizens.

The people have imbibed or assimilated the culture of their countries of residence. They speak their languages and intermarry with them. They are among the millions of people of African descent, men, women, and children, who were sold as slaves and transported to the United States of America and the West Indies, and who have naturalised or become citizens of the various countries where they reside. This will be shortly discussed in detail.

The second group of the Igbo Diaspora is second-generation Igbo migrants, who, on their own, left Igboland to sojourn in different parts of Nigeria or other countries of the world, either in pursuit of the golden fleece or in search of better means of livelihood. This group is a post-colonial creation, necessitated by both economic and political exigencies, which compelled and still compel many people to seek a better life outside their homestead.

People in this latter group still see themselves as part and parcel of their people back home. They share in the sentiments and aspirations of their people, in their successes, failures, or sufferings, either physically or psychologically. Some of them would occasionally return to Igboland to help build or seek the betterment of the Igbo nation, while others would remain at their respective bases and continue to be involved in issues affecting the Igbo in general.

The Transatlantic Slave Trade

The Transatlantic slave trade involved the capture and transportation of millions of Africans who were sold as slaves to the United States of America and the West Indies. The vast majority of these slaves were people from Central and West Africa, who were sold by other West Africans to Western European slave traders (with a small number being captured directly by the slave traders in coastal raids), who brought them to the Americas.

As far back as the 15th century, the Portuguese were already engaged in slave trading. Other European slave traders did not initially participate in the trade because Europeans in Sub-Saharan Africa had a life expectancy of less than a year from the time they arrived. The South Atlantic and Caribbean economies were particularly dependent on labour for the production of sugarcane and other commodities. This was viewed as crucial by Western European states that competed or vied with each other to create overseas empires.

The transatlantic slave trade actually began on August 18, 1518, when the King of Spain, Charles I, issued a charter authorising slaves' transportation directly from Africa to the Americas. Over the next four centuries, tens of millions of black Africans were transported from Africa to the United States of America and the Caribbean Islands through the Atlantic Ocean, with millions of others dying en route.

African slaves were first transported to Spain or Portugal before being transshipped to the Americas prior to King Charles issuing that charter. King Charles's decision to create a direct, more economically viable Africa-to-America slave trade fundamentally changed the nature and scale of this human trafficking industry (Keys, 2018).

In that August 1518 charter, the Spanish king gave one of his top Council of State members, Lorenzo de Gorrevod, permission to transport "four thousand negro slaves, both male and female" to "the (West) Indies, the (Caribbean) islands, and the (American) mainland of the (Atlantic) Ocean sea, already discovered or yet to be discovered", by ship "direct from the (West African) isles of Guinea and other regions from which they are to bring the said negros".

Due to this decree, in which King Charles launched Africa to America's transatlantic slave trade, shipments of slaves from Africa to the New World took place in 1519, 1520, May 1521, and October 1521. These four voyages were from a Portuguese trading station called Arguim (a tiny island off the coast of what is now northern Mauritania) to Puerto Rico in the Caribbean. The first three shipments carried at least 60, 54, and 79 slaves, respectively.

The Arguim story had its genesis more than 70 years earlier, in 1445, when the Portuguese established that trading post so that Portugal could acquire cheaper supplies of gold, gum Arabic, and slaves. By 1455, up to 800 slaves were being purchased there each year and then shipped back to Portugal. By the 1480s, Portuguese ships were already transporting Africans for use as slaves on the sugar plantations in the eastern Atlantic's Cape Verde and Madeira islands.

Spanish conquistadors took African slaves to the Caribbean after 1502, but Portuguese merchants continued to dominate the transatlantic slave trade for another century and a half, operating from their bases in the Congo-Angola area along the west coast of Africa. The Dutch became the foremost slave traders during parts of the 1600s, and in the following century, English and French merchants controlled about half of the transatlantic slave trade, taking a large percentage of their human cargo from the region of West Africa between the Senegal and Niger rivers (Encyclopedia Britannica).

The Transatlantic slave trade, which was a segment of the global slave trade that transported millions of enslaved Africans across the Atlantic Ocean to the Americas, was the second of three stages of the so-called triangular trade, in which arms, textiles, and wine were shipped from Europe to Africa; slaves from Africa to the Americas; and sugar and coffee from the Americas to Europe. The transatlantic slave trade is usually divided into two periods, known as the First and Second Atlantic Systems.

The first was the trade of African slaves to the South American colonies of the Portuguese and Spanish empires. This phase, which lasted from around 1502 to 1580, when Portugal was temporarily united with Spain, accounted for slightly more than 3% of all Atlantic slave trade. While the Portuguese were directly involved in trading the slaves, the Spanish empire relied on the asiento system, awarding merchants (mostly from other countries) the license to trade enslaved people to their colonies.

During this first Atlantic system, most of the traders were Portuguese, which gave them a near-monopoly. Some Dutch, English, and French traders also participated. But after the union with Spain, Portugal came under Spanish legislation that prohibited it from directly engaging in the slave trade as a carrier. It became a target for the traditional enemies of Spain, losing a large share of the trade to the Dutch, English, and French.

The Second Atlantic System was the trade of African slaves by mostly English, Portuguese, French, and Dutch traders. The Caribbean colonies and Brazil were the primary destinations during this period, as European nations established economically slave-dependent colonies in the New World. Slightly more than three percent of the slaves exported from Africa were traded between 1450 and 1600, and 16 per cent in the 17th century.

It is estimated that more than half of the entire slave trade took place during the 18th century, with the British, Portuguese, and French being the main carriers of nine out of every ten slaves abducted in Africa. By the 1690s, Britain had become dominant in the slave trade, shipping most of the slaves from West Africa. They maintained this position all through the 18th century and thus became the biggest shippers of slaves across the Atlantic.

As a result of the activities of various groups and organisations opposed to continuing slavery, the British Parliament abolished slavery in 1807, while the United States Congress outlawed it in 1808. But this did not bring an end to the slave trade, as trafficking in humans continued with increasing intensity. Between 1810 and 1860, over 3.5 million slaves were transported out of Africa, including 850,000 in the 1820s.

In the United States of America, Caribbean smugglers frequently violated the law until it was enforced by the Northern blockade of the South in 1861 during the American Civil War, while Great Britain used its warships to try to prevent slave-trading operations on the high seas. Brazil outlawed the slave trade in 1850, but the smuggling of new slaves into Brazil did not end entirely until the country finally enacted an emancipation law in 1888.

Perhaps, it may be necessary to state that slavery was abolished in Europe and the United States of America, not necessarily because of the philanthropy or goodwill of the European Christian missionaries championing the cause, but primarily because slavery was found to be no longer profitable. Slavery had become a fetter in the wheel of production, due to the introduction of machinery in production, or the so-called "Industrial Revolution", which revolutionised the production process in Europe. There were also frequent slave revolts, which made investments in the slave trade a burden.

During the early years of the transatlantic slave trade, the Portuguese generally purchased Africans who were taken as slaves during tribal wars. As the demand for slaves grew, they began to enter the interior of Africa to forcibly take captives. As other Europeans became involved in the slave trade, they remained on the coast and purchased captives from Africans who had transported them from the interior.

Raids, kidnappings, and warfare produced most captives brought to the Americas. There were also instances of African rulers selling their own subjects into bondage, in addition to those considered to be criminals, house servants, and debtors. Nevertheless, the majority of the slaves were captured in ethnic conflicts or kidnapped by slave traders.

Generally, European slave traders often relied on native Africans or middlemen to penetrate the interior of the continent and capture men and women to be sold along the coast. Once captured, the slaves were tied together by rope, and later marched hundreds of miles while suffering from thirst, hunger, exhaustion, physical injuries, and the anxiety of not knowing where they were going or their fate once they reached their final destination. Many did not survive the journey from the interior to the coast. Some died en route, while others were too emaciated and weak to endure the transatlantic voyage.

John Blassingame (1972) reported that once the captured Africans arrived on the coast, they underwent physical "examinations" in which they were made to jump up and down, and had their genital organs handled by a doctor. Those Africans chosen to make the voyage to the Americas were branded with the seal of the European companies that transported them.

The first slaves to arrive as part of a labour force in the New World reached the island of Hispaniola (now Haiti and the Dominican Republic) in 1502. Cuba received its first four slaves in 1513, while Jamaica received its first shipment of 4,000 slaves in 1518. Slave exports to Honduras and Guatemala started in 1526.

The first African slaves to reach what would become the United States arrived in July 1526 as part of a Spanish attempt to colonise San Miguel de Gualdape. The slaves later revolted and joined a nearby Native American tribe, while the Spanish abandoned the colony altogether. The area that would become Colombia received its first slaves in 1533. El Salvador, Costa Rica, and Florida began their stints in the slave trade in 1541, 1563, and 1581, respectively.

It has not been easy to estimate the number of Africans that were involved in the over 400-year period of slavery. Some estimates put the number at "between 100 million and 200 million". It is alleged that so many slaves died in the sea that sharks' travel patterns changed to feed off the bodies thrown overboard. While Ronald Segal (1995) estimated that "11,863,000 slaves were shipped across the Atlantic" for about five centuries, Patrick Manning (1992) put his own estimate at about twelve million slaves that were carried away during the Atlantic trade between the 16th and 19th centuries.

While approximately 10.5 million slaves arrived in the Americas, 1.5 million died on board ship, according to Manning. He also claimed that four million of those apprehended died within Africa, and that many more died young.

However, given that the slave trade had lasted for over 400 years and the fierce competition among various European countries - the Portuguese, the Spanish, the English, and the French, all trying to outwit the others in the illicit game, we believe that the number could be much higher.

Inside the African continent, the slave trade had devastating effects. Economic incentives for warlords and tribes to engage in the slave trade promoted an atmosphere of lawlessness and violence. Economic and agricultural developments were nearly impossible due to depopulation and a persistent fear of being imprisoned. A large percentage of the people taken captive were women in their childbearing years and young men who normally would have been starting families. The European slave traders usually left behind persons who were elderly, disabled, or otherwise dependent groups, who were least able to contribute to the economic health of their societies.

Life in Foreign Lands

African young men and women who were captured and sailed to the United States of America and the West Indies during the period of slavery already knew that they were not going on a picnic or sight-seeing. They had earlier been subjected to all sorts of torture and suffering when they were being carried away from the continent. They were therefore aware that they would be subjected to additional sufferings when they arrive at their final destinations.

Before they left the shores of Africa, the slaves would be branded with the marks of the companies or traders who had captured and sold them aboard slave vessels. In the Americas, they would again be branded with the marks of their new owners and given new names. The renaming process was aimed at severing links between them and their ethnic identity in Africa. This process by which African slaves became African Americans continually evolved throughout the duration of the institution of slavery.

Initially, clear distinctions were drawn between slaves born on the continent of Africa and those born in the Americas. The trauma of capture in Africa enslavement, and life on the plantations all contributed significantly to these slaves' perceptions of Africa. The "seasoning process," as this indoctrination came to be known, was aimed at conditioning African captives for their new status as slaves in the plantation zones of the Americas.

Meltzer (1993) states that 33 per cent of Africans would have died in the first year at the seasoning camps in the Caribbean. Jamaica held one of the most notorious of these camps. Dysentery was the leading cause of death. Around five million Africans died in these camps, reducing the number of survivors to about 10 million.

Atrocities and sexual abuse on plantations were widespread, as powerful white males took full advantage of their situation. Women were often subjected to unwanted sexual advances by their white captors and slave owners. Because these women were legally and socially considered property with no rights, there were no safeguards to protect them from harassment, rape, or long-term concubinage by masters and overseers.

The abuse was widespread, often producing mixed-race children, called creoles, who, due to the strict racial structure that defined anyone born to a slave mother as also a slave, or anyone with known or visible African ancestry as black, were caught between two diametrically opposed worlds.

Even in situations where black women seemed willing to partake in sexual relationships with wealthy white men in exchange for a home, prestige, education for children born to the union, and material possessions, in reality, the nature of plantation society and the racial hierarchy left her with little choice. Children born of interracial unions were also subject to long periods of servitude due to the taboos within colonial society against racial mixture between blacks and whites, particularly white women and black men.

For African born captives, their owners tried to present them as mixed-race or Creole slaves. The belief was that the creole slaves, because they were born in the Americas under conditions of slavery and therefore had no knowledge of an independent life in Africa, were more likely to accept their lot in life as slaves.

To help "Creolise" African-born captives, they usually shaved all of the hair from their bodies, washed them, and oiled them with palm oil. They were fed in small amounts and trained, often through violent coercion, not to resist having their body parts examined. In some instances, they were placed in work gangs for a few weeks in the West Indies before being sold in the American South to condition them to the back-breaking labour on the plantation.

Plantation owners imposed strict regulations on African religion and cultural manifestations such as dance, drumming, and language. The drum was specifically outlawed when it was discovered that its rhythms could be used as a form of communication among the slaves. Such repression did much to quell the number of revolts.

In addition to stripping the African of his freedom, ethnicity, religion, and original name, the seasoning process did much to diminish any possibility of unity among the slaves. Older Creole slaves were often put in charge of the seasoning process. These experienced slaves taught the basics of working in gangs, proper behaviour toward whites and other blacks within the slave hierarchy on the plantation, and more importantly, how to apply what they knew in Africa (agriculturally) to the American environment.

This did not mean that Africa had totally disappeared from the memory of these slaves, who would recast their culture and traditions in ways acceptable to their owners. They would take up European instruments and play them in distinct ways to replace the rhythm of the drum.

Occasionally, the slaves would assert their right to freedom, as evidenced by the numerous slave revolts and conspiracies that transpired throughout the period. In several instances, they had successfully revolted and taken over ships. The most famous of such incidents occurred in 1839 when a slave named Joseph Cinqué led a mutiny of 53 illegally purchased slaves on the Spanish slave ship, Amistad, and killed the captain and two members of the crew. The United States Supreme Court eventually ordered the mutineers to be returned to their homes.

Acts such as breaking tools, feigning illness, and destroying crops were also commonly used by slaves to halt work and alleviate the burden of slavery. Slave women equally used abortifacients or even engaged in infanticide to deny the planter class an increase in slave labour.

Despite being captured in the interior of Africa, sold along the coast, and enduring the Middle Passage and the seasoning process, African Americans and their descendants persevered to create a new reality that bore striking similarities to their former lives in Africa, which represented a new American reality. Hollywood films such as "Roots," based on the Alex Haley novel of the same name, and Steven Spielberg's "Amistad," based on the 1839 slave mutiny that questioned the legality of slave trafficking in the United States, have detailed the horrors of the trade in African captives to North America (Handley, et al 2006).

Countless books, articles, novels, and other mediums have also been employed to further the understanding of the nuances of the slave trade and its impact on the social, political, economic, and cultural spheres of past and present society. The Rastafari movement, which originated in Jamaica, where 92 percent of the population is descended from the Atlantic slave trade, also made efforts to publicise slavery and ensure that it was not forgotten, especially through reggae music.

The Igbo Diaspora in the Transatlantic Slave Trade

The Igbo Diaspora in the Transatlantic slave trade emanated from the Lower Guinea region of the Bight of Biafra, which stretched from the River Nun on the Niger Delta in the west to Cape Lopez in the south. This was one of seven regional coastal areas in West Africa from which slaves were recruited. The main ports in the area from where slaves were transported to the United States of America and the West Indies were Bonny, New Calabar, and Old Calabar. It is estimated that 14.6 per cent of the total African slaves were taken from this area. The net effect was that during the long period that slavery lasted, an estimated 1.7 million Igbo slaves were transported from the Bight of Biafra via European ships across the Atlantic Ocean (Chambers, 2013:4).

Similarly, it is estimated that more than 60% of these Igbo slaves ended up in various parts of the world during the time period, while approximately 25% of all African Americans were Igbo. This was in addition to a good number of Igbo people who occupied the West Indies and the Caribbean Islands, especially Jamaica and Haiti. This was because there were some Igbo slaves who were either too sick or on the verge of death to rebel and were too unruly to travel to the United States, and they were thus dumped off on these islands. There were also some other Igbo who were simply sold to the island plantations, and, therefore, were spread throughout these islands (Klein, etal. 1999: 103–139).

David Eltis et al (1999), report that a total of 2,944 voyages were made from the Bight of Biafra during this period, for which 941,463 captives were transported to the United States of America, with 760,242 surviving. Of this number, 218,007 slaves landed in Jamaica; 57,353 in Dominica; 51,982 in Barbados; 38,254 in Grenada; and 35,923 in St. Kitts.

A large number of Igbo slaves were also dispersed to Barbados. Olaudah Equiano, a famous Igbo author, abolitionist and ex-slave, was dropped off in Barbados after being kidnapped from his hometown near the Bight of Biafra. After arriving in Barbados, Equiano was promptly shipped to Virginia. At his time, 44 percent of the 90,000 Africans disembarking on the island (between 1751 and 1775) were from the Bight of Biafra. These Africans were mainly of Igbo origin. Barbados and the Bight of Biafra were linked in the mid-seventeenth century, with half of the African captives arriving on the island coming from there.

Other places where Igbo slaves were landed were Virginia, South Carolina, Louisiana, and Saint Domingue, now known as Haiti, where 30,000 Igbo slaves were transported from 1770 to 1790. It was these Igbo slaves that helped to influence the 1791 Haitian Revolution, which ultimately led to the abolition of slavery in the country in 1794.

In Jamaica, the bulk of Igbo slaves arrived relatively later than the rest of the other African arrivals on the island in the period after the 1750s. There was a general rise in the number of slaves arriving in the Americas, particularly in British Colonies, from the Bight of Biafra in the 18th century; the heaviest of these forced migrations occurred between 1790 and 1807. The result of such slaving patterns made Jamaica, after Virginia, the second most common destination for slaves arriving from the Bight of Biafra.

As the Igbo slaves formed the majority from the Bight of Biafra, they became largely represented in Jamaica in the 18th and 19th centuries. Igbo people in Jamaica were shipped by European slave traders onto the island between the 18th and 19th centuries as slave labour on plantations. David Eltis et al (1997), hold the view that Igbo people constituted a large portion of the African population of slaves in Jamaica.

However, there are differences in the actual identities of the slaves recruited from the Bight of Biafra, whether the slaves were a cohesive people in terms of manners and customs, and the proportion of Igbo-speaking people among the slave exports from the area. There is no doubt that Igbo society had kept slaves and that a large proportion of captives in the eastern Niger Delta came from Igbo areas, while most captives from the Bight of Biafra were Igbo speakers.

A contemporary source from the 1780s reckoned that 80 percent of the slaves exported from Bonny were Igbo. Sierra Leone registers of slaves captured by the British Navy after the end of the British slave trade in 1807 show that Igbos made up 60% of the captives on ships bound from the Bight of Biafra (Hall: 2007).

It is suggested, however, that because of the high proportion of Igbo exported as slaves, some non-Igbo people may have picked up the majority language, increasing Igbo influence over slave cargoes from this West African coastal region. During the Transatlantic slave trade era, West Central Africa was the leading departure region for captives, accounting for nearly 5.7 million slave embarkations. In second place was the Bight of Benin, which dispatched two million Africans, while the Bight of Biafra came in third place, with 1.7 million slave embarkations ((Falola, et al 2016).

The Bight of Biafra had contributed substantially to the "Guinea" traffic, which was achieved despite the area having mixed potential for slave trading. On the one hand, the Bight of Biafra was the most densely populated region along the West African coast in the 18th and 19th centuries. High population densities in the Igbo heartland, sustained by a balance between the sexes and good reproductive capacity, meant that large numbers of slaves could be supplied to ships without depleting the demographic stock. This appears to have remained the case for most of the two centuries (1650–1850) when the slave trade was conducted from the Bight of Biafra.

On the other hand, the coast of the Bight of Biafra had many creeks and mangrove swamps that made it hard to dock ships. Reefs made it hard to navigate, malaria was common, and local rulers forbade Europeans from living there. Similarly, the area had a higher mean loss rate for slaves exported than any other West African region, even though, as with those regions, there was a significant decline in slave mortality between 1650 and 1850.

There was also the propensity for loss of life on voyages from the main Biafran ports, Bonny, Old Calabar, and New Calabar. In the late 17th century, it was noted that "whosoever carries slaves from the New Calabar River to the West Indies, has need to pray for a quick passage, that they may arrive there alive and in good health." Old Calabar was the West African port of departure with the highest overall mean loss rate of slaves between 1597 and 1864, while Bonny was in second place.

Igbo slaves were often labelled as "bad slaves", "rascals", "lazy", "despondent", "ornery", "obstreperous", and "tending to bolt, and even to commit suicide" (Tete, 1938) They "are lazy and averse to labourious employment… sullen, and often make away with themselves rather than submit to any drudgery" (Long, 1774). As one slave merchant had reported:

> The greatest objection to the Eboes (Igbo) as slaves is their constitutional timidity and despondency of mind; which are so great as to occasion them very frequently to seek, in a voluntary death, a refuge from their own melancholy reflections. They require therefore the gentlest and mildest treatment to reconcile them to their situation; but if their confidence is once obtained, they manifest great fidelity, affection, and gratitude, as can reasonably be expected from men in a state of slavery (Roger et al 1983).

The categorisation of the Igbo as "bad slaves", as "lazy", "despondent", etc., is because they had refused to succumb to the evil of slavery; they refused to be enslaved, or to be slave-like. One would rather die or commit suicide than willingly accept being enslaved. You can enslave my body, but not my mind or my soul.

In 1803, at Dunbar Creek on St. Simons Island, Glynn County, Georgia, in the United States of America, a mass suicide was committed by captive Igbo people who had taken control of their slave ship and refused to submit to slavery. They were purchased for an average of $100 each by slave merchants John Couper and Thomas Spalding for forced labour on their plantations on Simons Island. The chained slaves were packed under the deck of a coastal vessel, the York, which would take them to St. Simons Island, where they were to be resold.

During the voyage, approximately seventy-five Igbo slaves rose in rebellion, took control of the ship, drowned their captors while singing in Igbo: *"Mmụọ mmiri du anyị bịa, mmụọ mmiri ga-edu anyị laa"* (the water spirit brought us here, the water spirit will take us home), and in the process caused the grounding of the ship in Dunbar Creek. They thereby accepted the protection of their god (Chiukwu) and death over the alternative of enslavement (Petley, 2018). Now known as "The Igbo Landing", it is the site of one of the largest mass suicides of enslaved people in history.

Because most historical information was passed down orally, the actual sequence of events is unknown. A common version credited to Roswell King, a white overseer on the nearby Pierce Butler plantation, is that the slaves, once ashore, walked into the creek in unison, singing and chanting in Igbo, under the leadership of someone who seemed to be like a high priest among them. This mutiny has been referred to in some quarters as the first major freedom march in America's history.

Several years later, in 1967, the Igbo people in Nigeria plunged into what looked like another mass suicide when they pulled out of Nigeria and declared their area an independent state of Biafra, rather than stay back and be wiped out in a carefully and systematically organised genocide. A horrendous war never known in the history of Africa, openly supported by some world powers, was unleashed on them to force them back to Nigeria. With practically nothing to prosecute the war except sheer will and determination to survive, the Biafrans stood their ground and were able to hold the enemy for thirty odd months. Such are the enigmatic Igbo.

Igbo slaves also participated in other violent revolts and conspiracies in the United States of America, including the famous 1822 rebellion in South Carolina. Before then, in 1816, in Western Jamaica, as many as 1,000 slaves, mostly Igbo, plotted a general insurrection and elected "a king of the Eboes" and two captains (Lewis, 1999:49-50).

A letter by the Governor of Manchester Parish to Bathurst on April 13, 1816, quoted the leaders of the rebellion on trial as saying "that 'he had all the Eboes in his hand', meaning to insinuate that all the Negroes from that country were under his control". The plot was thwarted, and several slaves were executed.

The 1816 Black River rebellion plot, according to Lewis, was carried out by only people of "Eboe" origin. This plot was uncovered on March 22, 1816, by a novelist and absentee planter named Matthew Gregory "Monk" Lewis (1834:22-28).

Lewis recorded what Hayward (1985) called a proto-Calypso revolutionary hymn, sung by a group of Igbo slaves, led by the "King of the Eboes":

Oh me Good friend, Mr. Wilberforce, make
we free! God Almighty thank ye!
God Almighty thank ye!
God Almighty, make we free!
Buckra in this country no make we free:
What Negro for to do? What Negro for
To do? Take force by force! Take force by force!

"Mr. Wilberforce" was in reference to William Wilberforce, who was a British politician and leader of the British abolitionist movement that fought for the abolition of the slave trade, while "Buckra" was a term introduced by Igbo and Efik slaves in Jamaica to refer to white slave owners and overseers.

The Igbo Culture Influence on the Americas

The long years of separation from Africa, the "seasoning process", and the brutalities by the slave masters, did not completely cut off African slaves in the United States of America and the Caribbean islands from their ancestral root on the African continent. They still retained some aspects of African culture. Instances of these retentions abound in the cultural traits exhibited among some elements both in the United States of America and the Caribbean.

In Virginia, the United States of America, possible Igbo names found among slave records include: Anica or Anakey, (mother is superior), *Nneka*, in Igbo; Breechy (an Nri-Igbo nobleman), *Mburichi* or *Mgburuichi*, in Igbo; Juba, (yam barn), *Jiugba*, in Igbo, etc. There are also practices like okra cultivation in Virginia, *Okwuru*, in Igbo; showing that there was Igbo presence in the area. The masking traditions of the *Okonko* secret society operated in the Igbo hinterland are also reminiscent of the Jonkonnu festivals. The maskers wear horns, which further show similarity to Igbo culture and the Ikenga deity.

In Barbados, the people refer to their home island as "Bim". The National Cultural Foundation of Barbados says that "Bim" was commonly used by slaves, and that it derives from the Igbo word *be m*, *be-mu*, which means, my home.

Haiti has a proverb that says, "The Igbo has hung himself," meaning, one would rather die than be forced to do something. They also have a folk song called "Ibu Lele." Anything in Haiti that has value is referred to as "Ibu."

There is also a place called Ibo Beach in Haiti. Among the Haitians, the Igbo left a great impression in their minds in terms of language, culture, idioms, etc. For them, 'ibo' is a synonym for 'greatness'. That is why in Haiti, anything great or enormous is labelled 'Ibo', such that their largest radio station is named 'radio ibo'. The people themselves have old-time tales of an Igbo-inspired revolution and their country's the independence. There is a song in Haitian Creole dedicated to their Igbo ancestors that is rendered as follows:

Ibo Granmoun O /
The Ibos are their own
Authority Granmoun O /
Their own authority
Ibo Granmoun O /
The Ibos are their own authority
Lakay Ibo /
In the Land of Igbos (strikingly similar to 'ala nke Igbo' in Igbo language)
Ibo Granmoun O /
The Ibos are their own authority

The history of Jamaica cannot be fully discussed without mentioning the influence of the Igbo. As recently as March, 2012, at an international conference on slavery held in Calabar, Nigeria, a Professor of History from Barbados, Hillary Beckless, categorically deposed that "in Jamaica, for instance, the settlers are Igbo, and that is why their pattern of life is Igbo. Even if you test Usain Bolt on a DNA now, he is likely to be an Igbo man" (Chambers,1913:2).

The Igbo influenced the culture, music, pouring of libation, "Ibo" style, idioms, language, and ways of life of the Jamaicans. Many of Jamaicans' way of life are quite similar to those of the Igbo, such that it is not uncommon to see Jamaicans watch Igbo Nollywood movies. The Igbo yam festival *Njọkụ Ji*, or *Ife-ji-ọkụ* has had a significant influence on the Jamaican *Jonkonnu* festival. There is even a town in Jamaica called "Ibu Town". Igbo idioms and proverbs abound in Jamaican patois.

Igbo and Akan slaves were said to have affected the drinking culture among the black population in Jamaica, using alcohol in ritual and libation. In Igboland and in Akan, palm wine is used on these occasions, which is substituted by rum in Jamaica because of the absence of palm wine. Much of Jamaican mannerisms and gestures and non-verbal actions are similar to that of the Igbo, such as "sucking-teeth" known in Igbo as "*ịma ọsụ*" or "*ịmụ ọsọ*" and "cutting-eye" known in Igbo as "*irọ anya*", non-verbal communication by eye movement.

Some Igbo words similar to those of the Jamaicans include:

Igbo	Jamaican	English Translation
Unu	Una	You people
Ịma Ọsọ	Ima Osu	To hiss by sucking your teeth
Akàrà	Akara	Bean cake
Sọọsọ	Soso	Only
Atu	Atoo	Chewing stick
Ọkwụrụ	Okra	A vegetable
Opoto-poto	Poto-poto	Muddy
Igbo	Eboe	Igbo
Sị	Se	Say

Proverbs are an important form of communication in both the Igbo and the Americas. They both use proverbs extensively. Some Igbo proverbs that are similar to those of Jamaica, to include:

> **Igbo**: "He who will swallow udara seeds must consider the size of his anus"
> **Jamaican:** "Cow must know 'ow 'im bottom stay before 'im swallow abbe (Twi 'palm nut') seed";"Jonkro must know what 'im a do before 'im swallow abbe seed."
> **Igbo:** "Where are the young suckers that will grow when the old banana tree dies?"
> **Jamaican** "When plantain wan' dead, it shoots (sends out new suckers)."
>
> **Igbo:** "A man who makes trouble for others is also making one for himself."
> **Jamaican**: "When you dig a hole/ditch for one, dig two."
>
> **Igbo**: "The fly that has no one to advise it follows the corpse to the grave."
> **Jamaican:** "Sweet-mouth' fly follow coffin go a hole"; "Idle donkey follow cane-bump (the cart with cane cuttings) go a (animal) pound"; "Idle donkey follow crap-crap (food scraps) till dem goa pound (waste dump)."

Igbo: "The sleep that lasts for four market days has become death."
Jamaican: "Take sleep mark death (Sleep is foreshadowing of death)" (Matzke, 2006).

Another set of African-American proverbs similar to that of the Igbo include:

Igbo: If one finger touches oil, it soils all the other fingers.
African-American: One bad apple can spoil the whole bunch

Igbo: Do not be the little bird, "Nza", who after a heavy meal, challenges its Chi to a wrestling bout.
African-American: Never bite the finger that fed you

Igbo: When a man says 'yes', his Chi also says 'yes'
African-American: Where there is a will, there is a way.

Igbo: Let the kite perch and let the eagle perch too. If one says 'no' to the other, let its wing break.
African-American: Live and let live.

Igbo: A child that has been stung by a bee, will run from any large fly.
African-American: A burned child dreads the fire.

Igbo: A chick that will grow into a cock can be spotted, the very day it hatches/A naghị amụ akaekpe na nka.
African-American: You do not learn to use your left hand in your old age.

Igbo: Do not let the monkey's hand into your soup pot, else it turns into a man's hand.
African-American: Don't put a snake in your bosom (Ndolo, 1995).

We can now see from the preceding discussions that the Igbo, as a race, can be found not only in Igboland, Nigeria, but also that many of the people with their cultural influences can be found outside the country's borders, in countries such as the United States of America and the West Indies, not just as migrants, but as full citizens of these countries where they now reside or domicile. This was due to the slave trade, which took place many centuries ago when millions of Igbo men, women, and children, were sold as slaves and transported to the Americas. Even though slavery had long been abolished and slaves set free, many of these freed slaves, because they could not trace their way back to Africa or Igboland, decided to remain in these countries as full citizens.

Separated by time and space, these former slaves, together with their descendants, did not entirely forget Igboland, or Africa, their original place of birth, but continued to look back with nostalgia on the continent through their various activities and behaviours expressed in words, symbols, gestures, proverbs, idioms, music, dance, etc., which are similar to those exhibited by the Igbo people in mainland Africa. These activities point to the undeniable relationship between these two groups: – the Igbo born in Igboland, and the Igbo born in foreign lands, the Diaspora Igbo, who were the products of the slave trade.

Towards a Global Igbo Solidarity

For centuries, the Igbo on both sides of the Atlantic, that is, the Igbo in mainland Africa, within Igboland, and the Diaspora Igbo, in particular, former slaves of Igbo origin, living in the United States of America and the West Indies, had been separated. They lived apart from each other, not only due to the natural barrier created by the expansive Atlantic Ocean, but particularly as a result of the evil machinations of the supremacist white oppressors who had put a wedge between the two groups.

The whites were not only content with plucking millions of black Africans from their roots and sold them as slaves in the Americas, but they also sought to strip these slaves of their cultural and ethnic identity so as to impose their own culture on them, while at the same time physically colonised their countries of birth and appropriated their resources.

The blacks, both in Africa and in the Diaspora, were therefore faced with double tragedies. While millions of them were uprooted from their homes in Africa, sold as slaves in foreign lands, and subjected to all forms of human indignities, those who remained in Africa were colonised, dispossessed of their resources, and treated as strangers in their own countries.

All through history, the blacks have been on the receiving end. The defining factor in the relationship between the blacks, both in Africa and in the Americas, was the colour of their skins. While the whites saw themselves as a superior race, as privileged people, and as specially created people destined to rule other races, they saw the blacks as an inferior species, less than humans, and incapable of performing any cognitive function. They propounded several theories to show that the cognitive membrane of the blacks was defective or inferior to that of ordinary humans, and concluded that the blacks might have descended from some lower animals, possibly apes.

That was why it was easy for the whites to use the blacks as slaves and to subject them to different forms of human degradation and indignities, and to also colonise the continent of Africa and appropriated her resources.

The Blacks both in the Americas and Africa only saw themselves through the whites' lenses: through their culture, way of life, art, language, religion, morals, and social behaviour. The blacks had no identity apart from what the whites told them, or what the whites determined for them. The blacks had no past, and they had no history, no culture, no art, no religion, and no separate identity. Therefore, for the blacks to live would be to live like the whites, to imitate and mimic them.

The blacks only knew about their past through the whites, through what they were told was their origin. The history of the blacks was like a blank sheet, a tabula rasa, containing nothing. The custom or the culture of the blacks was savage, nasty, and dirty. Their language was incomprehensible, sort of mumbo jumbo. Their religion was fetishistic, satanic, and devilish.

In schools, children learned only European history. They were taught in a foreign language, and forbidden from speaking in their mother tongue. In order to belong and have their own existence, the blacks must learn to live like the whites, to embrace their culture and way of life.

These were what led to the blacks' self-alienation: their self-denial, rejection, and acceptance of inferior status. Thus, the blacks began to hate themselves, the colour of their skin, their history, art, language, the names they bear, the God they worship, their religion, and their mode of dressing. They began to envy the whites and try to become like them. In consequence, some of them began to change the colour of their skin, to denounce the names they bear, and to take up foreign names. They spoke the language of the whites and worshipped their God.

Because the blacks were racially-segregated, discriminated against and subjected to different forms of human indignities, they were so engrossed in their existential being that they hardly realised the fate of each other across the Atlantic divides, or across the continents.

In other words, while the blacks in the United States of America, in the West Indies, and in different parts of Europe were contending with the problems of racial segregation and discrimination, they failed to see themselves as part of the sufferings of their fellow blacks in colonial Africa.

In the same vein, while the blacks in colonised Africa were suffering from political domination and or apartheid, economic exploitation, and the appropriation of their resources, they equally failed to associate themselves with the plight of the enslaved blacks in the United States of America, the West Indies, and Europe. In effect, the two groups, while suffering under the white dominion, stood parallel to each other, not coming together in unity to fight for their freedom.

The reason for this separation was because the blacks did not know their history. They were kept blind about their past. The whites did not want the blacks to know about the atrocities they had committed against the blacks over the years. They also would not want the blacks in the Americas to know of their roots in Africa, nor would they want the blacks in Africa to know about their relationship with the blacks in the Americas. They kept the two groups apart, since, were they to become conscious of their past relationship, they would come together and untie the fetters of their enslavement to fight for their common freedom and liberation.

In the nineteenth century, some African-Americans like George Padmore, W.E.B. Dubois, etc., came up to fight for the emancipation and social equality of the entire black race, both in the Americas and on the African continent. They tried to link up with some notable African nationalists, like Nnamdi Azikiwe, Kwame Nkrumah, etc., who were equally fighting for the unity and freedom of Africa, under the banner of Pan-Africanism.

But because the majority of African countries at that time were still under colonial rule and their leaders were fully engrossed in the fight for the independence of their individual countries, their efforts did not yield the expected results. Now that virtually all these African countries have gained political independence, the need to rekindle the fight for unity of the entire black race, whether in Africa, the Americas, or Europe, has not only become desirable, but necessary.

The emergence of Barack Obama as the 44th President of the United States of America in 2008 provided a boost or added impetus to blacks' struggle for self-worth, freedom, and equal opportunities. The excellent performance of Obama while in office had equally proved the fact that the blacks were capable of doing what the whites were able to do, and even to surpass them. However, whether Barack Obama, as President of the United States, effectively represented the interests of the black race and Africa in particular, that is, whether blacks benefited or not from the Obama presidency, is still debatable.

But for the Igbo, in particular, in their desire to conquer the world, they should take a cue from the success story of Barack Obama: his realisation of self-worth, and his "can-do spirit", which enabled him to overcome several man-made obstacles, to contest and win election as President of the United States of America, and thus became the first black man to occupy the American White House.

The Igbo have what it takes to rule the world. They are hard workers and entrepreneurs. They are ingenious and cosmopolitan. They are enduring, and have a Spartan spirit. They are global. They are everywhere, in every corner of the globe. The Igbo are also their brothers' keepers (*Onye aghana nwanne ya*). The only thing required of them, both at home and in the Diaspora, is proper coordination, sensitisation and mobilisation. These were what sustained the Biafran enterprise for as long as it lasted.

This would be simple to accomplish in today's digitalised world, information super-highway world, and easy means of transportation.. The world is now a global village: a mere click on the button could bring everybody together instantly, and the people would be talking to each other and sharing available information.

Both the Ohanaeze Ndịgbo and the World Igbo Congress should spearhead or champion this movement to reunite the Igbo globally, in different countries of the world, in the United States of America, in the Caribbean, in Europe, Asia and Australia, where the Igbo reside, so that the people would be on the same page, share their experiences, their plights and their aspirations, with a view to building a global Igbo unity, and the Igbo solidarity. These could be in the form of cultural exchanges, conferences, and seminars, primarily designed to promote better understanding and unity among the people.

The Igbo should borrow a leaf from the Jews, who are also all over the world and who occupy strategic positions both in world governments and in global non-governmental organizations. The Jews always use their privileged positions to influence key policies affecting their home government in Israel.

With an estimated more than thirty million Igbo presently living outside the shores of Igboland, a good number of them holding key positions in governments, in commerce and industry, and in technology and engineering, these Igbo could use their privileged positions to positively impact the well-being of their people at home in Nigeria, where the Igbo seem to be grossly marginalised in the scheme of things, and not getting their fair share.

During the Nigerian civil war, some influential Igbo people used their vantage positions to get the country of Haiti, which has a large Igbo population, to recognise Biafra. Just recently, on January 21, 2022, to be precise, a former Haitian Presidential Candidate, Senator Moise Jean-Charles, led a 10-man "home-coming mission to Enugu, the historic capital of the Igbo, to perform some conventional Igbo rituals such as the traditional naming ceremony and name adoption", after they had traced their roots to Igboland.

Senator Jean-Charles said after a reception organised for the team by the Enugu State Government that:

> I have not come here as a foreign person. I have come back home. Before I keep on talking, I want on behalf of all Haitians, all the blacks in Haiti, to thank you (Governor Ugwuanyi of Enugu State) for receiving us after 218 years. I have visited many countries, many places around the world, but this is the first time I have visited a country that everybody looks like me. (Vanguard, January 22, 2022)

The Igbo should follow up with this historic visit to establish more contacts between them and the people of Haiti, and indeed, with other countries of Igbo descent. Currently, in the United States of America, where an estimated more than six million Igbo reside, the people could use their numerical strength, in concert with other black people in that country, to determine who occupies the American White House, or to influence certain government policies that could be beneficial to the entire Igbo race. In general, the blacks in the United States support the Democratic Party because they believe that the Democrats were more liberal and civil rights oriented than the Republicans.

During the Nigeria-Biafra war, the Republican Party under President Richard Nixon, while claiming to be maintaining a policy of "neutrality", had closed their eyes to the genocide being committed against the Christian Igbo, who were being massacred in the most atrocious war ever witnessed in the history of Africa.

Curiously, under the Democratic Party of Obama's Presidency, the Igbo struggle for self-determination was made much harder as Barack Obama pursued his perceived United States' interest in standing behind the economic interests of a colonial power that gave no crap about how many Africans lost their lives so long as their colonial dividends were paid.

Obama had ensured the enthronement of a regime change in Nigeria, which seemed to encourage human rights abuses when they closed their eyes to various atrocities being committed by Fulani herdsmen wielding AK-47 rifles, ransacking towns and villages, burning down houses and farmlands, kidnapping, killing, maiming, and raping people at random.

The Igbo in America and elsewhere, all over the world, should therefore be clear-minded and actively involved regarding the interests of their homeland, while pursuing the politics of the respective countries where they reside. They should be more involved in issues that affect their own people than remain mere bystanders.

References

Abrahams, Roger D. and Szwed, John F. (1983, eds.), *After Africa: Extracts from British Travel Accounts and Journals of the 17th, 18th and 19th Centuries Concerning the Slaves, Their Manners and Customs in the British West Indies* (New Haven, Yale University Press)

Berlin, Ira. (1972) *Many Thousands Gone: The First Two Centuries of Slavery in North America.* (Cambridge, MA: Belknap Press)

Blassingame, John W. (1972) *The Slave Community: Plantation Life in the Ante-Bellum South*, (New York: Oxford University Press).

Booth, Thomas J. Chamberlain, Andrew T. and Pearson, Mike Parker (2015), 'Mummification In Bronze Age Britain', *Antiquity*, Volume

89 , Issue 347 , (October 2015) , pp. 1155 – 1173. Available from https://www.cambridge.org/core/journals/antiquity/article/mumification-in-bronze-age-britain/738F5B39B75741D162FD22E1B15 86E73

Chambers, Douglas B et al (2013), *Enslaved Igbo And Ibibio In America: Runaway Slaves and Historical Descriptions* (Enugu: Jemezie Associates)

Chambers, Douglas B. (2009), *Murder At Montpelier: Igbo Africans In Virginia* (Mississipi, University Press of Mississippi).

Christer Petley, (2018) *White Fury: A Jamaican Slaveholder and the Age of Revolution* (Oxford: Oxford University Press)

Long, Edward (1774) reproduced (1970) *The History of Jamaica or General Survey of the Ancient and Modern State of that Island*, (London, T. Lowndes,).

Eltis, David, Behrendt, Stephen D, Richardson, David, And Klein, Herbert S.(1999, eds.), *The Transatlantic Slave Trade: A Database On CD-ROM* (Cambridge, Cambridge University Press)

Eltis, David; Richardson, David (1997). Routes to Slavery: direction, ethnicity, and mortality in the transatlantic slave trade. (Abingdon, Routledge).

Encyclopedia Britannica

Equiano, Olaudah (2005), *The Interesting Narrative of the Life of Olaudah Equiano, or Gustavus Vassa, the African* (New York W.W. Norton & Company).

Eric Williams, (1944) *Capitalism & Slavery* (Chapel Hill, University of North Carolina Press), pp. 98–107, 169–177.

Falola, Toyin ; Chijioke, Raphael Njoku. (2016) *Igbo in the Atlantic World: African Origins and Diasporic Destinations*, (Bloomington, Indiana University Press)

Gwendolyn (2007) *Slavery and African Ethnicities in the Americas* (Chapel Hill, University of North Carolina Press).

Handley, Fiona J. L. (2006), 'Back to Africa: issues of hosting "Roots" tourism in West Africa' in , in Haviser, Jay B. MacDonald, Kevin C.(eds) *African re-genesis : confronting social issues in the diaspora* (London; New York : UCL Press)

Inikori and Stanley L. Engerman (eds, 1993), The Atlantic Slave Trade: Effects on Economies, Societies and Peoples in Africa, the Americas, and Europe (Duke University Press),

Jean-Charles, Moise (2022) 'Home-Coming Mission To Enugu', *Vanguard* newspapers, January 22

Klein, Herbert S., and Jacob Klein (1999) *The Atlantic Slave Trade* (Cambridge, Cambridge University Press) pp. 103–139.

Lovejoy, Paul E. (2003). *Trans-Atlantic Dimensions of Ethnicity in the African Diaspora*, (London, Bloomsbury Academic)

Manning, Patrick (1992), 'The Slave Trade: The Formal Demographics of a Global System' in Joseph E. Inikori; Stanley L. Engerman (1992, eds.), *The Atlantic Slave Trade: Effects on Economies, Societies and Peoples in Africa, the Americas, and Europe* (Durham, North Carolina, Duke University Press)

Meltzer, Milton. (1993) *Slavery: A World History*, (Cambridge, Massachusetts, United States, Da Capo Press).

Ndolo, Ike (1995) *Similarities Between Igbo and African-American Proverbs*'(Enugu: Okanga Magazine) pp. 35 -39

Richardson, David (1998), 'The British Empire and the Atlantic Slave Trade, 1660–1807', in Marshall, P. J. Low, Alaine, Roger Louis, Wm. (eds., 1998.), *The Oxford History of the British Empire: Volume II: The Eighteenth Century*, (Oxford, Oxford University Press)

Ronald, Segal (1995), *The Black Diaspora: Five Centuries of the Black Experience Outside Africa* (New York: Farrar, Straus and Giroux (1995), "It is now estimated that 11,863,000 slaves were shipped across the Atlantic." (Note in original:

Paul E. Lovejoy, "The Impact of the Atlantic Slave Trade on Africa: A Review of the Literature", in *Journal of African History* 30 (1989),

Smallwood, Stephanie E. Saltwater (2007) Slavery: A Middle Passage from Africa to American Diaspora. (Cambridge, MA: Harvard University Press).

Stephen Behrendt (1999). 'Transatlantic Slave Trade'. *Africana: The Encyclopedia of the African and African American Experience* (New York, Basic Civitas Books).

Tete, Allen (1938), *The Fathers*, (New York, G.P. Putnam's and Sons) pp. 53-54 Quoted in Chambers, B. Douglas (ed. 2013) *Enslaved Igbo And Ibibio In America* (Enugu: Jemezie Associates) p.1

The Capture And Sale Of Enslaved Africans: Available from www.liverpoolmuseums.org.uk

CHAPTER FIVE

The Igbo and their Neighbours

Introduction

Following the defeat of Biafra during the Nigerian civil war (1976-1970), it became necessary for some individuals and groups, particularly those around the border communities, to begin to distance themselves from the mainstream Igbo or to deny links to any relationship with the Igbo. This was due to their desire to gain acceptance and accommodation from the larger Nigerian society.

Before the war, the Igbo were the dominant, if not the most preferred ethnic group in the former Eastern Region, including the Niger Delta area, in most parts of the Mid-West Region, and in some areas in the Middle Belt zone. Many individuals and groups in these regions sought to identify with the Igbo through intermarriages, the names they gave their children, and the speaking the Igbo language itself.

But after the civil war, many of these groups began to retrace their steps and to distance themselves from the mainstream Igbo, perhaps out of fear or plain treachery. To them, the Igbo were the main group the Nigerian government was targeting for extermination: therefore, it was better to disown or abandon the Igbo and join the victorious Nigerian forces.

As a result, many of these groups began to assert their separate identities and to change the Igbo sounding names of their towns and villages to look different or distinct from Igbo towns. Towns like Umuokoro were changed to Rumuokoro, Umuola to Rumuola, Obigbo to Oyigbo (all in Rivers State), Igbuzo to Ibusa (in Delta State), Igbo-Akiri to Igbanke (in Edo State), etc.

Despite some of these border communities' attempts to distance or deny their Igbo heritage and language structures, population movements are important factors in determining group relationships. Language analysts, for instance, believe that most people living within the Niger-Benue confluence have a common affinity or relationship due to similarities in their languages. According to them, most people who live within this region belong to the Kwa subgroup, or the West Benue-Congo subgroup of the Niger-Congo language family, which dominates the West African subregion. They were said to have originally belonged to one big family before separating and speaking different languages.

Prominent among these language groups are the **Defoid** language cluster, which includes the *Akokoid and Yoruboid* language clusters, whose members are, Yoruba, Igala, and Itsekiri; the **Igboid**, spoken in South East Nigeria; the **Edoid,** spoken in Edo State; the **Cross River**, which includes the Ibibio, the Efik, the Annang, Khana, Ogbia, Loko, Mbembe, Obolo, and Gokana; the **Nupoid,** made up of the Nupe, the Gbagyi and Ebira; and the **Idomoid**, principally by the Idoma.

Hunting, fishing, and farming expeditions; religious proselytes: wars; slave raiders' activities, etc., equally play significant roles in shaping population movements and resulting in inter-ethnic relationships. In consideration of the above factors, we shall below, proceed to examine some of the Igbo neighbours and their relationships with one another.

1. Okrika

Okrika was a fishing village in the mangrove swamps of the eastern Niger River delta where slave trade activities took place. When slave trade was later abolished, the town served as a port for palm oil exportation.

Some people claim that most of the Okrika people were originally Igbo and that they migrated from Afam, a place beyond Ọbụ-akpụ in the interior Igboland, to settle in their present location. Many families in Okrika have Igbo names like Wachukwu, Ibanichuka, Olunwa, Amadị, Olungwe and Ọkụjagụ, which supports this viewpoint.

However, some other people counter this by arguing that "Okrika" was the British way of pronouncing "Wakrike", which in Ijaw means "we are not different". According to them, the people's close contact with the Ịbanị (Bonny and Opobo), on one side, and, to a lesser degree, with the Kalabari (New Calabar), on the other, who are offshoots of the Efik from Old Calabar, accounts for their dialect being affiliated to both of these groups, as well as to the Ijaw.

Although the Ịbanị and Okrika people speak the same dialect, they consider themselves to be of different origins, as do the New Calabar (Kalabari) and Brass. In Okrika today, there are parts with a mixture of Igbo language, and other parts where Okrika is spoken as a first language. In other words, while some families in Okrika could have migrated from some parts of Igbo land, others came from the Ijaw area. But the Okrika identity today is with the larger Ijaw nation, no doubt, as a result of the aftermath of the Nigerian civil war.

Notwithstanding, it should be noted that most of these island communities did not number more than a few thousands prior to the advent of the slave trade when thousands of people from the Igbo hinterland were brought there waiting for shipment to the Americas. It was these ex-slaves who helped to build the population of these areas, in addition to the Efik, Ibibio and Ijaw migrant traders and fishermen.

2. Kalabari

The Kalabari are a sub-group of the Ijaw people living in the eastern Niger Delta region of Nigeria. Originally, they were known as the Awome. The name Kalabari was derived from their ancestor, Perebo Kalabari, who was a son of Mein Owei. Their original settlement was spelled Calabar by the Portuguese, who pronounced it as Kalabari. This settlement (town) was abandoned as the people moved to other fishing settlements. Portuguese settlers continued to maintain the name, Calabari, which became surrounded by Efik people from Duke Town.

When the British came, Kalabari, was pronounced as Calabar (Kalaba) instead of Kalabari. At this time, the original Ijoid Kalabaris had moved to a new location, which became the new Calabar territory since the old Calabar was occupied by different people. With the passage of time, Old Calabar evolved into an Efik town known as Calabar.

Like the Okrika, the Kalabari are, to a large extent, bilingual, speaking Ijaw and Igbo dialects. At the same time, in Imo State, the Oguta people can speak Kalabari as well as their own language, while there is a Kalabari beach in Oguta, The Beach got its name from the fact that Kalabari palm oil merchants settled there to do business with the Igbo after the abolition of slave trade.

3. Ikwerre

The Ikwerre, known by the natives as "Iwhuruọha" (Amadi, 2018) are unarguably one of the largest Igbo ethnic groups in Rivers State. Ikwerre is bordered by Ohaji/Egbema in Imo State to the northeast, Ogba to the northwest, the Ekpeye and Abua to the west, the Ijoid groups of Degema, the Kalabari and Okrika to the south, the Eleme and Oyigbo to the southeast, and the Etche to the east. They speak the Ikwerre dialect of the Igbo language, which is sometimes considered a separate language in the Igboid family due to the civil war, which resulted in the people's quest for recognition as a separate ethnic nationality.

The Ikwerre inhabit the upland part of Rivers State, and are predominantly settled in the Ikwerre, Obio-Akpor, Port Harcourt, and Emohua local government areas of Rivers State. Ikwerre comprises four main groups, namely the Elele group (Ishimbam), the Igwuruta-Aluu (Ishiali) group, the Rumuji-Emohua-Ogbakiri (REO) or Risimini group, and the OPA group, that is, Obio/Port Harcourt/Akpor.

4. Opobo

Opobo, otherwise known as Opubu, is a city-state or kingdom, founded in 1870 by King Jaja, an Igbo man. Opobo comprises several islands and communities, mainly Opobo Town (Opuboama), Queenstown, Kalasunju, Oloma, Ayaminimah, Iloma, Minimah, Okpukpo, Iwoma, Ekereborokiri, Kalaibiama, and Epellema. A part of the city state is now in Akwa Ibom State, made up of Ikot Abasi and Kampa.

Opobo people speak the Igbo language, but with a different accent. A few of them speak the Ịbanị (an Ijoid language), which is similar to the Okrika and Kalabari languages, while some Opobo people also speak Efik. However, most of them bear Ibani names and have English last names. A few of them also bear Igbo names. In Opobo, a form of greeting/identification is "Ụmụ-afọ Ụbanị", which is Igbo.

Opobo (Opubo-ama, derived from the name of a revered Bonny king, Opubo the Great), is located east of the Kingdom of Bonny. Bonny and Opobo are of the same origin, both belong to the Ibani tribe. An Igbo man (who was subsequently initiated into the Ịbanị), called Jubo Jubogha, rose from slavery to lead the Anna Pepple chieftaincy house of Bonny.

In 1870, Jubo first arrived in what is now Opobo, having moved there due to a civil war in Bonny between his followers and those of Chief Oko Jumbo, the leader of the rival Manilla Pepple chieftaincy family. He was accommodated by the Nkoro leader, King Kpokpo, and formed what he called the "Kingdom of Opobo" soon afterwards. The king named his new state after Amanyanabo Opubo, "Pepple", Perekule the Great, a Pepple king in Bonny who had reigned there from 1792 to 1830.

Jubo Jubogha became involved in palm oil trading with Europeans. He started a trading post at Opobo Town, close to Ikot Abasi and four miles southwest of the Opobo River. Due to his dealings with them, he soon acquired the trade name "Jaja".

Jubo Jubogha was never on good terms with the Ngwa people to the north, or the Annang and the Ibibio to the east, as he declared himself the middleman in palm oil trading, thus asking them to stop trading directly with the Europeans. This resulted in a war (the Ikot Udo Obong War) between Jubo and the Annang and Ibuno people.

In 1887, Jubo Jubogha was deceived by the British when he was told to go and negotiate with the Queen of England. He was captured upon his arrival on the consul's flagship, and was sent into exile in Saint Vincent in the West Indies thereafter. He never returned.

5. Anaag

The Anaang (also spelled Annang), which comprises eight out of the present thirty-one local government areas in Akwa Ibom State (Abak, Essien Udim, Etim Ekpo, Ika, Ikot Ekpene, Obot Akara, Oruk Anam, and Ukanafun), and three of the seventeen local government areas in Abia State (Ugwunagbo, Obi Ngwa, and Ukwa East), is formerly located in the former Abak and Ikot Ekpene Divisions of the Anaang Province, and part of the former Opobo Division of the Uyo Province, which is located in the former Eastern Region of Nigeria.

The proper name for the Ika of Akwa Ibom is Ika-Annang. Based on 2018 estimates, there are about four million Annang speakers in Akwa Ibom and Abia States, and over one million speakers living outside these states.

6. Ibibio

The Ibibio people are a coastal people in southern Nigeria. They are mostly found in Akwa Ibom State, Cross River State, and the eastern part of Abia State. They are related to the Annang, Igbo, and Efik peoples. During the colonial period, the Ibibio Union asked for recognition by the British as a sovereign nation.

The Annang, Efik, Ekid, Oron, and Ibeno share personal names, culture, and traditions with the Ibibio, and speak closely related varieties (dialects) of Ibibio that are more or less mutually intelligible. The Ekpo/Ekpe society is a significant part of the Ibibio political system. The people use a variety of masks to execute social control. Body art plays a major role in Ibibio art.

The Ibibio people are reputed to be the earliest inhabitants of the south southern Nigeria. It is estimated that they arrived at their present home around 7,000 B.C. According to some scholars, the Ibibio people may have originated in the central Benue valley, particularly the Jukun influence in the old Calabar, at some point in history (Routledge & CRC Press Retrieved 2021-09-12)

Another version has it that the core Ibibio people were of the Afaha lineage, whose original home was Usak Edet in Cameroon. This was based on the fact that Usak Edet is commonly called Edit Afaha (Afaha's Creek) by the Ibibio people, which show that the Ibibio people are from Usak Edet.

After the first bulk of the people arrived in what later became Nigeria, they settled first at Ibom, then in Arochukwu. The Ibibio must have lived in Ibom for quite some time. As a result of clashes with the Igbo people culminating in the famous 'Ibibio War', which took place between 1300 and 1400 A.D., they left Ibom and moved to present-day Ibibio land (Udo, 1983).

7. Efik

The Efik are a sub-ethnic group of Ibibio located in the southern part of Cross River State. They speak the Efik language, which is a Benue–Congo language of the Cross-River family. Efik oral histories tell of migration down the Cross River from Arochukwu to found numerous settlements in the Calabar and Creek Town areas. Creek Town and its environs are often commonly referred to as Calabar, and its people as

Calabar people, after the European name Calabar Kingdom given to the state (Aye, 2000). Calabar is not to be confused with the Kalabari Kingdom in Rivers State, which is an Ijaw state to its west.

The Efik people also occupy southwestern Cameroon, including Bakassi. This area, which was formerly a trust territory of German Cameroon, was administered as a part of Nigeria's Eastern Region until it gained autonomy in 1954, thus separating the Efik people politically. As a result of a 1961 plebiscite, this separation was further extended when the area voted to join the Republic of Cameroon. Most of the area was immediately transferred, but in August 2006 Nigeria handed over the Bakassi Peninsula to Cameroon.

The Efik people occupy the basins of the Lower Cross River and down to the Bakassi Peninsula, the Calabar River and down to its tributaries, the Kwa River, Akpayafe (Akpa Ikang), and the Eniong Creek. The Efik are related to the Annang, Ibibio, Oron, Biase, Akamkpa, Uruan, and Eket people.

Although the actual origins of the Efik people are unknown, oral traditions provide accounts of their migration from Igbo and Ibibio territories to their present location. The bulk of them left for Uruan in present-day Akwa Ibom State, some to Eniong and surrounding areas. They stayed in Uruan for about a hundred or so years and then moved to Ikpa Ene and Ndodihi briefly before crossing over to their final destination in Creek Town (Esit Edik/Obio Oko).

There seems to have been three successive stages in the history of Efik migration and settlement: an Igbo phase, an Ibibio phase, and the drift to the coast. The people of Uruan were said to have given them the name "Efik", deriving from a verb, meaning to press or oppress, since they were alleged to be aggressive (Green, 1949).

Although their economy was originally based on fishing, the area quickly developed into a major trading centre and remained so well into the early 1900s. Incoming European goods were traded for slaves, palm oil, and other palm products. The Efik kings collected a trading tax called comey from docking ships until the British replaced it with 'comey subsidies'.

The Efik were the middlemen between the white traders on the coast and the inland tribes of the Cross River and Calabar districts. Christian missions were at work among the Efiks beginning in the middle of the 19th century. Mary Slessor, a Presbyterian missionary from Scotland, was concerned with eliminating the superstitious practise of killing twin babies.

In 1884, the Efik kings and the chiefs of the Efik placed themselves under British protection (Nair, 1972). The Efik, and indeed the people of the Old Calabar kingdom, were the first to embrace western education in present-day Nigeria, with the establishment of the Hope Waddell Training Institute, Calabar in 1895 and the Methodist Boys' High School, Oron in 1905. The first Primary School in Nigeria was founded in 1843 at Badagry - named St. Thomas Anglican Nursery and Primary School by Rev. Golmer of the Church Missionary Society (CMS). The first Secondary School was established in Lagos in 1859, also by the CMS.

8. Idoma

Apart from Benue State, where they are mainly domiciled, Idoma people are also found in Cross Rivers State, Enugu State, and Nasarawa State. Historical and linguistic evidences also suggest that the Idoma have ties with the Igala people to the west, concluding that the two nations came from a common ancestor.

As Michael Angulu Onwuejeogwu (1981) reported, Eri, the mythical father of the Umueri clan, had migrated from the Igala area and established a community in the middle of the Anambra River valley (at Eri-aka) in Aguleri, where he married two wives. The first wife, Nneamakụ, bore him five children, Agulu, Menri, Onugu, Ogbodulu, and a daughter called Iguedo. Oboli, his second wife, bore him Ọnọja, the only son who founded the Igala Kingdom in Kogi State.

Some people believe that the two ethnic groups fled the same kingdom at some point in history. Many traditional Idoma spiritual chants and "secret" tongues spoken during traditional ceremonies are actually Igala dialects and there are some Idoma who assert their Igala ancestry. Yet, other Idoma groups, notably in the southern regions, believe that their ancestors arrived at their present location from the northern fringes of Igboland as a result of land disputes.

The people of Ai-Aroga community in Owukpa district of Ogbadigbo Local Government Area in Benue State, and the people of Obollo-Eke in Enugu State, share a common border. They have everything in common except dialectical differences, arising from the fact that one speaks Idoma, while the other belongs to the Igbo language. For a novice, it would be hard to demarcate the thin line between the Idoma and Igbo communities at the fringes of Benue, Enugu, and Ebonyi states, considering the amount of mixing evident in these locations.

While many villages in Owukpa kingdom and Orokam districts of Ogbadigbo Local Government Area border the Igbo of Enugu State, the people of Agila, and parts of Igumale districts in Ado Local Government Area of Benue State, are bordered by the neighbouring Ebonyi and Enugu states, respectively. Basically, the people share a lot in common long before and after the Nigerian civil war. Although the Agila natives and their neighbouring Ngbo communities in Ohaukwu Local Government Area of Ebonyi State lost their peace at some point, and have been at each other's throats over perennial border disputes, those of Owukpa have continued to enjoy a harmonious relationship.

Also, many communities in Ogrute, Igbo Eze North Local Government Area of Enugu State, and Ai-Aroga, Itabono in Owukpa, among others, and Orokam districts of Benue State, share a walkable distance border with the Igbos of Obollo-Eke, Amala, Ikem, and Obollo-Afor in Enugu State. They bear the same names, such as Ugwu, Chukwu, Enyanu, Ada, Ngozi, Onyekachi, Okute among others, and there are huge cultural similarities.

9. Igala

The Igala ethnic group lives in Lokoja, east of the confluence of the rivers Niger and Benue. Their religious practise is broadly based on Christianity and Islam, with some sketches of African religion. In Igalaland, it is common to see a family where the father is a Muslim and mother, a Christian, or parents are Muslims and children are Christians or vice-versa.

The Igala population overflows outside their home base to regions like Anambra, Delta, Edo, and Enugu States. The Igala language is part of the Eastern Kwa sub-group or the West Benue-Congo sub-group of the Niger-Congo language family, where the Igbo also belong, depending on the school of thought of the observer. The Igala are identified by the old oral tradition of Western Igbo as the descendants of Igbo migrants who migrated westward during the expansion of the proto-Igbo peoples at the beginning of the first millennium.

According to oral tradition, Attah Ayegba Oma Idoko offered his most beloved daughter, Inikpi, to ensure the Igala won a war of liberation from the Jukuns' dominance, while Attah Ameh Oboni was known to be very brave and resolute, and he was revered for his stiff resistance of the British and his struggles to uphold some ancient traditions of the Igalas. When he got wind of a plan to depose and exile him by the British, he committed suicide by hanging himself to forestall the plan; for this and other numerous exploits recorded in his time, he is regarded by most Igalas as the last real traditional Attah Igala. The Igala word for king is 'onu'.

To seperate the Igala influence from the modern Igbo cultural evolution would be a historical travesty. According to several sources, the Igbo people evolved over a long period of time, from 4,000 BC to 500 AD in Igboland through waves of migration. Oral accounts stated that her northern neighbours migrated into her heartland in search of fertile land and rich marine life, the majority of whom were the Igala. The Igala settled among the locals east of the Niger, altering the historiography of many towns in today's Anambra State and parts of the present Oshimmili Local Government in Delta State.

For instance, in Anambra State, there are traces of Igala history in some communities of the local government councils of the state, such as Ayamelum, Ihiala, Oyi, Awka North/South, Aniocha, Dunukofia, Onitsha North/South, Ogbaru, Anambra East/West, and Njikoka, while a sizeable portion of Enugu State's communities have Igala ancestry as well. Thus, it is correct to call it a reverse migration, occurring about eight hundred years after which Eri was reported to have founded the modern Igbo nation with its set of unique religious doctrine. It was also a period during which one of his sons, Onoja, was said to have departed northward and founded the Igala land.

Eri's children were listed as Nri-Ifikuanim Menri, Agulu, Onoja, Ogbodudu, Onogu, and his only daughter, Iguedo. Together and respectively, his offsprings were instrumental in founding the towns of Aguleri, Igbariam, Ogbunike, Nando, Nri, Enugu-Ukwu, Nteje, Enugu-Agidi, and so many other settlements in the east and west of the Niger.

The Attah of Igala, His Royal Majesty, Dr. Michael Idakwo Ameh Oboni, in an interview with the Punch Newspaper, published on

August 26, 2017, revealed that a good number of the Igala people came from Wukari in the present Taraba State.

He said, "… talking about the origin of the Igala people, a sizable group migrated from Wukari in Taraba State, from where they came to Benue along the River Benue and continued very close to the confluence at a place called the Amagede by River Benue and slightly down from Amagede downwards to Idah, and they settled there. And there, they met a sizeable population of Yorubas, Benins and, to some extent, some Igbo. So, the migrant population from Wukari merged with them and produced a language called Igala as a people"

In Nsukka and the rest of Igboland, there is a popular masquerade called Agaba-idu, which is used to refer to an eminent man, while it is used to refer to a king in Igala. Also, Asadu is the word for 'kingmaker' among the Igbo, while it is called 'Achadu' among the Igala. Some other words that are signs of close cultural ties shared by both Igala and the Igbo, include Atama, which means, chief priest, in both languages. Ajogwu, means warrior among the Igala and the Igbo.

Both the Igbo and the Igala have four market days, which are – *Eke, Orie, Afor* and *Nkwo* in Igbo; and *Eke, Ede, Afor* and *Ukwo* in Igala. The two ethnic groups also eat *"Osikapa"* as rice, *"Abacha"* as cassava, *"Egwa"/"Agwa"* as beans, store their clothing in *"Akpati"*, (Box), while names like *Okolo, Oji, Okwoli, Akoh, Odiba,* etc., in Igala, are called *Okolo, Oji, Okoli, Ako* and *Odiba* in Igbo.

Indigenous Igbo People in Kogi State

Maazi Ogbonnaya Okoro (2021), linguist, writer, researcher, and historian, in a publication listed some aboriginal and indigenous Igbo communities that were mixed with Igala in the present Kogi State, based on extensive research work and interviews he conducted with both the Igbo and Igala people living in borderline areas. Among these communities were, according to Maazi Okoro, are the following:

i. Avurugo:

The Avurugo community is fully an Igbo community. This place had been their ancestral land before some individuals from other parts of Nsukka joined them. They have a market square called Eke Avurugo, which is open only on Eke market days. The language of the transaction is purely Igbo. There is no mixture of Igala and Igbo in the market. There is no speaking of English in the market, and their dialect is Nsụkka. Some parts of the market also have relationship with a few villages in the Ụzọ Ụwanị, and Okpuje area.

There is another market called Ahọ Ekwurugbo, or Afọ Ekwurugbo. The market opens only on Afọ days of the Igbo week. The communication language is also entirely Igbo without any other linguistic interjection. The people are farmers, and they produce everything they eat.

In Avurugo the names of their villages are all Igbo, among which are:

* Ụmụochịna
* Ekwurugbo
* Ụkpabiogbo
* Ụkpabioko
*Obinagụ
*Amaọhụrụ
*Nwa-Olieze
*Ere-Ane
*Ọzara
*Iheobune
*Nnọkwa
*Ekproko
*Alọme
*Agbataebiri
*Abụtaogbe
*Ọla
*Ịgabada
*Ọdọlụ
* Amaokwe

ii. Ikponkwụ

Ikponkwụ was previously located in the Okpuje area of Nsụkka, but is now located in Kogi State. Because of their beautiful land for agricultural activities, Ovoko moved there and would finally return after the war. Ovoko is located in the Igbo-Eze South LGA of Enugu

State. Some who could not return stayed back, while some even extend to Avurugo and settled among them.

iii. Akpanya

Akpanya is fully an Igbo community, but now in Kogi State. Akpanya has the same topography as Ụnadụ in Igbo-Eze South LGA. The first village by the boundary is Agbedo Akpanya, which shares the same dialect with Unadu. Its market is called Orie Akpanya. The market is always full on Orie market day of Igbo week. People come to the market from all over Nskka. Igbo is the language of communication in the market and throughout the village. They converse in Igbo and think in Igbo. If you leave Akpanya and go further, you will get to another community called Amaka.

iv. Amaka

Just as the name implies, Amaka is an indigenous Igbo people whose language and culture are Igbo, but as a result of state creation, they have been carved into Kogi State. Church services are conducted in Igbo.

v. Ọnịcha Igo

This is another Igbo-speaking community that can be found in the Ofu LGA of Kogi State. There are different villages there. They mix with Ịgala and intermarry. Some individuals are bilingual, speaking Igbo and Ịgala languages.

vi. Ịbaji

There are concentrated Igbo communities in Ịbaji. They don't deny their Igboness, especially those who never allowed state creation to demarcate them from their bloodline. The headquarter of Ịbaji is located at Odeke, which has an ancestral connection with Agụleri, now in Anambra State. They live close and share a common boundary.

During festivals, just as some would shout: "Igbo kwenụ!", the Odeke people will say: "Odeke-Agụlụ Kwenụ! Odeke-Agụlụ Kwenụ!"

The Ịbaji live in Enugu State and share common boundaries with the Ogurugu and Ụzọ Ụwanị in Enugu State and even share common boundaries with them

10. Bini

The Bini-Igbo relationship is on account of Eze Chima, an Aro native doctor, who, according to Michael Adjai Crowder (1962), left Arọchukwu for Bini during the Atlantic slave trade era to set up as an agent of *Ịbịnị Ụkpabi* (Long Juju of Arụchukwu) for the purpose of collecting slaves from the Bini Kingdom. Whenever, in the olden days, a native doctor travelled to a place, he, by custom, would, on arrival, report himself to the local chief or to the head of the society of native doctors of the land. He is either the guest of the head chief of the clan or puts up with the head of the local society of native doctors.

Accordingly, when Chima arrived in Bini, he reported himself to the Oba of Bini who accepted him as his guest. In time, Chima settled down and set up practice as a native doctor and agent of Arọ Oracle. He so impressed the Oba of Bini with his magical art that he gained great influence over the Oba. In consequence, the Oba installed Chima as chief in the palace of Bini. Thus, the plain, blunt, and ordinary native doctor who left Arọchukwu to establish an agency of the Long Juju earned a chieftaincy title and became Chief Chima or Eze Chima.

Having found his feet firm in Bini, Eze Chima sent for his brother, Ekensu, and other relatives from Arọchukwu and also set up an Arọ settlement in Bini similar to those the Arọ had set up in other areas throughout the former Eastern Nigeria.

With the march of time, Chima's practise in Bini expanded down to the Niger Delta area. The fame of the Arọ Oracle spread among the Urhobos and Itshekiris also, and clients from those areas trooped to him to consult the Oracle. The greatest index of Chima's influence on culture in Bini Kingdom is found in the fact that the Bini people adopted the Igbo week days of *Eke, Orie, Afọ* and *Nkwọ*, on which Chima made one sacrifice or the other or observed his abstinences and spiritual disciplines, as names also of Bini week days. Even today, the Binis' weekdays are known as the Igbo, *Eke, Orie, Afọ, Nkwọ* – as names of their week days (Egharevba 1960:13).

It was also suggested that the settlement of Eze Chima in old Bini was established in the area through which Siliku Street runs in present-day Benin City. As Eze Chima's influence increased, so did the population of his settlement. So influential was Eze Chima and his clan who were so powerful and well-integrated into society that there was almost nothing he and his people could not do on the basis of equality with Bini indigenes (Millar,1996:14).

Bini-Igbo Exchange of Culture

Having lived for some years in Bini as one of the Oba's palace chiefs, Eze Chima, the Arọ agent of the Arọ Oracle in Bini, and his people learnt the Bini chieftaincy institutions and titles. They adapted the Bini system to the administrative structures and customs of the place where they settled among other West Niger Igbo and in Ọnicha (Onitsha) on the east bank.

But as Eze Chima took away from Bini a copy of their chieftaincy institutions, so did he deposit in Bini, and the Binis adopted the Igbo weekdays of *Eke, Orie, Afọ, Nkwọ*, which are vital in determining appropriate days for abstinence in the spiritual and religious cultures of both the Igbo and the Bini. In other words, the West Niger Igbo borrowed Bini's chieftaincy traditions, just as the Bini borrowed the Igbo's religious traditions—through the agency of Eze Chima (Bondarenko, 1999).

Monarchies are the ones influenced by Bini. Onitsha has four ruling villages: Ụmụeze, Aroli, Okebụnabu (which include Umudei and Ogbabu) and Ọlọsị. The present Obi of Onitsha, Igwe Achebe, is the 21st Obi of Onitsha.

Inter-marriages have long existed between the Igala and the Bini. The people they met fishing at the bank of the River Niger were purely Igala. They were following the Niger all the way from their place to Onitsha. As a result, they rarely visit the upper land. They remained there. They have their buildings in their canoes. So, the Bini attracted them into coming to the hinterlands by intermarrying with them. Enubi, the mother of one of the outstanding monarchs of Onitsha, Obi Eze Aroli, is from Igala.

11. Yoruba

The ancient Igbo were said to be the original inhabitants of the present location of Ile-Ife in Oyo State. According to the story, the Ado-na-Idu Empire existed in the remote past, which had Ife as its headquarters. The Ado-na-Idu Empire comprised both the Igbo and the Edo people, and was bounded on the north by Nupe land, on the east by the Niger River, on the west by Dahomey (now known as Benin Republic), and on the south by the Atlantic Ocean.

An attempt by the immigrant Yoruba to usurp power in Ile-Ife, which the Igbo had opposed, led to conflict between the two groups, culminating in the eastward migration of the Igbo and kindred groups, from the territory. The last Igbo groups to leave Ile-Ife were the Onitsha people. That is why the people answer "Onitsha Ado". Onitsha people first migrated to Udo, the capital of the Kingdom of Idu (Edo), where they absorbed some aspects of the Bini culture, and later moved to Aboh, before crossing the River Niger (Eluwa, 2008:67).

Eminent historian and anthropologist, Professor Ade Obayemi (1972) stated that Ile-Ife was the cradle of the Yoruba people, but originally had Igbo settlers led by Obatala. According to him, the Igbo had installed and practised a culture based on their "ancient Odinala religion of peace, of the divine rights of the individual and not of kings, of the protection and validation of the weak and infirm, of an artistic and creative value rather than that of war and destruction".

He explained that the Igbo had been marked by the multiplicity of their settlements in Ile-Ife, which they knew by its more ancient name, "Igbo-Omoku." Obatala was a high priest in the mould of the Igbo priesthood, like Eze Nri, while some aspects of his priestly function were absorbed by the Ooni, who equally had absorbed the monarchical order that replaced the Igbo republican order of the Obatala era. The current Ile-Ife is therefore a hybrid system between the displaced Igbo culture and the settler order that replaced it. The war over Ife between the Igbo and the new wave of migrants to Ife was over two different ways of life: the freedom associated with the republic, or the order, and control associated with the monarchy.

The Obatala group was defeated, driven into exile, and scattered into places including as far as Ketu, Dahomey (Benin Republic), and Togo.

The republic disappeared, and the monarchy, as embodied by Oduduwa, replaced it. The rivalry between the Igbo and the Yoruba continues to mirror this. The war which the Igbo consistently levied against the new settlers is preserved and enacted even today in the Yoruba Egungun festivals, the Oreluere, the Obameri, the Moremi, and the Edi festivals.

The Egungun festival celebrates the canonisation of the era of peace as embodied by Obatala and the Igbo at a time of national regret, years later, when the Yoruba began to rue the tyranny of kings in their new order, and regretted the loss of the period of peace and creativity of the old order represented by the Igbo. They turned and memorialised the leader of the Igbo, Obatala, as a god, and the period of Igbo culture as the highest moment of creative fluorescence in the Yoruba world.

Thus, the Yoruba inhabit two souls: there is the fiercely republican Yoruba, many of whom find close affinity with the Igbo, and there is the Yoruba monarchist, who fiercely defends the settled order of kings.

The present Ooni of Ife, Oba Adeyeye Enitan Ogunwusi II, on whom the Yoruba tradition confers the authority of national memory, explained at a cultural festival in his palace that the ancient Igbo connections to Ife was evident in the traditions preserved in the oral narratives of Ife and in the extant lineages of the Igbo presence and habitation inside the Ooni's palace, such as "the Igbo quarters", which still exist in Ife (Nwakanma, 2019). According to the Ooni,

> From time immemorial, before the creation of humanity, it has been like that in terms of celebration of wealth. But, to the glory of God, a particular race actually discovered it first. If truth be told, the race that first discovered prosperity and wealth and really nurtured it, are the Igbo race.
> The Igbo first discovered it through their ancestral background, the lineage of Obatala. They discovered the prosperity of the world in terms of its divinity. And that is the reason why today the race of Igbo people is very particular, and they have good expertise when it comes to commerce. They are very distinct all over the world. There is no place in the world that you will not encounter an Igbo man. And the same goes with the Jews.
> There is the mistake the world usually makes. They make this mistake of believing that the Igbo descended from the Jews. No. It is actually the other way round. If truth is to be told, the first human race that

> existed was the Igbo race before the Jews. And they were all living together at the centre of the tropical rain forest, which is the heart of the whole thing. They were living together before they started moving clockwise. They started moving towards the eastern part of the world, where they started settling.
> So, the race of the Jews and the race of the Igbo are similar. But the Igbo are far older than the Jews. They are both commercially driven. They are both enterprise in nature. They are both driven by wealth because that is their ancestral belief. That is the race they belong to.
> In the Nigerian economy today and for the entire black race, if you don't give honour to the Igbo in terms of commerce and trade, you are just deceiving yourself. So, to be honest, let us go back to our history where we all come from.
> Ideally, the Igbo are supposed to join us to celebrate this festival because it belongs to them, the entire human race, and the Yoruba race. We are just the custodians because at some point, we were all living together here. So, let us realise what connects us.

However, it is argued that the assertion by the Ooni that the Igbo moved from Ile-Ife to their present settlement in Igbo land, was not true. This is because archaeological evidence proves that a place like Igbo-Ukwu is a much older settlement than Ife. So, in current Igbo historiography and assessment of their movements, Ife is a newer settlement of the Igbo and may have been part of a wave of migration leading to a pavement of Igbo history following an ancient catastrophe.

There is another view that suggests that the Igbo in their wave of migration following Amadioha's destruction of the ancient world, met an even older settlement in Ife, of people whom they absorbed, protected and introduced to a settled and peaceful way of existence. What this story points out is that human migration – settlements and resettlements have remained constant in man's development and search for security. There are many hypotheses about these settlements, and there is no doubt that the Yoruba and the Igbo were close and related. The language and the cultural patterns suggest points of very recent contacts and break-offs. The Idu, or Bini, is the middle culture between the Igbo and the Yoruba. Indeed, the Bini suggest that Izoduwa was Oduduwa, and they know precisely when he left Ani-Idu (Benin City). So, indeed, who are these people?

Again, there is the Nok hypothesis, which suggests a coagulation that broke off at the Niger-Benue valley, with the Jukun, the Igbo, the

Yoruba, and the Igala, and possibly the Idu, moving apart into their current settlements.

However, the value of Ooni Enitan's assertion is the necessity for strategic collaboration between these groups to understand that the Igbo, Yoruba, Igala, Nupe, Jukun, and so many cultures in West and Central West Africa have so much more in common, and must work together for their own security and prosperity.

Another hypothesis is that the Igbo-Nupe-Yoruba migrated from Egypt through the crags of air and settled in their current locations. Two studies published by the English colonial anthropologist M.D.W. Jeffreys, "The Winged Solar Disk, or the Ibo Itchi Scarification Marks" (1951), and "A Triad of gods in Africa," (1972), explore and affirm these links, and the possible Egyptian origin of the Igbo, and their worship of the Sun god.

The Igbo still call their first-born sons, "Opa-RA" (priest of the sun god, RA). MDW Jeffreys identifies in the symbols of the "Ichi" scarifications carved into the forehead and cheeks of the Igbo titled aristocracy, Ndi Nze, the "sun, moon, and wings and tail of the hawk" and the ram-headed symbol of the "Ikenga," as associated with ancient Egypt, particularly the winged solar disk symbol of Pharaoh Usertsen III. The problem is that Jeffrey thought the circulation of the symbols was from Usertsen's conquest of Nubia and the lands of the Meroetic Ridge, and may thus have been of a specific Egyptian colonial origin, rather than of Igbo origin.

He further writes that the Egyptian symbols bear an uncanny resemblance to the Nri-Igbo symbol, and raising the question of who borrowed from whom, and concluding that there is no evidence in Igbo of an independent invention of the symbol.

This is profoundly inaccurate because of Jeffery's project of attempting to sustain an idea of Egyptian cultural priority, or hegemony, and possibly maintain the fiction of a lack of cultural agency in Sub-Saharan Africa until it was brought from outside, a fiction that has long now been put to rest by works done by the likes of Cheik Anta Diop. There is no doubt that the Egyptian symbols may have Igbo origins.

The Igbo stories claim that the Igbo once ruled the world and destroyed it. They may have founded Egypt. The Igbo consider Igbo land "Ala-Nsọ" and established the code of Eje-Alọ. They are great travellers, but they always return, following the path of the Sun. Even the Egyptian priests, guardians of the Kemetic gnosis, affirmed in their teachings to Solon, the culture patriarch of the Athenians, that they had preserved in their temples, nine thousand years to the day Solon asked the question, the ancient knowledge of a people by the great Atlantic who had been destroyed in their quest to conquer the known world.

The Igbo themselves have the story of Kamalu, who took the impudent title "Amadiọha" – and who destroyed the ancient world, and was himself blown to smithereens as he and his scientists experimented with "orisha-Akalum" or the "ore of the heavens," or "Igwe" in his bid to create a powerful, all-conquering weapon of war. Amadiọha's recklessness remains a cautionary tale among the Igbo to this day, and you often hear the Igbo say, "onye emena ihe Ike" (let no one mess with energy), or "Anyị maara dowe ike" (We know the secret laws of energy, we just sealed it so no one should use it). Einstein discovered that ancient secret, and thus the atomic bomb.

Following Amadiọha's heresy, the Igbo abrogated the making of kings, forbade human sacrifice, and established a religion of peace. They dispersed in great numbers from their ancient habitations along the Atlantic in search of new one. Obatala and his group settled in Ife. And the story of these great Igbo settlements traverses the world.

There are five sub-nations of the Igbo: the Agbaja, the Oru, the Isu, the Nri, and the Idu. That is why they say, "Isee!" or "Ihi aa!" at the end of the kolanut ritual that commemorates this filial unity, its invocation of peace, and its summoning of the ancestral spirit. The Idu, who call themselves Bini today, are part of the larger Igbo, and are possibly the bridge with the Yoruba.

However, Prince Justice Faloye, President of the African Sociocultural Harmony and Enlightenment, presented another dimension to the Igbo-Yoruba relationship. In an article published in the Vanguard Newspaper of August 17, 2019, in response to the earlier postulation that the Igbo first occupied Ile-Ife before the Yoruba, he contended that the Yoruba predated the Igbo in existence.

According to the write-up, the Bantu Migration Theory, where the Igbo and Yoruba, among others, were said to come from, rests on the false premises that the origin of man occurred in East Africa, according to archaeologists, or in the southwest Namibian San homeland, according to geneticists. But there is now a strong case of the West

African coastal origin of humanity, which holds that the origins of man had to be along a coast, to account for the chemicals and attributes that could only have been derived from the ocean. Therefore, to fit their postulations, the East African origin advocates claim that man must have fed on shellfish and prawns off the Somali Coast, while the South African origin advocates point to the Cape Coast.

However, a recent study from Kyoto University (H. Yasuoka, 2013) proves that man evolved by picking wild yams, which are the foundations of Yoruba, Igbo, and other Southern and Middlebelt cultures. The global comparative genetic analysis of the world's major groups in the ten-year research known as the Human Genome Diversity Project, whose results were used and authenticated by the follow up project, the International HapMap Project, shows that Yoruba have the longest DNA strand, making it the oldest of all modern human groups.

The Yoruba came out with 93.2%, and as you move away from Yorubaland, it falls, with the Igala scoring 93.1%, the Igbo 92%, Cameroon's Ewondo 91.2%, and Ghana's Akan 90.1% – (Tishkoff SA 2009). The Harvard University's Simons Genome Diversity Project (Mallick S, Li H 2016) states that the Yoruba and San pygmies diverged around 87,000 years ago, being the first, while Marino Silva paper, 60,000 years of L2/Bantus states and that all other groups diverged from around 60,000 years.

Therefore, the question arises from where did man evolve, and where did Yoruba and the San pygmies diverge? If man evolved from East or South Africa, then where is the genetic and cultural trail from those areas into West Africa that houses the oldest genetic and cultural imprints of original Africans? What did they eat on their way to West Africa? What language did they speak? And why are there absolutely no oral traditions of East, South or Central Africa in Southern and Central Nigeria?

With the dynamics of genetic values and the cultural anthropological evidence that the first original African Information Retrieval System, the 16 sector knowledge bank, also known as Ifa-Afa-Iha- Eha, shared by all original Africans in Nigeria, we have to examine the southern Nigerian coasts as a conducive evolutionary spot and tie it to existing oral traditions. The Attah of Igala, Ameh Oboni, had categorically stated that Ifa is the link between all original Africans.

The beauty of the African Information Retrieval System, also known as Afa-Ifa-Iha-Efa, is that the Yoruba version traces their evolution to a place called Ife and clearly states that there have been several Ifes, as people relocated due to environmental conditions caused by the moving coastline during the Ice Age epochs. Ifa's history of evolution ties into the modern theory of evolution based on the evolution of hominids from monkeys to modern humans.

It states that Ijimere Baba Obo, the Patas Monkey master of all monkeys, clashed with Orunmila and the process of evolving into modern Man by playfully and wrongly applying the ointment on his buttocks and face only. Despite being left behind, the Yoruba and the Igbo revere Ijimere through Egungun/Egwugwu masquerades, being the link between humans and the spirit world.

The reference to Obatala as the first leader is faulted by the lack of distinction between the spirit, pre-human evolution, and modern humans. Oba Adeyeye Ogunwusi clarified in a recent interview, when asked how Oduduwa, at the beginning of humanity, could have lasted to the beginning of monarchy, that not only Oduduwa but also Obatala and others, were names tied to specific spiritual essences that repeat through history.

Obatala was the oldest spirit but not the oldest human because he failed in his assignment to solidify the Earth due to drinking palm wine and sleeping off, which made God send Oduduwa to complete the task and become the first human. Obatala remains the head of spirituality, religion, philosophy, and law, while Oduduwa continues to be a pioneer in human endeavours and leadership. The claim that Qbatala was republican and not monarchical, resulting in Igbo republicanism is unfounded. Since it began with priest-kings known as Eze based on Afa, the Igbo have followed the same advanced social organisation and development as others.

However, the Igbo did not join the 1500s imperialistic monarchies of the Benin, Oyo, and Igala, inspired by the 'arms for slaves' race. The Igbo were subjected to enslavement and division of their cultural sphere by the Benin, Igala, and Arọchukwu, which is a more probable cause of the republicanism and disdain for long-distance rulership from distant capitals.

Back to the issue of humanity's southern Nigerian origin, the coastline and bell-shaped rainforest between Lagos-Benin and Ife is the most probable point of evolution. It could be no further than Benin because the older Igbo groups are located to the north, and not on the delta, while the older Yoruba are to the south, not in Oyo. The most popular Igbo African origin is that of dispersal from Igalaland after a stopover from an unknown origin, which is backed by DNA and linguistic evidence.

This exercise is not about Yoruba-Igbo supremacy but to provide a well-articulated common genetic foundation, cultural origins, and linkages. This is why we have to take into account the oral traditions of the Ijaw, Nupe, Ewe, and others.

The Ijaw provide the most detailed picture of humanity's origins in southern Nigeria. The Ijoid language has the distinction of being the only linguistic group given a class of its own in the Niger Kongo ethnolinguistic family, meaning it only diverged from the parent Niger Congo mother tongue, with absolutely no proof of ever living in the hinterland.

In one of the Ijaw origin stories, it is said that an Idekoseroake, also known as Ojo/Ijọ/Ujo, anglicised to Ijaw, was an elder son of Oduduwa who migrated out of coastal Ife to its present Niger Delta homeland, which neatly ties in with the genetic and linguistic evidence for the people also known as Oru.

With the preponderance of genetic and cultural evidence, we rest our oars on a Southern Nigeria origin of humanity rather than the directionless migratory patterns from Tanzania Gorge or Namibia desert, in order to crystallise our true origin of African identity and unity required to empower and uplift the Black Race.

There are only two cultural spheres across Nigeria and Africa: the well-articulated Afro-Asian cultural platform of Hausa, Fulani, Amhara, and others, despite being products of Asian imperialism, and the unarticulated original Africans (Niger-Kongo ethnolinguistic family), despite having common origins and cultural foundations.

The ASHE Foundation[1] offers a clearer vision and template for uniting the 700 million-strong Niger Congo ethnolinguistic family, which dates back to the evolution of humanity in ancient Ife, where various groups diverged. While the Yoruba surround but do not live in the evolution bell-shaped rainforest called Igbo Irunmole, forests of ancestral spirits, the Ijaw stayed on the coast as groups migrated north, splitting into Igala, Nupe, Gwari, Idoma and Igbo.

The Volta-Niger linguistic family moved out of the bell-shaped rainforest into the central Nigerian grasslands, where the Nok civilisation evolved, followed by the Chad Sao civilisation, which linked to Egypt and Ethiopia, where the first king called Ori ruled in 4470 BC.

The new Jukunoid Benue-Congo language evolved and diverged up to the Benue and Chad into Cameroun, where the Beti-Pahuin family diverged and spread through the Chari and Sangha Rivers into Ugbangi-Kongo River basin, where the Bantus split into Western Bantus, which migrated towards the Coast to form the Kongo groups, and the East Bantus that migrated upstream to Rift Valley Great lakes, where they were known as Marshariki Bantus that diverged into Banda, Kikuyu, Sukuma and other Eastern Africans as well as the Zulu, Xhosa and other Ngunis of South Africa.

> ASHE Foundation is African Socio-cultural Harmony and Enlightenment Foundation (a think-tank to promote African sociocultural Harmony and Enlightenment in Nigeria, African and the Diaspora, which believes that from genetic and cultural anthropological studies, all the 2240 Niger-Kongo groups in Africa (517 in Nigeria) that accounts for over 70% of the population have common ancestry, cultural foundations and linkages, but due to colonialism, fail to realise their common cultural identity),

In all, what is important is not necessarily about who preceded the other in the order of existence, whether it is the Igbo, or the Yoruba, but that there is a link, or a relationship between these two major ethnic groups occupying large parts of southern Nigeria. The Igbo and the Yoruba, and many other ethnic groups in the south, belong to the same linguistic group and had, at one time or another, in the distant past, lived together as one people.

Therefore, like the present Ooni of Ife, Oba Adeyeye Ogunwusi, had said, which was reinforced by the Obi of Onitsha, Nnaemeka Achebe, the Igbo and the Yoruba should explore what unites them and should not allow some selfish politicians and other interest groups to drive a wedge in their relationship by throwing spanners into the system in order to dismember them. Personalities like Dim Chukwuemeka Odumegwu Ojukwu and Wole Sonyinka had proposed "a handshake across the Niger," by which is meant Igbo-Yoruba solidarity, but this seems to have been abandoned in pursuit of narrow political interests.

References

Ade, Obayemi (1972) *The Yoruba and Edo-speaking Peoples and their Neighbours Before 1600* (Ibadan, Institute of African Studies)

Amadi, Eric (2018) 'History of Ikwerre People In Nigeria', *Edo World*, June 20

Aye, E. U. (2000). *The Efik people* (Calabar, Glad Tidings Press).

Bondarenko, Dmitri; Roese, Peter (1999), 'Benin Prehistory: The Origin and Settling Down of the Edo'. *Anthropos: International Review of Anthropology and Linguistics*, 94: 542–552.

Crowder, Michael (1962) 'The Story of Nigeria, Igbo Primer popularly known as "Azu Ndu", approved by Government Education Department for infant classes of primary schools in the Igbo Provinces of then Eastern Nigeria page; Available from https://wap.org.ng/read/false-history-of-benin-ancestry-of-anioma-ikwere-onicha/

Egharevba J. U. (1960), *A short History of Benin* (Ibadan, Ibadan University Press)

Eluwa, B.O.N, (2008) *Ado-na-Idu, History of Igbo Origin* (Owerri: DeBonelsons Global Ltd)

Fan S. et al (2019), 'African evolutionary history inferred from whole genome sequence data of 44 indigenous African populations', *Genome Biol.* Apr 26;20 (1):82

Green, Margret Mackeson (1949). 'The classification of West African tone languages: Igbo and Efik'. *Africa: Journal of the International African Institute*. 19: 213–219.

Jeffery M. D. W. 'The Oreli Mask' *Nigerian Field*, Vol. 10, 1941, pp 140 - 142

Millar, Heather (1996), *The Kingdom of Benin in West Africa* (Salt Lake City, Benchmark Books)

Nair, K. K. (1972), *Politics and society in South Eastern Nigeria 1841 – 1906: A study of power, diplomacy and commerce in Old Calabar* (Evanston, North-Western University Press).

Obi Nwakanma (2019) 'Ooni of Ife and the Igbo-Yoruba relationship', *Vanguard* newspapers, August 11

Oboni, Michael Idakwo Ameh, Attah of Igala (2017), Interview with the *Punch* newspaper, August 26

Onwuejeogwu, M.A. (1981) *An Igbo Civilization: Nri Kingdom and Hegemony*,(London &Benin City Ethnographica and Ethiope)

Owonaru SK (Woyengidinikpete GY 2006, Alagoa EJ 1964), cited in Onuoha, Chris, 'RE: Ooni of Ife and Igbo-Yoruba Relationship', available at: https://www.vanguardngr.com/2019/08/re-ooni-of-ife-and-igbo-yoruba-relationship/

Faloye, Prince Justice (2019) 'Response to Obi Nwakanma', *Vanguard*, August 17

Behrendt, Stephen D. (Author), Latham, A.J.H. Northrup, David (2012), *The Diary of Antera Duke: An Eighteenth-Century African Slave Trader* (Oxford, Oxford University Press)

Forde, Daryll and Jones, G I (2019), *The Ibo and Ibibio-Speaking Peoples of South-Eastern Nigeria, Part III* (London, Routledge) This article incorporates text from the Calabar article in the Encyclopedia Britannica Eleventh Edition, a publication now in the public domain.

Udo, Edet A. (1983), *Who are the Ibibio?* Onitsha, Africana-Feb Publishers Limited. Onitsha, Nigeria. ISB N 9781750871

(see Journalist 101, WhatsAAP Platform, November 1, 2021).

CHAPTER SIX

The Igbo in Nigeria
A Panoramic View of Nigerian Environment

Nigeria, the name given to a large expanse of land lying on the coast of Guinea, which measures 923,768 square kilometres, is the most populous country in Africa, with between 180 million and 200 million inhabitants. The geography of the area is dominated by two great rivers: the River Niger, which has its source in the Futa Jallon highlands of Senegambia, and the River Benue, which rises from the Adamawa plateau of northern Cameroon. The two rivers joined themselves at Lokoja, where they form a letter 'Y', thus dividing the country roughly into three parts, before emptying themselves into the Atlantic Ocean through about twenty-two mouths that form a delta. Three main vegetation belts run parallel through the country.

First is the coast, screened from the sea by a sandy beach and occupied by lagoons and mosquito-ridden mangrove swamps that shade gradually into thick, deciduous bushes. Next is the forest belt, which varies in width and rises steadily from the mangrove side to about 6,500 feet above sea level. In the north is the savannah, which gradually shades into the thorn forests of the Sahara. The Atlantic Ocean and the Cameroon Mountains form the country's southern and eastern borders, respectively, while Chad, Niger, and Benin Republics border it on the north and west (Okoye, 1981).

Nigeria is by far the most populous, the largest, and the wealthiest of the former British African colonies. The country has gold, coal, lignite, tin columbite-tantalite, iron, lead, diamond, uranium, tungsten, petroleum, and palm oil, as well as cocoa, cashew, rubber, timber, groundnuts, benniseed, cotton, hides and skins, and fruits of various kinds.

Nigeria enjoys a heavy rainfall, reaching 150 inches or more annually along the coast, while the Atlantic winds temper a climate that otherwise would have been excessively torrid. The rivulets abound in fish, while the forest and savannah regions teem with wild animals of all descriptions. The temperature, soil, and resources of the country are diverse enough to give it economic self-sufficiency.

It is unfortunate that a country so richly endowed with such huge human and natural resources still has the majority of its citizens living in want and abject poverty. This is due to the failure of both the Nigerian government and its people to harness the country's huge recources. Their belief is that the easiest way to economic prosperity is only through revenues from petroleum which, was discovered in commercial quantity in the mid-1960s.

Some Pre-Colonial Traditional Institutions

Nigeria is a large country with a diverse population and culture. Virtually all the native races of Africa are represented in the country. It is in Nigeria that the Bantu and Semi-Bantu, migrating from southern and central Africa, intermingle with the Sudanese. Later, other groups such as the Shuwa-Arabs, the Tuaregs, and the Fulanis, who are concentrated in the far north, entered northern Nigeria in migratory waves across the Sahara Desert.

The earliest occupants of what is now known as Nigeria were said to have settled in the forest belt and in the Niger Delta region. Today, there are estimated to be more than 450 ethnic groups in the country. While no single group enjoys an absolute numerical majority, three major groups, however, constitute about sixty percent of the population. These are the Hausa-Fulani in the north, the Yoruba in the west, and the Igbo in the east. Other groups include the Kanuri, the Bini, Ibibio, Ijaw, Itsekiri, Efik, Nupe, Tiv, Idoma, Igala, Egbirra, Jukun, etc. Some of these groups had well established kingship systems before the arrival of the British colonial administration. Below is a summary of some of these groups.

i. The Kanem-Borno Empire

Borno's history begins in the ninth century AD, when some Arabic writers in North Africa first mentioned the Kingdom of Kanem east of Lake Chad. Bolstered by trade with the Nile region and trans-Saharan routes, the empire prospered. In the next few centuries, complex political and social systems were developed, particularly after the Bulala invasion in the 14th century. The empire moved from Kanem to Borno, hence the name. The empire lasted for about 1,000 years until the 19th century, despite challenges from the Hausa-Fulani in the west and the Jukun from the south.

ii. The Hausa-Fulani Emirate

To the west of Borno, around 1,000 A.D., the Hausa were building similar states around Kano, Zaria, Daura, Katsina, and Gobir. However, unlike the Kanuri, no ruler among these states ever became powerful enough to impose his will on the others. Although the Hausa shared common languages, culture, and Islamic religion, they had no common king. Kano, the most powerful of these states, controlled much of the Hausa land in the 16th and 17th centuries, but conflicts with the surrounding states ended this dominance. Because of these conflicts, the Fulani, led by Usman Dan Fodio, successfully challenged the Hausa states in 1804, setting set up the Hausa-Fulani Caliphate with headquarters in Sokoto, commanding a broad area from Katsina in the far north to Ilorin, across the River Niger.

iii. The Yoruba States

In the west, the Yoruba developed complex, powerful city-states. The first of these important states was Ile-Ife, which, according to Yoruba mythology, was the centre of the universe. Ife was the site of a unique art form, first uncovered in the 1930s. Naturalistic terracotta, bronze heads and other artifacts dating as far back as the 10th century showed just how early the Yoruba developed an advanced civilisation. Later, other Yoruba cities challenged Ife for supremacy, and Oyo became the most powerful West African kingdom in the 16th and 17th centuries. The armies of the Oyo king (Alafin) dominated other Yoruba cities and even collected forced tribute from the ruler of Dahomey. Internal power struggles and the Fulani expansion to the south caused the collapse of Oyo in the early 19th century.

iv. The Bini Kingdom

The Bini developed into a major kingdom during the same period that Oyo was becoming dominant in the west. Although the people of Bini are primarily Edo and not Yoruba, they share many of the same stories of origins with Ife and Oyo, and there is much evidence of cultural and artistic interchange between the two kingdoms. The King (Oba) of Bini was considered semi-divine and controlled a complex bureaucracy, a large army, and a diversified economy. Bini's power reached its apex in the 16th century.

The Nri Kingdom

The people of Nri have a creation myth of a patriarchal-king figure, Eri, who descended from the "sky" and was sent by (God) *Chukwu* to bring order to the universe. It was also claimed that Eri was one of the sons of biblical Jacob and one of the lost tribes of Israel. Archaeological discoveries suggest that Nri hegemony existed as early as the ninth century, with royal burials dating as far back as the 10th century (Onwuejeogwu, 1981:10)

Eri, the founder of Nri, was said to have settled in the region around AD 948, while the first *Eze Nri,* (King of Nri), Ifikuanim, started his reign around AD 1043. This was followed by the succession of other kings, each tracing his origin back to the founding ancestor, Eri. The Nri kingdom was a religio-political or theocratic state with several taboos used to educate and govern the subjects.

v. Akwa Akpa

The city-state of Akwa Akpa was founded in 1786 by Efik families (a branch of the Ibibio tribe) who left Creek Town further up the Calabar River. They settled on the east bank in a position where they were able to dominate traffic with European vessels that anchored in the river, and they soon became the most powerful Ibibio merchants in the region. The Europeans gave this city the name "Old Calabar" for unknown reasons.

The city became a centre of the slave trade, where slaves were exchanged for European goods. Most slave ships that transported slaves from Calabar were English; about 85 per cent of these ships were owned by Bristol and Liverpool merchants. The Igbo were the main ethnic groups taken out of Calabar as slaves, despite not being the dominant ethnic group in the area. Many were taken there for sale from the interior wars (Glyn, 2009:21-22).

vi. The Igbo and the Delta States

The Igbo, like several other Nigerian groups, did not develop into centralized monarchies. Becauseof the size of their territory and density of population, Igbo societies were organised in self-contained villages or federation of village communities, with a society of elders and age-grade associations sharing various governmental functions.

Like the Igbo, the Ijaw of the Niger Delta and some people of the Cross River area, where secret societies played prominent roles in administration and governmental functions, had no developed kingship system. But by the 18th century, overseas trade had begun to encourage the emergence of centralized systems of government in these areas.

The Contact with Europe

It would be foolhardy to believe that the first European ship that sailed to Africa was on a mere jolly ride or picnic. On the contrary, the driving motive of all the European voyages to Africa was economic, or the quest for exploitation of the human, natural, and mineral resources of Africa. From 1434 to 1807, the Niger coast in what is now Nigeria was a hub of activity between Africa and various European traders.

The Portuguese were the first to come. They were followed by the Dutch and then, the British. Portuguese traders who sailed southeast along the Gulf of Guinea in 1472 landed on the coast, where they traded with Nigerians from the trading posts they had set up along the coast. They exchanged items like brass and copper bracelets for such products as pepper, cloth, beads, and slaves – all part of an existing internal Nigerian trade.

Domestic slavery was common in Nigeria well before European slave buyers arrived. Black slaves were captured or bought by Arabs and exported across the Saharan Desert to the Mediterranean and the Near East. In 1492, a Spaniard, Christopher Columbus, 'discovered' for Europe a 'New World', now known as the United States of America. The discovery proved disastrous not only for the 'discovered' people, but also for Africans. It marked the beginning of a triangular trade between Africa, Europe, and the United States. European slave ships, mainly British and French, took people from Africa to the New World. They were initially taken to the West Indies to supplement local Indians decimated by the Spanish Conquistadors.

The slave trade grew from a trickle to a flood, particularly from the seventeenth century onwards. Chambers (2005) contended that many of the slaves taken from the Bight of Biafra across the Middle Passage would have been Igbo. These slaves were usually sold to Europeans by the Aro Confederacy, which kidnapped or bought slaves from Igbo villages in the hinterland. He further maintained that most Igbo slaves were not victims of slave-raiding wars or expeditions, but were sometimes debtors and people who committed what their communities considered to be abominations or crimes.

Portugal's monopoly in the obnoxious trade was broken in the sixteenth century when England, France, and other European nations, entered the trade. The English pioneered the transport of young Africans from their home countries to work in mines and till lands in the Americas.

The British, like other newcomers to the slave trade, found they could compete with the Dutch in West Africa only by forming national trading companies. The first of such effective English enterprises was the Company of the Royal Adventurers, chartered in 1660. It was succeeded in 1672 by the Royal African Company. Only a monopoly company could afford to build and maintain the forts considered essential to hold stocks of slaves and trade goods. In the early eighteenth century, Britain and France destroyed the Dutch hold on West African trade, and by the end of the French Revolution and the subsequent Napoleonic Wars (1799-1815), Britain had become the dominant commercial power in West Africa.

It is not easy to estimate the number of Africans that were lost to Europe and the United States of America due to slavery. However, conservative estimate put the figure at more than ten million people – men, women and children. This occurred over a long time period of more than five centuries, between the 15th and 19th centuries.

In 1807, the British Parliament enacted legislation prohibiting British subjects from participating in the slave trade. The legislation forbade ships under British registry to engage in the slave trade. Other countries more or less reluctantly followed the British lead. The British Royal Navy maintained a prevention squadron to blockade the coast, and a permanent station was established at the Spanish colony of Fernando Po, off the Nigerian coast, with responsibility for patrolling the West African coast. Slaves rescued at sea were usually taken to Sierra Leone, where they were released (Uzoigwe: 1974:80).

However, we observe that the decision to abolish slavery by the British Parliament was made not so much out of the British government's goodwill or philanthropy as it was because slavery was no longer profitable and had become a stumbling block in the wheel of progress. The introduction of the use of machinery in factories and on farms, otherwise known as the "Industrial Revolution", revolutionalised the production process and brought about a massive increase in production.

Similarly, the high mortality of slaves, coupled with frequent slave revolts, which led to the founding of Haiti, was equally responsible for the outlawing of slavery. The campaign to eradicate the slave trade and substitute for it with trade in other commodities increasingly resulted in the British interventing in the internal affairs of Nigeria during the 19th century. This was what led to the annexation of Lagos in 1861.

The annexation of Lagos was made easy by an internal struggle for the throne between two brothers, Oba Kosoko, and his uncle, Akintoye. The British sided with the latter, deposed Oba Kosoko, and made Akintoye their puppet with a promise to help him eradicate slavery. It was Akintoye's son, Dosunmu, who later ceded Lagos to the British Crown in 1861, making it a British colony.

Lagos, which was founded as a colony of Benin in about 1700, was bombarded by the British in 1851 from Fernando Po, which was then the headquarters of the Bights of Benin and Biafra, with John Beecroft appointed as its consul in 1849. The slave trade was one of the major causes of the devastating internecine strife in southern Nigeria for three centuries, until abolition occurred in the mid-1800s. Most of what is now known as Eastern Nigeria was brought under British control between 1824 and 1895 through the activities of various European explorers, traders, and missionaries like John Beecroft, W. B. Baikie, and George Taubman Goldie.

Following the abolition of slavery and its substitution with "legitimate trade", Britain became primarily interested in opening markets for its manufactured goods and expanding commerce in palm oil in Africa. Uzoigwe (ibid) further reports that by 1864, there were as many as twenty-one British companies operating in the Niger Delta area alone. It was necessary for the British to usurp the power of the coastal chiefs in order to secure these firms and ensure British monopoly in the oil and ivory trades. That was why some of the local chiefs who could not be recruited as allies after being bamboozled with some worthless gifts from Europe were either deposed or sent into exile. Among those 'recalcitrant chiefs' were King Jaja of Opobo and Nana of Itsekiri. They were both deposed and sent into exile, where they later died.

The Scramble for Africa

Apart from the issue of how to check the activities of African middlemen who had been trying to break their monopoly of trade, Britain was equally troubled by the rising commercial war raging in several parts of the Lower Niger, not only between different British companies in the area, but particularly by the increasing French and German activities trying to supplant her in the region.

France did not initially show much enthusiasm for Africa, particularly for exploration of the continent, but after its defeat by Prussia in 1871, along with its loss of Alsace-Lorraine, she began to revive interest for empire in Africa. In 1874, France created the "Commission for Scientific and Literary Voyages and Missions" for the purpose of exploiting the continent.

The new French attitude coincided with Colonel Louis Briere de Isle's Governorship in Senegal, who already was consolidating for France, several areas in the region. It was Colonel Louis Briere who revived the so-called Faidberbe's Niger policy, through which France extracted many treaties from several African chiefs. With these treaties, France took control and annexed several cities in the region, among which were Bamako, Mourgoula, Porto Novo, Cotonou, and Dahomey. These activities by France, no doubt, posed a serious threat to British influence in the Lower Niger region.

Germany, on her part, was not initially interested in the "scramble for Africa", because after the German victory over France in 1871, Chancellor Bismarck boasted that Germany was a satiated power, and that his map of Africa lay in Europe. But after realising that she was being beaten to the race by other European powers, Germany woke up from her slumber and decided to colonise Namibia, then known as South West Africa; Cameroun, Togo, and parts of East Africa.

In response to these European challenges, Britain girded her loins and decided to move steadily from the coastal areas into the hinterlands. The arrival, on the scene of George Taubman Goldie was intended to greatly bolster British efforts in the area. Goldie was a "ruthless" and no-nonsense man who wasted no time in reorganising British trading companies operating in the Niger Delta region aimed at expanding the scope of their activities and playing a more vigorous role in the affairs of the territories. Between 1877 and 1879, Goldie succeeded in securing the amalgamation of the rival British companies, which he called the United African Company (UAC). Among the aims of this new company were "to end the excess competition that was throttling trade, to thwart French ambitions on the Lower Niger, and to supplant the monopoly of the African traders with that of the company". (Uzoigwe, 1974:80).

In June 1882, Goldie carried out further reorganisation of the UAC. He renamed it the National African Company (NAC). Goldie's interest in Africa was both commercial and political. He recognised the fact that the attainment of the second goal was necessary for the actualisation of the first objective, which was commercial. In that regard, he focused his efforts to the hinterland and began a policy of negotiating treaties with African leaders in exchange for territories ceded to the National African Company. Goldie employed twenty gunboats with which he bombarded recalcitrant African rulers, and by 1884, he had succeeded in collecting thirty-seven dubious treaties of protection from these leaders.

In 1884/85, all the countries of Europe scrambling for African territories gathered in Berlin, Germany, to broker peace. In applying morality to banditry, or the robbery of Africa, they decided to use contour maps to partition the continent and share it among themselves. While they endorsed their belief in the virtues of "Free Trade", these European vampires declared that every colonial power must establish effective occupation of a territory before declaring it annexed.

Following the 1884-85 Berlin Conference, and largely due to the energetic efforts of Taubman Goldie and his National African

Company, Britain rightly laid claim to the large expanse of territory now called Nigeria. This was in spite of the reluctance of the British Government to assume political responsibility for the area in the face of mounting French and German activities.

By 1886, when Goldie's conglomerate, the National African Company, was granted a charter under the name of the Royal Niger Company (RNC), he had led several successful military expeditions in different parts of the territory. More often than not, he had used sheer force of arms, manipulation, or intimidation on the people and thus succeeded in collecting as many as 237 dubious treaties from several African leaders on behalf of the British government. Goldie extended British influence to all parts of what was then known as Western Sudan, now Northern Nigeria, through various agreements with French and German companies.

Establishment of a Military Force

As far back as 1863, Britain had established an auxiliary force largely made up of runaway slaves to augment its military forces in rivalry with French forces for the scramble for Africa. The force was also used to protect British interests in the Lower Niger.

The auxiliary force was organised by Captain, later Sir John Glover, who returned to Lagos overland after his ship was wrecked at Jebba. It numbered about one hundred men, and was variously known as the "Glover Hausas", the "Hausa Militia", and the "Lagos Constabulary".

Upon the proclamation of the Oil Rivers Protectorate in 1891, Sir Ralph Moore established the "Oil Rivers Irregulars", which was later changed to the "Niger Coast Constabulary", following the proclamation of the Niger Coast Protectorate on August 13, 1893, with headquarters in Calabar.

Lagos, which from 1861 was administered as a British colony, had the "Lagos Constabulary". In 1895, a separate body known as the "Hausa Force" was carved out of the Lagos Constabulary, while in 1900, after the revocation of the charter granted to the Royal Niger Company, the Lagos Constabulary became known as the "Southern Nigeria Regiment".

Up North, Sir Frederick Lugard who was appointed High Commissioner for the Northern Protectorate changed the name of the

"Royal Niger Constabulary" to the "Northern Nigeria Regiment". With the amalgamation of the Northern and Southern Nigeria Protectorates in 1914, all these military forces were brought together and named the "Nigerian Regiment of the West African Frontier Force". That was the origin of what we know today as the Nigerian Army, the Nigerian Navy, and the Nigerian Air Force (Eze, 2008:26).

These military forces were used by the colonialists to conquer Nigeria, subjugate her people, colonise, and dispossess them of their resources. Recruitment into these forces generally was from the more backward parts of the country, and the soldiers were quite ready to suppress any rebellion that might arise against colonial rule. They were excellent soldiers, loyal to their comrades, their regiment, and the British Empire.

The soldiers, at that time, had a very poor image or reputation because they were easily identified with the occupation forces, and were noted for their brutality against the native population. N.J. Miners (1971) reports that "the military forces in these territories had been created not to defend the inhabitants against foreign attacks, but to assist the foreigners to conquer the country".

He further explained how the former Premier of the defunct Northern Nigeria, Sir Ahmadu Bello, Sarduana of Sokoto, recalled with nostalgia the general mood in the North concerning these soldiers. "Within sight of the school, we could see the square fort and the sentries behind the parapets ... we did not like the soldiers, they were our own people and conquered us for the strangers and had defeated our people on the plain just before us", the Sarduana had lamented.

The Making of Nigeria

Following the deposition of King Jaja of Opobo and pockets of petty pushbacks from Calabar to Kano, Sapele to Sokoto, Mushin to Maiduguri, etc., the British Government then assumed direct overlordship of Nigeria as a colonial territory, on January 1, 1900, with the revocation of the charter granted to the Royal Niger Company, which had previously administered the territory. It took a few more years to subdue the 'recalcitrant' Igbo, especially the entrenched and widespread mercantile Arọ and the theocratic Nri spheres of interests, and bring the Igbo into the fold.

Early colonial Nigeria did not have much contact with the United States of America. Most of the people who sought to further their studies travelled to Great Britain to do so. The British had instilled in the emerging Nigerian elites that America had little to offer but institutionalised intolerance and vile violence.

In Igboland, no known Igbo parents had sent their children to study outside Nigeria until after over twenty years of colonisation, when King Onyeama N'Eke sent his son (Henry) and Simon Onwu (first Igbo western-trained medical doctor) to the United Kingdom. The Yoruba already had graduates returning home from Britain before 1900. History credits Nnamdi Azikiwe with being the first Nigerian to study in the United States of America, even though Eyo Ita and Ibanga Udo Akpabio, were already in the United States at the time.

By the turn of the century, it had become clear to Britain that she could no longer administer these territories by proxy or through a surrogate, if she was to effectively discharge her imperial responsibilities. She was also aware of the abundant raw materials and other natural resources in the area that could feed her industries at home, and the need to create a wide market for her manufactured goods.

Accordingly, in December 1899, Britain revoked the charter earlier granted to the Royal Niger Company, which had hitherto been responsible for the political administration of the other parts of the territory not yet under the control of either the Colonial Office or the Foreign Office, so that she could assume direct control of the territories.

Prior to the taking over of Nigeria by the British Government in 1900, the territory was organised into three distinct colonial administrative units bearing three different names. These were:

- The Colony of Lagos and the Protectorate Territories of Yorubaland, which was under the administrative control of the British Colonial Governor in Lagos;
- The Niger Coast Protectorate, which comprised largely the present South-East and South-South geopolitical zones, including Edo and Delta states, with headquarters at Old Calabar, which was administered by the Foreign Office in London, through a Consul-General;

- The Sokoto and Kanemi Emirates in the north, as well as the areas lying around the confluence of the Rivers Niger and Benue, with headquarters at Asaba, which was under the supervision of the Royal Niger Company(Okonjo, 1974:4).

The Unholy Wedlock

In 1900, with the revocation of the charter granted to the Royal Niger Company, the British Government formally took over direct administration of the territory. But not finding any suitable name to give to these diverse areas, or how the territory could be identified, Britain decided to fall back on a name earlier suggested by Miss Flora Shaw, a journalist with the *London Times* Newspaper, who, in an article published in January 1894, referred to all these territories, which were then under the influence of the British Empire, as *"The Niger Area."* Flora Shaw was later to become Lady Flora Lugard, upon her marriage with Lord Frederick Lugard, the first High Commissioner of the Northern Protectorate and later, the first Governor of Nigeria.

Ironically, Nigeria has continued to stick with this name, which was suggested to her by a British woman. Other countries with similar historical situation or circumstance had since changed their names. For instance, Ghana used to be called Gold Coast; Ethiopia was formerly called Abyssinia; Burkina Faso was formerly known as Upper Volta; and Benin Republic formerly called Dahomey. In the same vein, Namibia was previously called South West Africa; Malawi's former name was Nyasaland; while Zambia was known as Northern Rhodesia; Zimbabwe was formerly known as Southern Rhodesia; and Mozambique known as Lorenzo Marc. There is something in a name one bears or answers.

While some of these other countries could, perhaps, point at one or two things that linked them in the past, historians are yet to tell us the relationship between the Bantu, the Semi-Bantu, the Sudanese, the Shuwa-Arabs, the Tuaregs, the Fulanis, etc., that make up present-day Nigeria. Before the British colonisation of Nigeria, all the kingdoms, ethnic groups, and elements that currently make up the territory had lived on their own, and had nothing to do with each other.

It was the British colonialists who gave the country the name "Nigeria", brought together these diverse elements into one political union, but made no serious effort to make them one nation. Obafemi Awolowo, former Premier of Western Region, following Flora Shaw or Lady Lugard above, described Nigeria as "a gepgraphical expression" (Awolowo, 1966:56).

With the formal taking over of Nigeria by the British government, the country was divided into three administrative units. These were the Colony and Protectorate of Lagos; the Protectorate of Southern Nigeria; and the Protectorate of Northern Nigeria. While the Colony and Protectorate of Lagos was ruled by a governor, assisted by a local legislative council with an official majority; a civil service, patterned after the British model, even if imperfect, and a judiciary, which took after the judicial system in London, the Protectorates of Southern and Northern Nigeria were each governed by a High Commissioner, answerable to the Secretary of State for the Colonies in London, for the orderly administration and development of each of the areas.

The High Commissioners had the authority to rule without consulting the people, but only by proclamation, and were thus answerable to no one, though they could be overruled by the authorities in London. This was a very serious lapse since the people were denied participation in their own government.

In May 1906, the colonial authorities took a decisive step towards the unification of the territory when they brought together the Colony and Protectorate of Lagos and the Protectorate of Southern Nigeria into one administrative unit, with Sir Walter Egerton as the Governor. Egerton then proceeded to reorganise the new administration into the Western, Central, and Eastern Provinces, placing each under the supervision of a Provincial Commissioner. He further divided each province into a number of divisions, each headed by a District Commissioner.

The British Government's desire to create a big commercial centre in Nigeria for the growth of its home industry came to fruition on January 1, 1914, with the amalgamation of the Northern and Southern Protectorates, which had their headquarters in Kaduna and Lagos, respectively, with Lagos doubling as the capital of the whole country. Frederick Lugard, who had been the High Commissioner for the Northern Protectorate, was made the Governor of the whole country, while each of the two protectorates was governed by a Lieutenant

Governor, who was reporting directly to Lugard as Governor of Nigeria.

In 1926, to ensure effective administration of the territory, the colonialists divided the country into 24 provinces and 88 divisions and shifted the administrative headquarters of the Southern Provinces from Lagos to Enugu. These 24 provinces were evenly distributed between the northern and southern parts of the country, each with twelve provinces. The Northern Provinces comprised Adamawa, Bauchi, Benue, Bornu, Ilorin, Kabba, Kano, Katsina, Niger, Plateau, Sokoto, and Zaria, while the Southern Provinces, excluding Lagos, were Abeokuta, Benin, Calabar, Cameroun, Ijebu, Ogoja, Ondo, Onitsha, Owerri, Oyo, Rivers, and Warri.

Of the 88 divisions, the North then had 39 divisions, while the South had 40 divisions. Lagos still remained the administrative capital of Nigeria, while Kaduna was the capital of the Northern Provinces. In 1939, the Southern Provinces were split into two – the Eastern and Western Provinces, with Enugu as the capital of the Eastern Provinces and Ibadan, as the capital of the Western Provinces, while the North was left intact.

Looking back at the 1914 amalgamation, one would simply regard it as a fraud, an imposition, an unholy wedlock contrived in deceit and debauchery. The amalgamation was arranged by the British colonialists for purposes of creating a big market for British industries at home. Nigerians were not involved, and they were never consulted, directly or indirectly, but were simply made passive recipients of the system.

Another reason why Britain decided on amalgamation was because of the financial and economic difficulties the colonial administration was facing at the time in running the Northern Protectorate, where for instance, the North was always run on deficit budgets, but the South had budget surpluses. Specifically, in 1913 alone, while the Southern Protectorate had "collected a comfortable revenue of one million, one hundred and thirty-eight thousand British pounds", in the Northern Provinces, where the "importation of trade spirits had been prohibited, the colonialists relied solely on direct taxation and government grants averaging three hundred and fourteen thousand, five hundred pounds, for the eleven years up to 1912, in order to balance its budget" (Okoye, ibid:55)

In other words, Nigeria's 1914 amalgamation was motivated by British selfish interest or a desire for centralised economic control in which the colonialists would use revenues collected from the South to service the North.

Again, the amalgamation of the Northern and Southern Protectorates was necessitated by lack of personnel to run the administration and the inability or unwillingness of the British colonial authorities to spend time and resources in a colonial territory. This was what forced Lugard to introduce the indirect rule system.

Under the indirect rule system, some stooges of the colonialists were fished out from the local population and made "warrant chiefs", thereby empowered them to run the day-to-day affairs of government at the local level, while the British authorities, who sat at the remote centres of the administration, kept a watchful eye. In a society where the chieftaincy institution was strange or did not exist, particularly in the South or the Igbo area, the indirect rule system caused a lot of dislocations in the polity, which led to its abrogation.

Even with the amalgamation of the Northern and Southern Protectorates, the administrative individuality of the two areas was still maintained. For instance, while the South had its laws made by a legislative council dominated by appointed British officials, the North was ruled by proclamations made by the Governor. Lugard, as Governor-General, was the only bond of unity between the two protectorates. It was only after the Richards' Constitution of 1945 that a central legislative council began to legislate for the entire country. Thus, while the South opened its doors to accept the influences of Western civilisation, the North was shielded from such influences. This had resulted in imbalances in the process of social mobilisation between the South and the North.

Struggle for Nigeria Independence

From the beginning, the Nigerian people never wanted the foreigner, nor did they acquiesce to his rule of oppression. They had fought him, but were only overpowered by the European's superior firepower. But the people did not surrender. They continued to struggle and put up resistance, both individually and collectively. This ranged from King Jaja of Opobo, who was exiled in 1884 for refusing to allow the British companies to enjoy monopolies of trade in his domain; to the "Egba Uprising" of 1918, when the people openly rose against the White man's tax, but had 500 of them gunned down; to the "Aba Women's Riot" of 1928, when fifty defenceless women were slaughtered for opposing any attempt to include them in paying tax to the colonialists in the face of the biting economic hardships prevalent in the land; and to the 1949 Iva Valley Strike in Enugu, when 21 coalminers were gunned down for daring to ask for a marginal increase in their wages, etc.

Everywhere, there was resentment against colonial rule. But then, there was no organised resistance, and there was no identified leadership. Resistance had always been spontaneous, initiated by affected individuals or groups, or prompted by events. This had resulted in frequent eruptions of violence all over the place.

Frantz Fanon (1977: 44-56) made a fine analysis of the use of violence in decolonization. According to Fanon, since colonialism was a violent phenomenon, the "violence of the natives" equally compensated for the "violence of the coloniser". He further says that violence is "a cleansing force. It frees the natives from their inferiority complex and from their despair and inaction".

Even though there was no organised resistance at the initial stage of decolonisation, the message had been sent, which was that through violent reactions, the people had passed a vote of no confidence on the system. This caused the colonisers to panic, to begin to put in place some semblance of democracy here and there, and to establish reform programmes aimed at pacifying the people, lest the situation spiral out of control.

In 1923, the colonial administration came up with the Clifford's Constitution, which provided for a legislative council consisting of four elected members (three for Lagos, and one for Calabar), fifteen unofficially nominated members representing various interests, and twenty-nine European heads of government departments. The Clifford's Constitution was meant only for the southern part of the country, where the wind of change was blowing incessantly. The North was not included, but was ruled by proclamations made by the Governor – one country, two systems of government, one would observe.

The need for a platform to run for election to the proposed legislative council prompted veteran nationalist, Herbert Macaulay, to establish the Nigerian National Democratic Party (NNDP) in 1922. But the purview of the NNDP did not go beyond Lagos. At that time, the NNDP was opposed by the People's Union led by Dr. J.K. Randle and Dr. Akinwade Savage, as well as by the Union of Young Nigerians led by Dr. Orisadipe Obasa and Ayo Williams. At the end of the Lagos election, the NNDP cleared all the three elected seats reserved for the area, while the Calabar National League clinched the only seat meant for Calabar. That was the beginning of organised resistance against colonial rule in the country.

In 1934, the Lagos Youth Movement (LYM), led by Dr. V.C. Vanghan and Mr. Ernest Ikoli, a veteran journalist, was formed. It later changed its name to the Nigerian Youth Movement (NYM) in 1937, and attracted membership from such eminent personalities as Professor Eyo Ita and Dr. Nnamdi Azikiwe, who had just returned from the Gold Coast (Ghana), where he managed a successful newspaper outfit, the *African Morning Post*.

Azikiwe's membership in the NYM revolutionalised the Nigerian political scene and greatly boosted the fortunes of the party, which in no time succeeded in displacing the NNDP from the monopoly of Lagos politics. Through Azikiwe's oratorical prowess, political sagacity, and the setting up of his *West African Pilot* Newspaper, the fire of nationalism was ignited throughout the country, as the *Pilot* became a thorn in the flesh of the colonialists and did not give them any breathing space.

A crisis that rocked the leadership of the NYM forced Azikiwe to resign his membership in the party to join the NNDP. In 1944, Zik, as he was then popularly called, along with Herbert Macaulay, H.O. Davis, and Olu Alakija, among others, seized the opportunity of a rally organised by the National Union of Nigerian Students (NUNS) to form the National Council of Nigeria and the Cameroons (NCNC), The party later changed its name to the National Council of Nigerian Citizens in 1962, when the Eastern Cameroun joined the Cameroun Republic, and ceased to be part of Nigeria. Macaulay was made the chairman of the new party, while Azikiwe was appointed the secretary general.

Among the aims of the NCNC were the extension of democratic principles to all Nigerians, political freedom and economic security, social equality, and religious tolerance. The NCNC was in its upbeat state when the Second World War ended in 1945 and when the colonial administration imposed on the country, a new constitution called the Richard's Constitution of 1946. The war had in no small way helped to demystify the claims of the Whiteman to be superhuman, as many Nigerians who fought alongside the Europeans in the jungles of Europe and Asia saw to their surprise that the Whites were not what they had claimed to be. On their return to Nigeria at the end of the war, many of these demobilised soldiers wasted no time in enlisting in the national struggle and particularly joined the NCNC, which they considered to be the only authentic national political party in the country.

The NCNC went on a tour of all parts of the country to explain to Nigerians the implications of Richard's Constitution and to raise funds to enable the party to send delegates to London to protest the imposition of that constitution. While members of the party were touring the country, Macaulay became ill and died on May 7, 1946, in Lagos, at the age of 82. Azikiwe was then asked to take over the leadership of the party.

Under Richard's Constitution, both the Northern and the Southern Protectorates sat together in one legislative council for the first time since the 1914 amalgamation. The Richard's Constitution however provided a grand base for Nigerian regionalism when, apart from the central legislature in Lagos, there were regional houses of assembly for the North, the East, and the West. Members of these regional houses of assembly were not even elected by the people, but were selected from the native authorities, from which five members were in turn selected as representatives to the central legislature in Lagos.

The Richard's Constitution fueled ethnic cleavages that were waiting for available opportunities, which resulted to the formation of political parties based on ethnic sentiments. The first of these ethnically based political parties was the Action Group (AG), which metamorphosed from *Egbe Omo Oduduwa* (the Children of Oduduwa), a Yoruba cultural organisation. Led by Chief Obafemi Awolowo, a Yourba lawyer, the Action Group, which favoured decentralisation, believed that the best way to build a nation was to start at the base and go progressively up the ladder. The formation of the Action Group led to the influx of members of the Nigerian Youth Movement (NYM) into the group, which brought back the old rivalries and feud between the NYM and the NNDP, whose members had joined the NCNC. While the Action Group favoured decentralisation, the NCNC stood for a more centralised form of government.

The Northern People's Congress (NPC), which on its part, metamorphosed from *Jamiml'uyyar Mutenen Arewa Ayan,* led by Sir Ahmadu Bello, Sarduana of Sokoto, made no pretences of representing only the interest of the North, and in particular, the interest of the Hausa/Fulani oligarchy. The slogan of the party was "One North, One People".

The criticisms against the Richard's Constitution led to the setting up of the Macpherson Constitution in 1951, which later formalised Nigerian regionalism. While the constitution provided for a two-chamber legislature for the North and the West, made up of the House of Assembly and the House of Chiefs, it provided only one legislative chamber for the East, the House of Assembly. In the elections held under that constitution, while the North voted overwhelmingly for the NPC, the NCNC won in both the West and the East.

However, in the West, on the day of inauguration of the House, some NCNC members, in an unprecedented manner, crossed over to the Action Group, which was led by Chief Obafemi Awolowo, and thereby denied the NCNC the expected majority in the legislature. In consequence, Azikiwe, the NCNC leader, who would have assumed leadership of the Western House of Assembly, was forced to rush back to the East, "from whence I come". That was the beginning of tribal politics in Nigeria, whereby the Hausa/Fulani saw the NPC as their own political party; the Yoruba, embraced the Action Group as their own party; and the Igbo pitched tent with the NCNC.

In 1953, Chief Anthony Enahoro, a federal parliamentarian and member of the Action Group, moved a motion in the legislature: "that this House accepts, as a matter of primary political objective, the attainment of self-government for Nigeria in 1956". The motion was supported by both the Action Group and the NCNC members in the House. In response, the leader of the NPC, Sir Ahmadu Bello, Sarduana of Sokoto, proposed an amendment to the effect that self-government should be considered "as soon as possible", which had always been the official position of the British colonial administration.

The debate on the motion was explosive and led to a walkout by members of both the Action Group and the NCNC in the House, leaving behind only members of the NPC. The NPC members were later booed on the streets of Lagos and called stooges of the colonial government. However, the Northerners paid back the Southerners with their own coin, when they attacked a mass rally of the Action Group members led by Chief S.L. Akintola in Kano, leaving forty-six people dead and three hundred others injured (Okoye, op cit 161).

At the same time, while many frontline nationalists were fighting for the exit of the colonialists to enable Nigerians to take their destiny into their own hands, some minority ethnic groups, however, were expressing mixed feelings regarding their possible fate in an independent Nigeria, where the three major ethnic groups – the Hausa/Fulani, the Igbo, and the Yoruba, would be in charge. To allay their fears, the British government set up the Willinks Commission, otherwise known as the "Minorities Commission", to look into this problem.

While noting the unproportionate size of the federal units and the substantial powers granted to regional governments, the "Minorities Commission", however, considered the fears of the minorities to be unfounded and therefore recommended against the creation of new states for the minorities. It stressed that the interests of the minorities would be adequately protected within the existing three-regional structure (see Commission's Report in addendum). Thus, before Nigeria was granted political independence on October 1, 1960, after ninety-nine years of colonial rule, the country was already polarised as before when it was colonised, no thanks to the failure of the colonialists to make it one nation.

The Post-Independence Crises

At independence, Nigeria was a time bomb, ready to explode at any time. The election held in 1959 to usher in political independence was a patchwork of expedients, a time bomb, or marriage of convenience between the NPC and the NCNC. The election had failed to produce a clear winner, which necessitated the NPC, with 150 seats in the parliament, to go into alliance with the NCNC with 90 seats, so as to form the central government, leaving the Action Group with 72 seats in opposition. Under the arrangement, while the NPC produced the Prime Minister with executive powers, in the person of Alhaji Abubakar Tafawa Balewa, the NCNC produced the ceremonial Governor General, in the person of Dr. Nnamdi Azikiwe, with the Queen of England still the Nigerian Head of State.

In 1963, Nigeria became a republic, thereby removing all vestiges of colonial rule. Azikiwe changed from Governor General to President, albeit still a ceremonial President. That arrangement was a time-bomb laid by the colonialists, which did not take long to explode, and when it did, Nigeria went down the doldrums.

In a recently declassified information, a former British civil servant who worked in Nigeria during the colonial era, Harold Smith, revealed how he was recruited by the colonial authorities in Nigeria to help rig the pre-independence election in favour of the North, whose leaders were seen to be pliable and ready to do their bidding. But because he had refused to be part of the scheme, in spite of all the material enticements, including the offer of a royal knighthood, he was subjected to all sorts of victimisation and humiliation by the British authorities (see The Guardian of London, 1992).

While the Action Group leader, Chief Obafemi Awolowo, was satisfied with being the leader of opposition at the centre, other members of the party led by his deputy and Premier of the Western Region, Samuel Akintola, did not like the arrangement. They preferred to be part of an all-inclusive federal government so as not to be marginalised. They therefore went into secret talks with the Prime Minister, Abubakar Tafawa Balewa, without involving Awolowo, who was still the party leader.

A crack had developed in the wall of the Action Group. At the party's caucus meeting where the issue was to be discussed, Awolowo managed to secure the majority vote of the party members to expel Akintola from the party, which also meant removing Akintola as Premier of the Western Region. He was to be replaced with Alhaji D.S. Adegbenro. Akintola left the Action Group and formed his own political party, the Nigerian National Democratic Party (NNDP), but refused to relinquish the premiership of the Western Region.

On May 29, 1962, when the decision of the Action Group was to be tabled before the Western House of Assembly for debate, supporters of the new party, the NNDP, rose from their seats and began a weird dance on the floor of the House. One of them seized the mace, the symbol of authority in the House, aimed it at the Speaker, missed him, and got the mace broken on his table. There was pandemonium, chaos and confusion. The police moved in and dispersed the members with tear gas.

As a result of this development, the Federal Government declared a state of emergency throughout the Western Region and appointed a federal minister, Dr. Majekodunmi, as Administrator to oversee the region. A battalion of the Nigerian Army was dispatched to the region to enforce the emergency. At the end of the emergency, which lasted one year, Akintola, in spite of his unpopularity, was restored as the premier of the region. This was deeply resented by the people. The matter was not helped by Akintola's alleged vindictive stance, when he resorted to dissolving local government councils and demoting some recalcitrant traditional rulers (Eze, op cit:176).

While all these things were going on, the Action Group Leader, Obafemi Awolowo, and some of his supporters were charged with treasonable felony for plotting a popular uprising against the federal government through armed insurrection. Awolowo was alleged to have sent people to Nkrumah's Ghana to train for the uprising. He was also alleged to have imported arms into the country specifically for this purpose. It was a celebrated trial that lasted several months, at the end of which, some of the suspects were found guilty and sentenced to various terms of imprisonment, ranging from two to ten years. Awolowo was jailed for ten years.

Meanwhile, the first national census after independence was conducted in 1962, but due to several allegations of malpractices, the exercise was nullified and another one was fixed for 1963. The NCNC, which was already in control of both the Eastern and the Mid-Western Regions and maintained a relative strength in the West, was confident that with the 1963 census figures about to be released, which could give the South a greater population, and hence more constituencies, it would win the elections fixed for 1964 and form the federal government. However, when the census results were released, the North maintained its lead with 55 percent of the population. This was rejected by both the NCNC and the Action Group, as well as several other organisations like the trade unions and students associations.

To contest the 1964 elections, the Action Group faction in the West loyal to Akintola, teamed up with the NPC in the North, and formed the Nigeria National Alliance (NNA), while the other Action Group faction loyal to Awolowo, teamed up with the NCNC and formed the United Progressive Grand Alliance (UPGA). When the Federal Electoral Commission called for the filing of nomination papers from interested contestants, NNA supporters in the North refused to allow UPGA candidates there to file their papers.

UPGA challenged this and called for the extension of the deadline to enable its candidates to file their papers. This was turned down by the Chief Electoral Commissioner. Three of the six electoral commissioners disagreed, and resigned their appointments. UPGA called for a boycott of the election. This was effectively observed in the East and Lagos, but partially observed in the Mid-West and the West, and not observed at all in the North. The result was that the NNA was able to win all but five of the 167 seats in the North, and the majority of seats in the West. This gave the party an overall majority. UPGA was furious and called the election a hoax, and urged the President not to accept the result.

In his reaction, the President, Nnamdi Azikiwe, in a prepared speech, said he was not bound to accept the result of the election literally and re-appoint Tafawa Balewa as Prime Minister, "because of reports of irregularities". But Balewa countered that if there were irregularities, they were matters for the courts to decide. Four days of uncertainty and confusion saw Balewa and Azikiwe making contacts with the military and soliciting their support. The President also consulted with the Federal Attorney General and the Chief Justice of the Federation, who advised him against assuming "executive powers" and appointing "a caretaker prime minister" to conduct fresh elections. For those four days, there was praticallyy no government in Nigeria, and the country was on the brink of collapse.

On January 4, 1965, the President yielded to various pressures, when he re-appointed Tafawa Balewa, Prime Minister. Elections were later held in the East and Lagos, where UPGA's boycott was observed. In the spirit of reconciliation, UPGA ministers in the central government were assigned portfolios, while the Prime Minister announced the promotion of Brigadier J.T.U. Aguiyi-Ironsi to the rank of Major-General, and named him the General Officer Commanding the Nigerian Army to succeed the British-Born Major-General Welby-Evarard, who was leaving the country in February of that year. (Eze, ibid 179-182).

The last straw that broke the camel's back was the October 1965 Western Nigeria election. The NNDP/NNA alliance and the Action Group/UPGA alliance were each determined to win the election at all costs. The campaign for the election was fierce and violent. In the end, the NNDP managed to rig itself into power.

Electoral officers disappeared or refused to receive nomination papers from opposition candidates and declared the NNDP candidates elected unopposed. Those who agreed to accept opposition candidates' nomination papers had had their appointments revoked. Ballot papers were found in the hands of unauthorised persons on election day.

Returning officers refused to declare the election result after the count, enabling false returns to be broadcast from the regional radio station at Ibadan. The chairman of the electoral commission resigned in protest, listing these malpractices as his grievances.

In some constituencies where the Action Group candidates were declared elected and issued certificates of return, the radio still announced NNDP candidates as winners. The result was that the NNDP was declared the winner in 73 out of 93 seats in the regional House of Assembly.

As expected, the Action Group refused to accept the results of the election, while its supporters launched a campaign of rioting, arson, and murder against the NNDP government and its supporters. Houses were set on fire, and NNDP leaders matcheted. On several occasions, the police were forced to open fire on the protesters. The army was also drafted to the region to help the police track down the protesters.

While all these were going on, the federal government stood aloof or remained unconcerned. To divert people's attention from the deteriorating situation in the Western Region, the Prime Minister called a meeting of the Commonwealth Prime Ministers' Conference in Lagos for January 1966 to discuss the Unilateral Declaration of Independence (UDI), in Rhodesia, now Zimbabwe, by Rhodesian Prime Minister, Ian Smith, and many people were amazed.

The January 1966 Coup and the Nigeria-Biafra War

On January 12, 1966, the Commonwealth Prime Ministers' Conference, hosted by Nigeria ended in Lagos. Three days later, on January 15, 1966, the unexpected happened. The military launched attacks on the political leadership and rendered it impotent. In the process, some top government functionaries, like the Federal Prime Minister, Tafawa Balewa, the Finance Minister, Festus Okotie Eboh; the Premiers of the Northern and Western Regions, Ahmadu Bello and Samuel Akintola, respectively; as well as some top military officers, were killed. In the ensuing circumstances, Major General J.T.U. Aguiyi Ironsi emerged as the new military head of state, thus truncating democratic governance in the country.

As fate would have it, since the preponderance of the military officers that took part in that coup were of Igbo origin, the majority of those killed during the exercise were non-Igbo, and the new military head of state was an Igbo man, it was easy to ethnicise the January 1966 uprising and brand it "an Igbo coup". The matter was not helped by the banning of all ethnic associations in the country and the promulgation by the new military regime of "Unification Decree No. 34" of May 24, 1966, which abolished the federal structure of government and replaced it with a unitary system.

Five months into the administration, the country was in flames. It started as mere demonstrations by students of the Institute of Administration, Zaria, and those of Ahmadu Bello University, also in Zaria, against Decree No. 34 promulgated by the Ironsi regime, but later snowballed into full scale killings and massacres of people of Igbo origin living in different parts of Northern Nigeria between May 29 and 30, 1966. Approximately 3,000 people were killed or injured at the end of the Holocaust, and valuable property was looted or vandalized. As a result, a large number of Igbo people living in the North returned to their homeland, while some sent their wives and children home. But following assurances of their safety by some prominent traditional and religious leaders, the majority of those who left returned to the North.

Two months later, specifically on July 29, a worse catastrophe happened. An army mutiny took place, which resulted in the abduction and killing of the Head of State, General Ironsi, who was on tour to the

Western Region. He was killed along with his host, Colonel Francis Adekunle Fajuyi, Military Governor of the Western Region.

In what has been described as "a revenge coup", the mutineers also descended on other Igbo military officers and men across the military formations in the country, eliminating them in large numbers and forcing others to go into hiding. They later put forward the then Lieutenant Colonel Yakubu Gowon as the new military Head of State. By August 9, when the killing had subsided, "27 Igbo officers, 12 non-Igbo officers, 154 men of other ranks from the East, and 17 from the West and the Mid-West had been killed and many others injured" (Luckham, 1971:43).

As a result of the May and July killings, the Federal Government decided to convene an Ad Hoc Constitutional Conference in Lagos in September 1966 to discuss the future of Nigeria. This even led to more killings of the Igbo in different parts of the country outside Igboland, following which the Constitutional Conference was unceremoniously called off. Okwudiba Nnoli (1978:244) reports that

> Between September 29 and the end of November 1966, over 50,000 Igbo were gruesomely murdered, usually under inhuman conditions, maimed, or horribly mutilated, and over two million others who survived the killing and maiming became refugees in their ethnic homeland.

It was the failure or inability of Nigerian military leaders to amicably resolve their differences that led to the January 1967 meeting at Aburi, Ghana, under the auspices of the then Ghanaian military Head of State, Lieutenant General Joseph Ankrah. The atmosphere at the meeting was said to be friendly and cordial, leading to a number of resolutions that could have amicably resolved the lingering Nigerian crises. Unfortunately, no sooner had the military leaders left Ghana than they began to sing discordant tunes and gave the "Aburi Accord" different interpretations, which led to its non-implementation. And Nigeria continued to drift.

The climax was on May 27, 1967, when Yakubu Gowon unilaterally divided the country into twelve states, three of which were from the Eastern Region. It was a masterstroke designed to severe eastern unity and isolate the landlocked Igbo from the region's minority ethnic tribes. Almost immediately, the Eastern Consultative

Assembly, still in session, mandated the Military Governor of the East, Colonel Chukwuemeka Odumegwu Ojukwu, to pull Eastern Nigeria out of Nigeria at the "earliest practicable time".

Then, on Tuesday, May 30, 1967, Colonel Ojukwu, in an early morning broadcast, proclaimed Eastern Nigeria a sovereign and independent nation under the name of the "Republic of Biafra", and thus severed links between the Eastern Region and the rest of the Federal Republic of Nigeria.

But why did the Eastern Consultative Assembly and Ojukwu decide to take such extreme action as secession? Chinua Achebe (2012) provided a good answer:

> A government that failed to safeguard the lives of its citizens has no claim to their allegiance and must be ready to accept that the victims deserve the right to seek their safety in any other ways.

Since the disturbances that began in various parts of Northern Nigeria in May 1966, when thousands of Igbo people were massacred and millions were displaced, the Nigerian federal government had shown no remorse and had done nothing concrete to ensure the safety of Igbo lives and property. And as Lambert Ejiofor (1989) had remarked:

> In that circumstance, there appeared to be no option left for the Igbo other than to take their destiny into their own hands.

Gowon's immediate reaction to the declaration of Biafra was to proclaim it a "rebellion" that must be crushed at all costs. On July 6, 1967, Nigeria therefore declared war on Biafra. It was supposed to be a "police action", which would end in a matter of weeks, if not days, but the war later dragged on for thirty odd months, and took its toll. Over two million lives were lost, several other millions became homeless and unquantifiable private and public property was destroyed.

The war was fought in a most unconventional manner of modern warfare, not respecting the sanctity of women, children, the sick, or the elderly, who were made the prime targets of attacks. Hundreds of unarmed civilians were massacred by the Nigerian federal forces. For instance, in Asaba in September 1968, as many as seven hundred men who had joyfully come to welcome the Nigerian soldiers to the town, were lined up in one day and executed (Okocha, 1994)

It was indeed a war of genocide, which, apart from the use of ground forces to massacre innocent civilians, and fighter jets to bomb and destroy churches and market places, also killed as many women and children as possible, and as well involved imposition of economic blockades to ensure that there was no Biafran survivor at the end of the war, since, according to the often quoted saying of then Nigerian Deputy Head of State and Finance Minister, Chief Obafemi Awolowo, "starvation is a legitimate weapon of war".

From the beginning, Biafra was the underdog. With inferior material means, insufficient weapons, and ill-trained soldiers, several Biafran towns fell to the rampaging Nigerian federal forces. This was due to the open support given to Nigeria by such powerful countries as Great Britain, the Soviet Union, and most countries in the Arab world, which supplied the country with sophisticated weapons, fighter jets, military personnel and technical advisers. They also ensured that the economic blockade imposed by Nigeria against Biafra was strictly enforced so that nothing would enter the Biafran enclave either by land, by air, or by sea, thereby causing untold hardship to the people of Biafra.

But Biafra itself was not a pushover. Despite the numerous odds stacked against them, Biafran soldiers displayed great valour in the battlefield, and with their Spartan spirit, the spirit of endurance, they put up strong resistance and brought the enemy to a halt. They even made some incursions into some Nigerian territories, like in the Mid-West Region, and up to Ore and Okitipupa in the Western Region.

The Biafran scientists had also put on their thinking caps and fabricated all sorts of weapons, rockets, land mines (*Ogbunigwe*, also called Ojukwu Bucket), submarines, machine guns, etc. They had equally refined petroleum products and manufactured different kinds of goods. The Biafran Land Army ensured that every inch of the remaining land in Biafra was effectively cultivated for massive production of food to help ward off the lingering starvation in the enclave. It was a war of survival, and everybody at whatever level, had thrown in his weight.

The war dragged on till January 15, 1970, when Biafra finally capitulated, no thanks to external support given to Nigeria by Britain, the Soviet Union, some Afican countries like Egypt, the entire Arab world, as well as the conspiracy of silence by the international community on the sufferings in Biafra.

The Wonders and Miracles of Biafra War

The Biafra War (July 6, 1967 – January 15, 1970) had gone through different stages during the period, and the people of Biafra always rose to meet its challenges. It started with the following song.

> Armoured car,
> Shelling machine,
> Heavy artillery,
> Ha enweghi ike imeli Biafra.... (All These will not be able to defeat Biafra)

The story is long, but we will try to make it short. Unless we were born before or during the Biafran war, most of us may not have heard the above song. But we always remember this song as if it were yesterday. It was one of the popular songs that gave the Biafran soldiers courage and the belief that no weapon on the surface of the earth could defeat Biafra.

Indeed, it was such songs that gave Biafran soldiers the courage to confront Nigeria, which had the entire country's pre-war military weapons with only 150 rifles at the start of the war. Some of these songs were also the reason Biafra troops surprised the world in the first few weeks of the war by advancing as far as Ore, a few kilometres to the Nigerian seat of government in Lagos, at the time.

That move forced Nigeria to place embargo on all categories of shipping, with the exception of oil tankers, suspecting that Ojukwu was importing arms through the channel. As Biafra kept pressurising Nigeria, the Nigerian government was forced to include oil tankers in the blockade. They thought that Ojukwu was buying weapons with oil money.

The blockade spurred more Biafran support for the war. Thousands of Biafran youths abandoned their parents, traders closed their shops, and secondary and university students left their schools and trooped into the streets, chanting war songs and begging Ojukwu to give them more guns and machetes to face the enemy.

> Ojukwu nyem egbe, (Ojukwu give me gun)
> Nyem nma, (give me cutlass)
> Ka'm gbagbuo Gowon, gbagbuo Hassan.... (So I can kill Gowon, Kill Hassan)

But there were no guns to give them. Poor boys. You won't blame them. They thought that the war was a war between just two African nations, Nigeria and Biafra. At that point, Biafran local blacksmiths from Awka, Ebenebe, Ezeagu, Dikenafai, etc., embarked on mass fabrication of dane guns and local cannon guns for Biafran boys.

With these local weapons, Biafran troops continued making waves. In panic, the Nigerian government quickly ran to Britain and America, who were inseparable allies, for weapons, which they quickly arranged for them. As soon as Nigeria took delivery of the foreign weapons, Gowon chided Ojukwu that if Biafra failed to surrender immediately, the Igbo would be wiped out from the face of the earth within one month.

After the threat, Biafran troops became more resolute and swore to swim and sink with Ojukwu. Knowing that in war, death was inevitable, and knowing the new capability of the enemy, they were ready to die, as captured in an emotional but defiant war chant:

> Save my bullet when I die
> Oh Biafra!
> Save my bullet when I die
> Alleluia, if I happen to die in the battle field
> Save my bullet when I die.

Touched and inspired by these songs, Biafran scientists rose to the challenge. They manufactured Biafran armoured personnel carriers, nicknamed Biafran Red Devils. They converted local canon guns, *"Mkpo n'ani"* (the Igbo traditional gun fire), to land mines, which they later perfected into the famous *Ogbunigwe* (mass killer). Nigerian soldiers nicknamed it "Ojukwu bucket" while their foreign mercenaries called it "Biafran Wonder." There was no African country who had accomplished this feat since then.

Biafran scientists later upgraded the *ogbunigwe* to the flying *ogbunigwe*, a rocket-propelled missile that became a terror to Nigerian troops. The flying *ogbunigwe* became the first rocket propelled missile to be wholly designed, developed, mass-produced, and launched in Africa.

When Nigeria perceived that Biafra could match them artillery for artillery on land, they switched to sea battle with a fresh supply of modern warships from Britain and America. Biafran scientists went back to the drawing board and came out with the famous shore battery, a sophisticated piece of naval equipment that destroyed scores of Nigerian warships.

In October 1967, the Nigerian Second Division, under the command of Murtala Muhammed, invaded Onitsha through Asaba and tried to cross the River Niger but was severally prevented by the Bifaran shore battery. They eventually entered Onitsha but were quickly routed by Biafran troops under the command of Major Joseph Achuzie and Col. Assam Nsudoh, who captured and killed most of the Nigerian soldiers.

In December 1967, the Nigerian Second Division and the Sixth Battalion re-crossed the Niger River at Idah and made their way again to recapture Onitsha, but were again held up in a gruesome battle by Biafran troops.

On March 31, 1968, the division with over 6,000 troops, supported by over forty trailer loads of weapons and armoured cars, attempted to link up with the First Division at Enugu. It was an ill-fated journey, as the entire division was completely decimated by Biafran forces. This forced the Nigerian government into another panic, resorting to air battle with the aid of Russian war planes and professional mercenary pilots from Egypt.

As Russia joined the war with her highly sophisticated MIG jets and professional pilots hired from Egypt to pilot the machines, Nigerian troops were thrown into jubilation, certain that the Russian air raids would finally seal the fate of Biafra. Biafran soldiers reacted very emotionally to this new situation, again expressing their readiness to pay the supreme sacrifice for Biafra in spite of all odds.

> My Father, don't you worry
> My mother, don't you worry
> My brother, don't you worry
> My sister, don't you worry
> If I happen to die in the battle field
> Never mind, we shall see again

Touched by this heart-rending song, Biafran scientists went back to the laboratory and fabricated the Biafran Babies, locally manufactured military aircrafts that dealt several hits on Nigerian military bases in Makurdi, Kaduna, and Kano. It was the first instance of black pilots manning war planes without expatriate accompaniment.

Yes. Biafra may not have won the Nigeria-Biafra war. But they gave a good account of themselves, to the amazement of both Nigeria and the world. This made Yakubu Gowon, the Nigerian Head of State, to declare the *No Victor, No Vanquished* at the end of the war. Apart from the ingenuity exhibited by Biafran scientists in the local manufacture of a wide variety of war weapons under the famous RAP, short for Research and Production Unit, they also achieved other feats in the area of war logistics and human survival that utterly confounded Nigeria and the world.

The Biafran scientists also converted local palm oil to crude oil and processed it into motor fuel, diesel, kerosene, lubricants, and other motor oils. They converted and processed coconut water into break fluids and gear oil. After the fall of Port Harcourt and later Enugu, which cut off vital Biafran airforce services, Biafran civil and aero engineers and technicians quickly converted a tarred road at Uga into an emergency airstrip within 48 hours of the fall of Enugu airport. They later constructed a more standard airport at Uli, which landed all categories of aircraft that flew in relief materials and weapons, mostly at night.

When Nigerian bomber planes followed Biafran pilots in the air, the Biafran pilots radioed the airport control tower personnel to turn off landing lights and other airport lights to avoid detection by the enemy jets, and still landed safely in the dark. Unbelievable ingenuity!

Each time a Nigerian bomber plane collided with and damaged the airport runway, Biafran technicians repaired the damaged runway and repaired the potholes in a matter of hours, using an improvised cement device, and flights resumed. Biafran scientists used all available sources of protein and carbohydrates, including cassava leaves, lizards, and rodents, to produce food formulas to supplement supplies from the Red Cross, Caritas International, and other foreign food donor organizations.

The local food production helped to drastically reduce malnutrition and Kwashiorkor, especially on Biafran children, preventing the kind of situation we now have in IDP camps in Nigeria.

To combat the dearth of drugs in Biafra, especially in military hospitals, Biafran pharmacists stormed the bushes and came out with tonnes of herbs and vegetables of all types, like *ogirisi igbo, onugbu, azam* and other crops, which they analysed and processed into drugs for all types of cures. They processed some of these herbs into drips for the emergency treatment of war casualties and other accidents. They processed palm oil, firewood, charcoal, and ash into highly effective orthopaedic accessories like Plaster of Paris (POP) and other medical appliances.

For the most part of the war, several schools in Biafra were in session until about 1969, when the volume of refugees reached an all-time high, forcing many schools to vacate their buildings to accommodate refugees, while some were converted to hospitals.

Markets, churches, farmlands, name it, all were booming in spite of regular air raids by Nigerian jets, but did not daunt the Biafran spirit. Civil servants, including refugee civil servants, continued to receive their monthly salaries as and when they were due for the majority of the war, even when Umuahia was the only remaining Biafran centre of government. One of Ojukwu's many war magics.

Business and trading, for which the Igbo are known, were in full swing, as many Biafran businessmen and women criss-crossed the Nigerian cities of Lagos, Jos, Makurdi, and Enugu and Biafra in the popular "*afia attack*" (smuggling) to supply Biafrans with essential commodities of all types, including the latest wears for boys and girls.

The Biafran commandos and militia outfits, variously known as BOFF (Biafra Organisation of Freedom Fighers), and Rangers, operated "behind the enemy lines" i.e., within Nigeria held Biafran territories, where they attacked Nigerian barracks and looted armouries, which they dispatched to Biafran military units "across the line".

For all intents and purposes, Biafra was not defeated in the war until Ojukwu left Biafra to seek "peace" and "freedom for Biafra". As far as we know, Ojukwu, as the symbol of Biafra, did not surrender. Even his deputy. General Phillip Effiong who was reported to have surrendered, did not say that Ojukwu had directed him to surrender

When Ojukwu eventually came back from exile in 1982, he did not surrender to anybody. All he said was that he wanted to lead the Igbo back to the Nigerian mainstream, which was why he joined the then National Party of Nigeria (NPN) and contested for the Senate. Even at that, the Nigerian government was still afraid of him and preferred him to keep a safe distance.

What else could be said except that Biafra and Biafrans had lived up to the ideals and vision of their national anthem as composed by the Great Zik of Africa:

> Land of the rising sun, we love and cherish,
> Beloved homeland of our brave heroes;
> We must defend our lives or we shall perish,
> We shall protect our lives from all our foes;
> But if the price is death for all we hold dear,
> Then let us die without a shred of fear. (Omeife 2021)

How Enugu Rangers Won the War for the Vanquished

Football is the greatest instrument that unites Nigerians. Whenever the national team, the Super Eagles, is on song, all Nigerians become united in an astonishing togetherness. There was the Nigeria-Biafra war of 1967-1970 that could have divided the country forever. At the end of the war in 1970, then Head of State, General Yakubu Gowon made the famous pronouncement of "No Victor, No Vanquished". Of course, the vanquished ones knew themselves as they sauntered back into Nigeria, hungry and broken, after the end of the Biafra struggle.

The eminent Nigerian football administrators of that time, notably the iconic Oyo Orok Oyo, stressed at the end of the war that a team from the erstwhile rebel section must be involved for a true national champion to emerge. The reigning champion, the Nigerian Army football team, had to face the team from the East. In the pulsating match, the boys from the East defeated the Nigerian Army team 2-1, a clear case of the vanquished turning the table on the victors.

A key player from the Nigerian Army team, Paul "Wonder Boy" Hamilton, recalled that Olusegun Obasanjo was so enraged when he saw the Army team in the office of the team coordinator, George Innih, that he nearly had them flogged for "losing to those hungry boys".

The Eastern boys may have been hungry, but they were quite determined, such that one of their star players, Dominic Nwobodo, who had his head broken and bloodied, completed the match with a completely bandaged head that earned him the nickname "Alhaji".

It was from the ruins of the war that the Enugu Rangers were formed in 1970, and the team represented Nigeria in the 1971 African Cup of Champions Clubs, reaching the quarterfinals before losing to the ASEC Mimosas of Cote d'Ivoire. The pioneer Rangers team of 1970 comprised Cyril Okosieme in goal, Ernest Ufele and Johnny "Wheeler" Nwosu as full backs, Peter Okeke as defensive midfielder, Skipper Godwin Achebe as central defender with Luke "Jazz Bukana" Okpala as his partner, while the forward players were Mathias Obianika, Kenneh Abana, Dominic Nwobodo, Chukwuma Igweonwu and Shadrack Ajaero.

The Rangers team got to the final of the 1971 National Challenge Cup but lost to WNDC (IICC, 3SC) of Ibadan, with WNDC's goalie, Adisa Amusa, saving the penalty of Skipper Achebe. A major addition to Rangers team thereafter was the goalkeeper, Emmanuel Okala, who took over from Cyril Okosieme.

In the spirit of rising from the ruins of the war, the schoolboys of East Central State won the 1971 Manuwa/Adebajo Academical Cup, and star players from the team such as Godwin Ogbueze, Dominic Ezeani, Kenneth Ilodigwe, and Christian Chukwu were immediately drafted into the Rangers team. Crack centre-half, Dominic Ezeani, who had displaced Skipper Achebe in the gold-winning national team, the Green Eagles, at the 1973 All-Africa Games staged in Lagos, equally took over from the legendary Achebe as captain of Rangers and henceforth led the team to winning the double, that is, the League and Challenge Cup, in 1974.

The 1974 Challenge Cup final was between Rangers and the Mighty Jets of Jos, a team from the Head of State Yakubu Gowon's Plateau State. Aloysius Atuegbu, who was playing for the Mighty Jets, recalled that Gowon came to his home and promised to buy him a Volkswagen Beetle if he could help beat the Rangers. Aloy played like a possessed man. Rangers skipper, Ezeani, advised Aloy that he would get injured if he continued playing like mad. In Aloy's next move, Rangers hard defender Harrison Mecha gave him a wicked tackle, such that Aloy was stretchered out for good. Rangers beat the Mighty Jets 2-0 and lifted the coveted trophy. No Volkswagen for Aloy!

Rangers won the coveted Challenge Cup three years on the trot, beating Shooting Stars of Ibadan 1-0 in 1975, and Alyufsalam Rocks of Ilorin 2-0 in 1976, and a team remarkably made up of ten Ghanaian players and only one Nigerian! Rangers were unable to defend the cup in 1977, due to a fixture overload.

Playing too many matches caught up with Rangers in 1978, when, after playing tough matches against Canon Sportif of Cameroun in the African Champion Clubs Cup and replaying the Challenge Cup semi-final with Raccah Rovers of Kano, the team eventually succumbed 3-0 to Bendel Insurance of Benin in the final. Rangers had played some truly remarkable matches, like when the team lost 1-0 to Mehalla of Egypt in the 1975 semi-finals of the Champions Cup only to trounce the Egyptians 3-0 in the return leg played in Enugu, even after one of the players, US-import Kenneth Ilodigwe, had been sent off by the referee. The match was aptly described as "Mehalla saw wahala in Enugu!"

Rangers lost the 1975 African Champions Cup final in Lagos to Hafia FC of Guinea after having waited in vain in Enugu for the match to be played there, only to be ferried to Lagos at the 11th hour. In the match, Rangers' main thrust of attack, Nwabueze Nwankwo's long throws were continuously disallowed by the referee. Rangers were defeated 3-1 on aggregate.

Rangers won the African Cup-Winners Cup in 1977, beating Canon of Cameroun 5-2 on aggregate, and ending up as the only African team to win a competition without losing a match! The semi-final matches of the competition against the Nigerian reigning champions, the IICC Shooting Stars of Ibadan, nearly caused a tribal war. The first leg was played in Lagos, but the second leg had to be rescheduled for Kaduna, where Rangers won through a heart-stopping penalty shootout.

Rangers International of Enugu helped the Igbo people regain their pride of place after the debacle of Biafra. Rangers had no time for fancy, and their players would readily tell you: "There are no goal posts in the midfield!" (Mbah, et al, 1993).

References

Achebe, C, (2012) *There Was a Country* (London, Penguin Books)
Awolowo, Obafemi (1966) *Thoughts on Nigerian Constitution* (Ibadan: Oxford University Press)
Chambers, Douglas B. (2005), *Murder at Montpelier: Igbo Africans in Virginia*, (Mississippi, University Press).
Ejiofor, LU., 'Azikiwe and the Nigerian Civil War' in Olisa, MSO and Ikejiani, OM (1989,eds.) *Azikiwe and the African Revolution* (Onitsha, African Fep Publishers Limited)
Eze, Dons (2008) *Africa In Turmoil* (Enugu: Linco Press)
Fanon, Fratnz (1977) *The Wretched of the Earth* (London: Pengun Books)
Glyn Leonard (2009), *The Lower Niger and Its Tribes* (Charleston, South Carolina, Biblio Bazaar, LLC)
Hrbek, Ivan; Fāsī, Muḥammad (1988), *Africa from the Seventh to the Eleventh Century.* (London: UNESCO).
Luckham, Robin (1971) *The Nigerian Military* (Cambridge: Cambridge University Press)
Mbah, S. et al (1993) *Rangers International* (Enugu: Reynods Publishers)
Miners, NJ (1971) *The Nigerian Army 1956-1966* (London: Matheu & Co. Ltd)
Nnoli. Okwudiba (1978) *Ethnic Politics In Nigeria* (Enugu: Fourth Dimension Publishing Co. Ltd) p.244.
Ogundiran, Akinwumi (2005), 'Four Millennia of Cultural History in Nigeria (ca. 2000 B.C.–A.D. 1900): Archaeological Perspectives;, *Journal of World Prehistory.* 19 (2): 133–168.
Okocha, Emma (1994) *Blood On The Niger* (Port Harcourt: Sunray Publications Ltd.) pp. 23-34.
Okonjo, I.M (1974), *British Administration In Nigeria 1900-1950* (London:Nok Publishers) p. 4.
Okoye, Mokwugo (1981), *Storms on the Niger* (Enugu: Forth Dimension Publishers) p.10
Omeife Omeife (2021) 'The Biafra Story', *Daily Star*, February 10.
Onwuejeogwu, M.A. (1981) *An Igbo Civilization: Nri Kingdom and Hegemony,*(London &Benin City Ethnographica and Ethiope)
Remi Anifowose (1982) *Violence And Politics In Nigeria, The Tiv And Yoruba Experiences* (New York: Nok Publishers)
Ryder, A.F.C. (1969) *Benin and The Europeans*, (London, Longmans)

Smith, Harold (1992) 'The Politics of Ignorance: Nigeria and the CrossStreet Hacks' in, *The Guardian*, (London) March 12.

Her Majesty's Stationary Office (1958), *The Willinks Commission on the Fears of the Minority Groups*

Uzoigwe, GN (1974) *Britain and the Conquest of Africa* (New York: Nok Publishers International)

CHAPTER SEVEN

The Igbo in Nigerian Politics
The Dramatic Rise of the Igbo

In his book, *The Trouble with Nigeria*, Chinua Achebe (1983) claimed that Nigerians of all other ethnic groups will probably achieve consensus on no other matter than their common resentment of the Igbo.

Elaborating, Achebe averred that had the Igbo been a minor ethnic group of a few hundred thousand, their "menace" would have been easily contained. However, they have millions of members

The rise of the Igbo as a strong force in Nigeria surprised many people. This is due to their late arrival in the Nigerian political scene, in addition to their late contact with the outside world. As late as the nineteenth century, when many Igbo people were still holed up inside their very thick forests, the Yoruba, for example, had produced several lawyers, doctors, engineers, surveyors, journalists and so many other professionals, while the Hausa had produced many Islamic scholars, judges, and doctors as far back as the thirteenth century.

According to Coleman (1958:142), "as early as in the 1920s, the Yoruba had twelve practising barristers, and eight medical doctors, while the Igbo had none". Frederick Schwarz (1965) also reports, that

> The Yoruba had been exposed to western education at a much earlier date than any other group in Nigeria. They were the wealthiest Nigerians, with a substantial middle class based on cocoa farming, and their cities, Lagos, Abeokuta, and Ibadan, were Nigeria's intellectual and political centres.

As for the Hausa ethnic group, there were reports of how Katsina and Kano had received the Islamic faith and civilisation way back in the thirteenth century through a very powerful and influential king named, Mansa Musa, who in 1324, went to pilgrimage in Mecca with "six hundred thousand men dressed in brocade and Persian silk and a baggage train of eighty camels, each carrying three hundred pounds' weight of gold dust". In the same vein, Leo Africanus, who visited

Jenne, Mali, Gao, Kano, Katsina and other states, recorded in his *History and Description of Africa,* "a great store of doctors, judges, priests, and other learned men, that are bountifully maintained at the king's expense." (see Okoye 1981)

Notwithstanding this early contact of the Hausa with the outside world, when the British colonialists came to Nigeria, they would not open up the North to Western education. Rather, they preferred to rule the people through their traditional authorities, the Emirs, thus perpetuating, rather than changing the indigenous authoritarian political system. As a concomitant of this system, Christian missionaries were excluded from the area, which became equally closed to European civilisation. During the ensuing years, the Northern Emirs maintained their traditional political and religious institutions while reinforcing their social structure.

Even among their eastern neighbours, the Igbo were still far behind. For instance, the first African principal of Dennis Memorial Grammar School (DMGS), Onitsha, was SJ Cookey from Opobo; the first African principal of Government College, Umuahia, was Erekosima, a Kalabari; and the first African principal of Government Secondary School, Owerri, was Kombo, a Nembe. In the same vein, at the Government Secondary School, Afikpo, Mr. Mboto, from Itigidi, was in charge, while the first African Chief Dental Surgeon of Eastern Nigeria was Dr. Ernest Dublin Green, from Bonny; as the first Chief Architect of Eastern Nigeria was Chief AG Spiff, from the present Bayelsa State, who was killed on the sea in the 1990s in one of the Kalabari/Nembe crises. At the time of all these appointments, no Igbo man was qualified to head any of the institutions. In the 1950s, very few Igbo lawyers could compete with the Douglas family of Abonema.

How then did the Igbo come to dominate the East, in particular, and move forward to assert themselves vigorously in other parts of the country?

The Igbo took education seriously from the 1930s on, invested in it, and then started to reap its benefits. The successes achieved by the Igbo were based on individual efforts, and of course, their belief in mentorship.

In Igboland, because of the difficulties the British colonialists had in penetrating the thick mangrove-malarious forests of the area and establishing firm control over the highly autonomous and individualistic Igbo, who very often rose to challenge any attempt at depriving them of their independence, it was the Christian missionaries, who came with cunning and material enticements around 1857, that succeeded in winning the hearts of the people. The missionaries had brought along with them both the Christian religion and western education, which the Igbo came out to embrace with an overwhelming interest. As a result, several Igbo communities and cultural associations began to compete with one another to build schools and colleges for their children and wards, as well as to sponsor their brilliant sons and daughters to educational institutions abroad. Cyril Onwumechili (2000) reports that

> ...within ten to fifteen years of the last Igbo village being subjugated by the British, some Igbo were already working and settling in various parts of Nigeria. The Igbo took their destiny into their own hands. All over Nigeria, they were very active in the public and private sectors, mainly as clerks, teachers, and members of the security forces, artisans, petty traders, and domestic servants to foreigners. Even without their kindred in high positions as godfathers, they began to improve their positions by dint of hard work ...
> The Igbo in the cities organised traditional assemblies of people to form the same village, town, or clan associations. The assembles at home and "abroad" (away from the clan) rendered mutual help to their members, promoted development in their clans of origin, and often awarded scholarships to their sons and daughters. They joined various clan assemblies in a city federated to become an Igbo city union, especially in cities outside Igboland. Some of the unions built Igbo schools in the cities of abode...

The net effect of these efforts was that before the Nigerian civil war in 1967, the Igbo, who previously were late comers in the Nigerian project, had not only succeeded in bridging the educational imbalance between them and the Yoruba, but also in overtaking many of those who were there before their arrival. As B.J. Dudley (1966) had shown:

> Statistics for students' enrolment in Nigerian universities for the former four regions of Nigeria between 1965 and 1966 showed that the "Midwest Region had 111 students, the Northern Region had 275, the Western Region had 901 students, and the Eastern Region (mainly Igbo), 1,180 students.

Eastern Nigeria was also the first of the then three regions of Nigeria to establish a full-fledged university, the University of Nigeria, with campuses in Nsukka and Enugu, in 1960, which aroused the desire for hundreds of youths in the area to begin to seek university education.

Under the colonial setting, western education was accompanied by cash economy, which led to the emergence of such economic activities as banking, mining, manufacturing, commerce, etc., not to mention the civil service. These opened new horizons for the adventurous and newly educated Igbo to seize upon. And they began to see opportunities beyond their immediate environment. This led to mass migration of the Igbo from their homeland to explore new opportunities in the cities, where they were employed as clerks, either in the civil service or in commercial firms, or became self-employed artisans, traders, craftsmen, political elites, etc. As they moved out to these new areas, they settled there with their wives and children.

Unfortunately, rather than embrace this open-minded approach of the Igbo, which would have led to national integration, where every Nigerian would appreciate each other as members of the same family, the Igbo were looked upon with a jaundiced eye or suspicion. They were resented and accused of economic parasitism, dominance, selfishness, and acquisitive tendencies.

Not only were the Igbo resented or discriminated against by their various host communities, there was also stiff competition for the slice of "the national cake" among the three major ethnic groups in the country – the Igbo, the Hausa, and the Yoruba — between the Igbo and the Yoruba on one hand, for jobs in the federal civil service and other industrial and commercial establishments, and between the Igbo and the Hausa-Fulani on the other, for the political control of the federal government of Nigeria. These remain some of the major challenges that confront every political administration in the country.

The general resentment of the Igbo, or the Igbo "scare" across the country, was not limited to most of the ethnic groups in Nigeria, but equally extended to the relationship between the Igbo and the English-speaking Cameroun, which was part of Nigeria. According to Ihechukwu Madubike, fear of dominance drove the British Cameroon to opt out of Nigeria during the United Nations referendum on February 11, 1961. He wrote:

The fear of Igbo dominance in all the sectors of social and political life in the former German and British territories was given as a major factor. Kumba, Mamfe, Bamenda, Tiko and Victoria, had a large number of Ndigbo who dominated the economy. This led to local resentments, which politicians like Dr. E.M.L Endeley, Chief Manga Williams, and J.N. Foncha exploited for selfish interests.

Madubuike however observed that stereotyping the Igbo did not change their natural disposition "to hard work, aggressiveness, showiness, and ethnic pride, all of which may be interpreted as the Igbo hubris, which, in literary parlance, is a tragic flaw" (therepublicannews.com).

Several reasons have been adduced as to the dramatic rise of the Igbo in the Nigerian political arena. Apart from the initial stimulus provided by the Christian missionaries who brought in western education, which the Igbo embraced with enthusiasm and open arms, there was also the free enterprise of the Igbo, or their "can do" spirit, their belief in success based on personal merit or achievement, as well as their adventurism, which made many of them began to try their hands on "something new". Unlike the Hausa-Fulani or the Yoruba, whose systems were more or less based on inheritance and over-dependency, the Igbo believe in their own self-worth, in their ability to surmount any obstacle ahead of them.

Comparing the Hausa with the Igbo, Robert LeVino (1971:182) wrote:

> The ideal successful Hausa man seems to have been the office holder who faithfully supported his superior and rewarded his followers; the Ibo ideal appears to have been the energetic and industrious farmer or trader who aggrandised himself personally through productive or distributive activity.

Mention must equally be made of the role played by the Igbo State Union (1934-1966) in awakening the consciousness of the Igbo of the need for unity and self-actualization, in addition to various Igbo town unions and other cultural associations that built schools and colleges and awarded scholarships to their deserving sons and daughters.

Another factor that was responsible for the rise of the Igbo in Nigeria was population pressure, which forced thousands of Igbo young men and women to move out of their homeland to other parts of the country and beyond in search of work. According to Okwudiba Nnoli (1978:59),

> Igboland is one of the most densely populated areas of the world. In some areas, the population density exceeds 1,000 people per square mile. Moreover, the soil is comparatively poor because it is highly leached and acidic. Hence, a large number of Igbo-speaking people have migrated to colonial life.

Inter-Ethnic Rivalries

One major issue that has long plagued Nigeria and contributed to its numerous setbacks is tribalism, or what we now call ethnicity. This problem not had retarded her economic progress, but also her political development. For instance, Nigeria, which started the process of decolonisation from Britain along with Ghana, had to wait for three more years, in 1960, to deal with the problem of "ethnic minorities", while Ghana gained political independence in 1957.

Apart from that, just six years after independence in 1960, the country was faced with a catastrophic situation when its boat was rocked by the military, which hinged their reason for intervening in the political process on "tribalism and nepotism". Nigeria has suffered several other setbacks, principally due to quarrels among the various ethnic groups that make up the country.

It is claimed that there are over 450 ethnic groups in Nigeria, each of which fights to assert its own identity and thereby struggles to pull the country apart. According to Chinweizu (2005), Nigeria is a *"noyau",* a French word, which he interpreted to mean

> A society of inward antagonism, one held together by mutual internal antagonism, one which could not survive if its members had no fellow members to hate.

Chinweizu claimed that while Britain had created "a Nigerian State", she failed to create "a Nigerian nation". Thus, for each of the over 450 ethnic groups in Nigeria, the nation is the ethnic group or clan, or even the religious community, and not Nigeria.

During colonial rule, Nigerians were made to see or recognise themselves as belonging only to their tribes or language groups. To many of them, the tribe or ethnic group was primary, while the

Nigerian nation was secondary. The people were made to keep apart from each other and to see members of other tribes or ethnic groups as potential enemies and competitors for the common patronage.

J.S. Coleman (1978:59), claims that the British colonial administration in the country took every opportunity to spread the myth and propaganda that Nigerians were "separated from one another by great distance, by differences of history and traditions, and by ethnological, racial, tribal, political, social and religious barriers".

No doubt, Coleman canvassed this view based on the assertion by a former colonial Governor of Nigeria, Sir Hugh Clifford, who had equivocally stated that his administration would seek to secure "to each separate people the right to maintain its identity, its individuality, and its nationality, its chosen form of government; and the peculiar political and social institutions which have been evolved for it by the (wisdom and accumulated experiences of generations for its forebears" Okonjo, 1974:123). This, therefore, is proof that the colonialists never wanted a united Nigeria or to build a strong Nigerian nation.

Since it was the colonialists who held the key to every success in life, Nigerians hoping to make it, were made to assert themselves as individuals within their language group or tribe. Therefore, to enroll or register their children and wards in schools, to seek for jobs in the civil service or in industrial and commercial establishments, and even to access medical services in hospitals, they were made not only to put down their names, but also to indicate their tribes of origin and religion.

In the same vein, Nigerian immigrants to colonially created urban centres or places of economic activity were made to live not with their host communities, but to live separately as strangers in the same town. In many cities in Northern Nigeria, Nigerian immigrants lived in separate, designated areas known as Sabon Gari (strangers' town).

There is no doubt that the main purpose for which the colonialists had introduced tribalism or ethnicity as part of their machinery of governance in Nigeria was to keep the people divided or quarelling while appropriating their resources. And the best way to do this was to create artificial scarcity in terms of available vacancies in schools, job opportunities, residential houses, allocation of market stalls, service deliveries, etc., so that the people would continue to quarrel and fight among themselves while the colonialists were exploiting them.

Okwudiba Nnoli (1978) conceives tribalism or ethnicity as a product of colonial and post-colonial order in the context of an urban setting. According to him, before colonial rule, each of the ethnic groups in the country existed as fragmented units, having little or nothing to do with each other. Individual members of these groups even fought each other and carried out trade and other businesses with members of other ethnic groups without seeing themselves as being Igbo or Yoruba, Hausa, Tiv, Idoma, or any other ethnic group.

Only during the colonial cash economy, when Nigerians began to migrate to urban centres in search of paid jobs as clerks, miners, artisans, technicians or traders that they began to see themselves as belonging to a particular language group, and others as being different from them. In the process, they began to bind themselves in groups for purposes of protecting their special interests and providing for their various needs.

The Igbo as Nigerian Guinea Pigs

The Igbo are in a precarious situation in Nigeria. Because of their upward mobility, their desire to always try their hands on something new, many of them migrate to other parts of the country and beyond in search of alternative means of livelihood. They thus constitute the second largest ethnic group in every city or town outside Igboland. Besides, due to their ingenuity and resourcefulness, the Igbo are capable of making oceans in the desert and turning dust into gold. They can take up any business no matter how menial, once they are convinced that something positive will come out of it.

Therefore, when the Igbo, through hard work and determination, begin to prosper, or to make success in their ventures, it begins to attract envy, hatred, and resentment, not only from their host communities, but also from different other Nigerians. They are vilified and called all sorts of names, and are blamed for everything that goes wrong in any part of Nigerian community and are made to pay dearly for it with their lives and their property.

For instance, if there is an economic recession and many people are finding it difficult to eke out a living – no jobs, no food on the table, and traders are not selling their wares, etc., it will be blamed on the ubiquitous *Omo Kobo-kobo*, the *Nyamiri*, (the Igbo), who have monopolised everything, hoarded the goods, and dominated the political space. They will be molested and attacked, their wares looted, and their market stalls vandalised. At the governmental level, they are usually seen as menace, and forced to relocate, their wares seized, and their stalls demolished.

In the same vein, if the politicians fail to agree on how to divide their spoils and begin to haggle and quarrel over who occupies which position in government, and thereby causing dislocation in the polity, it will be blamed on the "selfish" Igbo who will want to reap where they did not sow, causing confusion and anarchy in the country. They are chastised and vilified.

Similarly, whenever there is religious misunderstanding between Mohammed Abubakar, a Muslim cleric, and James Adamu, a Christian minister of the gospel, who are all Northerners, over which of their respective religion is superior or more authentic, and thereby sowing seeds of hatred and discord among their followers, it will be the vulnerable Igbo residents in the area that will be descended upon. They will be physically attacked, killed or maimed, their houses and property destroyed or looted. This has been the lot of the Igbo all through the history of Nigeria – a people often despised, not wanted, and yet who will not be allowed to leave.

In 1932, there was a near breakdown of law and order in Jos Metropolis, primarily due to an attempt by the Hausa immigrants to drive away the Igbo living in the metropolis and take over their property. This was occasioned by the scarcity of various food items in the height of the Depression years prior to World War II, which was blamed on the Igbo.

Similarly, during the 1945 general strike, when life was unbearably difficult for many people in the country – no jobs, no food, – the Igbo were made to bear the brunt. The Igbo, who lived in a section of "Native Town" in Jos, called Sarkin Arabs Ward or "Igbo Quarter", were attacked by the Hausa, who accused them of causing the food shortages. For two days, the battle raged between these two ethnic groups. In the end, two people were confirmed dead and several others injured. It took a combined team of the army and police drafted from Kaduna to quell the crisis. The shock of the riot compelled the Igbo to move from "Native Town" to inside Jos Township (Nnoli, 1978:233)

In 1953, Chief Anthony Enahoro, a member of the Action Group, had moved a motion in the House of Representatives that Nigeria be granted independence in 1956, which was supported by both the

Action Group and the NCNC members in the House, but which the NPC members were reluctant to support. Members of the NPC were later booed, jeered, and called unprintable names on the streets of Lagos. Thereafter, a plan by the Action Group delegation led by Chief Samuel Akintola to hold a rally in Kano led to attacks, not on the Yoruba, Akintola's ethnic group, but on the Igbo living in the northern city, by irate northerners. For four days, from May 16, 1953, to May 19, 1953, the war raged, during which 36 people were confirmed dead – 15 Northerners and 21 Southerners, with 241 people wounded (Report on 1953 Kano Disturbances, 1953).

The attack on the Igbo was not just spontaneous or accident, but simply a premeditated and carefully planned action by the northern political establishment. This was because the then Secretary of the Kano Branch of the Northern People's Party (NPC) and later Minister of Works in the Federal Cabinet of Prime Minister Alhaji Abubakar Tafawa Balewa, Mallam Inua Wada, was reported to have convened a meeting of the Native Authority sectional heads at the Works Depot in Kano, where he treated them to a most provocative speech as follows:

> Having abused us in the South, these very Southerners have decided to come over to the North to abuse us, but we are determined to retaliate for the treatment given us in the South. We have therefore organised 1000 men ready in the city to meet force with force.

In spite of the fact that the planned Akintola rally in Kano had been banned and that Akintola himself never showed up in the town, on Saturday, May 16, 1953, the organised crowd of Northerners swooped in on a bloody massacre of innocent citizens. The irony of the whole incident was that the rioters switched their attack from the Yoruba, Akintola's ethnic group, whom they hardly touched, to the Igbo, whom they butchered with a "universally unexpected degree of violence".

A Commission of Inquiry later set up by the Northern Regional Government condemned the riots in these terms:

> No amount of provocation, short term or long term, can in any sense justify their behaviour", warning that the "seeds of the trouble that broke out in Kano on May 16, 1953, have their counterparts still in the ground. It could happen again, and only a realisation and

acceptance of the underlying causes can remove the danger of its occurrence.

In course of time, more prominent Northerners did not hesitate to openly voice out their grievances, resentment and hatred of the Igbo, and accordingly began to plot and to incite their people to rise against them, which resulted to the 1966 pogrom.

Vendetta Policies and the Politics of Exclusion

With the Biafran surrender on January 15, 1970, Yakubu Gowon, as head of the Nigerian federal government, declared the war "no victor, no vanquished" and granted "amnesty" to all those who fought on the side of Biafra. He further announced the introduction of what was generally referred to as the '3Rs' – Reconstruction, Rehabilitation and Reconciliation, which were aimed at reconstructing the war-ravaged infrastructure in Biafra, rehabilitating the displaced former Biafrans, and reconciling them with the rest of Nigerians. This was hailed as magnanimous and statesmanship by the international community.

But hardly had Yakubu Gowon finished with these pronouncements than the federal government began to renege on them and formulate policies specifically aimed to hurt the Igbo and bring them down on their knees. Chinua Achebe (2012: 234) observed that there were hawks in Gowon's cabinet who were bent on exacting maximum punishment on the Igbo and who would want to have the Biafran pound of flesh. According to him, "there were hardliners in the federal government of Nigeria who would cast the Igbo in the line of treasonable felons and wreckers of the nation."

These were the people who got the federal government to adopt a banking policy that nullified any bank account that had been operated during the war by Biafrans and approved a flat sum of twenty pounds for each Igbo depositor of Nigerian currency, regardless of the amount of the deposit. Through this policy, millions of former Biafrans, still smarting from the horrific effects of the three-year war, lost all their life-long savings. The measure was to handicap the Igbo economically and make it difficult for them to re-enter the mainstream of the Nigerian economy.

Furthermore, the federal government had banned the importation of stock fish and secondhand clothes, two products in which the Igbo were actively engaged, and which would have easily corroded their economy at that crucial period in their lives.

Also, sensing that the presence of federal troops in Igboland had led to demand for goods and services in the area and was therefore beginning to earn money for the Igbo, the federal government ordered a quick and massive withdrawal of troops from Igboland.

In the same vein, just two years after the end of the war, the federal government decided to auction out its business enterprises to private individuals under the 1974 Enterprises Promotion Decree, also known as the Indigenisation Decree, being well aware that the Igbo did not have the financial wherewithal to participate in the exercise. Apart from excluding them from the ownership of these companies, it also meant that the Igbo would lose many of the jobs and positions that they previously occupied in these establishments.

At the end of the war, Igboland was almost completely devastated, with many roads and bridges, hospitals, schools, industries, and private homes completely destroyed. Instead of the federal government declaring a Marshal Plan on rebuilding and developing war-ravaged Igboland, the Igbo were left to shoulder the burden all alone. It does not matter that the federal government had earlier proclaimed the so-called 3Rs – Reconstruction, Rehabilitation and Reconciliation, at the end of the hostilities, which later turned out to be only a pipe dream. It was only through self-help efforts that the Igbo were able to rebuild these damaged infrastructures.

At the same time, many Igbo who fled for their lives from other parts of the country during the 1966 disturbances, leaving their houses behind, had these properties declared "abandoned" at the end of the war and confiscated by some state governments.

The Igbo were equally denied two key industries that were originally slated to be located in the area. These were the iron and steel complex, and the petrochemical industries, which had been located in Ajaokuta and Lagos, respectively. Furthermore, there is the high incidence of infrastructural deficit in Igboland, owing primarily to the absence of federal presence in the region. Uchenna Anyanwu (1999) reports that "out of 91 national industries, only 16 were sited in the entire east".

In addition to the loss of their savings, the Igbo people also found themselves discriminated against by other ethnic groups as well as the federal government. In desperation, some Igbo sub-groups, particularly those on the fringes, started distancing themselves from the larger Igbo population by changing the names of both their people and their places to non-Igbo-sounding words. For instance, a town like Umuibekwe was changed to Rumuibekwe, while Igbuzo was changed to Ibusa, Igbonke to Igbo-akiri, etc. These people were encouraged and rewarded immensely by the federal government as a means of curbing a future Biafra.

As a result of discrimination, many Igbo had problems finding employment, and they became one of the poorest ethnic groups in Nigeria during the early 1970s, with thousands of them, especially the middle class, migrating en masse to various towns outside Igboland, and to many countries in Europe, the United States, and other African countries, in search of better means of livelihood.

In spite of the general amnesty proclaimed by Yakubu Gowon at the end of the war, only a negligible number of Igbo military and the police officers were reabsorbed into the Nigerian Armed Forces and the Nigerian Police Force, while a policy of stunting upward mobility for Igbo military officers and their early retirement to ensure that high-ranking Igbo military officers and the police do not stay there for a long time, was introduced. As claimed by Nsukka Analyst (1994), "out of 154 military officers of the rank of brigadier general and above, as at February 1989, only eight were Igbo".

More than six decades after the Nigeria-Biafra war, which was proclaimed "no victor, no vanquished", the Igbo are still being treated as second-class citizens and as conquered people. They are not considered fit to be entrusted with sensitive or key positions in government. They are excluded from top commands in the military and police.

To attest to the reality of this assertion, below is a table of illustration showing the distribution of high government positions occupied by the two other major ethnic groups in Nigeria – the Hausa and the Yoruba, during the successive military administrations in the country, vis-à-vis the Igbo.

Military Regime	Hausa/Fulani	Yoruba	Igbo
Gowon Regime (Supreme Military Council)	9	8	1
Murtala/Obasanjo (Supreme Military Council)	10	7	1
(Governors)	6	4	0
(Ministers)	6	7	2
Buhari Regime (Supreme Military Council)	9	2	1
Babangida Regime (Armed Forces Ruling Council)	11	8	1
(National Defense and Security Council)	5	5	0

Source: Nsukka Analyst, in *Nsukka Journal of the Humanities*, No. 10, June 1999

The Igbo are also regarded as unqualified to serve as President of Nigeria. Rather, they are always fit to play second fiddle. For instance, Dr. Alex Ekwueme was Vice President of Nigeria during the Second Republic. Under the National Party of Nigeria's zoning formula, Ekwueme would have gone for the presidency at the end of President Shehu Shagari's second term in office. But in order to prevent Ekwueme, an Igbo man, from going for the presidency, the Hausa/Fulani controlled military quickly staged a coup d'état and overthrew that civilian administration.

Again, it was through the courageous efforts of Dr. Alex Ekwueme, who led "G. 34", that the military was forced to vacate the political scene. But when it was time to contest for the Presidency in 1999, the highly politicised retired and serving Nigerian military officers sidelined Ekwueme and brought out Olusegun Obasanjo from prison, where he was serving a jail sentence for treason, and imposed him on the People's Democratic Party (PDP), to contest and win the Presidential election.

The Creation of states and local government areas had been skewed against the Igbo, so much so that the Igbo or the South East is the only zone with five states; while other zones have six or seven states. Out of 774 local government areas in Nigeria, the Igbo, with more than one-third of the country's population, have only 95 local government areas, while the North West zone has 186 local government areas; The South West, 137 LGAs; the South South, 123 LGAs; the North Central, 121 LGAs; and the North East, 112 LGAs. The three states of Kano, Kaduna, and Katsina have a total of 101 LGAs, six more local government areas than the entire South East Zone.

The implications of this capricious and arbitrary creation of states and local government areas are obvious. With more states and more local government areas, more federal revenues and resources are channeled to the areas. The same goes for appointments in the federal public service, such as permanent secretaries, ministers, ambassadors, membership of boards and parastatals, and heads of extraministerial departments and agencies.

Is it not an irony of fate that by 1983, the old Anambra State with 23 LGAs had more local government areas than the old Kano State, which then had 20 LGAs, but with the capricious creation of local governments by the military between 1985 and 1999, the table turned against the old Anambra State with a total of 47 local government areas as against old the Kano State with a total of 71 local government areas? The same applies to the old Imo State, which had 21 local government areas in 1983, as against the old Kaduna State, which had just 14 local government areas. Today, the old Kaduna State has 57 local government areas, while the old Imo State has 49 LGAs.

One of the contradictions of the Nigerian political arrangement is that Nigeria is perhaps the only country in the world where its population increases as you advance towards the arid zone, but decreases as you move towards the coastal area. At least, that was what our demographers had led us to believe. That is why they now tell us that there are more people living in the North than in the South, which accounts for why there are more states and more local government areas in the North; more electoral constituencies in the North; more ministers from the North; more legislators in the National Assembly from the North, etc.

The present security challenges across the country stem from the perceived injustice and animosity borne against the Nigerian nation by certain groups and individuals who feel that they are being shortchanged by the system. As a result, when some disgruntled Igbo youths banded together under the banner of IPOB (Indigenous Peoples of Biafra) or MASSOB (Movement for the Actualisation of the Sovereign State of Biafra) and began to vent their rage on the system, some people dismissed them as insane. But they are not. Rather, they are protesting against a system that fails to accord them equal dignity and respect: where a former majority tribe was overnight turned into a minority through a dubious structural political arrangement that deprives them of their fair share of the country's common wealth. Since these youths have found the Nigerian environment harsh and suffocating, they have no option but to ask for the dissolution of the so-called marriage that was contracted on their behalf some one hundred years ago, and they begin to look back with nostalgia on their lost el dorado, the Biafran Republic!

The Underdevelopment of Igboland

What would have helped the economic development of war-ravaged Igboland at the end of Nigeria-Biafra war in 1970 would have been if the Federal Government was faithful to the implementation of the 3Rs - Rehabilitation, Reconciliation and Reconstruction, enunciated by Yakubu Gowon. Before the outbreak of the civil war, the Eastern Regional Government under the Premiership of Dr. Michael Okpara (1959-1966), had maintained an economic growth rate of 12.5 percent per annum, which was the fastest in the entire country. But the war had damaged everything – roads and bridges, electricity, school buildings, health institutions, water facilities, etc., in addition to all the government and privately owned industrial establishments, business ventures, and farm settlements. In other words, it would be starting all over again if any progress could be made.

The expectation was that if the Nigerian Federal Government would be faithful to the 3Rs' implementation and helped the East Central State administration rebuild their damaged infrastructures and also build up the manpower needs of industrial establishments in the area, Igboland would be eyeing Dr. Okpara's 1966 feat of 12.5 per cent annual growth rate from 1966. But that did not happen. Rather, the Federal Government left the people of East Central State to shoulder the burden of rebuilding these infrastructures alone, never mind that every Igbo man who survived the war and who made deposits in banks was given twenty pounds (£20), no matter the amount of money one had deposited in such banks before the outbreak of the war.

Thus, as a result of the unfriendly business environment in Igboland arising from the failure of the Federal Government to assist in the reconstruction of the war-damaged infrastructures and industrial establishments in the area, a good number of Igbo people, since there was nothing tangible for them to do in Igboland to make ends meet, decided to take their £20 and jumped into the next available vehicle to take them to other parts of the country to begin to manage their lives there. With the traditional Igbo industry, hard work, and determination, many of these Igbo people began to make successes of their efforts, and it was not long before their £20 began to multiply into larger dividends, with which they began to set up gigantic businesses at their various places of abode.

During the ill-fated Biafra Republic, for less than three years, the people were making their own rockets and calculating their distances. They were distilling their own oil and making aviation fuel, creating chemical and biological laboratories, discovering new cures for diseases like cholera, shaping their own spare parts, and doing all sorts of technological innovations. At the end of the war, the Administrator of the former East Central State, Ukpabi Asika, decided to bring these Biafran scientists and engineers together and set up the Project Development Institute (PRODA), headed by Professor Godwin Ezekwe, to absorb them. The initiative led to the design of industrial machinery models and prototypes for the East Central State Industrial Masterplan. But with the coming of the Murtala/Obasanjo military regime in 1975, the federal government took over PRODA by decree, starved it of funds, and basically destroyed its aims.

Either through externally induced egotism or selfish interests, the governments of states of the former Eastern Region or the various Igbo states will not work together to chart a common economic development agenda, and have allowed their joint venture investments to go moribund.

At the end of the Nigeria-Biafra war in 1970, and following the creation of states in 1967, the Head of State, General Yakubu Gowon, by decree, set up the Eastern States Interim Assets and Liability Agency (ESIALA) to manage the assests and liabilities of states created out of the old Eastern Region. At present, there are nine states: Abia, Ebonyi, Akwa Ibom, Bayelsa, Cross River, Imo, Anambra, and Enugu.

Before the Eastern Region was split into various states, it was very rich in terms of mineral resources and industries. Among the various industries established by the government were the Nigerian Cement Factory (NIGERCEM), Nkalagu; the African Continental Bank; the Eastern Marketing Board; the Eastern Nigeria Development Corporation; the West African Institute for Oil Palm Research; the Nigerian Breweries Stout Factory at Aba; the Tobacco and Glass Making Plant at Port Harcourt; farm settlements at Ohaji, Igbariam, Boki, Ulonna, Erei, Uzo-Uwani, and Egbema; the Nigerian Coal

Corporation in Enugu; as well as rice farms at Abakaliki and Ogoja; and many other projects.

Under Decree 39, which Gowon signed on June 24, 1970, the University of Nigeria, Nsukka, which was founded by Dr. Nnamdi Azikiwe and opened on October 7, 1960, was listed as one of the assets of the Eastern Interim Assets and Liability Agency.

The Premiers of the old Eastern Region, Nnamdi Azikiwe and Michael Okpara, and their political party, the NCNC, had laboured hard to establish these properties and institutions. Unfortunately, since the creation of states, which started in 1967, the various state administrations had not been able to keep these institutions afloat or come together to discuss their economic development. This was unlike what is obtained in both the former Northern and Western Regions, which set up a common investment agency that binds them together, like the Arewa Holdings in the North and Oodua Properties in the West.

Aside from these, the absence of an investment-friendly environment in many parts of Igboland due to the lack of basic infrastructure like good roads, energy, and access to seaport, has forced many investors to leave Igboland and seek green pastures elsewhere.

The Igbo and their Quest to Rule Nigeria

Nigeria began her political tutelage of Western democracy with the promulgation of the Clifford Constitution in 1923. The constitution provided for four elected members and fifteen nominated members in the Legislative Council, which legislated for only the Southern Provinces, while the North, which was ruled by proclamations by the Governor, was excluded. Out of these four elective seats, three were for Lagos, while the remaining one was for Calabar. In the election to fill the seats, the Nigerian National Democratic Party (NNDP) led by Herbert Macaulay won all three Lagos seats, while the Calabar National League won the one seat reserved for Calabar.

The leading members of the NNDP at that time, apart from Macaulay, included Adeniyi Jones, Eric Moore, Egerton Shyngle, Wynter Shackleford, Thomas Horatio Jackson, J.T. White, Adeyemo Alakija, and Karimu Kotun. For fifteen years, the NNDP had dominated Lagos politics until the birth of the Lagos Youth Movement (LYM) in 1934, later changed to the Nigerian Youth Movement

(NYM) in 1937, with J.C. Vaughan, Eyo Ita, Ernest Ikoli, Samuel Akinsanya, and H.O.Davis, as its leaders.

Emergence of Dr. Nnamdi Azikiwe

Dr. Benjamin Nnamdi Azikiwe was perhaps, one of the greatest Igbo that ever lived. For a very long time, he had dominated the Nigerian political scene. In 1937, Azikiwe returned to Nigeria from Ghana where he managed a successful newspaper outfit, the African Morning Post (1935-36), and immediately joined the NYM. He also established the West African Pilot newspaper which had become the darling of Nigerian nationalist agitators because of its incisive reportage and hard-hitting articles against colonialism. Soon, the West African Pilot began to compete with the Daily Service, which was then edited by Ernest Ikoli with H.O. Davis as manager.

In the 1938 elections, the NYM, for the first time, defeated the NNDP and won all the seats in the Legislative Council as well as three out of the four seats in the Lagos Town Council. In 1941, disagreements among the leaders of the NYM over the selection of candidates that would fly its flag for the forthcoming election led to the resignation of Dr. Nnamdi Azikiwe from the party. He later joined the NNDP along with many eastern members of the NYM. This exacerbated the media war between the West African Pilot and the Daily Service, now edited by Chief S.L. Akintola, a Yoruba, thus precipitating a cold war between the Igbo and the Yoruba.

In November 1943, a youth rally organised under the auspices of the National Union of Nigerian Students (NUNS), later metamorphosed into the National Council of Nigeria and the Cameroons (NCNC) on August 26, 1944, with Herbert Macaulay emerging as its president and Nnamdi Azikiwe appointed the general secretary. The NCNC, which was the first national political party in Nigeria, campaigned vigorously against the proposed Richards Constitution. Members of the party later decided to to tour the country to educate the public about the dangers inherent in the proposed Constitution and to raise funds to enable it to send a delegation to London to protest against it. It was while the party members were on tour that Macaulay fell sick in Kano and later died in Lagos on May 7, 1945. Azikiwe then took over as president.

On February 16, 1946, the Zikist Movement, with radical and idealist young men comprising Raji Abdullah, Kola Balogun, M.C.K. Ajuluchukwu, Nduka Eze, and Abiodun Aloba, as leading members, was formed as part of the NCNC. It had Kolawole Balogun as its first president, and M.C.K. Ajuluchukwu as its secretary general. While pledging positive action to defend Dr. Nnamdi Azikiwe against attacks by opponents, the Zikist Movement sought to galvanise Nigerian youths to rise in opposition against the Richards Constitution in particular and colonialism in general. The Zikist Movement drew its inspiration from the published work of Dr. Azikiwe's Renascent Africa, written in 1937, and from Dr. Nwafor Oziru's Without Bitterness.

The rising nationalist agitations, with both the NCNC and the Zikist Movement at the vanguard, soon began to give the colonialists sleepless nights, and they began to look for ways to disorganize the nationalists and break their rank and file. Accordingly, in 1947, while the NCNC delegation comprising Dr. Azikiwe, Dr. Olorun-Nimbe, Adeleke Adedoyin, Nyong Essien, P.M. Kale, Abubakar Dipcharima, and Mrs. Funmilayo Ramsone-Kuti were in London to protest against the Richards Constitution, the colonialists instigated quarrels among them, which later developed into a major crisis that led to the split of the party.

At the NCNC convention held in Kaduna in April 1948, Dr. Azikiwe mustered the support of party members to expel Olorun-Nimbe, Adeleke Adedoyin, and Magnus Williams from the party for precipitating in the London quarrels. Following their expulsion, they joined the NYM. Thereafter, a Yoruba movement, Egbe Omo Oduduwa (children of Oduduwa), was launched in London with Sir Adeyemo Alakija as President and Obafemi Awolowo as General Secretary.

The NCNC and the NYM had always used the press as platform for waging their war, but on September 3, 1947, this nearly blossomed into what would have been a full-scale war, when the Igbo and Yoruba residents of Lagos planned a public demonstration to show each other's case and strength. A club joke by Mr. C.D. Onyeama that "the Ibo domination of Nigeria is a matter of time" was seized upon by the NYM-supported Daily Service to stir up war between the two ethnic groups resident in Lagos. Mokwugo Okoye (1981:117) explains it this way,

...for some years, the Yoruba had been dominant in business, the professions, and the civil service, following in the wake of the Brazilians, West Indians, and Sierra Leoneans, but now the Ibos were pushing forcefully ahead in all walks of life. This objective situation was exploited by rival politicians on both sides to precipitate a tribal vendetta that has for many years plagued Nigerian politics.

However, before the war could openly explode, the government promptly intervened and banned all public meetings for that day.

To divert public attention from the simmering tribal politics and focus on the real problem facing the nation, which was colonialism, the Zikist Movement, on October 27, 1948, came out with a public lecture entitled "A Call for Revolution", with Osita Agwuna as principal speaker and Anthony Enahoro as Chairman. The colonial authorities were not pleased with that lecture and proceeded to file sedition charges against some of the group's members. A meeting was later convened at the Glover Memorial Hall, Lagos, on November 7 to acquaint the NCNC members with the issue and enable them to take an informed position. Dr. Azikiwe, who would have chaired the meeting, excused himself after travelling to Ijebu Ode on another mission, so Oged Macaulay, who presided over the meeting, was later to share in the punishment that was lined up for the Zikists.

In February 1949, some members of the Zikist Movement who participated in that public lecture were tried and convicted on various terms of imprisonment and fines, while Osita Agwuna, the principal speaker, was to serve three years in prison. Raji Abdallah was jailed for two years, Oged Macaulay, one year, and Anthony Enahoro, six months. Both Ralph Aniedobe and Ogoegbunam Dafe were fined £25 each, or serve in prison for three months. Even the editor of the African Echo newspaper, which carried an editorial supporting the Zikists' action, Smart Ebbi, did not escape the colonialists' hammer. He was jailed for one year.

As a result of increasing Zikists' activities across the country, on February 8, 1950, the colonial government swooped on their offices nationwide, searched them, and arrested some of the movement's principal officers. In the excitement that followed these arrests, a young employee of the Post and Telegraph Department, Heelas Ugokwe, pulled a jackknife and aimed to stab the Government Chief

Secretary, Mr. H.M. Foot, but was promptly arrested, charged to court and subsequently sentenced to twelve years' imprisonment. He was released after serving six years in prison, only to die of tuberculosis two years later.

On April 12, 1950, the government promulgated an Order-in-Council banning the Zikist Movement. According to the government's statement: "conclusive evidence has been obtained from many parts of the country that the Zikist Movement is an organisation that aims to stir up hatred and malice and to pursue seditious aims by lawlessness and violence. The movement has a membership of only a few hundreds, and its teachings are condemned by the overwhelming majority of the people of Nigeria, who wish to maintain law and order and pursue economic and political progress without resorting to violence. Although the movement is small and unrepresentative, its purposes and methods are dangerous to the good of the government of Nigeria, and it is essential to make it quite clear that such purposes and methods will not be tolerated" (Okoye, ibid 147).

Azikiwe described the Zikists as "fissiparous lieutenants and cantankerous followers" According to him, the Zikist Movement was "just one out of the two hundred member-unions of the NCNC", and added that the group had acted without his authority and "retarded national progress." (Okoye, 1979:19)

Many people saw Azikiwe's action as stabbing the Zikists in the back, a great betrayal. Nnamdi Azikiwe had, by that action, missed the opportunity of immortalising his name and climbing the political ladder. He chose to squander the opportunity offered by the Zikists and fell to the colonialists' trap. With his chain of newspapers firing on all cylinders and the Zikist Movement giving him cover fire, he was indeed a thorn in the flesh of the colonialists. But the colonialists duped him into believing that if he softened his anti-colonial stance and distanced himself from the radical groups fighting for the immediate abolition of colonialism, he would be handed over Nigeria "on a platter of gold" That was a scam, and he fell for it.

It was also a lost opportunity for the Igbo to have produced a Nigerian president. Members of the Zikist Movement were neither interested in tribe nor religion. They believed themselves to be Nigerians, irrespective of where one came from or the religion one professed, and they saw Azikiwe as their ideal.

Having succeeded in getting Azikiwe to tone down his anti-colonial stance and acquiesce to the disbandment of the Zikist Movement, the colonialists proceeded to sponsor the emergence of political parties based on tribal or ethnic leanings. In the West, Egbe Omo Oduduwa was transformed into a political party, called the Action Group (AG), while the North floated the Northern People's Congress (NPC). These political parties and a dozen others based on ethnic leanings were to compete against the NCNC, which had now been presented as the political party for the East, or the Igbo, in particular.

Not done, the colonialists went further to sow seeds of discord between Azikiwe's ethnic group, the Igbo, and other ethnic groups in the country, where the Igbo were said to be ambitious and domineering. Thus, Azikiwe had lost on all fronts. He lost his main support base, the Zikist Movement, and he lost his Pan-Nigerian stature, becoming identified as a tribal leader. The much he later got in post-colonial Nigeria was Governor General, or President without power.

In the election conducted in 1952 under the Macpherson Constitution, the NCNC won in both the Eastern and Western Houses of Assembly. But in the West, on inauguration day, when Azikiwe would have assumed office as the Leader of Government Business, some elected members of the NCNC crossed over to the Action Group, thereby, leaving Azikiwe and his party in the minority. In frustration, Azikiwe scurried back to the East, "from whence I come", ejected Eyo Ita, his deputy, who then was the leader of Government Business, and took over the position. That was the genesis of the sour relationship between the Igbo and their southern minority brothers, and the minorities never forgave the Igbo.

The 1959 Pre-Independence Election

In preparation for Nigeria's independence in 1960, parliamentary elections were held throughout Nigeria on December 12, 1959. The result was a hung parliament with no clear majority to form a government. The National Council of Nigeria and Cameroons (NCNC), led by Dr. Nnamdi Azikiwe came first with a total of 2,594,557 votes, but got only 81 seats in the parliament; the Action Group (AG), led by Chief Obafemi Awolowo, came second with 1,992,364 votes, but got 73 seats; while the Northern Peoples Congress

(NPC), led by Sir Ahmadu Bello, Sarduana of Sokoto, came third with 1,922,179 votes, and got 134 seats out of the 312 seats in the House of Representatives, despite getting less public votes. As a result, none of the three major political parties mentioned above received enough seats in parliament to form a government. An alliance had to be formed to determine who would rule the country.

Curiously enough, while the two major political parties in the South, the NCNC and the AG combined, garnered more than four million votes but only got 154 seats in the parliament, the NPC in the North, with less than two million votes, secured 134 seats. The implication is that the North might have been allocated more parliamentary seats than the South, put together.

This was confirmed by a former British colonial civil servant, Mr. Harold Smith, who worked in Lagos and who had participated in the 1959 federal election. He disclosed that the British authorities had allocated more parliamentary seats to the North because of their false claim that over fifty per cent of the country's population lived in the region.

In an overview of the research work carried out by K.W.J. Post, titled: "The Nigerian Federal Election of 1959", and published in the London Guardian Newspaper of February 9, 1992, Harold Smith wrote:

> The British backed up the Northerners' demand for 50% of the federal parliamentary seats by stating in the 1950s' that the North did indeed have over 50% of Nigeria's population. At that time, I was in charge of statistics at the Department of Labour's Headquarters in Lagos, and I did not believe a word of it.

Commenting on the outcome of the election, which gave the North 89.2% voter turnout, the East 74%, and the West 71%, Harold Smith wondered why "the politically inexperienced North and apathetic peasants in remote rural areas with few, if any attribute of civilisation – tarred roads, clean water, schools or medical provision, would produce a percentage poll of 89.2%", while the East and the West, "with higher literacy and political awareness" scored the lower figures of 74% and 71%, respectively.

Nevertheless, had Azikiwe's NCNC and Awolowo's Action Group (which won 81 seats and 73 seats respectively, and thus came first and second), come together to form an alliance, they would have comfortably formed the government. It was even alleged that Awolowo had volunteered to be the Deputy Prime Minister or Finance Minister in a coalition government, while Azikiwe would become the Prime Minister. This was because the NCNC had more public votes and more seats than the Action Group.

At the same time, it was also alleged that while Dr. Azikiwe, the NCNC leader, had invited Awolowo's AG team to Asaba, the gateway between the Western and Eastern Regions, for talks on a possible coalition government, he also sent another team up north to hold talks with the NPC leader, Sir Ahmadu Bello, on the same issue. At the end of the NCNC/NPC talks, Alhaji Tafawa Balewa, emerged as the Prime Minister of Nigeria, while Azikiwe became a figure-head Governor General.

Many people were surprised and shocked that Azikiwe would accept this non-functional Head of State arrangement considering his towering personality and the contributions he made towards Nigerian independence.

However, this was defended by Azikiwe's concern for Nigeria's unity, rather than a narrow personal interest or what would benefit the Igbo in particular. If he had accepted the NCNC/Action Group alliance and the two southern political parties formed the federal government, the North would have been isolated, which would ultimately lead to the breakup of the country. But he decided to forgo the lure of becoming Prime Minister in the interest of Ngerian unity. How right he was is for history to judge.

The Second Republic

During the politics of the Second Republic (1979-1983), the Igbo were divided over what to do. While one group had favoured the Igbo, just coming out of the war, teaming up with other Nigerians to form a national political party, the other group preferred that the Igbo form their own political party, and then seek the support of other Nigerians. Thus, while the mainstream Igbo, or "timber and calibre", belonged to the National Party of Nigeria (NPN), which had offered the Igbo its Vice-Presidential ticket in the person of Dr. Alex Ekwueme, the mass of the Igbo joined Dr. Nnamdi Azikiwe and formed the Nigerian Peoples Party (NPP). The NPP then nominated Dr. Azikiwe as its presidential candidate.

At the end of the 1979 presidential election, the NPN clinched the position, while Dr. Azikiwe and his NPP came in a distant third. The most the NPP got were three state governorship positions in Anambra, Imo, and Plateau, in the middlebelt. However, the NPP went into alliance with the NPN and formed the Federal Government. In 1984, the NPN repeated the same feat by winning the presidential election, and this time around, the strength of the NPP was reduced to two states – Imo and Plateau states.

The Fourth Republic

The other period in which the Igbo would have made it was in 1999, at the onset of the present political dispensation. Dr. Alex Ekwueme, former vice president during the Second Republic under the defunct National Party of Nigeria (NPN), was a towering political figure. To his credit is the current division of the country into six geopolitical zones, which he negotiated during the 1995 Constitutional Conference.

Ekwueme had led a group of other Nigerians, known as the "G-20", to challenge the continued occupation of the political space by the General Sani Abacha military dictatorship. When the military finally exited the political scene, the "G-20" was transformed into a political party known as the People's Democratic Party (PDP). Ekwueme thus became the acknowledged leader of the political party and would have naturally won the presidential ticket of the PDP but for the subterfuges and intrigues of both the serving and retired military officers who brought out one of their own, General Olusegun Obasanjo, from prison and imposed him on the party and subsequently on Nigerians.

At the same time, in the rival All Peoples Party (APP), Dr. Ogbonnaya Onu, another Igbo, emerged as the party's presidential candidate. But the same forces that destroyed Ekwueme lured him into agreeing that the APP go into alliance with the Alliance for Democracy (AD), which already had Chief Olu Falae as its presidential candidate. In the process of harmonisation between the two political parties to choose one single presidential candidate that would slug it out with the PDP in the election, Ogbonnaya Onu was made to step down for Olu Falae, who then picked the APP/AD Presidential ticket.

The resultant outcome was that there were two Yoruba presidential candidates, in the persons of Olusegun Obasanjo and Olu Falae, for the PDP and the APP/AD, respectively. At the end of the presidential election in May 1999, Obasanjo won the presidency.

Alex Ekwueme attempted to challenge President Olusegun Obasanjo for the PDP presidential ticket again in 2003, but was unsuccessful. In 2007, Chief Chukwuemeka Odumegwu Ojukwu also contested for the presidency on the platform of the All Progressives Grand Alliance (APGA), but he came in a distant third.

An interesting development in the 2023 presidential election is the surprise emergence of former Anambra State Goverenor, Mr. Peter Obi, as a top contender in the Presidential race. Obi was running mate to Alhaji Atiku Abubakar of the Peoples Democratic Party (PDP) in the 2019 Presidential election, but the PDP did not win the election. At the onset of the 2023 exercise, Peter Obi indicated interest to contest for the Presidency under the PDP, but he was not allowed a foothold in the party. In annoyance, he left the PDP and joined the Labour Party, where he picked its Presidential ticket.

At first, many people did not take him seriously, and they mocked him that he was on a wild goose chase since he had "no political structure". But Obi was not worried. He had a message of hope for Nigerians. With sound analysis of the country's economic and political problems, and their possible solutions, he became the toast of many Nigerians, irrespective of creed or ethnic background. Like whirlwind, the Obi phenomenon began to blow across the length and breadth of the country. Peter Obi did not make himself an Igbo Presidential candidate. Rather, he presented himself as candidate of the youths and the marginalised Nigerians.

References

Achebe, C, (2012) *There Was a Country* (London, Penguin Books)

Achebe, C. (1983) *The Trouble With Nigeria* (Enugu, Fourth Dimension)

Anyanwu, U. (1999) 'The Igbo-Yoruba Relations and Problems' in Njoku, ON (ed.) *Nsukka Journal of the Humanities*, No. 10, June 1999.

Chinweizu (2005) 'The Reconstruction of Nigeria: Four Delusions on Our Strategic Horizon', *The Guardian* newspapers, June 24

Coleman, J.S. (1958) *Nigeria: Background to Nationalism*, (Berkeley and Los Angeles, University of California Press)

Dudley, BJ (1966), *Instability and Political Order: Politics and Crisis In Nigeria* (Ibadan: University

LeVine, R. (1971) 'Dreams and Deeds: Achievement Motivation in Nigeria' in Melson and Wolpe, (eds.) *Nigeria: Modernization and the Politics of Communalism* (Michigan State University Press, Quoted in H.N. Nwosu, (1977) *Political Authority & the Nigerian Civil Service* (Enugu: Fourth Dimension Publishers. p. 182)

Nnoli, Okwudiba (1978*) Ethnic Politics In Nigeria* (Enugu: Fourth Dimension Publishing Ltd.)

Nsukka Analyst (1994) 'Marginalization in the Nigerian Polity: A Diagnosis of the Igbo Problem and the National Question', *Nsukka Analyst*, Vol .I, No. I, December.

Okonjo, I.M. (1974) *British Administration in Nigeria 1900-1950* (New York: Nok Publishers) pp. 87-89

Okoye, Mokwugo (1979) *A Letter to Dr. Nnamdi Azikiwe: A Dissent Remembered* (Enugu: Fourth Dimension Publishing) p.19.

Okoye, Mokwugo (1981) *Storms on the Niger* (Enugu: Fourth Dimension Publishing) p. 29

Onwumechili, CA (2000) *Igbo Enwe Eze: The Igbo Have No Kings* (Owerri, Ahiajioku Lectures)

Schwarz, FAO, (1965) *The Tribe, the Nation or the Race, The Politics of Independence*, (Cambridge: MIT Press)

Smith, Harold (1992) 'The Politics of Ignorance: Nigeria and the Cross Street Hacks' *The Guardian*, March 12).

Kaduna State Government (1953), *The Northern Region of Nigeria, Report on the Kano Disturbances, 16, 17, 18, and 19 May'*, (Kaduna: Government Printer)

CHAPTER EIGHT

Quest for a United Igbo Front

Introduction

Ethnic unions, communal associations, etc., like ethnicity itself, were products of colonial order in the context of the urban setting. Colonialism had forced many people to migrate from the rural areas to the urban centres in search of opportunities for participation in the cash economy introduced by the colonial administration, either as paid employees in the civil service or in commercial establishments, or as self-employed artisans, like businessmen, traders, contractors, carpenters, masons, etc. There was also a concentration of modern social facilities and amenities in urban areas, such as electricity, pipe borne water, schools, health centres, good roads, modern markets, and modern recreational faciliates and relaxation spots, which equally attracted migrants from the rural areas.

As a result of the uncertainty and insecurity in this strange environment, the migrants began to bind themselves into unions or associations, not only as a strategy for collective engagement in the provision of social services in these urban centres but also for the protection of their individual interests and welfare. In addition, the unions served as frames of reference for newcomers from the same ethnic group, community, or village, to the urban centres and equally contributed to the education, economic, social, and physical development of their home areas or communities.

During the colonial era, several of these unions or associations metamorphosed and were scattered in many big cities across Nigeria. For the Igbo nation in particular, prominent among these groups, up to the period prior to the military takeover of government in January 1966, was the **Igbo State Union,** which served as an umbrella organisation for all the other Igbo associations in the country.

The Igbo State Union

What came to be known as the Igbo State Union (ISU) had its history in the early 1930s, when some Igbo people who were living in Lagos came together to form an association, which they called the "Igbo Union."

At the dawn of colonial administration in Nigeria, the Igbo occupied a very lowly position in the scheme of things. E.N. Ota (1999:56) reports that

> ...the Igbo people who went to Lagos to seek means of livelihood were mostly "employed as labourers, houseboys, cooks and stewards to Europeans, Indians, Brazilians, and Yoruba. They were looked down upon as people from the backwaters and were derisively called Kobo kobo aje ayo, by the Yoruba", (the equivalent of cannibals).
> They were taunted in very degrading manners and the ego of the average Igbo was greatly deflated by such humiliating remarks and references. As a result, some Igbo people began to dissociate or even refused to be identified as Igbo, while some began to change their names to camouflage their Igbo identity.

In due course, however, some few educated Igbo migrants in Lagos began to kick against such degrading and humiliating remarks as well as the menial and lowly jobs being assigned to their people due mainly to their low level of education. Therefore, they decided to come together to form an association called the Igbo Union, which was aimed at promoting their cultural identity, advancing the social, cultural, economic, and educational improvement of their members and their respective communities.

Already, the idea of forming ethnic-based socio-cultural and political organisations was gaining ground in Nigeria. The Ibibio State Union was the first of such ethnic-based organizations, formed in the early 1930s. Such developments stemmed from the increasing realisation that the most decisive forces in the power struggle in a multi-ethnic society like Nigeria were the ethnic groups, and not individuals. As such, there must be some organisational instruments to defend and promote the interest of each ethnic group.

However, before this period, there were several pan-Igbo unions and organisations around the world, formed primarily by some ex-slaves, such as the Igbo Union in Bathurst, The Gambia, which was founded in 1842 by a prominent Igbo trader and ex-slave, Thomas Refell; the Igbo Union, Freetown, Sierra Leone, founded in 1860 by the Igbo Community in that town, and which had a renowned Igbo anti-colonialist leader, Africanus Horton, a surgeon, scientist and soldier, as one of the active members.

One of the greatest achievements of these Pan-Igbo organisations was the promotion of Igbo identity, which initially flowed from the fact that they shared a common language, a common culture, and shared values, all of which eventually led to the search for the common ancestral origins of the Igbo as well as discovering the link between the Igbo and other ethnic groups in Africa in general and Nigeria in particular.

Proceeding from this noble objective, the Igbo Union, Lagos, was formally inaugurated in 1934, following a reception organised for the first Igbo university graduates, namely Dr. Nnamdi Azikiwe, Dr. Simeon Onwu, and Dr. Francis Akanu Ibiam. The union brought together several towns, clans, and divisional organisations in Lagos. Among the principal officers of this union were:

Mr. Dennis Osadebay	President
Mr. H.U. Kaine	Vice President
Mr. Henry Kanu Offonry	General Secretary
Mr. B.O.N. Eluwa	Assistant Secretary

The Igbo Union began to garner momentum following the establishment of the West African Pilot by Dr. Nnamdi Azikwe, which gave the union enormous publicity and support. By 1943, it changed its name to the Igbo Federal Union and began to expand to all the regions, with strong branches in many towns across the country. The union united the Igbo and instilled in them the consciousness of being Igbo, teaching them to always consider the development and progress of their homeland and also contributing to the good of their host communities.

The Igbo Federal Union had basically the same officers as the Igbo Union and had as its specific objectives the building and running of thirty schools all over Igboland and establishing an Igbo national bank. The Igbo Federal Union was a loose form of association that brought together a multitude of voluntary mutual aid groups formed to foster civic welfare in the home communities of Igboland and the Igbo settler communities in the urban centres.

However, the weakness of the Igbo Federal Union was due mainly to the fact that it was merely an association of town, clan, and divisional unions in cities. Its influence was therefore limited, as it was unable to mobilise people in towns, clans, or divisions in Igboland.

In December 1948, a pan-Igbo conference was held in Port Harcourt, which was attended by several Igbo unions in various cities in Nigeria, including representations of home-based unions in Igboland. The aim of the conference was "to organise the Igbo linguistic group into a political unit". The conference led to the formation of a new association called the Igbo State Union.

Membership in this union was opened to all towns and clans in Igboland as well as those in various non-Igbo cities throughout Nigeria. The founders of the union had anticipated that Nigeria would be reorganised into states based on cultural and linguistic affinity, and that the Igbo State would be a member of the Commonwealth of Nigeria (Aguomba, 2005).

The Port Harcourt conference also saw the need to galvanise all segments of Igbo society to "counter the virulent and ethnically chauvinistic Yoruba anti-Igbo reports and impressions that portrayed the Igbo as aggressive and rambunctious". It was also claimed that "it was against the climate of Yoruba-Igbo hostility" that the Port Harcourt conference was held. "Igbo leaders at the conference were quite familiar with the poignant injustice of subordination that colonial rule was meting out to the Igbo ethnic group vis-à-vis the Efik and the Yoruba. They also realised that nothing could serve as enough psychological compensation except the coming together of various segments making up the Igbo nation" (Ota, op cit 1999).

At the conference, the following officers were elected to pilot the affairs of the union:

Dr. Nnamdi Azikiwe	President
Barrister A.C. Nwapa	Deputy President
Mr. Raymond Amanze Njoku	First Vice President
Mr. Mike O. Ajegbo	Second Vice President
Mr. H. U. Kaine	Third Vice President
Barrister Jaja Wachukwu	Principal Secretary
Mr. B.O.N. Eluwa	Permanent Under Secretary
Mr. M.I. Onwuka	Treasurer

Dr. Nwafor Orizu	Political Adviser
Chief Mbonu Ojike	Economic Adviser
Dr. Akanu Ibiam	Medical Adviser
Dr. K.O. Mbadiwe	Cultural Adviser
Mr. E.I. Oli	Educational Adviser

However, Dr. Azikiwe did not stay long as President of the Igbo State Union as he later resigned the position due principally to a conflict between his towering statures as a Nigerian leader and his leadership of an ethnic or tribal organisation. He was succeeded by Chief Z. C. Obi, who remained in that position till the military takeover of the government in January 1966.

The constitution of the Igbo State Union, as amended and later adopted in Aba in 1951 and 1953 respectively, had outlined its main objectives as follows:

- To devise ways and means whereby all the sons and daughters of Igboland at home and abroad, shall be brought together under one union.
- To promote cultural understanding among the various groups in Igboland at home and abroad.
- To bring within the influence of the union, all Igbo men and women organizations at home and abroad.
- To encourage the educational progress of the Igbo at home and abroad.

The constitution extended membership of the union to all Igbo communal associations at home and abroad, town unions, clans, or district unions on payment of some specified amounts in registration fees.

As an agent of cultural revival, one of the responsibilities that the Igbo State Union assigned to itself was the encouragement and promotion of Igbo ethnic identity and solidarity. This was to be realised through the observation and celebration of "Igbo Day". Beginning in 1954, Igbo Day was designated as a public holiday for the Igbo people on the first Saturday of October. Each town or village union would present its traditional dances and served local dishes to celebrants and visitors from other ethnic groups. S.N. Nwabara (1977:228) claims that the Igbo Day had sought to "immortalise the role of the Ibo in the crusade for a new order, so that the present and future generations could refer to the Ibo people with pride".

The Igbo Day was equally an occasion to celebrate brotherhood and oneness of the Igbo, as the people were reminded of the need to always appreciate and tolerate one another for the overall interest and development of Igboland. Apart from affording the Igbo the opportunity to reflect on Igbo cultural heritage, the Igbo Day also "helped in reducing the psychological pressures of urban living".

Conscious of the importance of Western education as a passport for winning gainful employment and for participation in the colonial economic system, the Igbo State Union also encouraged its affiliate unions and other Igbo communal associations to build primary and secondary schools in their various localities for the education of their sons and daughters and awarded scholarships to some of its principal officers to study abroad. The result was that before the attainment of independence by Nigeria in 1960, according to Okwudiba Nnoli (1980), "the Igbo, who in the 1920s had no single university graduate (except, perhaps, James Africanus Horton, a Sierra Leonean medical doctor of Igbo parentage), had as many university students as the more advanced Yoruba".

Similarly, the Igbo State Union, through its intervention and encouragement, ensured that the Igbo were able to maintain their traditional values and lifestyles while at the same time adapting to and incorporating the new values introduced by the British colonial administration.

Following the military takeover of government in January 1966, the Igbo State Union, along with all other ethnic or tribal unions in the country as well as the political parties, were proscribed by the military administration.

Looking back at the Igbo State Union's three decades of existence, Chinua Achebe (1983:47) dismissed it as a "paper tiger" that served neither the Igbo elite nor the Igbo masses. According to him,

> ... the Igbo State Union was a paper tiger whose bogey value may have been exploited by a handful of self-appointed leaders in places like Lagos and Port Harcourt; but it was largely a joke among the Igbo elite, and for the Igbo masses, it was quite unknown.

Notwithstanding this criticism, however, some analysts argue that the Igbo State Union had not only served as a rallying point for the Igbo, but also served as a theatre for the training of Igbo leadership. They pointed out that those who had served as functionaries of the union had, through it, acquired the necessary exposure and experience that prepared them for their future political roles.

For instance, people like Nnamdi Azikiwe, Dennis Osadebay, A.C. Nwapa, Raymond Njoku, Mike Ajegbo, Jaja Wachukwu, Nwafor Orizu, Akanu Ibiam, Mbonu Ojike, K.O. Mbadiwe, etc., who were former key functionaries of the Igbo State Union, were later to occupy important political offices in either the federal or the regional governments. On that note, Richard L. Sklar (1983) observes that

> ... the founders of the Igbo State Union were no less politically motivated than were the organisers of the Egbe Omo Oduduwa; at least nine of the thirteen inaugural members of the union's provisional committee rose to high offices in the NCNC, and seven of them have attained ministerial rank in the Eastern, Central, and Federal governments". However, he contends that Azikiwe's weakness as an organiser led to his failure to sustain the needed political equilibrium between the National Council of Nigerian and the Cameroons (NCNC), of which he was President, and the Igbo state Union.

The formation of the Igbo State Union also led to the emergence and consolidation of Igbo ethnic identity in Nigeria. Before then, the Igbo did not seem to have any compelling traditional loyalty beyond their village. The union, therefore, was able to reduce inter-group suspicion while emphasising self-respect and the prospect of integration.

The Post-War Era

i. Introduction

Unlike during the First Republic, when there was only one umbrella Igbo cultural organization, towards the tail end of the military adventurism in politics between 1979 and 1999, more than a dozen different Igbo unions had metamorphosed, with each claiming to have the Igbo interest at heart, or to have been motivated by the desire to lift the Igbo to greater heights. This is a manifestation of the republican nature of the Igbo, which does not repose supreme knowledge or authority on any single individual or institution.

Among these unions were Ọhanaeze Ndịgbo, Aka Ikenga, Mkpoko Igbo, Odenigbo Forum, the Eastern Mandate Union, the South East Movement, Igbo National Assembly, Igbo Peoples Congress, Ala Development Foundation, the Igbo Salvation Front, the Igbo Redemption Council, the Igbo Question Movement, etc.

There were also some Igbo youth organisations like the Igbo Youth Congress, the Igbo Youth Movement, and the Federated Council of Igbo Youths, in addition to such radical groups as the Movement for the Actualization of the Sovereign State of Biafra (MASSOB), the Biafra Zionist Movement (BZM), the Biafra Independent Movement (BIM), the Indigenous People of Biafra (IPOB), etc. Outside the shores of the country, there is the World Igbo Congress (WIC), etc. Each of these groups believes itself to be a Moses that was bestowed with the divine mandate to lead the Igbo to the Promised Land. Today, many of these groups no longer exist or merely exist on the pages of newspapers and the internet.

We shall proceed to examine some of these groups to see how far they have helped or are helping to advance the Igbo cause.

i. Ọhanaeze Ndigbo

Soon after the Nigerian civil war ended in January 1970, some Igbo leaders came together to consider their possible fate in the new united Nigeria where they now found themselves. Since the ban on the Igbo State Union along with several other ethnic and political associations by the military in 1966, there had been a vacuum as far as the Igbo interest was concerned. No other organisation represented or spoke for the Igbo. Considering the displacement of the Igbo during the war and its aftermaths, Igbo leaders at the meeting thought it necessary to form an umbrella organisation that would speak for the people, which they called the Igbo National Assembly (INA). But the Federal Military Government at that time did not take kindly to the formation of the organization, and hence, it promptly banned it, probably due to fear, or a grand suspicious agenda being cultivated by the Igbo.

However, following the lifting of the country's ban on political activities in 1976, in preparation for the military's handover of power to a civilian administration in 1979, Igbo leaders banded together once more and formed what they called **Ọhanaeze Ndịgbo**. Among notable Igbo personalities that championed and supported the organisation at that time were Dr. Kingsley Ozumba Mbadiwe, Dr. Michael Iheonukara Okpara, Dr. Pius Okigbo, and Chief Jerome Udoji, who servedas its first Secretary General (www.ohanaeze.org).

The General Assembly is the highest policy-making organ of Ọhanaeze Ndigbo, at the national level of the organisation's organisational structure. This was followed by the *Imeobi* (Inner Caucus), and the Council of Elders, which were serviced by the Executive Committee and various other standing committees. This structure was equally replicated at the state and local government levels.

Ọhanaeze currently comprised the five core Igbo states of Abia, Anambra, Ebonyi, Enugu, and Imo, as well as the Igbo-speaking areas of Delta and the Rivers States, which produce its leadership in alphabetical order. The organisation's constitution, as amended in 1999, allowed for integration of both the youth and women wings.

Ọhanaeze is conceived as a socio-cultural organisation, but it equally serves as a clearing house in matters affecting the interest and general welfare of the Igbo in Nigeria and worldwide. The organisation believes in a democratically-oriented government that is accountable to the people, which allows for equal opportunities for all its citizens. It also stresses that if the Nigerian society is free and fair to all its members, irrespective of religious or ethnic origin, the Igbo, considering their adventurous spirit, determination, courage, confidence, and freedom, the country will work for the good of all.

At its formative stage in 1979, as the military was in the process of vacating the political scene and handing over power to a democratically elected civilian government, Ọhanaeze Ndigbo found itself in a dilemma regarding what would be its possible position in the emerging scheme of things. That is to say, the problem as to whether Ọhanaeze should align with the Igbo solidarity and teamup with a predominantly Igbo political party, the Nigerian Peoples Party (NPP) led by Dr. NnamdiAzikiwe, just as the Igbo State Union did for the NCNC in the First Republic; or to seek for the integration of the Igbo into the mainstream of Nigerian politics and join forces with a perceived pan-Nigerian political party, the National Party of Nigeria (NPN), which had even offered one of their own, Dr. Alex Ekwueme, the Vice Presidential ticket of the party.

After weighing the two options, Ohanaeze chose the latter, thus alienating itself from the majority of the Igbo population who supported the Nigerian Peoples Party (NPP). Members of the organisation were then largely seen as the Hausa/Fulani oligarchy, while Ohanaeze itself became "largely recognised by many as the Igbo wing of the NPN operating under a different name" (Onuoha, 2014).

However, at the tail end of military's involvement in politics, Ohanaeze came out strongly to canvass for more states to be created in Igboland. This resulted in the creation of Enugu, Abia, and Ebonyi states in the core Igbo area, as well as Delta State across the River Niger and the new Rivers State, both of which have a high percentage Igbo population.

Nonetheless, many people believe that Ohanaeze Ndigbo is undemocratic and elitist, comrpised mainly of people with established interests, and that the organisation was not doing enough to fight for the Igbo interests, particularly on such issues as the "Igbo Question", the despising or hatred of the Igbo by virtually all the ethnic groups in the country; the "Power Shift" or the "Igbo Presidency Project"; the Igbo marginalisation in virtually all spheres of the polity, in political appointments, in siting of industries, in allocation of resources, etc.

Furthermore, Ohanaeze is not well known among the Igbo masses because of the perception that it neither spoke nor championed their cause. It is also not popular among majority of the educated elites, who regard it as one of the parastatals of the governments of the south-eastern states. For instance, in September 2017, when the Nigerian Army under its code name, "Operation Crocodile Dance Smile II", unleashed a reign of terror on the leadership of the Indigenous People of Biafra (IPOB), by invading the home of its leader, Nnamdi Kanu, and killed many people in the process, Ohanaeze Ndigbo allegedly sided with the federal government of Nigeria and the Governors of South East states in proscribing the organisation.

It is also alleged that Ohanaeze never raises an eyebrow, even when the Igbo are openly persecuted, maligned, robbed and denied their rightful positions. It continues to preach "turning the other cheek". Many of these critics see Ohanaeze Ndigbo as nothing more than a Trojan horse that neither barks nor bites.

Defending these accusations, a former President-General of Ohanaeze Ndigbo, Professor Joe Irukwu (2007:66), explained that the organization "is driven and guided by the *'ako-na-uche'* philosophy, which is less confrontational, subtle, tactful and democratic". According to him, "*ako-na-uche* calls for sound judgment in dealing with issues and situations, but more importantly, it symbolises the value of approaching issues with the ancient wisdom of (Igbo) ancestors, dressed up with a lot of tact, diplomacy, and respect for the interests and intelligence of others".

There is no doubt that most of Ohanaeze Ndigbo members witnessed and fought in the Nigerian civil war. They had suffered and experienced the horrors of the war, and they would not want a repeat occurrence. Besides, majority of them had various investments scattered all over Nigeria and would therefore not want to rock the boat. In their wisdom, there is need to tread with caution. In other words, Ohanaeze believes in the concept of "one Nigeria", but not as it is presently constituted. Nigeria must be restructured to allow for true federalism.

Before the intrusion of the military into the country's internal politics, each of the then existing four regions was semi-autonomous. Each of them had its own constitution, which clearly defined its roles, duties, and limitations, as well as its earnings and its obligations to the central government, etc. Now, everything has been bastardised. The various state governments are no more than the departments of the federal government, and every month they would go cap in hand to Abuja to solicit for funds to run even their most minute activities.

Ohanaeze Ndigbo equally believes that the Igbo would be better off in Nigeria rather than to opt out of it. According to the former President General of the organization, Chief John Nnia Nwodo (Vanguard, 2017)

> ...no ethnic group has more stakes in the Nigerian project than Ndigbo, and as such, cannot consider breaking up as a viable option. There is no part of the country where Ndigbo have not invested their resources, even without any corresponding investment from others in Igboland.

ii. The World Igbo Congress (WIC)

The World Igbo Congress (WIC) is the apex Igbo organization in the Diaspora. Registered in the United States of America in 1994 as a non-profit corporation, WIC is an organ for the unity, dignity, and welfare of the Igbo, who at that time were still feeling the impact of the Nigerian civil war. The World Igbo Congress was established as an organ for the expression of the right to fair treatment of the Igbo in the community of ethnic nationalities in Nigeria. It was incorporated in 1997 as the World Igbo Congress Foundation, with the added function of developing and implementing approved projects.

According to the organization, the operations of the World Igbo Congress cover the interests of Igbo people in the diaspora and in their homeland, especially in Abia, Anambra, Delta, Ebonyi, Enugu, Imo, and Rivers states. Conscious of the fact that the Igbo live with numerous other ethnic groups such as the Ibibios, the Kalabaris, the Ijaws, the Itsekiris, the Urhobos, etc., the WIC does not discriminate in dealing with the Igbo and their neighbours in the South-South region, since all these people will equally benefit from its activities.

The operations of the group cover all aspects of youth, community, and infrastructural development. In addition, the World Igbo Congress connects the Igbo people to the world through partnerships at all levels. Membership in the organisation includes community organisers, health practitioners and economic development practitioners from affiliates in most United States metropolis and elsewhere.

The World Igbo Congress does not believe in the Igbo severing links with the Federal Republic of Nigeria. Instead, the Igbo should seek a better deal within the context of the Nigerian nation. Accordingly, it collaborates with the Ọhanaeze Ndịgbo and with other organisations with similar objectives to ensure that the interests of the Igbo are protected in the country and everywhere in the world.

Through its annual conventions, which were hosted by various Igbo communities in different cities of the United States of America, and which usually attract eminent Igbo personalities from all over the world, the World Igbo Congress x-rays various problems confronting the Igbo nation and proffers solutions to them.

iii. Ala Igbo Development Foundation (ADF)

The Ala Igbo Development Foundation (ADF) is an intellectual, research-oriented group registered with the Corporate Affairs Commission (CAC) of Nigeria as a non- governmental organisation that brings together Igbo intelligentsia, elders, clergy, patriotic public figures, women, and youth, both at home and abroad. Its main aim was to protect and ensure the survival of the Igbo, their culture, and civilisation as well as the development of Igboland. The group's membership included people from Africa, Europe, and America. Membership of the group cut across the continents of Africa, Europe and America (www.alaigbo.com).

The founding of the organisation came as a result of an international colloquium on "The Igbo", which was held in Enugu between March 11 and 14, 2014. The colloquium, which attracted participants from the United States of America, Canada, the United Kingdom, Germany, Australia, South Africa, Ghana, etc., was conceived in the light of persistent socio-political situation in Nigeria, which had continued to fuel national and international debate over the future of the country. It was the absence of internal cohesion and national focus within Igboland, as well as the extreme physical and political vulnerability of her citizens, that made the colloquium a timely and urgent wake-up call.

In the words of the founding president of the Alaigbo Development Foundation, Professor Timothy Uzodinma Nwala, a political philosopher and one popularly regarded in academia as the father of African philosophy, "while the Igbo nation confers on the Igbo their natural citizenship and identity, the Nigerian federation confers on them an acquired citizenship and identity". This is what makes for competitiveness in a federal system.

For three days, the over two thousand, five hundred eminent Igbo sons and daughters deliberated over the persistent century-old predicament of the Igbo in Nigeria, over which the entire Igbo, youths and elders, men and women, at home and in the Diaspora, kept groaning by the day.

Participants at the colloquium examined ways and means of overcoming the persistent Igbo predicament so that her citizens could live a life of dignity and self-confidence as well as co-exist and live at peace with their neighbours. They equally discussed how the Igbo could protect and guard their lives, their collective and individual interests, as well as how the people could apply their God-given talents without let or hindrance.

Alaigbo Development Foundation (ADF) does not consider itself a rival or a replacement for *Ohanaeze Ndigbo*, the apex Igbo cultural organisation, rather, as an affiliate of *Ohanaeze Ndigbo*. ADF supports the organisation whenever and wherever her support was needed. It also works with governments, various bodies, and individuals in Igboland and the Igbo Diaspora to help sharpen the vision of the founding fathers of *Ohanaeze Ndigbo*.

The organisational structure of Alaigbo Development Foundation comprises the Board of Trustees, which is the registered custodian of its assets, and the Working Committee, which is responsible for the day-to-day management of ADF affairs, in addition to supervising its Secretariat, its various standing committees, as well as proposing agenda for the various organs of the group. *Alaigbo* Council is the supreme organ of ADF and is responsible for its general policy, the conduct of election of the working committee, financial control, and approval of its budget.

In addition, there is the *Alaigbo* Trust Fund, established for the purposes of promoting activities pertaining to its basic objectives, namely, the protection and advancement of Igbo culture and civilisation as well as the development of the Igbo nation. *Alaigbo* Trust Fund has a management board comprising between twelve and fifteen members of highly respected Igbo citizens of proven integrity.

Among the standing committees of ADF are Research and Documentation, Finance and Budget, Contact and Mobilization, Publicity and Information, Diaspora and International Relations, Electoral, Projects, Legal, and Security. ADF holds an annual congress where various issues pertaining to the predicament, the general welfare and the progress of the Igbo both in Nigeria and in the Diaspora are deliberated upon and extensively dealt with.

iv. The Movement For The Actualisation of the Sovereign State of Biafra (MASSOB)

The Movement for the Actualization of the Sovereign State of Biafra (MASSOB) was founded in September 1999 by Ralph Uwazuruike, an Indian trained lawyer. MASSOB is a secessionist movement whose goal was to actualize an independent State of Biafra. Though its leaders had portrayed MASSOB as non-violent in its operations, and advertised a twenty-five stage plan to achieve its goal through peaceful means, the Nigerian government did not see it that way.

Since its formation, there had been several conflicts between the group and the Nigerian government, which had resulted in the deaths of several MASSOB members. In 2005, the leader of the group, Ralph Uwazuruike, was arrested and detained on treason charges by the federal government led by President Olusegun Obasanjo. He was released two years later, in 2007, following several outcries by well-meaning Nigerians. The Nigerian government saw MASSOB as determined to disrupt the country's peaceful existence.

At its formation, MASSOB had adopted two levels of governmental administration, namely, the "Biafra Government in Exile", represented by the Federal Republic of Nigeria, and the "Shadow Government of Biafra", represented by the Republic of Biafra. According to the group, the Nigerian government was *de jure* and was diminishing each passing day, while the Biafra Republic was *de facto*, a state in the making.

In its organogram, aside from Uwazurike, the national leader of the movement, MASSOB had national and regional directors of information, finance, agriculture, among others, which were the equivalent to Ministers or Commissioners, and local government area administrators, chief security officers, etc.

At its inception, MASSOB concentrated on organising rallies and peaceful protests, which culminated in the hoisting of Biafran flags at different locations in the South East. In 2005, the organisation re-introduced the old Biafran currency into circulation. This sparked a lot of excitement, especially as the currency was being freely exchanged at the border communities of Togo and the Republic of Benin, while in 2009; MASSOB launched "the Biafran International Passport" in response to persistent demands by Biafrans in diaspora.

Despite MASSOB's claim to be a peaceful organisation, the Nigerian government's response to its activities had been mass arrests and alleged killings of its members by security agents. For instance, as of May 2008, MASSOB claimed that a total of 2,020 of its members had been allegedly killed by security agents since 1999. In addition, in June 2012, the Human Rights Writers' Association of Nigeria accused the Nigerian government of allegedly killing sixteen MASSOB members by security agencies in Anambra State.

Similarly, in February 2013, MASSOB claimed that several unidentified corpses found floating on the Ezu River on the boundary of Anambra and Enugu States were those of its members who had previously been arrested by the police and executed without trial. As Kodilinye Obiagwu et al. (2015) had reported:

> In the last fourteen years, no movement or organization has lost as many members to violent death as MASSOB. In the same vein, no movement has attracted as many arrests and incarcerations, deaths at the hands of security personnel, and clashes with law enforcement as the movement. Yet, it has remained unyielding and undaunted in its quest for the seeming chimerical actualization of the sovereign state of Biafra.

Thus, in spite of mass arrests, detentions, and killings of hundreds of MASSOB members by government security agents, the group refused to bulge. Thousands of Igbo youths, and even the elderly, continued to pour into the organisation, yearning for the realisation of their dream republic. "Only till we achieve the declaration of a State of Biafra can we say that we are free. We must break away from Nigeria, we are not wanted here", vowed one of the enthusiastic members of the group in an interview in Enugu.

The MASSOB member also revealed that they met in their cell once every month to discuss at the residence of a senior member. "We talk about things that affect our welfare and plan how the organisation would move forward', he intimated. Indeed, many Igbo youths were very sentimental about MASSOB, with the Biafran flag, the "Rising Sun", usually stuck on top of their vehicles, motorcycles, and tricycles, just to show their enthusiasm about the project.

Aside from working for the actualisation of the Biafran Republic, MASSOB had embedded itself in the consciousness of the people and had never shied away from responding to any threat to the maltreatment of the Igbo in any part of Nigeria. MASSOB had fashioned itself as the Igbo's protector and the South East's policeman. For example, when some Igbo people were killed in Kano following a religious crisis in the city, MASSOB hired buses to convey back to Igboland those whose lives were still threatened and who desired to return home. The group equally offered comfortable accommodations to the returnees who had no immediate homes in their villages.

MASSOB had also cried against the visible injustice meted out on the Igbo by successive administrations in Nigeria, like discrimination in political appointments, the non-siting of industries in Igboland, the sinister and cold-blooded murder of the Igbo in different parts of Nigeria at the least provocation, the absence of infrastructural development in the South East, such as the absence of an international airport in the zone, the foot-dragging effort by the Nigerian government to construct the second Niger Bridge, and the dilapidated road infrastructure in the area.

On several occasions, MASSOB tested its strength among the populace amidst threats by the Nigerian government when it variously issued a sit-at-home order on the people of the South East to protest the alleged marginalisation and several injustices meted on the Igbo by successive Nigerian governments, and on each of such occasions, the order was effectively observed.

The Movement for the Actualisation of the Sovereign State of Biafra (MASSOB) was founded as a nonviolent ethnic and social justice organisation. It got off to a great start and was very popular among its ethnic group. It came at a time when some other Igbo oriented groups were formed to challenge the alleged marginalisation of the Igbo in the scheme of things in Nigeria. It equally came at a time when the Igbo nation was battling to restore the sanctity of their values and traditions.

MASSOB's operation was then well grounded in the context of Nigeria's socio-political realities, which had refused to be tailored along the country's pluralistic nature, leading to gross lopsidedness in the social scheme of things, including insecurity of the Igbo nation, her sons and daughters, as well as gross and uneven distribution of the country's resources, both human and material.

Ordinarily, the method MASSOB adopted was regionally and internationally not in conflict with the law and right norms, particularly in the context of 'rights to self-determination and that of indigenous peoples' using non-violence.

However, things began to fall apart for MASSOB following a factional clash that occurred at its headquarters in Okwe, Onuimo Local Government Area of Imo State, in 2014, which resulted in the deaths of four of its members under controversial circumstances. The leader of the group, Ralph Uwazuruike, was accused by some of his colleagues of importing thugs numbering about 5,000 to dislodge their members seeking to take over the administrative secretariat of the organisation, and in the process, many people were killed and several others wounded.

Uwazurike was also accused of financial impropriety and of withdrawing about N20 million every month from MASSOB's account, which was money contributed by members and meant for the upkeep of the movement.

Uwazuruike was said to have acquired properties in Dubai, Germany, and the United Kingdom, where he bought a house for his son who was in school there, and that he was collecting between N200 million and N300 million every month from the Presidential Villa in Abuja, drove in convoy of cars and lived like a king in his palatial home. This was at a time when about 5,800 MASSOB members had perished in the process of fighting for Biafra. According to one aggrieved member of the organisation:

> Uwazuruike has lost track of the actualisation of Biafra. He can't deliver on Biafra anymore. Uwazuruike cannot deliver Biafra. He is a dreamer who sees himself as the master of Igboland for selfish, political and pecuniary pursuits. He lives like a king and emperor, driving in a long convoy of luxury cars, with MASSOB members (Igbo youths) serving as security aides lining the streets and pavements as he strolls. He prefers to be godfather to governors in Igboland, and his boys are bitter.

However, investigations revealed that the crisis that rocked MASSOB could be traced to the infiltration of the group by some politicians who sought to make capital gains out of the movement. For instance, it was alleged that the sum of N200 million donated to MASSOB by a candidate in the Anambra State governorship election was at the root of the crisis, which led to the factional fighting at the MASSOB headquarters in 2014. There was also the allegation that the MASSOB leader had been going around collecting money from some other top politicians in Igboland.

In the same vein, many Igbo leaders objected to some of MASSOB's operational modalities or activities, such as, when the group asked the people of the South East not to participate in any election in

Nigeria, and also not to present themselves for counting during the national census exercise.

There was also the issue of Uwazuruike not opening up the group to intellectualism. Many members of MASSOB, including some top directors of the organization, were known to have no visible means of livelihood and equally had limited education.

Again, the *modus operandi* of MASSOB was far from being tailored within the confines of modern ethno-social struggles, using non-violent means. Uwazuruike was therefore accused by some of his colleagues of being a pacifist who believed that his dream republic could still be realised without taking up arms.

All these allegations and pitfalls led to disenchantment among many members of MASSOB. In the ensuing crisis, one of Uwazuruike's top directors, Mr. Uchenna Madu, claimed to have wrestled the organisation's leadership from his former boss. Other splinter groups that emerged from the system included the Biafra Zionist Movement (BZM) and the Indigenous People of Biafra (IPOB). Uwazuruike was then forced to lead the other faction, which he called the Biafra Independence Movement (BIM).

v. The Biafra Zionist Movement (BZM)

The Biafra Zionist Movement (BZM) is a breakaway group from the Movement for the Actualization of the Sovereign State of Biafra (MASSOB), agitating for the restoration of Biafra and its independence from Nigeria. The movement's main goal is to restore the Sovereign State of Biafra to its pre-colonial statehood. BZM was formed in 2010 to give "seriousness" to the actualization of the Biafran dream (www.biafrazionistmovement.com).

The Biafra Zionist Movement was led by Benjamin Onwuka, a tough-talking London-trained lawyer and former member of MASSOB who hailed from Item in Bende Local Government Area of Abia State. Onwuka cited the plight of the Igbo in Nigeria as the reason behind the formation of the group. According to him, the security of the lives and property of the people of Biafra in the entity called Nigeria was no longer guaranteed. He claimed that the rights of the Biafran people to peacefully practise their religion and freedom of association as enshrined in the United Nations Charter were no longer safe and guaranteed in Nigeria.

Onwuka drew the attention of followers and supporters to his side because his *modus oparandi* differed significantly from MASSOB. With the moral support of other pro-Biafra groups abroad that had aligned with his organization, he returned to Nigeria to physically get involved in the cause for the actualisation of Biafra. He criticised Uwazuruike for his pacifist approach, arguing that his method was not likely to lead to the actualistion of Biafra. He accused Uwazuruike of deviating from the goals and mandate of MASSOB and claimed that with the support of countries like Britain, his group would realise Biafra by 2015.

In August 2012, Onwuka filed an application with the United Nations Secretary General seeking observer status for the Republic of Biafra. He equally wrote to the African Union, asking for independent status and requesting that it to convene a meeting of the heads of state and government of the organisation. In the application, Onwuka claimed that the insecurity of lives and property, as well as religious freedom for the Igbo was no longer guaranteed in Nigeria.

Members of the Biafra Zionist Movement chose a more aggressive approach, marching through major streets of Enugu in the early hours of April 10, 2013, hoisting Biafran flags. However, they were apprehended by police in the city's Coal Camp area where some of them were arrested and chased away.

The first major sign that MASSOB's non-violent approach to issues regarding the affairs of the Igbo was testing the patience of BZM was on March 8, 2014, when the group invaded the Enugu State Government House, hoisted its flag, and threatened to invade other government houses in the South East. They followed this up on June 4, 2014, when Onwuka personally led some members of the group to besiege the Enugu State Broadcasting Service (ESBS) radio station with the aim of broadcasting an "overthrow" of the government of Enugu State. In the wake of the invasion, some policemen and members of the group were killed. Some members of the group were later arrested by the police.

Parading the invaders before newsmen, the police said the group had planned to make a live broadcast announcing its overthrow of Enugu State government and possibly burn down the radio station. They claimed that those arrested had carried arms, machetes, petrol, empty beer bottles, and one Biafran Zionist flag. When confronted, they shot and killed a police sergeant, and one of them was killed. Onwuka was declared wanted and later arrested and detained by the police. He was released two years later.

Many Nigerians, including the apex Igbo socio-cultural organization, *Ohanaeze Ndigbo*, condemned the Biafra Zionist Movement for forcibly occupying Enugu State Government House and the State Broadcasting radio station. According to one member of *Ohanaeze Ndigbo*, "we abhor the use of force by any group because we have worked and sacrificed so much for the unity and progress of this country. This is not the kind of struggle we are preaching. You don't storm a radio station to begin to broadcast or invade a government house to hoist flags when we have not discussed and agreed on it.

> The truth is that, whether anybody likes it or not, the South East is one and we are capable of deciding how we want to live here. We supported and participated effectively at the National Conference because it is our desire that this country be restructured to give every zone a sense of belonging.

Since the arrest and incarceration of the BZM leader, Benjamin Onwuka, not much has been heard of the organisation, safe from a few newspaper and online publications.

vi. *The Indigenous People of Biafra (IPOB)*

The Indigenous People of Biafra (IPOB) is a political self-determination movement group led by Mazi Nnamdi Kanu, Director of the London-based Radio Biafra. IPOB believes that the people of Biafra had the right to self-determination in accordance with the United Nations Charter and the Charter of African Union on Human and People's Rights, which clearly states that "indigenous people have the right to self-determination". By virtue of that right which Nigeria has signed and domesticated into local laws, IPOB insists that Biafrans are free to determine their political status and pursue their economic, social, and cultural development. In that regard, the main purpose of IPOB was to liberate the people of Biafra, who were forced into an unholy union with the Nigerian State.

More importantly, IPOB wants a referendum to be conducted for the people of Biafra to enable them to determine where they wish to belong. They insist that the people should boycott all further elections in Biafran territories, which they claim covered the whole of the former Eastern Region as well as parts of Delta and Benue States, until the referendum is conducted.

IPOB was launched in Enugu on May 30, 2014, to coincide with the 47th anniversary of the declaration of the Republic of Biafra on May 30, 1967, by Dim Chukwuemeka Odumegwu Ojukwu. At its maiden commemoration of Biafra Day at Ngwo in Enugu State, IPOB leader, Nnamdi Kanu, claimed that Nigeria as a nation would cease to exist by December 2015.

Before the ageing war veterans who gathered at the unveiling of a multi-million-naira cenotaph in memory of the fallen Biafra heroes who died during the Nigeria-Biafra war, Nnamdi Kanu, a former member of the Movement for the Actualization of the Sovereign State of Biafra (MASSOB), declared that no national conference could solve Nigeria's problem because of the deep-rooted hatred of the Igbo among the nation's ethnic nationalities. For him, the only panacea to Nigeria's problems was to split the country into different regions, and he called on the Igbo nation to keep faith with Biafra, which he said, would soon become a reality.

Describing Nigeria as "a failed nation, where nothing works," Kanu called on Igbo people to join the crusade of putting in place the Biafra Republic, citing as an injustice to the Igbo, the painful refusal by the Federal Government to pay entitlements and benefits to soldiers who fought on the Biafran side, whereas their counterparts in the North and West had benefitted. He further lamented that despite the slogan of *'no victor, no vanquished'* after the civil war in 1970, successive governments in Nigeria, including the then Jonathan administration, had continued to make life unbearable for the Igbo nation.

Kanu then urged all genuine Igbo to join the crusade to establish the Biafra Republic. "There is no going back," he said, "by December 2015, Nigeria would have ceased to exist; we shall get Biafra, if they don't give us Biafra, no human being will remain alive in Nigeria by that time; we shall turn everybody into corpses."

Earlier, in a telephone interview with Ikenna Onyekwelu from his London base, Kanu accused MASSOB leader, Ralph Uwazuruike, of jeopardising the integrity of the Biafra movement. According to him, "Uwazuruike has impugned the integrity of the entire Biafra movement, which is a holy mission. He has brought fraud into it. They left what they were supposed to do to dabble in fraud and criminality, by joining corrupt politicians" (Guardian, 2015)

He claimed that Biafra was a righteous enterprise that could only be obtained by men and women of unimpeachable character and integrity, and that the Indigenous People of Biafra (IPOB) were more prepared and determined than ever before to ensure that Biafra came, "not just any Biafra, but the Biafra of truth and honesty."

Commenting on the decision by the Jonathan administration to commence payment of pensions to Biafran war veterans, Kanu, while expressing satisfaction with the decision, however, asserted that the agitation for Biafra must continue. "We are relentless. Relentlessness is the word. We don't retreat. We don't surrender. We intend to go on until every injustice that had been meted out to Biafra people spanning many decades is corrected".

He said that the only way to redress that injustice was by amending the country's constitution so that any of its constituent units that wished to leave would be allowed to do so. "There has to be a referendum to ask the people what they want", he said, insisting that the general election slated for 2015 should not hold.

"All the elections they have been holding these years, what have they produced?" he asked, and pointed out that the elections were only able to produce "a few millionaires with their bank accounts abroad, who don't even trust the financial institutions in Nigeria. They steal money from the people". He therefore asserted that the United Nations should be invited to supervise any further elections in Nigeria so as to ensure that the people's democratic right to choose their leaders was no longer subverted.

The IPOB leader attracted both national and international attention when he was arrested in Lagos in October 2015 by the Muhammadu Buhari administration, and was later charged in court on an allegation of treason. In spite of different court rulings and several appeals by many prominent Nigerians for Kanu to be released, the administration obstinately kept him in prison. This attracted sympathy for Nnamdi Kanu, and made him sort of a cult hero, with thousands of Igbo youths adoring him and flocking to the side of IPOB. Everywhere, Kanu and his IPOB became the talk of the day. As a result, the Nigerian Federal Government became worried and uncomfortable. In the process, they began to hunt down and kill IPOB members by the hundreds, even though they bore no arms.

Some human rights organisations, including Amnesty International, began to condemn and accuse the Nigerian security agencies of cold-blooded murder of unarmed IPOB members. Specifically, and with video evidence, Amnesty International showed how no less than one hundred and fifty IPOB members were massacred by the Nigerian Army at Nkpor in Anambra State, from May 29 to May 30, 2016, while the group was celebrating Biafra Remembrance Day; and also at Ngwa High School in Abia State, on February 8, 2016, while they were on a prayer session.

Notwithstanding the high-handedness of the Nigerian government toward IPOB, members of the group were undaunted. They refused to give up, but remained resolute and faithful to their cause, even with their leader, Nnamdi Kanu, still in detention.

On April 25, 2017, a Federal High Court sitting in Abuja granted bail to Nnamdi Kanu, but with very stringent conditions, among which were the signing of his bail bond by a serving Nigerian Senator and a Jewish rabbi (since Kanu claims to profess a Judaic religious faith), who each must deposit one hundred million naira to the court. In addition, Kanu must deposit his own international passport with the court and must not be seen in the company of more than ten people at a time. This posed a challenge to some Igbo political leaders, who promptly rallied themselves to see that these stringent bail conditions were met.

When Kanu was eventually released, he decided to move around the country to meet with his supporters. At every place he visited, he talked about Biafra and the necessity for a referendum to enable the people to decide where they wished to belong. He equally insisted that there should be no election anywhere in the South East, and in particular, the governorship election slated for Anambra State on November 18, 2017, until the referendum was conducted.

As Kanu continued to move around to sensitise and mobilise his supporters, the IPOB came up with a sit-at-home order issued to all Biafrans for May 30, 2017, marking the 50th anniversary of the declaration of the Republic of Biafra. The sit-at-home order was strictly observed in most of the major cities in the South East and in some parts of the South South zone, where all the major streets and market places were deserted.

Reacting to that "sit-at-home" order issued by IPOB, some youths from the northern part of the country, issued quit notice to Igbo people residing in different parts of Northern Nigeria to vacate the area before

October 1, 2017. At the same time, the Federal Government of Nigeria, through its Attorney General, filed an application before an Abuja High Court asking it to revoke the bail granted Nnamdi Kanu, on the allegation that Kanu had flouted the bail conditions granted him. The Attorney General further alleged that the IPOB had constituted a threat to national security by raising a standing army known as the Biafra Security Service (BSS).

Other bail conditions which the federal government claimed Nnamdi Kanu had violated included alleged incitement of his supporters "to disrupt, disallow, and boycott elections in the South East states, starting with the Anambra State governorship election scheduled for November 18, 2017, should the government fail to hold a referendum for the realisation of the state of Biafra", and that Kanu had been seen in company of more than ten persons at a time.

The IPOB, on its part, denied these allegations, stating that it had not raised any standing army but that the Biafra Security Service (BSS) was only a vigilante group set up to monitor and ensure the safety of Biafrans returning from the North. "With October 1, 2017 (the deadline given by some Northern youths for the Igbo to leave the North) looming, it has fallen on the IPOB to ensure the welfare, safety, and well-being of Biafrans returning home to prevent what happened in 1966 from happening again... That's why BSS was inaugurated, to gather intelligence", said the group.

It further claimed that the IPOB was a peace-loving group that would never resort to armed struggle to achieve its objectives. The "IPOB can never be militarised because we are naturally peace-loving people. More importantly, we consider peaceful agitation to be far more potent than armed struggle. So, IPOB will never resort to armed struggle", it affirmed.

Fearing the implications of the Indigenous People of Biafra (IPOB)'s renewed activities, which could put the group in collision course with the federal government, the governors of the five South East states, along with the leadership of *Ohaneze Ndigbo*, invited Nnamdi Kanu to a meeting at the Government House, Enugu, on August 30, 2017. The meeting was to seek ways and means of containing the crisis without letting it get out of hand so as not to jeopardise the interests of the Igbo in general, and in particular, their kith and kin living in the northern part of the country, who were given "quit notice".

The Igbo leaders were said to have pleaded with Nnamdi Kanu to end his agitation for Biafra and the IPOB's threat to stop further elections in the South East. Kanu was alleged to have refused to yield to these demands, on the ground that he alone could not take such a decision. He was equally said to have insisted that the Igbo political leaders should extract something tangible from the federal government, its readiness to address the cause of Biafra agitation, before anything could be reviewed.

The South East governors, along with the leadership of *Ohaneze Ndigbo*, were accused of conspiring with the federal government to "deal decisively" with Nnamdi Kanu and IPOB. Accordingly, on September 14, 2017, the federal government dispatched its military forces, under the code name of "Operation Python Dance Smile II", to states in the South East, and in particular, to Nnamdi Kanu's country home of Afaraukwu, near Umuahia, Abia State, to kill a fly with a sledgehammer. Virtually all the streets in the South East were filled with stern-looking heavily armed soldiers who were ready for action at the least provocation.

In the process, the Nigeria Union of Journalists (NUJ) State Secretariat in Umuahia, Abia State, was descended upon by the soldiers, while some journalists found there were badly beaten and their communication equipment and other working gadgets smashed. At the same time, Nnamdi Kanu's country home at Afaraukwu was invaded, with several people allegedly killed and properties destroyed, while Kanu, his father, and some other members of his immediate family went missing, or fled to unknown places. Almost immediately, the federal government declared IPOB a terrorist organisation and proscribed it, despite the fact that most people knew that members of the group bore no arms, and were going about their agitation peacefully.

For almost one year, the whereabouts of Nnamdi Kanu, his father, and other members of his family were unknown, until late 2018 when Kanu was seen on a praying wall in Jerusalem, Israel. He later relocated to London and began to broadcast on Radio Biafra. Kanu's parents also later resurfaced, but died in quick succession shortly after.

In December 2020, the IPOB established the Eastern Security Network (ESN), which it said was "to protect the people of South East against incessant attacks by bandits". On June 26, 2021, Nnamdi Kanu was abducted in Kenya by Nigerian security forces, perhaps, in connivance with Kenyan government officials, and repatriated to Nigeria to continue with his court trial.

Even though many Igbo people share the sentiments expressed by Nnamdi Kanu and the Indigenous People of Biafra (IPOB) that the place of the Igbo in Nigeria was less than satisfactory, the people nevertheless are not comfortable with the method adopted by the IPOB in pursuing their goal and objective. Specifically, many people do not agree that the Igbo, or the people of the South East in particular, should not take part in state and national elections or in national headcount until a referendum is conducted, which the IPOB had insisted. They were also not happy with the "sit-at-home" orders declared by the IPOB in the South East, which had decapitated the economic life of the zone.

Equally unsatisfactory is the choice of words often used by the IPOB leader, Nnamdi Kanu, in addressing both his elders and people in government. They felt that Nnamdi Kanu should have been cautious in his choice of words in addressing those who were his seniors in accordance with the traditional Igbo respect for elders.

In the same vein, the people observe that there was a deliberate effort by the leadership of IPOB to avoid the educated or intelligentsia in its rank and file who would have helped enrich its programme content. Rather, the IPOB prefer to settle for jobless youths and artisans, most of whom did not witness the horrific effects of the Biafra war. Since the bulk of membership of the IPOB possessed limited education, majority of them were easily swayed or brainwashed by the leadership, as they had very often refused to see beyond their nose by dabbling into some dangerous activities that could lead to another disaster.

Again, the arrest and detention of the IPOB leader, Nnamdi Kanu, had exposed the weakness of the organisation as lacking in leadership structure, due to several orders and counter orders issued from the organization. Very often some criminals had capitalised on this confusion to cause mayhem in various parts of the South East.

References

Achebe, C. (1983) *The Trouble with Nigeria* (Enugu, Fourth Dimension Publishing Company) p. 47)

Aguomba, C.de (2005) *Akanu Ibiam: His Life and Times* (Port Harcourt: Falcon Publishing Company)

Ahonotu, A (1982), 'The Role of Ethnic Unions in the Development of Southern Nigeria: 1916 to 1966' in Boniface I. Obichere (ed.1982), *Studies in Southern Nigerian History* (London: Frank Cass & Co. Ltd).

Irukwu, J.O (2007) *Nation Building and Ethnic Organizations: The Case of Ohanaeze in Nigeria* (Ibadan, Spectrum Books). P.67

Nnoli, O. (1980) *Ethnic Politics in Nigeria* (Enugu: Forth Dimension Publishing Co. Ltd).

Nwabara, SN (1977) *Iboland: A Century of Contact with Britain, 1860 to 1960*, (London: Hodder & Stoughton) p. 228

Obiagwu, K. et al (2015) 'MASSOB: No Longer at Ease for an Ethnic Militia" (*The Guardian* newspapers, (Lagos, June 13)

Onuoha, G. (2014) 'The Politics of "Hope" and "Despair": Generational Dimensions to Igbo Nationalism in Post-Civil War Nigeria', in *African Sociological Review* Vol.18 1.

Onyekwelu, Ikenna (2014) 'Uwazuruike Jeopardized Integrity of Biafra Movement', Interview with Nnamdi Kanu, *The Guardian* newspapers, (Lagos), June 25.

Ota, EN 'The Igbo State Union and the Evolution of Igbo Ethnic Identity in Nigeria, 1936-1966,' in Njoku ON (ed.) 1999, *Nsukka Journal of the Humanities*, No. 10 June. P. 56

Sklar, R.L. (1983) *Nigerian Political Parties* (Lagos, NOK Publishers International)

Onwuka, B (nd),. 'Biafra Zionist Movement', Available from www.biafrazionistmovement.com.

CHAPTER NINE

Way Forward for the Igbo

Introduction

The Igbo have come a long way. From fragmentary independent acephalous units living inside some thick forests and being wary or suspicious of outside intrusion as late as the early 19th century, the people, as soon as they became convinced of the new social, economic, and political order brought in by colonialism, bought into the system and wholeheartedly threw themselves into the bargain. They quickly spread like bees across the country and beyond, take up residences and began to do any work, no matter how lowly, menial, or undignified. Through dint of hard work and perseverance, the people began to build themselves up the ladder and emerged as a strong force to be reckoned with in the country and even beyond, virtually attempting to upstage those who were there before them.

But some other ethnic groups in the country were not happy with the sudden rise of the Igbo, and became uncomfortable. They became envious and jealous of the Igbo, and began to see them as enemies, and as obstacles to the realisation of their own growth and development. In course of time, these other Nigerians began to discriminate against the Igbo, conspired against them, pushed the people out of the country which they laboured so hard to build, and later levied war against the Igbo people.

Despite being defeated in a war which was declared *'no victor, no vanquished',* the Igbo were only allowed to draw twenty pounds from their bank accounts out of the money they deposited before the war, but the people did not succumb. They did not surrender. They were undaunted. They persevered and refused to give up. From the ashes of the war, they began to build themselves up the ladder once again.

This again attracted envy and hatred for the Igbo from these other ethnic groups and from the Nigerian state itself, which was discriminating against the people. In consequence, many of the Igbo people began to feel that they were no longer wanted in Nigeria. As such, they were no more enthusiastic about the Nigerian project. They became disenchanted and disillusioned. They were disturbed about how they were being pushed out of the house they had laboured so hard to build, and treated like pariahs, endangered species, or second-class citizens in a country where they thought was their own.

The Igbo people were not happy about the way they were always made scapegoats for everything that went wrong in the country, and compelled to suffer for the sins they did not commit. They knew and believed that there was an unwritten law or an organised conspiracy against the Igbo in Nigeria, aimed at denying or preventing the people from getting their rightful position in the scheme of things or from ascending to the highest office in the land, which is the Presidency, and rising beyond some certain positions in the security services.

No less a person than a former Nigerian President, Olusegun Obasanjo, had confirmed this unwritten law against the Igbo in Nigeria. In an interview he granted the British Broadcasting Corporation (BBC, 2018), Obasanjo stated that the Igbo do not feel themselves to be actually wanted in Nigeria due to decades of official marginalisation, which should either be stopped or the people be allowed to take their chances in a new nation. According to the former president:

> Nigeria has placed an embargo on an Igbo man becoming Nigerian's president, and the Igbos understand this… They knew about the glass ceiling against the Igbos. After the Nigerian civil war, despite the 'no victor, no vanquished' programme, Nigeria placed a glass ceiling against the Igbos. The reconstruction programme was more visible in the breach. There was the 'abandoned' property programme that was induced to drive a wedge between components of the former South East Nigeria.
> While the country was too embarrassed to put the discrimination programme down in an official gazette, it was there for anyone who cared to look. It was evident when no Igbo was qualified to become the Inspector General of Police or lead any division in the armed forces. It was there when 'sensitive' or 'lucrative' positions were shared in Nigeria and the Igbos were conspicuously absent… It was there when Buhari appointed 47 people to key positions in his government, and none of whom were from the South East.
> Go to the South East today. Since the 1970s and the oil boom, Nigeria has invested in commercial industries. None has been sited in the South East. None. Refineries, steel plants, cement firms, any industry. The South East was systematically deindustrialised. Even when it was the best location for any industry, there was a reason it should not be sited

there. What this means is that any Igbo man who wanted to work in any commercial federal establishment would have to leave the East' Obasanjo had stated.

One might however ask Obasanjo what he did to improve the situation of the South East during his eight years as President of Nigeria. Did he appoint an Igbo man to any sensitive position, or did he site any commercial industry in Igboland?

The precarious situation in which the Igbo had found themselves in Nigeria had led to different perspectives or viewpoints regarding the path the Igbo should take to work out their salvation. While one group favours the complete severing of links between the Igbo and the rest of Nigerians so as to give the Igbo unfettered freedom to chart their independent course of existence; the other group prefers that the Igbo remain in Nigeria and fight for their salvation there. These two opposing viewpoints, dubbed *"The Igbo Outside Nigeria",* and *"The Igbo Inside Nigeria"* had put many Igbo leaders in dilemma and sometimes, on a collision course. We shall now proceed to discuss them.

Between the Young and the Old Brigades

The emergence of some Igbo youth organisations in recent years agitating for the resurrection of the defunct Republic of Biafra appears to be a vote of no confidence in some established Igbo elite groups, in particular, on the apex Igbo socio-cultural organisation, *Ohanaeze Ndigbo,* and on the governors of the five South East States, who openly show support for the continued membership of the Igbo in the Nigerian federation, albeit in a restructured form. For these youth organisations, there was no point seeking palliative because, in their belief, Nigeria had gone beyond redemption as the position of the Igbo in Nigeria since the end of the Nigeria-Biafra war had become intolerable, unbearable, and beyond reformation. What is needed, according to them, is the complete severance of links between the Igbo and Nigeria under the aegis of the Republic of Biafra.

The Igbo youth groups would not fail to berate and severely criticise the "old brigades" for not doing enough to mitigate the long sufferings of the Igbo in Nigeria. They would label them opportunists, traitors, and clientele groups that were ever ready to sell their people at whatever price; so far, their interests were assured and guaranteed.

Therefore, for these youth organisation, while members of the established order would claim to be fighting the Igbo cause, they actuality, were only out to protect their personal interests and investments in Nigeria.

On their part, the "old brigades" would criminalise the youth organisations and accuse them of irresponsibility in both their actions and utterances and of being hell-bent on plunging the country into another civil war. They would go further to castigate members of these youth groups, most of whom were poorly educated, and who were born after the horrendous civil war in the country, as naive, immature, and irrational both in their words, attitudes, and behaviours, and hence, would tryas much as they could to distance themselves from them.

Among these militant youth organisations, which have become ubiquitous in many parts of the country, and particularly in Igboland, were the Igbo Youth Movement (IYM), the Movement for the Actualisation of the Sovereign State of Biafra (MASSOB), the Biafra Independence Movement (BIM), the Biafra Zionist Movement (BZM), the Indigenous People of Biafra (IPOB), etc., whose *modus operandi* significantly differed from the established elite Igbo groups like Ohanaeze Ndigbo. Godwin Onuoha (2014) describes the relationship between these two groups as "inter-generational struggles between youth-led and elite-led Igbo groups". According to him, while

> ... the old(er) generation seeks to continuously hold on to their authority, power, and status, the young(er) generation is radically defining the status quo and exploiting the democratic conditions for potential gains. The young(er) generation aligns with ethnic militia groups and crime syndicates within the expanded 'democratic' space, one that is emerging as a reaction to the allegedly corrupt old(er) generation that wields authority and power.

It is thus an unending war between these two groups, who see each other from different perspectives, and as cogs in their respective plans to realise their set goals.

To many people, the disagreement between these two groups is unhealthy and has negative implications for the Igbo's struggle for a better deal in Nigeria. They also see it as the result of the Igbo's inability to speak with one voice, to forge a united front against a common enemy in order to free themselves from their oppressors and their oppressive rule. They believe that it would have been preferable if these two groups had swallowed their pride and selfish interests and banded together to advocate for their needs.

In reality, that would be ideal. But when it is realised that the Igbo are by nature republicans, not recognising a divinely ordained leader, the reason for this multiplicity of groups may not be far-fetched. Thus, in the absence of a towering political, leader as was the case in the 1940s, 1950s and 1960s, when the Azikiwes, the Nwafor Orizus, the Ozumba Mbadiwes, etc., came back from the United States of America with their foreign university degrees; or during the period of national emergency like the Nigerian crisis of between 1966 and 1970, when the fate of the Igbo was hanging in the balance, and an Odumegwu Ojukwu emerged to provide effective leadership, the possibility of a single person emerging as the Igbo leader may be very difficult to come by.

But that is not to suggest that the Igbo should not strive to build a cohesive unit while trying to meet the challenges of modern society, which would be in consonance with the age-old Igbo belief of *Igwe bu ike* (Unity is Strength). The problem of the Igbo in today's society is so complex that it requires every hand to be on deck to be able to salvage the situation. The existence of several splinter groups, virtually working at cross purposes, with every one of them claiming to be the champion of the Igbo cause, has even worsened the position of the Igbo in the country, as the people always failed to speak with one voice.

The Igbo outside Nigeria

This is an extreme viewpoint held by a good number of Igbo people, both young and old, which was borne out of desperation and frustration. Those who hold the view go further to describe Nigeria as a fraud that was contrived by the erstwhile British colonialists through a dubious treaty of amalgamation executed in 1914, without seeking the view or consent of any of the proposed partners in marriage.

The group refers to the different cultural backgrounds of various inhabitants of the country, which, it says, makes unity very difficult and contends that, having managed the relationship for over one hundred years without success, the best thing would be to dissolve the marriage so that each partner could go its own way without further disturbing the system. In particular, they reject or deprecate the servant-master relationship, which they claim, currently exists between the Igbo and the rest of other Nigerians, and hold that the membership of the Igbo in a conglomerate called Nigeria had never been rosy but had resulted in harrowing experiences where the Igbo were always at the receiving end.

For these advocates of the "Igbo-must-opt of Nigeria", this would be the panacea to the problems of the Igbo in the country, in particular, to the unresolved *Igbo Question*, where the Igbo were always made to carry the blame for everything that went wrong in the system, and where the people were always physically attacked and their property and shops destroyed or looted at the least provocation. As a result, the Igbo would be better off, or in a better position, to realise their potential, if they chose to leave Nigeria and establish their own country.

They lamented that Nigeria was suffocating the Igbo and had stifled the people's development as a race, citing the Biafran period, when the Igbo demonstrated their mettle and ingenuity by producing and manufacturing every conceivable item under the sun, including refining petroleum products and fabricating various weapons of weapons of war, like sardines, rocket launchers, landmines or the weapon of mass destruction, called *Ogbunigwe*.

They believe that Biafra would have been a very powerful nation had it survived the war and would have compared favourably with a country like Israel, which, though very small in population and virtually living in a desert, yet was able to produce enough food for its population, and at the same time, squarely faced and defeated all its surrounding Arab nations.

The group recalled how the engineers and scientists who wrought 'miracles' in Biafra were ignored at the end of the war and not brought together to replicate the same "miracles" in Nigeria. According to them, the Nigerian environment was hostile and suffocating and not friendly to Igbo enterprise, the "can do spirit" of the Igbo, since the people were forced to live with such obnoxious Federal Government's policies like "Quota System", "Federal Character", "Geographical Spread", etc., which promoted mediocrity rather than encouraged meritocracy.

The Igbo inside Nigeria could be compared to the Biblical Jonah in the womb of a whale, where the whale swallowed Jonah. Even though Jonah did not die inside the whale's womb, he would not make progress. Three days later, when the whale vomited Jonah out, he became a transformed person. He was no longer the timid and coward prophet that he was. He became bold and began to deliver the divine message to the people of Nineveh.

In the same vein, the Igbo inside Nigeria are in a backwater, in a state of unrealised potential. They would not realise their potential or make progress in Nigeria. Nigeria is holding them back. Nigeria is a stumbling block. The people are discriminated against, and they suffer all sorts of indignities. The Igbo can only realise their potential or make progress when they are separated from Nigeria.

The majority of these "the Igbo must-opt-out of Nigeria" campaigners were youths who were frustrated by the system, and saw no hope in Nigeria. They had gone through the crucibles of acquiring Western education or had acquired professional skills in various trades, yet at the end of the day, they had nothing to show for it. They remained jobless, with no hope for the future. In other words, for millions of jobless, frustrated, and dissatisfied Igbo youth, Biafra had become an ideal, a dream, and an imagined better place than a Nigeria that had shuttered opportunities for them. Biafra, therefore, is a dream, founded on a shared sense of loss, grief, and victimhood.

Thus, they see in a nation called Biafra as their only hope, due to its expected limitless opportunities. For them, Biafra is an el dorado, a new Jerusalem, a land full of milk and honey, where every good thing abounds. They are prepared to endure any hardship or suffer any deprivation and inconvenience in the land of their dreams, rather than continue to take insults and be subjected to humiliation and indignities in a country called Nigeria, where everything is placed upside down.

The method for realising this lofty ideal, that is, the Biafra of their dreams, would be through a referendum to be conducted among those agitating for Biafra, or in designated areas of Biafra. This would determine the acceptability or otherwise of the agitation. However, this proposal was opposed by the Nigerian authorities, who contended that the country's constitution did not have any provision for a referendum. But the Biafra agitators would have none of it. They continued to press for it, which brought them into confrontation with the Nigerian government.

These, notwithstanding, even if the proposal for a referendum by the Biafra agitators is accepted by the Nigerian federal government, it is still fraught with some difficulties that may need to be straightened out before putting it into effect.

Number one, if the referendum is conducted and the majority of the Igbo vote to opt out of Nigeria and the people eventually become a separate and independent nation, what would be the relationship between the new Igbo country and what is left out as Nigeria? With the long standing historical and cultural relationships among the people, how would the two countries relate to each other? Will a resident of Enugu in the new Igbo nation, for instance, who wishes to travel to Lagos or Abuja to do business or meet with his relatives apply as a foreigner and have his visa approved each time he wants to undertake such a journey, and vice versa? This could however be sorted out through ECOWAS protocols, where citizens of member states do not require entry visas.

Number two, there are some Igbo people who were born and bred outside of Igboland, and who are completely assimilated into the culture and language of the parts of Nigeria where they reside. Some of them know little or nothing about Igboland and seldom visit the region. They also hardly speak the Igbo language, and as a matter of fact, they rarely think of themselves as Igbo. What will be the status or position of these people in the new independent Igbo nation? Will they stay back in Nigeria and be seen as foreigners, or are they going to trace their way to the new Igbo nation? The same question may be asked of those other Igbo who are married to non-Igbo. Are they going to naturalise, or will they be treated as foreigners?

All these, notwithstanding, a Nigeria that fails to guarantee full citizenship rights to all its citizens will remain an arena of endless protests and conflicts. And that Nigeria is unlikely to realise its full potential and reach its destination.

The Igbo inside Nigeria

Those who hold the view that the Igbo should remain and continue to be part of Nigeria are mainly the elderly, in particular the establishment class, those with vested interests in Nigeria who occupy prominent positions in the country's economic and political order, and who have their investments scattered all over Nigeria. Some of them had participated in or experienced the horrendous effects of the civil war and wished that such things would never happen again. At the moment, they feel fairly comfortable with the existing social and political arrangements in the country and fear that they might lose their privileged positions should the Igbo leave Nigeria and become a separate country.

While they reluctantly acknowledge that successive administrations in the country have done and continue to do injustice to the Igbo, this group believes that such injustices can be sorted out or ameliorated within the confines of one Nigeria, if everyone is sincere and honest. They also believe that Nigeria is large enough to accommodate and absorb all its constituent units, the Igbo inclusive.

According to this group, the solution to the problems of the Igbo in Nigeria is not necessarily to opt out of the country and go for a separate state. Rather, the solution to the Igbo problem could be found by tinkering with the country's grand norm, that is, its Constitution. They insist that the Igbo have invested too much in building Nigeria, and therefore, the people could not afford to leave the country to any other group(s) of people.

In the same vein, the mainstream Igbo politicians represented by political office holders, at both the federal and state levels, believe that the Igbo would be better off in an indivisible entity called Nigeria, which must be built on "love, fairness, equity, and justice." As a result, they believe that it would be more profitable, or that the Igbo would enjoy a bigger dividend in a wider Nigerian political environment.

Another of their arguments is that the Igbo are cosmopolitan and travel a lot. The Igbo are entrepreneurial. They are ubiquitous. They are in every part of Nigeria and beyond. They have built houses, mansions, estates, hotels, and established industries and businesses in all parts of Nigeria, in Lagos, Ibadan, Benin-City, Abuja, Minna, Kaduna, Kano, Jos, Sokoto, Maiduguri, Yola, Bauchi, and in so many other cities.

Some Igbo entrepreneurs are estimated to own between eighty and ninety per cent of all hotels in Abuja, for example. What will happen to these investments if the Igbo pull out of Nigeria? In other words, what will be the likely fate of these investments in Nigeria, if they leave the country? Will the Nigerian government, for instance, treat these investments as 'foreign' owners, or will the government acquire or take over these investments? In fact, many of these property owners and investors would not wish a situation where they would be separated from their property or investments, and therefore, they are naturally opposed to the Igbo opting out of Nigeria.

In any case, is it not a matter of concern that the majority of the Igbo entrepreneurs prefer to have their investments outside of Igboland, not minding what happened during the Nigeria-Biafra war, when many properties belonging to the Igbo in some parts of Nigeria were declared "abandoned" and confiscated by some state governments? Apart from that, some of these investments outside Igboland would have given employment to millions of teeming Igbo youths who have been roaming the streets in search of non-existent jobs.

Apart from these Igbo investors and property owners, those who also are strongly opposed to the Igbo leaving Nigeria are those who rose to positions of prominence in various capacities in the country, such as governors, senators, ministers, legislators, judges, ambassadors, directors general, captains of industries, bank executives, etc. They are reluctant or unwilling to sacrifice their privileged positions in favour of uncertainty in an independent Igbo nation.

Rather than opting out of Nigeria, they contend, the Igbo should strive for a Nigeria that works for everyone, a Nigeria that works for all of us, a Nigeria where no one's right to full citizenship is abridged or circumscribed in any way, whether wittingly or unwittingly by race, religion, or ethnicity, or by the government; a Nigeria with constituent parts that have respect for each other.

But for the Igbo to have a respectful place in Nigeria, they should be well focused. They should be united. They should build a strong home base while not isolating themselves from the mainstream of Nigerian politics. They should have a proper agenda, and a well focused goal. They should know what they want in Nigeria and how to go about achieving that goal.

The Igbo should stop crying about being marginalized, or that they lost a war. These are no longer necessary. The Igbo may feel "marginalised" because they have not produced a Nigerian president of Igbo extraction or are not holding positions of command in the security agencies. But the Igbo are not marginalised in the sector in which they know best – COMMERCE.

The Igbo are ruling the commercial sector of Nigeria. They are everywhere, all over the country. Can you imagine Lagos, Abuja, Kano, Kaduna, Jos, Ibadan, Benin, Calabar, Bauchi, Maiduguri, and even the remotest part of Nigeria without the Igbo, who trade on motor spare parts, pharmaceuticals, electronics, computer accessories, etc? These towns would not have added up, or would have simply collapsed.

The problem is that the Igbo do not know the power they have, or how to make use of it. The Fulani, because they rear cattle, formed the Miyetti Allah Cattle Breeders Association, which protects and champions the interests of cattle herders across the country. They appoint some powerful individuals in the country as their patrons. Because of this, the Fulani have the audacity to traverse to all parts of the country, with their cattle destroying farmlands, raping and killing people in their farms without anybody doing anything to them.

The constant harassment, looting, and destruction of their goods in various regions of the nation would cease if Igbo traders throughout the nation could unite to form an umbrella organisation as powerful as the Miyetti Allah. Besides, such an association would enable them make strong statements on any action or direction they wish to take, be it political or economic.

References

Obasanjo, O (2017) 'Hard Talk', interview with BBC on September 11, is available from: https://www.bbc.co.uk/programmes/n3ct2kl7

Onuoha, G. (2014), 'The Politics of "Hope" and "Despair": Generational Dimensions to Igbo Nationalism in Post-Civil War Nigeria', in *African Sociological Review* Vol.18 1.

CHAPTER TEN

The Igbo Icons

Introduction

The Igbo are ingenuous, both as a collective and as individuals. The people are enterprising. They are explorers. They are hard-working and resilient. They are everywhere, all over the world, and wherever they are, they will not fail to register their mark, notwithstanding the condition in which they may find themselves.

Over the centuries, the Igbo nation, both at home and in the Diaspora, has produced men and women of honour, those who towered above their peers and who distinguished themselves in their various individual callings, in the arts, in science, in the military, and in governance, and thereby helped to change the course of events, not only within the African continent but also outside the shores of the continent. These were the Igbo icons, men and women, who exhibited the well-known Igbo qualities of excellence, resilience, exploration, enterprise, industry, and hard work.

We hereby proceed to discuss just a few of these people.

1. Olaudah Equiano (1745 – 1797)

Olaudah Equiano was born around 1745 in Iseke, an Igbo community in Oshimmri (now the River Niger), and died on March 31, 1797, in London, England. In his acclaimed autobiography, "The Interesting Narrative of the Life of Olaudah Equiano; or, Gustavus Vassa, the African", written by himself in 1789, Olaudah Equiano recorded his early childhood.

According to him, in 1757, he was kidnapped at the age of 11 and shipped across the Atlantic to the Americas, specifically the West Indies. One of his American slaver captors named him 'Gustavus Vassa' after the 16th century Swedish king, in accordance with the cultural cleansing criminality that characterised chattel slavery in the Americas.

From the West Indies, Equiano went to Virginia, where he was purchased by a sea captain, Michael Henry Pascal, with whom he travelled widely. He received some education before he bought his own freedom. He was sold twice more, but finally purchased his freedom in 1766.

While working on ships and sailing the world, Equiano did some on-the-side trading in the spirit of Igbo entrepreneurial expertise. He saved enough money within three years to buy himself out of bondage for 40 pounds - a bondage he was forced into while chilling in his father's estate.

As a free man, Equiano sailed to wherever ships would go, up to the Arctic! He ended up in London, and, using his own experiences, he began to preach freedom and the abolition of the abduction of Africans, which was terribly termed the "slave trade."

After 20 years of working to stop slavery, he joined the movement to abolish slavery in 1786 in London. He worked with 'Sons of Africa,' a group of twelve African activists advocating for the outlawing of evil human trafficking. Three years later, Olaudah Equiano wrote and published his book, a testament against slavery. The book was a runaway success that brought him publicity and loads of money. He travelled extensively, promoting the book and preaching the cause of abolitionists.

Olaudah Equiano was probably the foremost African civil rights activist, the forerunner of Frederick Douglass and Dr. Martin Luther King, Jr. Operating in London did not diminish Equiano's American connections. In fact, he reportedly insinuated birthplaces in America on two occasions, which was probably done to facilitate the issuance of certain documents freeing him from bondage.

After he settled in England, he became an active abolitionist, agitating and lecturing against the cruelty of British slave owners in Jamaica. He briefly was commissary to Sierra Leone for the Committee for the Relief of the Black Poor; his concerns for the settlers - some 500 to 600 freed slaves – and for their ill treatment before their journey ultimately led to his replacement.

The publication of his autobiography was aided by British abolitionists, including Hannah More, Josiah Wedgwood, and John Wesley, who were collecting evidence on the sufferings of slaves. In that book, and in his later Miscellaneous Verses (1789), Equiano idealises Africa and shows great pride in the African way of life, while attacking those Africans who trafficked in slavery. As a whole, Equiano's work shows both broad human compassion and realism.

Equiano did not live to see the official abolition of slavery, as he died on March 31, 1797. However, his efforts contributed to the efforts of William Wilberforce, who supported the campaign that later led to the Slavery Abolition Act of 1833. The Act abolished slavery in most of the British Empire. Transatlantic European abductors were driven out of the abomination known as "slave trade" forty years after Olaudah's death. Thus, the people of Igbo extraction have been involved in the politics of the Americas and the western world. Though the history of slavery in the Americas is marred by politics and pogrom, it made a significant contribution to the character and constitution of America.

The eventual abolition of slavery in Europe, following the realisation of its repugnancy, as advocated by Olaudah Equiano, took many years and many bloody events in the United States of America. So many stories exist about the forced coming of West Africans to the Americas since the early 1600s. In the late 1700s, Olaudah's book opened a window.

Equiano is often regarded as the originator of the slave narrative because of his firsthand literary testimony against the slave trade. Despite the controversy regarding his birth, "The Interesting Narrative" remains an essential work both for its picture of 18th-century Africa as a model of social harmony defiled by Western greed and for its eloquent argument against the barbarous slave trade. Equiano's book, with its strong abolitionist stance and detailed description of life in Nigeria, was so popular that in his lifetime it ran through nine English editions and one United States printing, and was translated into Dutch, German, and Russian.

Olaudah Equiano was not only the first African to write about slavery, he is considered the father of American autobiography. No other American before him had chronicled his or her journey to the New World with such global acclaim. Equiano married an English woman named Susannah Cullen in 1792, and they had two daughters. He died in 1797 in Westminster.

2. Henri Christophe (1767-1820)

Henry Christophe (October 6, 1767 – October 8, 1820) was a key leader in the Haitian Revolution and the only monarch of the Kingdom of Haiti. Claims about Henri Christophe's place of birth and life before coming to prominence have been contested since the early nineteenth century. He was born Christophe Henry, a former slave of Bambara ethnicity in West Africa, and of Igbo descent. As an adult, Christophe may have worked as a mason, sailor, stable hand, waiter, or billiard maker; if so, most of his pay would have gone to his master.

One popular story claims that he worked in and managed La Couronne, a hotel restaurant in Cap-Français, the first capital of the French colony of Saint-Domingue and a major colonial city. There, the legend goes, he became skilled at dealing with the grand blancs, as the wealthy white French planters were called. He was said to have gained his freedom from slavery as a young man, before the Slave Uprising of 1791. Sometime after he had settled in Haiti, he brought his sister Marie there; she married and had children. The political skills he learned as a hotelier also served him well when he later became an officer in the military and a leader in the country.

Beginning with the slave uprising of 1791, Christophe distinguished himself as a soldier in the Haitian Revolution and quickly rose to be a colonel during the revolutionary years. In 1779, he may have served with the French forces as a drummer boy in the Chasseurs-Volontaires de Saint-Domingue, a regiment composed of gens de couleur (mixed-race residents of Saint-Domingue). They fought at the Siege of Savannah, a battle during the American Revolutionary War. It is claimed that Christophe was wounded in this battle. He fought for years in the North with Toussaint Louverture, assisted in the defeat of French colonists, the Spanish, British, and finally French national troops, and became commander-in-chief at Cap-Français. By 1802, Louverture promoted him to the rank of general.

The revolution succeeded in gaining independence from France in 1804. In 1805, Christophe fought alongside Jean-Jacques Dessalines in the capture of Santo Domingo (now the Dominican Republic) from Spanish forces as part of the Treaty of Basel. Christophe was in charge of the northern division of the country, where he notably supervised the first steps of the construction of Citadelle Laferrière. General Nicolas Geffrard, commander in the South, later approached Christophe with a plot to kill Dessalines; seeing an opportunity to seize power, he did not warn the self-proclaimed Emperor.

Christophe's influence and power in the North were such that Dessalines, though aware of opposition brewing against him in the highest circles of power, found himself unable to strike against his general. The conspiracy involved the majority of Dessalines' senior officers, including Dessalines' Minister of War and Navy, Etienne Elie Gérin, General Alexandre Pétion, Commander-in-Chief of the Second Division in the West, General Nicolas Geffrard and many others.

On April 6, 1805, having gathered all his troops, General Christophe took all male prisoners to the local cemetery and proceeded to slit their throats, among them Presbyter Vásquez and 20 more priests. Later, he set on fire the whole town along with its five churches. On his way out, he took along, fashioned like a herd, 249 women, 430 girls, and 318 boys, a steep figure considering the relatively low population of the town at that time. Alejandro Llenas wrote that Christophe took 997 from Santiago alone, and "Monte Plata, San Pedro, and Cotuí were reduced to ashes, and their residents either had their throats slit or were taken captive by the thousands, like farm animals, tied up and beaten on their way to Haiti."

The Haitian General Henry Christophe (referred to as Enrique Cristóbal in Spanish-language accounts), under Dessalines, attacked the towns of Moca and Santiago. The barrister, Gaspar de Arredondoy Pichardo wrote, "forty children had their throats cut at the Moca's church, and the bodies found at the presbytery, which is the space that encircles the church's altar..." This event was one of several documented accounts of atrocities perpetrated by General Christophe, under the orders of Dessalines; they retreated from the Spanish-ruled side of the island after their failed invasion attempt of 1805.

On October 16, 1806, they signed a proclamation entitled "Resistance to Oppression," that declared the necessity to overthrow Dessalines' government and proclaimed Christophe head of the provisional Haitian government. Dessalines was assassinated the next day, October 17, 1806.

After Dessalines was assassinated, Christophe retreated with his followers to the Plaine-du-Nord of Haiti, the stronghold of former slaves, and created a separate government there. He suspected he was also at risk of assassination in the South. On February 17, 1807, he declared himself "President and Generalissimo of the armies of land and sea of the State of Haiti". Pétion became President of the "Republic of Haiti" in the south, where he was backed by General Jean-Pierre Boyer, a personne de couleur, who controlled the southern armies.

On March 26, 1811, Christophe created a kingdom in the north and was later proclaimed Henry I, King of Haiti. He also created nobility and named his legitimate son, Jacques-Victor Henry, prince and heir. He renamed Cap-Français as Cap-Henry, while Jacques-Victor Henry, his son, became heir apparent. He gave him the title of Prince Royal of Haiti. His second son was a colonel in his army.

Christophe built six châteaux, eight palaces, and the massive Citadelle Laferrière on a mountain near Milot. It has now become a UNESCO World Heritage Site because of the remains of the Sans-Souci Palace.

As king, Christophe created an elaborate Haitian peerage (nobility), originally consisting of four princes, eight dukes, 22 counts, 40 barons, and 14 knights ("chevaliers"). Christophe founded a College of Arms to provide armorial bearings for the newly ennobled. For his personal coat of arms, Christophe chose a crowned phoenix rising from flames and the motto 'Je renais de mes cendres' (I rise from my ashes), presumably in reference to the rebirth of Cap Henry after he himself burned it in 1802 to repel the invading French army.

The two parts of Haiti struggled to increase agricultural production to recover from the expensive and damaging wars. The United States had only recently ended its arms and goods embargo against Haiti and had begun war with Great Britain in the War of 1812. Christophe had to choose whether to enforce a version of the slave plantation system to increase agricultural production or to subdivide the land into parcels for peasants' subsistence farming. The latter was the policy of President Pétion in the South. King Henry chose to enforce corvée plantation work, a system of forced labor, in lieu of taxes, but also began his massive building projects. During his reign, Northern Haiti was despotic, but the sugar cane economy generated revenue for the government and officials.

After Napoleon abdicated in April 1814, King Louis XVIII attempted to take back St Domingue. The Treaty of Paris, ratified on May 30, gave Spanish San Domingo back to newly restored Bourbon France and granted an extra five years of slave trade in which to recoup losses entailed by the abolition of slavery.

In October 1814, Henry I's ministers made public evidence of French schemes to try and recover its former colony in the form of letters carried by French agents captured on the island. In the ensuing uproar, the nation mobilised for the expected French invasion and began an international public relations campaign. From November on, reprints of Haitian pamphlets, newspapers, and open letters appeared in print media across the Atlantic world. Such broadsides and editorial interventions were accompanied by critical theoretical texts on race and colonialism, such as Pompée Valentin Vastey's The Colonial System Unveiled (Le Système colonial dévoilé). Simultaneously, Henry established contact with the most prominent English abolitionists: his letter to William Wilberforce arrived on January 5, 1815, and began a new level of engagement between Great Britain and the Kingdom of Haiti.

Despite promoting education and establishing a legal system called the Code Henry, King Henry was an unpopular, autocratic monarch. His realm was constantly challenged by Petion's government of the South, which was ruled by gens de couleur. Toward the end of Christophe's reign, public sentiment opposed what many considered his feudal policies of forced labor, which he intended to use to develop the country. Ill and infirm at age fifty-three, King Henry committed suicide by shooting himself with a silver bullet rather than risk a coup and assassination. His son and heir was assassinated 10 days later.

King Henry was buried within the Citadelle Laferriere. His descendants continued to be among the powerful of Haiti. Pierre Nord Alexis, President of Haiti from 1902–1908, was Christophe's grandson. Michèle Bennett, who married to Jean-Claude Duvalier and served as First Lady of Haiti during his administration (1980 to 1986), is Christophe's great-great-great-grand daughter.

3. James Africanus Beale Horton (1835-1883)

James Africanus Beale Horton, surgeon, scientist, soldier, and political thinker, was the first man to propose a modern independent nation of the Igbo in 1865. He published and sent to the British government his proposal titled,

> The Empire of the Eboes/Hackbous/Heebos/Iboes/Igboes/Egboes, with the requirements necessary for establishing that self government recommended by the Committee of the House of Commons, 1865: and a vindication of the African Race.

This proposal included a plan for a self-governed, independent nation

- An army,
- Currency
- Support for modern civilisation and economic empowerment.

His proposal was based on his research, which demonstrated that the Igbo race was the "most emulative, intelligent, and adaptable race" in West Africa, and that with modern support, they would vindicate the black race. He also supported the hypothetical but controversial Jewish migration origin of the Igbos at that time.

Horton was born in then British colonial Sierra Leone, near Freetown. His parents were former receptive Igbo slaves. Horton lived in Gloucester and began studies at a local school in 1845. In 1847 he moved to Freetown to attend the local Church Missionary Society School (CMS). In 1853, he was moved to Freetown's Fourah Bay Institution to train for a ministry in the Church of England. His seminary studies ended two years later when the CMS selected him to study medicine in preparation for a medical career in the British army.

In 1855, along with William Davies and Samuel Campbell, Horton received a British War Office scholarship to study medicine in Great Britain. He studied at King's College London and Edinburgh University, qualifying as a medical doctor in 1859. While a student, he took the name "Africanus" as an emblem of pride in his African homeland. He published his dissertation, "The Medical Topography of the West Coast of Africa" in 1858.

Upon completion of his studies at Edinburgh, Horton was commissioned as an officer in the British Army and was made a staff assistant surgeon, becoming one of the earliest Africans in the officer cadre of the British Army. When he returned to Sierra Leone, he was posted to serve in Ghana in the West Indian Regiment. In his army career, he was posted to various locations within the British colony, including Lagos, the Gambia, Sierra Leone, and Ghana.

Horton became more concerned with politics during his military service in West Africa. He refuted the derogatory racial theories about Africans rife in Victorian Britain and its empire. However, Horton also considered himself a loyal subject of the British establishment and envisioned that Britain should have a strong cultural and technological influence on the development of Africa. Thus, his philosophies, radical when colonial powers were dominant, have acted as a basis for the future advancement of African independence and nationalist ideologies.

At age 45, Horton retired and returned to Freetown, where he continued to promote African education as the key to self-governance, and provided further scholarships to hopeful young Africans. He also took keen interest in Africa's technical and economic development and opened a bank called the Commercial Bank of West Africa. His business and gold mining exploits made him one of the richest men in Africa by 1880'

Although his dream of an independent, self-governed Igbo nation was not realised in his lifetime, his political thoughts shaped African political thoughts during Africa's colonisation after his death. James Africanus Beale Horton died in Freetown, Sierra Leone, in 1883.

Africanus Horton worked toward African independence, a century before it occurred. In his varied career, he served as a physician, an officer in the British Army, a banker, and a mining entrepreneur. In addition, he wrote a number of books and essays, the most widely remembered of which is his 1868 "Vindication of the African Race", an answer to the white racist authors emerging in Europe. His writings looked ahead to African self-government, anticipating many events of the 1950s and 1960s. Horton is often seen as one of the founders of African nationalism and has been called "the father of modern African political thought".

Horton's first two publications: "The Political Economy of British West Africa: with the Requirements of Several Colonies and Settlements" (1865) and "West African Countries and Peoples" (1868), were a defence of Africans against the racist views of some European anthropologists that Africans were physically and intellectually inferior people whose development stopped centuries ago. He argued that all races have the faculty to acquire knowledge about philosophy, science, and technologies that civilizations have developed over the ages.

Horton was the first modern African political thinker to openly campaign for self-government for the West African colonies and championed the cause of what he referred to as "African nationality". He was an advocate of an elected monarchy in which a king would be elected by universal suffrage and a bicameral legislature. In regards to the economic development of Sierra Leone, he proposed the annexation and commercial development of surrounding land in an effort to raise the revenue necessary to implement various economic and social development plans.

In another of his publications, a compilation of letters called "Letters of the Political Condition of the Gold Coast" since the exchange of territory, Horton wrote about hostilities between ethnic groups in the Gold Coast and offered his views about solving the hostilities, including the continuation of education in Africa.

Horton was one of the first West Africans to demand the establishment of a medical school and higher education institution in the region. He recognised the value of an indigenous institution and believed that it should be headed by an African, believing that they would be more invested in the progress of the country than a European. In 1861, he wrote a letter to the War Office in London, stating the need for a tropical medical school in the region. After his retirement from the army, Horton started a finance institution called the Commercial Bank of West Africa.

Horton married on two different occasions while living in Freetown. He first married Fanny Marietta Pratt, daughter of the prominent Pratt family of Igbo origin. Marietta died at age 22 years, and Horton then, on May 29, 1875, went on to marry Selina Beatrice Elliott (1851–1910), the daughter of John Bucknor Elliott, who was the manager of the Western Area of Freetown. The Elliotts were a Nova Scotian settler family of African-American descent.

4. Edward Wilmot Blyden (August 3, 1832 – February 7, 1912)

Edward Wilmot Blyden, educator, writer, diplomat, and politician, was born on August 3, 1832, in Sankt Thomas, Danish West Indies (now known as the US Virgin Islands), to free black parents who claimed descent from the Igbo area of present-day Nigeria. Between 1842 and 1845, the family lived in Porto Bello, Venezuela, where Blyden discovered a facility for languages and became fluent in Spanish.

According to the historian, Hollis R. Lynch, in 1845, Blyden met the Reverend John P. Knox, a white American, who became pastor of the St. Thomas Protestant Dutch Reformed Church. Blyden and his family lived near the church, and Knox was impressed with the studious, intelligent boy. Knox became his mentor, encouraging Blyden's considerable aptitude for oratory and literature. Mainly because of his close association with Knox, the young Blyden decided to become a church minister, which his parents encouraged.

In May 1850, Blyden, accompanied by Reverend Knox's wife, went to the United States to enroll in Rutgers Theological College, Knox's *alma mater*. He was refused admission due to his race. Efforts to enroll him in two other theological colleges also failed. Knox encouraged Blyden to go to Liberia, the colony set up in the 1830s by the American Colonization Society (ACS) in West Africa, where he thought Blyden would be able to use his talents. Later in 1850, Blyden sailed to Liberia, and soon became deeply involved in its development.

Blyden soon began working in journalism. From 1855 to 1856, he edited the *Liberia Herald* and wrote the column "A Voice from Bleeding Africa." He also spent time in British colonies in West Africa, particularly Nigeria and Sierra Leone, writing for early newspapers in both colonies. He equally worked as an editor at *The Negro* and *The African World*. He maintained ties with the American Colonisation Society and published in their *African Repository and Colonial Journal*.

Starting in 1860, Blyden corresponded with William Ewart Gladstone, who would later become a significant Liberal leader and Prime Minister of the United Kingdom. Gladstone offered Blyden an opportunity to study in England in 1861, but Blyden declined due to his obligations in Liberia. In 1861, Blyden became professor of Greek and Latin at Liberia College. He was selected as president of the college, serving from 1880 to 1884 during a period of expansion.

As a diplomat, Blyden served as an ambassador for Liberia to Britain and France. He also travelled to the United States, where he spoke to major black churches about his work in Africa. Blyden believed that by returning to Africa and assisting in its development, black Americans could put an end to their racial discrimination. He was criticised by African Americans who wanted to gain full civil rights in their birth nation of the United States and did not identify with Africa.

In suggesting a redemptive role for African Americans in Africa through what he called "Ethiopianism", Blyden likened their suffering in the diaspora to that of the Jews. He supported the 19th-century Zionist project of Jews returning to Palestine. Later in life, Blyden became involved in Islam and concluded that it was a more "African" religion than Christianity for African Americans and Americo-Liberians.

Participating in the development of the country, Blyden was appointed the Liberian Secretary of State (1862–1864). He was later appointed Secretary of the Interior (1880–1882). Blyden ran for President for the Republican Party in 1885, but lost to incumbent, Hilary R.W. Johnson.

From 1901 to 1906, Blyden directed the education of Muslims at an institution in Sierra Leone, where he lived in Freetown. He became passionate about Islam during this period, recommending it to African Americans as the major religion most in keeping with their historic roots in Africa.

As a writer, Blyden is regarded widely as the "father of Pan-Africanism" and is noted as one of the first people to articulate a notion of "African personality" and the uniqueness of the "African race." His ideas have influenced many twentieth-century figures, including Marcus Garvey, George Padmore and Kwame Nkrumah.

His major work, *Christianity, Islam, and the Negro Race* (1887), promoted the idea that practising Islam was more unifying and fulfilling for Africans than Christianity. He argued that the latter was introduced chiefly by European colonisers, and believed that it has a demoralizing effect. Although Blyden continued to be a Christian, he however thought Islam was more authentically African, as it had been brought to sub-Saharan Africa by people from North Africa. His book was controversial in Great Britain. At first, many people did not believe that a black African had written it; his promotion of Islam was disputed. In later printings, Blyden included his photograph as the frontispiece.

His book included: 'Let us do away with the sentiment of Race'; 'Let us do away with out African personality and be lost, if possible, in another Race'; 'This is as wise or as philosophical as to say, let us do away with gravitation, with heat and cold and sunshine and rain'. Of course, the race in which these persons would be absorbed is the dominant race, before which, in cringing self-surrender and ignoble self-suppression, they lie in prostrate admiration.

Blyden married Sarah Yates, an Americo-Liberian from the prominent Yates family. She was the daughter of Hilary Yates and his wife. Her paternal uncle, Beverly Page Yates, served as Vice President of Liberia from 1856 to 1860 under President Stephen Allen Benson. Blyden and Sarah had three children together.

Later, while living for several years in Freetown, Sierra Leone, Blyden had a long-term relationship with Anna Erskine, an African-American woman from Louisiana. She was the grand daughter of James Spriggs-Payne, who was twice elected president of Liberia. Blyden and Erskine had five children together.

Blyden died on February 7, 1912, in Freetown, Sierra Leone, where he was buried at Racecourse Cemetery. In honour of him, the 20th-century pan-Africanist, George Padmore, named his daughter, Blyden.

5. Edward James Roye (February 3, 1815 – February 11, 1872)

Edward James Roye served as the fifth President of Liberia from 1870 until his overthrow and subsequent death in 1871. He had previously served as the 4th Chief Justice of Liberia from 1865 until 1868. He was the first member of Liberia's True Whig Party to serve as president. Born in 1815 in Newark, Ohio, Roye was of Igbo descent.

In 1846, attracted by the American Colonisation Society's promotion of the relocation of African Americans to the colony of Liberia in West Africa, Roye emigrated to the colony with his family at the age of 31. There, he set up business as a merchant. The next year, the colony gained independence. Within three years of his arrival, Roye became active in Liberian politics, serving as a representative and Speaker (1849-1850) of the Liberian House of Representatives and as Chief Justice of the Supreme Court of Liberia. Roye was inaugurated as President of Liberia on January 3, 1870.

In the decades after 1868, escalating economic difficulties weakened the state's dominance over the coastal indigenous tribal peoples. As conditions worsened, the cost of imports was far greater than the income generated by exports of its commodity crops: coffee, rice, palm oil, sugarcane, and timber. Liberia has tried desperately to modernise its largely agricultural economy.

In 1871, Roye tasked the Speaker of the House of Representatives, William Spencer Anderson, with negotiating a new loan from British financiers. Anderson secured $500,000 under strict terms from the British Consul-General, David Chinery, but was heavily criticised and eventually arrested. Anderson apparently tried again the following year for his part in securing the loan. He was found not guilty, but he was shot to death while leaving the courtroom.

Roye was removed from the presidency on October 26, 1871, in what some allies called a coup d'état. The circumstances surrounding his removal from office, however, remained murky and highly partisan. What is known is that he was jailed for several months following his ouster and soon died under equally mysterious circumstances.

His unpopular loans with Britain as well as fears from the Republican Party that he was planning to cancel the upcoming presidential election were among the reasons for his forced removal. No specific historical record is available about the date and circumstances of Roye's death. Various accounts indicate that he was killed on February 11 or 12, 1872.

Another account suggests that he drowned on February 12, 1872, while trying to reach a British ship in Monrovia harbor. The portrait of President Roye in the gallery of the Presidential Mansion in Monrovia notes his date of death as February 11, 1872. Edward James Roye's picture can also be found on Liberia's five- dollar note.

6. King Jaja of Opobo (1821–1891)

Mbananso Okwara Ozurumba, popularly known as Jaja of Opobo, was born in 1821 in Umuduruoha, Amaigbo, in present-day Imo State and rose against the odds of poverty and colonial rule to become Nigeria's first international trader and millionaire in the 19th century. The founder and king of a prosperous city, he is popularly known as Jaja of Opobo, a name given to him by the British, which later became his household name. He is known as Jaja Jubogba or Jo Ubam by the Igbo.

Jo Ubam, (some say "Jibuno Jibuoha"), was regarded as a hero who left an indelible mark on the history of Nigeria and West Africa. At about the age of twelve years, Jaja was kidnapped, sold into slavery, and taken to Bonny Island in the present Rivers State. He was adopted by Mgborie Igonidon of the Opubo (Annie Pepple) trading house. It was his first owner who gave him the name Jubo Jubogha.

Jaja worked very hard for his master and was very humble until he was sold again to Chief Alali, who was the ruler of the Opubo Anne Pepple Royal House. It was here that the British, who could not pronounce his name properly, gave him the name "Jaja".

In those days, the Bonny Empire was a flourishing kingdom in ancient Nigeria that gained its wealth through trade and business in the slave trade. Slaves were granted their freedom if they had successful businesses and could rise in the social classes to become prominent people in society as well as the ruling kingdom. Jaja worked for the chief and ran businesses on the side until he was able to buy his freedom and become a man of his own.

With his newly found freedom and already flourishing businesses, Jaja concentrated on running his businesses well and learned the tricks and wits of working as a trader, especially with the British. At a very young age, he had earned for himself high social status and an enviable name in the trading business in West Africa.

At the death of his former enslaver, the ruler of the Opuba Anne Pepple Royal House, there was no one interested in taking up the throne because of the debts the royal house had incurred over the years. Seeing it as both a business opportunity and a way of honouring the late chief, Jaja boldly took up the role and paid off the debts in a matter of two years.

Under the rule of Jaja, the Anne Pepple Royal House became the richest and strongest trading house under the Bonny Empire. But in 1859, Jaja was forced to leave the royal house after a fire outbreak, allowing the envious Manilla Pepple House to take over the Anne Pepple House. In the same year of 1859, Jaja established the Opobo city-state.

Through his intelligent administration and expansion of trade links, the Opobo city-state became powerful, had control over the traditional sources of palm oil in the region, and took over fourteen of the eighteen trading houses under the Bonny Empire.

Jaja was very opened to western social development and learned to speak very fluent English, building schools in Opobo, and other social amenities which quickly developed the city. Jaja employed many African Americans to teach in his schools, providing quality education to students.

Despite being open to western trade and social development, Jaja was greatly against the political ambitions of the British Empire and protected his city for as long as he could.

As time went on, the oil trade business in Opobo land began to expand, and the ambitions of the Europeans to dominate this market grew, thus creating a conflict between Jaja and British top sales and business tycoons, one of whom was John Holt of Liverpool. While Jaja evaded attempts by John Holt to penetrate Jaja's market in Qua Ibo

River, Liverpool members of the African Association were pressing for strong action against Jaja over what they described as "falling rates of profit".

In the course of "national interest", King Jaja dealt severe blows to the Qua Ibo people in 1881. He raided about seven of their villages, captured many, and executed about 100 people for engaging in direct trade with the Europeans. Even when the British came up with funny tricks and laws to outrun Jaja in the quest of control of the oil region, he always checkmated them, and this angered the British the more.

It only took a while for Jaja to be labelled as a tyrant by the British who tried to get rid of the powerful King and businessman who was in charge of several of West Africa's biggest trading businesses. To prove to the British that an African was capable of being great without their help, Jaja started exporting palm oil directly to the United Kingdom through his own ships, thereby pioneering Nigerian export trade and becoming the first Nigerian and West African to directly export to the West.

Jaja became a millionaire and caused the western trade to fall in West Africa. Through his monopoly over importation and exportation of oil, foreign traders especially the British were forced to pay taxes.

Apart from the fact that he was a wealthy merchant and a very diplomatic man, Jaja was also a man of honour and power. This is exemplified when he aided the Queen of England in a battle in the Gold Coast (the Ashanti war) and was awarded a sword of honour from Queen Victoria in 1871.

Through his wealth, King Jaja also became a powerful politician and owned a strong military which was sent out to help the British during the Anglo-Ashanti wars in 1875 to which Queen honoured him. Jaja had many wives and children who he took pride in him as a very responsible father. He sent all of his children to the best schools in West Africa and the West.

At the 1884 Berlin Conference, however, the other European powers designated Opobo as British territory, and the British soon moved to claim it. King Jaja of Opobo was made to sign a peace treaty with the British under the orders of Consul Hewet. The treaty made Opobo city a protectorate under the British. King Jaja only agreed to the treaty after it was agreed that the clause under the treaty that allowed free trade and unlimited access to the city be removed.

A year later, the British Empire declared the Gulf of Guinea a British protectorate, allowing free trade, and Jaja opposed this ruling, declaring that his city would not be affected by such rules. He was labelled a terrorist and accused of illegal trade and plans to rid his city of the British.

When King Jaja refused to cease taxing British traders, in September 1887, Henry Hamilton Johnston, a British vice-consul, invited him to negotiations, which he accepted after several appeals. Johnson brought a "Warship" named HMS Goshawk to Opobo and invited Jaja on board. He assured Jaja that nothing would happen to him.

When he went on board the ship, he was given two bad choices by Johnson. One was that if he would not allow the Europeans access, he could go back and face immediate bombardment from the British navy, while the other was that he would go into exile. Jaja, being a man of strong values and principles chose not to back down, the British arrested him and tried him in Accra in the then Gold Coast (Ghana). Later, they took him to London for some time, where he met Queen Victoria and was her guest at Buckingham Palace.

No one knew what transpired between King Jaja and Queen Victoria, but after some time, he was finally deported to the West Indies. While in exile in the Caribbean, his presence was alleged to be the cause of immense civil unrest among the people of Barbados.

Barbadians, mostly of African (Nigeria) descent, had heard rumours that an African king had been apprehended and was on his way to the island. They rallied themselves together to give him a befitting reception. It was quite an interesting episode of his life in Barbados. The British brought him and wanted to try him on the Island for his "crimes", but the people of the Island felt insulted about how an African King had been subjected to such ridicule and shame.

Just when the ship made berth at the water side, the people of the island rushed and camped at the waterside to avoid the British bringing King Jaja to the colonial courthouse, which was in the middle of the Village's square. They literally camped at the water side throughout the night.

The next day, which was a Sunday, the people of the island held their church service on the waterside, right by the ship. Jaja came out before the service was over, and the women greeted him as a King from their ancestral land with a loud cry. The crowd went berserk and hysterical. The British feared that they might plan an escape plan for Jaja, so they got their bags and sailed back to St. Vincent.

King Jaja was moved from one place to another, around the West Indies so that his family lineage could not be traced in St. Vincent (Saint Vincent and the Grenadines). It was said at a time that he got married and had children.

"Jaja", in the West Indies (Barbados and St. Vincent), is a common slang term for someone who is arrogant and who carries himself or herself with an air of pride and dignity. This is coined after the way King Jaja held his head up high while he was on the island.

After years of campaigning for his freedom, Jaja was moved to the Island of São Vicente, Cape Verde, off the coast of West Africa, to prevent the possibility of a revolt. He eventually won his liberty after years of fighting against his wrongful abduction, and it was agreed by the British Parliament that he could be repatriated to his kingdom state of Opobo. Jaja now well advanced in age, longed to see his beloved Opobo land again.

In 1891, after several appeals to the British Empire against his unfair treatment, King Jaja was granted permission to return to his city-state of Opobo, but he died on his journey home. It is widely speculated that he was poisoned to death after being served a cup of tea with strict orders to be given to him. His body was shipped instead to Tenerife in the Canary Islands, where he was buried.

Following his exile and death, the power of the Opobo state rapidly declined, the land was plagued with slave raids, riots and the British exploited the land for her natural resources. After many years of clamour and protest, his body was properly exhumed and sent back to his beloved Opobo kingdom, where he was laid to rest. His remains are now a sacred (grave) shrine behind the Palace of the Amanyanabo of Opobo.

7. Onyeama N'Eke (Circa 1970 – 1933)

Onyeama was born in the 1870s. He was the youngest of the ten children of Özö Omulu Onwusi, a polygamous titled man of means, and the only son of his mother – Chinazungwa Ijeonyeabo of the nearby Ebe community. At the age of seven years, Onyeama's father initiated him into the masquerade society, a puberty rite of passage that showed the promise of the young man. Onyeama's father died thereafter. His mother also died, probably killed for poisoning a man who had threatened her son, Onyeama, with violence.

Brought up by his half-brother, Amadiezeoha Nwankwo Onwusi, Onyeama worked hard and made his mark in business. Probably as a slave merchant, he travelled to the famous Arọ-controlled trading centres, including Abiriba, Arọchukwu, Arọndizuọgụ, Bende, Oguta, Uburu, etc. When British rule reached Eke in 1908, Onyeama was rich enough to buy his way into the Ọzọ title society and to marry a local beauty, Afịa Nwirediagụ, and later Gwachi Ebue.

Slowly but surely, Onyeama got the colonists to award him the "Warrant Chiefdom" of Eke. He took power and defined it. Onyeama saw himself as an absolute ruler whose authority could not be easily flouted. But the King of Onitsha, Obi Okosi I, also reigned. No Igbo king questioned the might of the supreme monarch of Onitsha, let alone supposedly "lesser chiefs" from northern Igboland.

Onyeama signalled quite early that the reign of the Obi of Onitsha was history turned upside down, because he considered the entire monarchy of Onitsha a sub-colonial setup of recent immigrants from the Benin Kingdom. If anything, he (Onyeama) was in the league of the Oba of Benin or Ooni of Ife, the Yoruba monarch. This set the stage for a looming showdown between the kings of the northeast Igbo (called the Wawa) and southwest Igbo (called the Ijekeebé).

And so, it was that in 1928 at the gathering of all major Igbo kings and chiefs in the old Onitsha Province (including Enugu) and beyond, in Enugu, the then capital of the Southern Provinces, to welcome Captain W. Buchanan-Smith, the recently appointed Lieutenant-Governor. The Obi of Onitsha, Chief Okosi I, naturally occupied the highest seat of honour reserved for the supposed traditional ruler of Igbo nation. When Onyeama came in later with his entourage of security men, chiefs, and Igbanküda drummers, he was outraged by the Obi's assumed position of supreme authority in his domain. He ordered the immediate removal of the powerful king of Onitsha.

A scene had ensued, with the district officer trying to placate Onyeama. Furiously, as legend had it, he uttered: "Wa" (the local linguage for "No"); for emphasis, and as a mark of immutability, he shouted: "Wa–wa!" [Never!], and turned and decreed to the colonial officers: "If that man is still occupying that seat when I come back, the leopard will eat him." Onyeama got his way, and prevailed as the greatest king in town!

Chief Okosi was persuaded to think that because the colonial administration had put Enugu under Onitsha Province, he had automatically become the Chief of entire Igboland. This was a mistaken belief because, as was later pointed out to him, Chief Onyeama was equally a colonial recognised chief.

Considered an upstart by those who have had longer socio-economic intercourse with the British, Onyeama did not make himself many friends. A record was waxed in the 1930s accusing him of burying an unfaithful wife alive! A court order forced the German company that waxed the slanderous record to withdraw it from circulation. This and many other image-destructive stories of absolute tyranny, wife-snatching, and even murder have never removed from the legend of Onyeama. His people looked at him with a mixture of awe and admiration. His secret police (made up of hand-picked, local wrestling champions) struck so much fear into both chiefs and commoners that generations still respect the might of this great king.

Generally regarded as the King of Agbaja, Onyeama N'Eke was the greatest king in northern Igboland. He was probably the greatest Igbo king in living memory. From his palace in Eke, Onyeama reigned over the entire Agbaja, from the Oji River through Udi and Ezeagu to the present-day political capital of Igboland, Enugu, and even the Nkanu and Ogui communities.

It was Chief Onyeama that brought Christianity, in particular, Catholicism, and Western education to northern Igboland. Stories had it that the Church Missionary Society (CMS), was the first to come, and because they were teaching in Igbo language, Onyeama jettisoned them and went to Igbariam to fetch the Catholics, who were using both Latin and English languages. He wanted something different. He gave the Catholics land where they built both the church and school.

Onyeama was also instrumental to the establishment and growth of Enugu Colliery. He led the "Udi Chiefs" that signed agreement with the colonial government for the exploration and exploitation of coal mining in Enugu. He also created a conducive environment for the mining and ensured that labour was promptly and constantly supplied to the Colliery Management.

8. Nnete Okorie-Egbe Nwanyereuwa (Leader Of 1929 Aba Women 'Riot') (1866 - 1968)

Princess Nnete Okorie-Egbe of Akwete was the fearless leader in the 1929 women's riot of Aba, protesting unfair taxation of women. She used her time, talent, and enthusiasm to enrich the lives of others and make a difference in her society. She was imprisoned by the British colonial administration for two years in Port Harcourt, but was later released to a hero's welcome as the colonial administration backed down and reversed itself, by abolishing taxation on women.

The Aba Women's Riot featured women rebelling against economic and socio-political oppressions in Bende, Umuahia, and other regions of Igboland. Over 10,000 women came out to protest, from majorly six ethnic groups: Ibibio, Andoni, Ogoni, Bonny, Opobo, and Igbo.

The Aba women's riot did not just happen. It had months of tension leading up to it. The power situation in Igbo land had a very large disparity between it and other parts of Nigeria. The Igbo did not have a unified political institution as in the Northern and Western parts of the country; hence it was harder to enforce the Indirect Rule system of administration instituted by Lord Lugard in 1914 in Igboland.

The indirect rule system in Igboland involved the appointment of "warrant chiefs", who were not necessarily people that were respected by the communities. But they became an enforced symbol of power. They became increasingly oppressive within a few years as a result of their vested interests.

Direct taxation on men was introduced in 1928 without major incidents, thanks to the careful propaganda during the preceding twelve months. In September 1929, Captain J. Cook, an assistant district officer, was sent to take over the Bende Division temporarily from the serving district officer. Upon taking over, Cook found the slated nominal rolls for tax inadequate because they did not include details of the number of wives, children, and livestock in each household. He decided to revise the nominal roll to include these.

The "Aba Women's Riot" was sparked by a dispute between a woman named Nwanyeruwa and a man, Mark Emereuwa, who were helping to make a census of the people living in the town controlled by the Warrant Chief Okugo. Nwanyeruwa was of Ngwa ancestry, and had been married in the town of Oloko. In Oloko, the census was related to taxation, and women in the area were worried about who would tax them, especially during the period of hyper-inflation in the late 1920s. The financial crash of 1929 impeded women's ability to trade and produce, so they sought assurance from the colonial government that they would not to be required to pay taxes. Faced with a political a political impasse, the women agreed not to pay taxes or have their property appraised.

On the morning of November 18, 1929, Emereuwa arrived at Nwanyereuwa's house and approached Nwanyereuwa since her husband, Ojim, had already died. He told the widow to "count her goats, sheep, and people." Since Nwanyereuwa understood this to mean, "how many of these things do you have so we can tax you based on them", she was angry. She replied by saying: "Was your widowed mother counted?" meaning, "that women don't pay tax in traditional Igbo society."

The two exchanged angry words, and Emeruwa grabbed Nwanyeruwa by the throat. Nwanyeruwa went to the town square to discuss the incident with other women who happened to be holding a meeting and to tell them about the issue of taxing women. Believing they would also be taxed based on Nwanyeruwa's account, the Oloko women invited other women by sending palm fronds from other areas in the Bende District, as well as from Umuahia and Ngwa. They gathered nearly 10,000 women who protested at the office of Warrant Chief Okugo, demanding his resignation and calling for a trial.

Nwanyereuwa played a major role in keeping the protests non-violent. Under her advice, the women protested in song and dance, "sitting" on the Warrant Chiefs until they surrendered their insignia of office and resigned. As the revolt spread, other groups followed this pattern, making the women's protest a peaceful one. Other groups came to Nwanyeruwa to get in writing the inspirational results of the protests, which, as Nwanyeruwa saw them, were that, "women will not pay tax till the world ends and chiefs are not to exist anymore."

Women from Oloko and elsewhere brought monetary contributions to Madam Nwanyeruwa for helping them avoid paying taxes. Unfortunately, many women rioted and attacked chiefs, destroying their homes, thus causing the revolt to be marked as violent.

Women would gather at the compound of the man in question, sang and danced while detailing the women's grievances against him.

The women would often bang on his hut, demolish it, or plaster it with mud. Actions like mistreating his wife or violating women's market rules were punishable by being "sit on." If necessary, these practises were continued until he repented and changed his ways. The women also used nakedness as a weapon. The nakedness of women was considered a taboo in many African communities, indicating the power women possessed to stop the malfeasance.

When it came to the warrant chiefs, along with singing and dancing around the houses and offices, the women would follow their every move, invading their space and forcing the men to pay attention. The wives of the warrant chiefs were often disturbed, and they too would put pressure on the warrant chiefs to listen to the demands of the women. This tactic of "sitting on the warrant chiefs," that is, following them everywhere and anywhere, was very popular with the women in Igboland, and used to great effect. Through the choice of clothing, the use of body language, and the choice of song, they draw attention to the role and status of women in Igboland, particularly in the protection of the good of the land.

The result was that women were able to transform "traditional methods for networking and expressing disapproval" into powerful mechanisms that successfully challenged and disrupted the local colonial administration. The women's protests were carried out on a scale that the colonial state had never witnessed in any part of Africa. The rebellion extended over six thousand square miles, containing all of Owerri and Calabar provinces, home to roughly two million people.

Until the end of December 1929, when troops restored order, ten native courts were destroyed, a number of others were damaged, houses of native court personnel were attacked, and European factories at Imo River, Aba, Mbawsi, and Amata were looted. About 46 women attacked prisons and released prisoners. But the response of the colonial authority was also decisive. By the time order was restored, about fifty-five women had been killed by the colonial troops.

In addition, the positions of women in society were greatly improved as women were appointed to serve as warrant chiefs in some areas. The Aba Women's Riot remains an important historic event that speaks about the underestimated strength of women who came together and showed courage, bravery, rebellion, and even sacrifice while fighting an oppressive system. Nwanyeruwa died in 1968, during the Nigerian/Biafra Civil War, at the age of 102.

9. Simeon Ọnwu (December 28, 1908 - June 4, 1969)

Simeon Ezievuo Ọnwụ was a Nigerian physician and the first medical doctor from the Igbo ethnic group in Eastern Nigeria whose prominence is credited with hastening the formation of the Igbo Union. He was born on December 28, 1908, in Affa, in the Udi Local Government Area of Enugu State. Simon Onwu was the son of Chief Amadị Ọnwụbụnta and Madam Nwalute Ọnwubụnta of Amozalla Affa in Udi Local Government Area.

Dr. Onwu began his elementary schooling at St. Mary's School, Onitsha, where he was brought up as a Catholic. He then attended Wesley Boys' High School, Lagos before transferring to King's College, Lagos. However, he did not complete his secondary education in Lagos, for in 1924, he accompanied Chief Onyeama Onwusi of Eke as his personal confidant on an extended trip to the United Kingdom. He returned to Britain in 1925 to study, and in 1927, obtained his London Matriculation Certificate. Later that year, he went to the University of Edinburgh Medical School and obtained the degrees of MB and ChB in July 1932, thus becoming the first medical doctor from the Igbo ethnic group in Eastern Nigeria. He also obtained the Diploma in Tropical Medicine and Hygiene from the University of Liverpool in 1932. After that, he went to Coombe Hospital in the Republic of Ireland and got his Licentiate in midwifery.

Dr. Simeon Onwu returned to Nigeria in 1933 and joined the Colonial Civil Service as a junior medical officer in Port Harcourt, where he spent the next two years. His return to Eastern Nigeria coincided with the emergence of political activities among the Igbo in the new urban setting of colonial Nigeria. It is on record that the first time in which Port Harcourt's Igbo acted in concert and upon awareness of their common linguistic and cultural heritage was the occasion of the "welcome home" reception held for Dr Onwu by prominent Igbo there. The success of the Port Harcourt reception was instrumental in the decision to transform the reception committee into a permanent Igbo Union in Port Harcourt. His return also inspired the formation of similar cultural organisations in Lagos and elsewhere in the country.

He worked as a medical officer in different parts of Nigeria for the next 27 years. In 1948, he returned to Britain for a postgraduate course, and in 1950, he became Senior Medical Officer in Aba. He was promoted two years later to the grade of Deputy Director of Medical Services in the Eastern Region. In 1957, Dr. Onwu became the first African Director of Medical Services in the Eastern Region, holding the post along with that of Permanent Secretary in the Ministry of Health until he retired from the public service in 1963.

In 1953, Dr Ọnwụ was awarded the Coronation Medal, and in 1954 and 1956, Queen Elizabeth II of England conferred upon him the Order of the British Empire (OBE) and Member of the Royal Vatican Order, respectively, in recognition of his contributions and achievements. In recognition of his devout life as a Catholic, he was awarded the Papal Order of the Knight of Saint Sylvester by Pope Paul VI. In 1968, Dr. Onwu was again honoured by the Vatican by having his name enrolled in the Papal Scroll of Honour.

In June 1964, Dr. Ọnwụ was appointed Chairman of the Eastern Nigerian Housing Corporation, a post he held until his death. In 1965, he was elected the first African Vice-President of the International Union of Building Societies. He travelled extensively, visiting the United States of America, the former Union of Soviet Socialist Republics (USSR), Germany, and India under the auspices of the World Health Organization (WHO), and represented Nigeria in many world conferences.

Dr. Ọnwụ was Chairman of the Red Cross Society, Eastern Nigeria; Chairman of Cosmas and Damain; and Vice-Patron of the Society for the Prevention of Cruelty to Children.

During the Nigerian civil war, he suffered from a prolonged illness that made him to travel to London for medical treatment. He died at St. Bart's Hospital, London, on June 4, 1969.

10. Robert Benjamin Ageh Wellesley Cole (March 7, 1907 – October 31, 1995)

Robert Benjamin Ageh Wellesley Cole was a Sierra Leonean medical doctor who was the first West African to become a Fellow of the Royal College of Surgeons of England. He was born at No. 15 Pownall Street, Freetown, Sierra Leone, to Wilfred Sydney Wellesley Cole and his wife, Elizabeth Cole (née Okorafor-Smart).

The Wellesley-Cole family had three other children, including Dr. Irene Ighodaro. The Okorafor-Smart family was a prominent Creole family whose members were mostly liberated Igbo Africans. Wilfred Cole was a successful engineer and the first Sierra Leonean to serve as an assistant for the Public Water Works Department in Freetown. The Wellesley-Cole family was a middle-class Creole family, and Robert Wellesley-Cole grew up in a household of relative comfort and privilege.

Wellesley-Cole was educated at the Government Model School in Freetown, Sierra Leone, where he was taught by teachers such as William Campbell. Following the completion of his primary education, Wellesley-Cole was enrolled as the first student of the Government Model Secondary School, currently known as the Prince of Wales Secondary School. He completed his studies at Prince of Wales and then proceeded to the CMS Grammar School, currently known as the Sierra Leone Grammar School, where he eventually became Head Prefect in his final year. He passed the Cambridge Entrance Certification in 1925.

Wellesley-Cole obtained upper-second class honours from Fourah Bay College and proceeded to attend Newcastle University Medical School. He was the first West African to become a member of the Royal College of Surgeons of England. Due to discrimination in the West African Medical Service, Wellesley-Cole mainly practised in the United Kingdom, Ibadan, Nigeria, and Sierra Leone. Following Sierra Leone's independence on April 27, 1961, the then Prime Minister, Milton Margai, offered Wellesley-Cole the position of senior medical officer.

11. Nnamdi Azikiwe (November 16, 1904 – May 11, 1996)

Nnamdi Benjamin Azikiwe, generally referred to as "Zik of Africa", was a Nigerian statesman and political leader who served as the first indigenous Governor-General of Nigeria (1960-1963) and first President of Nigeria (1963-1966), though in non-executive positions. Azikiwe was born of Igbo parents in Zungeru, in present day Niger State, and spoke fluently the three main Nigerian languages of Hausa, Igbo, and Yoruba.

Considered a driving force behind the nation's independence, Zik came to be known as the "father of Nigerian nationalism." He travelled to the United States, where he was known as Ben Azikiwe, and attended Storer College, Columbia University, the University of Pennsylvania, and Howard University. He returned to Africa in 1934, where he began working as a journalist in the Gold Coast (Ghana). In British West Africa, Azikiwe advocated Nigerian and African nationalism as a journalist and a political leader.

Azikiwe's initial goal was to get a position commensurate with his education, but after several unsuccessful applications, he accepted an offer from a Ghanaian businessman, Alfred Ocansey, to become the founding editor of the *African Morning Post*. He was given a free hand to run the newspaper, and he recruited many of its original staff.

As editor, Azikiwe promoted a pro-African nationalist agenda. He also criticised those Africans who belonged to the 'elite' of colonial society and favoured retaining the existing order, as they regarded it as the basis of their well-being. During his stay in Accra, Azikiwe advanced his new Africa philosophy, which was later explored in his book, Renascent Africa.

Azikiwe's philosophic ideal was a state where Africans would be divorced from ethnic affiliations and traditional authorities and transformed by five philosophical pillars of: "spiritual balance, social regeneration, economic determinism, mental emancipation, and risorgimento nationalism". Azikiwe did not shy away from Gold Coast politics, and the paper supported the local Mambii Party.

The *African Morning Post* published a May 15, 1936 article titled: "Has the African a God?" by I. T. A. Wallace-Johnson, and as Editor, Azikiwe was tried for sedition. He was originally found guilty and sentenced to six months in prison, but his conviction was overturned on appeal.

Azikiwe returned to Nigeria in 1937 and founded the *West African Pilot*, a newspaper that he used to promote nationalism in Nigeria. In addition to the Pilot, his Zik Group established newspapers in politically and economically important cities throughout the country. The group's flagship newspaper was the *West African Pilot*, which used Dante Alighieri's "Show the light and the people will find the way" as its motto. Other publications were the *Southern Nigeria Defender*, in Warri (later Ibadan), the *Eastern Guardian*, in Port Harcourt, and the Nigerian *Spokesman*, in Onitsha. In 1944, the group acquired Duse Mohamed's Comet.

Azikiwe's newspaper venture was a business and political tool. The Pilot focused less on advertising than on circulation, largely because expatriate firms dominated the Nigerian economy. Many of his newspapers emphasised sensationalism and human interest stories; the Pilot introduced sports coverage and a women's section, increasing coverage of Nigerian events compared with the competing *Daily Times* Newspaper (which emphasised expatriate and foreign news service stories). The Pilot's initial run was 6,000 copies daily; at its peak in 1950, it was printing over 20,000 copies.

Azikiwe revolutionised the West African newspaper industry, demonstrating that English language journalism could be successful. By 1950, the five leading African-run newspapers in the Eastern Region (including the Nigerian Daily Times) were outsold by the Pilot.

On July 8, 1945, the Nigerian government banned Azikiwe's *West African Pilot* and *Daily Comet* for misrepresenting information about a general strike. Although Azikiwe acknowledged this, he continued publishing articles about the strike in the Guardian. At his death on May 11, 1996, The *New York Times* commented that Azikiwe "towered over the affairs of Africa's most populous nation, attaining the rare status of a truly national hero who came to be admired across the regional and ethnic lines dividing his country."

Azikiwe became active in the Nigerian Youth Movement (NYM), the country's first nationalist organisation on his return to Nigeria from Ghana. Although he supported Samuel Akisanya as the NYM candidate for a vacant seat in the Legislative Council in 1941, the NYM executive council selected Ernest Ikoli. Azikiwe resigned from the NYM, accusing the majority Yoruba leadership of discriminating against the Ijebu-Yoruba members and the Igbo. Some Ijebu members followed him, thus splitting the movement along ethnic lines.

Azikiwe entered formally into politics in 1944, co-founding the National Council of Nigeria and the Cameroons (NCNC) with Herbert Macaulay as President, and himself as Secretary-General. As a result of Azikiwe's support for the 1945 general strike and his attacks on the colonial government, his *West African Pilot* was suspended. During the strike, Azikiwe raised the alarm about an assassination plot by unknown individuals working on behalf of the colonial government. His basis for the allegation was a wireless message intercepted by a Pilot reporter. After receiving the intercepted message, Azikiwe went into hiding in Onitsha. The Pilot published sympathetic editorials during his absence, and many Nigerians believed the assassination story.

A militant youth movement, known as the Zikist Movement, led by Osita Agwuna, Raji Abdalla, Kolawole Balogun, M.C.K. Ajuluchukwu, and Abiodun Aloba, was established in 1946 to defend Azikiwe's life and his ideals of self-government. Inspired by his writings and Nwafor Orizu's "Zikism" philosophy, members of the movement soon began to advocate for positive and militant action to bring about self-government. Calls for action included strikes, the study of military science by Nigerian students overseas, and a boycott of foreign products.

In 1945, a British Colonial Governor, Arthur Richards, presented proposals for a revision of the Clifford's Constitution of 1922. Included in the proposal was an increase in the number of African members nominated to the legislative council. However, the changes were opposed by nationalists such as Azikiwe. NCNC politicians opposed the unilateral decisions made by Arthur Richards and a constitutional provision allowing only four elected African members, while the rest would be nominated candidates.

Another source of criticism was the lack of input into the advancement of Africans to senior civil service positions. The NCNC prepared to argue its case to the new Labour government in London. A tour of the country was begun to raise awareness of the party's concerns and to raise money for the UK protest. During the NCNC tour, President Herbert Macaulay died, and Azikiwe assumed leadership of the party. He led the delegation to London and, in preparation for the trip, travelled to the US to seek sympathy for the party's case. Azikiwe met Eleanor Roosevelt at Hyde Park, and spoke about the "emancipation of Nigeria from political tyranny, economic insecurity, and social disabilities."

The UK delegation included Azikiwe, Funmilayo Ransome-Kuti, Zanna Dipcharima, Abubakar Olorunimbe, Adeleke Adedoyin, and Nyong Essien. They visited the Fabian Society's Colonial Bureau, the Labor Imperial Committee, and the West African Students' Union to raise awareness of their proposals for amendments to the 1922 Constitution. Included in the NCNC proposals was consultation with Africans about changes to the Nigerian constitution that would give more power to the regional houses of assembly and limit the powers of the central legislative council to defence, currency, and foreign affairs. The delegation submitted its proposals to the Colonial Secretary, but little was done to change the Richards' proposals.

Under the Richards' Constitution, Azikiwe was elected to the Legislative Council in a Lagos municipal election from the Nigeria National Democratic Party (NNDP). He and the party representative did not attend the first session of the council, and agitation for changes to the Richards' Constitution led to the Macpherson Constitution. The Macpherson Constitution took effect in 1951 and, like the Richards' Constitution, called for elections to the regional House of Assembly. Azikiwe opposed the changes, and contested for the chance to change the new constitution. Staggered elections were held from August to December 1951.

In the Western Region, where Azikiwe stood, two parties were dominant: Azikiwe's NCNC and the Action Group led by Chief Obafemi Awolowo. Elections for the Western Regional Assembly were held in September and December 1951 because the Constitution allowed an electoral college to choose members of the national legislature; an Action Group majority in the house might prevent Azikiwe from going to the House of Representatives. He won a regional assembly seat from Lagos, but the opposition party claimed a majority in the House of Assembly, and Azikiwe did not represent Lagos in the federal House of Representatives.

In 1951, he became leader of the opposition to the government of Obafemi Awolowo in the Western Region's House of Assembly. The non-selection of Azikiwe to the National Assembly caused an uproar in the west. An agreement by elected NCNC members from Lagos to step down for Azikiwe if he was not nominated broke down. Azikiwe blamed the constitution and wanted changes made.

Azikiwe moved to the Eastern Region in 1952, and the NCNC dominated regional assembly made proposals to accommodate him. Although the party's regional and central ministers were asked to resign in a cabinet reshuffle, most ignored the request. The regional assembly then passed a vote of no confidence on the ministers, while the appropriation bills sent to the ministry were rejected. This created an impasse in the region, and the Lieutenant Governor dissolved the regional house. A new election returned Azikiwe as a member of the Eastern House of Assembly. He was selected as Chief Minister and became Premier of Nigeria's Eastern Region in 1954, when it became a federating unit.

Azikiwe became Governor-General of Nigeria on November 16, 1960, with Abubakar Tafawa Balewa as Prime Minister. He also became the first Nigerian to be named to the Privy Council of the United Kingdom. When Nigeria became a republic in 1963, he was its first President. In both posts, Azikiwe's role was largely ceremonial.

Azikiwe and his civilian colleagues were removed from office in the January 15, 1966, military coup, and he was the most prominent politician to avoid assassination after the coup.

Azikiwe was a spokesman for Biafra and advised its leader, Chukwuemeka Odumegwu Ojukwu, during the Biafran War (1967–1970). However, he switched his allegiance back to Nigeria during the war and appealed to Ojukwu to end the war in pamphlets and interviews. The *New York Times* said about his politics, "Throughout his life, Dr. Azikiwe's alliance with Northerners put him at odds with Obafemi Awolowo, a socialist-inclined leader of the Yoruba; the country's other important southern group."

After the war, Azikiwe was appointed Chancellor of the University of Lagos from 1972 to 1976. He joined the Nigerian Peoples Party in 1978 and made unsuccessful bids for the presidency in 1979 and 1983. He left politics involuntarily after the December 31, 1983 military coup. Azikiwe died at the age of 91 on May 11, 1996 at the University of Nigeria Teaching Hospital in Enugu after a long illness and was buried in his native Onitsha.

Nnamdi Azikiwe established the University of Nigeria, Nsukka, in 1960, while Queen Elizabeth II appointed him to the Privy Council of the United Kingdom. He was honoured with the title of Grand Commander of theFederal Republic (GCFR), Nigeria's highest national honour, in 1980.

12. Nwafor Orizu (July 17, 1914 – 1999)

Prince Abyssinia Akweke Nwafor Orizu was Nigeria's second Senate President from November 16, 1960 to January 15, 1966 during the Nigerian First Republic. He also served as Acting President of Nigeria from late 1965 until the January 1966 military coup. Orizu was a member of the Nnewi Royal Family. The Nwafor Orizu College of Education in Nsugbe, Anambra State, is named after him.

Nwafor Orizu was born in 1914 into the royal house of Nnewi, Anambra State. He went to the United States in 1939, earning a degree in government at Ohio State University and an M.A. degree at Columbia University. He was an advocate of the "horizontal", broad system of

American education, as opposed to the narrow "perpendicular" British system, and earned the nickname "Orizontal", a play on his name and a reference to his constant discussion of the theme. As discussed in his 1944 book, Without Bitterness, Orizu was a passionate advocate of introducing the American system in Nigeria. He established the American Council on African Education (ACAE), which obtained numerous tuition scholarships from American sources for the benefit of African students.

Around 1949, Orizu bought the Enitona High School and Enitona Printing Press from a supporter for only £500, which he borrowed. Another supporter sold him a luxury bus on an installment plan. He established a newspaper known as The *West Africa Examiner* and became the managing director, while M. C. K. Ajuluchukwu was the editor. Orizu went to Enugu to console the striking miners after the shooting of 21 coal miners on November 18, 1949. Possibly in reaction to a fiery speech that he made there, the British colonial authorities sentenced him to seven years in jail for allegedly misappropriating the funds of the ACAE. But later, Roy Wilkins, chairman of ACAE in the US, wrote a letter to Nnamdi Azikiwe, exonerating Dr Nwafor Orizu of any financial impropriety.

Orizu ran successfully for election as an independent candidate to represent Onitsha Division and became the chief whip in the Eastern House of Assembly. Later, he joined with other independent candidates to form the National Council of Nigeria and Cameroon (NCNC). He played a central role in helping Zik become Premier of the Eastern Region, using his influence in the NCNC to persuade Professor Eyo Ita to resign as Premier of the Region. Azikiwe appointed Nwafor Orizu the Minister of Local Government.

When Nigeria attained independence on October 1, 1960, Nwafor Orizu became the President of the Nigerian Senate. When the President of Nigeria, Nnamdi Azikiwe, left the country in late 1965, first for Europe and then on a cruise to the Caribbean, under the law, Orizu became Acting President during his absence and had all the powers of the President.

On January 15, 1966, a coup was launched by a group of dissatisfied young military officers led by Major Chukwuma Kaduna Nzeogwu. The army quickly suppressed the revolt but assumed power when it was evident that key politicians had been eliminated, including the Prime Minister, Abubakar Tafawa Balewa; the Premier of the

Northern Region, Sir Ahmadu Bello; and the Premier of the Western Region, Chief Samuel Ladoke Akintola.

On January 16, Nwafor Orizu, made a nationwide broadcast, after he had briefed Dr. Nnamdi Azikiwe on the phone on the cabinet's decision and announced the cabinet's "voluntary" decision to transfer power to the armed forces. Major General Johnson Aguiyi-Ironsi then made his own broadcast, accepting the "invitation". On January 17, Major General Ironsi established the Supreme Military Council in Lagos and effectively suspended the constitution.

After the coup, Nwafor Orizu faded from the political scene but remained active in education. Before the civil war, he had set up a high school, the Nigerian Secondary School, in Nnewi. He remained its proprietor until the state government took over all the schools after the defeat of Biafra. After that, he continued as a teacher and an educator, publishing several books.

13. Dennis Osadebay (June 29, 1911—December 26, 1994)

Dennis Chukude Osadebay, politician, poet, journalist, and former premier of the defunct Mid-Western Region of Nigeria, which now comprises Edo and Delta States, was one of the pioneering Nigerian poets who wrote in English. As a politician, he detested party politics and tried to form unbiased opinions on important matters of the period. He was also a leader of the movement to create a Mid-Western Region during the Nigerian First Republic.

Osadebay was born in Asaba to parents of mixed cultural backgrounds. He attended the Asaba Government School in Asaba, the Sacred Heart School in Calabar, and the Hope Waddell Training Institute. He joined the labour force in 1930 as a customs officer working in Lagos, Port Harcourt and Calabar. He subsequently went to England to study law during the 1940s. It was while studying that he started publishing poetic verses. He was called a newspaper poet at the time because most of what he wrote was printed in the *West African Pilot* and a few other newspapers.

In his writings, Osadebay used both his personal life and public events as inspiration. In "Africa Sings", a collection of poems, he delved into themes from a personal point of view, such as a sullen poem written about his 25th birthday and the coming of middle age. However, his best work in the volume was written from an impersonal viewpoint.

In his adventurous poem "black man troubles", he used Pidgin English to lament the plight of black Africans in colonial Africa and social injustice. His poems were also notable for faithfully representing modern poetic rhythm.

Dennis Osadebay was one of the founding members of the National Council of Nigeria and the Cameroons (NCNC) in 1944. He left the country to study law a few years later. After completing his studies, he returned to Nigeria, established a law practise in Aba, and was also made the legal adviser to the NCNC. He ran for and was elected to the Western Region House of Assembly in 1951, which was dominated by the rival Action Group (AG). From 1954 to 1956, he was the region's opposition leader, but he handed over the reins to Adegoke Adelabu in 1956. After the death of Adegoke Adelabu, he took on his familiar oppositional role in 1958.

In 1960, Osadebay became the President of the Nigerian Senate, and upon the creation of the Mid-Western Region in 1963, he became the pioneer Premier of the newly created region. He remained as Premier till the military takeover on January 15, 1966. He died on December 26, 1994.

14. Mbonu Ojike (C 1914 - November 29, 1956)

Mazi Mbonu Ojike was a nationalist, writer, choirmaster, organist, and a teacher in an Anglican school. He was also a student in America and then a cultural and economic nationalist. In 1951, Ojike served as the Second Vice President of the National Council of Nigeria and the Cameroons (NCNC) and as the Deputy Mayor of Lagos. He was popularly known as the "boycott king" because of his slogan, 'boycott the boycottables' by which he advocated for the boycott or rejection of foreign cultures.

In the United States of America, Mbonu Ojike spent eight years in intellectual pursuit and improving outsiders' knowledge of Africa, speaking from an African perspective. Upon his return to Nigeria, he promoted his brand of Africanisation, a persistent consumption of African forms of clothing, food, dress, religion, and dance while also believing in the selective benefits of foreign amenities. Ojike made common the use of the word, "Mazi" as a substitute for "Mr."

Among his publications were "My Africa" and "I Have Two Countries." Ojike was a sophisticated critic who was passionate about "economic nationalism." He was sometimes outspoken, which earned him some enmity.

Ojike was born to the family of Mgbeke and Mbonu Emeanulu in Arondizuogu, in present day Imo State. Despite his father's protestations, Ojike attended Anglican schools, and had his primary education at CMS School, Arondizuogu. In 1925, he was a pupil teacher at Arondizuogu and Abagana Anglican Central School. In 1929, he entered CMS Teachers Training College, Awka, to train as a teacher, finishing training in 1931.

Ojike soon gained employment at Dennis Memorial Grammar School (DMGS), Onitsha, where he was choirmaster, Sunday School Supervisor, and school organist. He gradually became dissatisfied with the missionaries' form of education, criticising it as not paramount to African development and suppressing African culture. Soon, he left the school and worked as an agent for the *West African Pilot* newspaper. Motivated by the writings of James Aggrey and Nnamdi Azikiwe, Ojike decided to pursue further education abroad.

In November 1938, Ojike left Nigeria with eleven other students for higher education. He started college at Lincoln University (Pennsylvania) before leaving for the University of Illinois at Urbana-Champaign and finishing his studies at Ohio State University with a bachelor's degree in economics. He subsequently earned a master's degree in education and administration. In the United States, Ojike lectured extensively about his experience living in an African cultural environment and his views about colonialism and racism. He wrote rejoinders to articles that portrayed Africa in a negative light, in addition to writing two books and a pamphlet on African culture. His books explained cultural practises and debunked the notion of African inferiority.

In "My Africa", Ojike introduced Americans to his culture partly as a way to promote cultural relationships between the two cultures. In America, he embraced and learned about a democratic system of governance. He was also passionate about cultural and political nationalism. He opposed colonialism as harmful to democracy, and the notion that African society is a passing fad.

Though a cultural nationalist, Ojike did not believe in the rejection of all forms of Western culture, but in the notion of 'cultural plasticity' where Africans borrow certain aspects of a foreign culture but still retain the core social and political values that promote stability, progress, and dignity. In 1941, Mbonu Ojike, K.O. Mbadiwe, and John Karefa-Smart established the African Students Association of the United States and Canada. Among the objectives of the organisation were the welfare of African students and the interpretation of African culture for a western audience.

Ojike was also a member of two pan African organizations, namely the American Council for African Education and the African Academy of Arts and Research. The latter was founded by Ojike, Mbadiwe, Orizu, and Lawrence Reddick. The academy sponsored a series of well received dance events between 1943 and 1945. In 1945, Ojike attended the United Nations Conference on International Organisations as a member of these organisations.

Upon his return to Nigeria, one of his early ideas was the establishment of a university based on the American higher education model. A primary strategy of the university was to save cost by providing education to students locally instead of going abroad to earn degrees. However, the idea never came to fruition.

Between 1947 and 1948, Mbonu Ojike was the general manager and a columnist for the *West African Pilot*, and wrote two columns: "Weekend Catechism" and "Something to Think About". In 1948, he left the Pilot to start a business venture, the African Development Corporation. He raised capital and bought a popular bakery formerly owned by Amos Schackleford.

After the death of 21 striking coal miners in Enugu in 1949, Ojike, in response, wrote a column calling for concerted action against colonial authorities. The article was interpreted as sedition, and Ojike was fined. The shootings also motivated him to co-found a broad organisation called the National Emergency Committee, with Akinola Maja as chairperson. The organisation briefly existed for a year and was a national voice opposing racial discrimination before political rivalry broke it up.

Ojike was a supporter of a federal system of governance in Nigeria. At a general conference in Ibadan organised to draft the Macpherson Constitution, Ojike and Eyo Ita co-wrote a minority report criticising the adoption of a regional government system and the introduction of the House of Chiefs instead of a federal system composed of states with ethnic borders and the removal of vested interests in governance.

Ojike played an important role in the activities of the National Council of Nigeria and the Cameroon (NCNC), particularly in their rallies. He was an agent for mass mobilisation, and his "Freedom Song" was a popular tune at NCNC rallies. He was the Second National Vice President of the party and contested and won a seat to represent Lagos at the Legislative Council, where in 1951 he was appointed Deputy Mayor of Lagos.

In 1953, Mbonu Ojike became involved in Eastern Nigeria politics and development when he was elected to the Eastern regional assembly. He was first appointed regional Minister of Works in 1954 before moving to finance in the same year. As a minister, he supported the introduction of "Pay as You Earn" taxation and was involved in the establishment of the Eastern Region Finance Corporation and road construction.

However, allegations of corruption swirled about his involvement in the corporation's purchase of shares in the African Continental Bank while he was the sitting Minister of Finance. He resigned his position in 1956. At the Foster-Sutton Tribunal, which was investigating the activities of the corporation, Ojike was resolute in his loyalty to Azikiwe, the founder of the bank and NCNC leader, especially when the arguments were framed in the form of economic freedom for the people or extending Western imperialism.

Ojike believed in selective importation and imitation. He wanted Africa to be economically free and politically independent. One of his slogans was "boycott the boycottables", which called for a reduction in consumption of Western goods and investments in education and other economically productive ventures. He preferred palm wine to imported gin and promoted the wearing of African clothes among elite civil servants. He voiced support for the introduction of an African national costume and supported African music and dance. His interest in African music led to the founding of the All African Dance Association.

Ojike married two wives and had five children. He was a member of the Reformed Ogboni Society. He died on November 29, 1956, at Parklane Hospital, Enugu, and was buried the next day.

15. Michael Okpara (December 25, 1920 – December 17, 1984)

Dr. Michael Iheọnụkara Ọkpara served as Premier of Eastern Region from 1959 to 1966 during the First Republic. At the age of 39, he was the nation's youngest Premier. Okpara was a strong advocate of what he called "pragmatic socialism" and believed that agricultural reform was crucial to the ultimate success of Nigeria.

Michael Okpara was born on December 25, 1920, at Ụmụegwu Ọkpụala, Ọhụhụ, Umuahia, in present-day Abia State. Although he was the son of a labourer, he was able to attend mission schools and later went to Uzuakoli Methodist College, Umuahia, where he won a scholarship to study medicine at Yaba Higher College, Lagos. After completing his medical studies at the Nigerian School of Medicine, he worked briefly as a government medical officer before returning to Umuahia to set up a private practice.

Okpara became interested in the Zikist Movement, a militant wing of the National Council of Nigeria and Cameroon (NCNC), while working in his practice. After rioting workers were shot by police at the Enugu coal mines in 1949, Okpara was arrested for his alleged complicity in inciting the riot, though he was soon released. After the granting of internal self-rule in 1952, he was elected to the Eastern Nigerian House of Assembly on the platform of the NCNC. Between 1952 and 1959, he held various cabinet positions in the Eastern regional government, ranging from Minister of Health to Minister of Agriculture and Production.

In 1953, when NCNC legislators revolted against the party leadership, he remained loyal and joined forces with Azikiwe. In November 1960, when Azikiwe left active politics to become Nigeria's first African Governor-General, Okpara was elected leader of the NCNC. His outspoken manner led to a severe strain in relations between his party and the ruling Northern Peoples Congress (NPC).

Okpara was the leader of the NCNC and Premier of Eastern Nigeria during the First Republic from 1959 to 1966. Although he was one of the politicians detained soon after the military coup of January 1966, he survived the army revolt, in which the two premiers of the North and the West, Sir Ahmadu Bello and Chief S.L. Akintola, respectively, were killed.

As Premier, Okpara ceded the day-to-day running of the NCNC to his old friend Dr G. C. Mbanugo; the civil service, to Sam Oti; the intelligentsia to Professor Kalu Ezera; and the economic domain, to Sir Louis Odumegwu Ojukwu.

A strong advocate of what he termed "pragmatic socialism", Okpara believed that Nigeria's salvation depended on a revolution in agriculture. To this end, he acquired and managed a large farm in his hometown, called Umuegwu Okpuala Mixed Farms, which inspired many Eastern Nigerian leaders to follow suit.

He also established a number of farm settlements, in Adani and Igbariam; established industries such as Golden Guinea Breweries and Ceramic Industries in Umuahia; Turners Asbestors and Nigergas in Emene, Enugu; a Textile Mill in Onitsha; and built the Hotel Presidential in Enugu and Port Harcourt, etc. Okpara also championed the educational and infrastructural development of the Eastern Region.

Michael Okpara never owned a house of his own while he was in government. When the Nigerian civil war ended, he went into exile in Ireland. Before his return from exile in 1979, his close associates and beneficiaries took up a collection to build him a house in his village, Umuegwu. Okpara died on December 17, 1984.

Michael Okpara was a member of the Royal Academy of Physicians of Great Britain. Michael Okpara Way, in Abuja, is named after him, as well as Michael Okpara University of Agriculture in Umudike, and Okpara Square in Enugu.

He received the award of Grand Commander of the Order of the Niger (GCON), one of Nigeria's highest honours in 1964. There is a statue of him in Enugu, and there is also another statue of him in Umuahia.

16. Akanu Ibiam (November 29, 1906 – July 1, 1995)

Sir Francis Akanu Ibiam, as he then was, KCMG, KBE, was a distinguished medical missionary who served as Governor of the Eastern Region of Nigeria from December 1960 until January 1966 during the Nigerian First Republic. He was first known as Francis Ibiam;
from 1951 to 1967 as Sir Francis Ibiam; and Dr. Akanu Ibiam, following his renunciation of British knighthood during the Nigeria-Biafra war.

Ibiam was born on November 29, 1906, in Unwana, Afikpo, in present-day Ebonyi State to Igbo parents. He was the second son of Chief Ibiam Aka, a traditional ruler of Unwana. He later ascended to the position of traditional ruler, Eze Ogo Isiala I of Unwana and Osuji of Uburu.

Ibiam attended the Hope Waddell Training Institute, Calabar, and King's College, Lagos, and was then admitted to the University of St. Andrews, graduating with a medical degree in 1934. He was accepted as a medical missionary of the Church of Scotland, in which role he established Abiriba Hospital (1936–1945) and later superintended mission hospitals at Itu and Uburu.

Ibiam was never ordained as a minister, but he was elected and ordained as an elder of the Presbyterian Church. He was appointed an honourary officer of the Order of the British Empire (OBE) in 1949 in honour of his work as a medical missionary for the Church of Scotland and was appointed an honorary Knight Commander of the Order of the British Empire (KBE) in 1951. Ibiam was president of the Christian Council of Nigeria from 1955 to 1958.

In 1957, he was appointed principal of Hope Waddell Institution, and in 1959, he became president of the University College of Ibadan. On a visit to then Northern Rhodesia, now Zambia, Ibiam was refused service at a café reserved for whites, an affair that became notorious. In 1962, he was chairman of the committee that established the Protestant Chapel called Christ Church Chapel at the University of Nigeria, Nsukka Campus.

In the lead-up to Nigeria's independence, Ibiam served in the Eastern Regional House of Assembly and in the legislative and executive councils. After Nigeria gained independence in 1960, Ibiam was appointed Governor of the Eastern Region. On August 24, 1962, he was appointed a Knight Commander of the Order of St. Michael and St. George (KCMG). He held the office until the military coup of January 15, 1966, that brought Major General Johnson Aguiyi-Ironsi to power.

During the Nigerian Civil War of 1967-1970, Ibiam actively assisted the Biafrans, helping to obtain relief supplies through his church contacts. As one of the six Presidents of the World Council of Churches (WCC), Ibiam spoke at the WCC meeting in Upsalla, Sweden, in July 1968, where the problem of relief for refugees was discussed. He was instrumental in ensuring that the nightly air lift of relief into Biafra was started. In 1969, he travelled across Canada to raise humanitarian aid and support for the people of Biafra. Ibiam returned his knighthood and renounced his English name, Francis, in protest against the British government's support of the Nigerian federal government.

Immediately after the war, Ibiam went to General Yakubu Gowon and threatened to call the Biafrans back to arms if his government continued to treat them as conquered people. He continued to work on reconstruction and hospital services and was responsible for the Bible Society of Nigeria and the Christian Medical Fellowship. Later, he became President of the All Africa Conference of Churches. Ibiam died on July 1, 1995. More than 20,000 people attended his funeral in Unwana.

17. Johnson Umunnakwe Aguiyi-Ironsi (March 3, 1924 –July 29, 1966)

Major General Johnson Thomas Umunnakwe Aguiyi-Ironsi, MVO, MBE, was the first Military Head of State of Nigeria. He seized power amid the ensuing chaos following the January 15, 1966 military coup, which decapitated the country's leadership.

Ironsi ruled from January 17, 1966 until his assassination on July 29, 1966 by a group of mutinous Northern Nigerian officers and men who were led by Major Murtala Mohammed and included Captain Theophilus Danjuma, Lieutenant Muhammadu Buhari, Lieutenant Ibrahim Babangida, and Lieutenant Sani Abacha, in a revolt against his government, in what was popularly called the July Counter Coup.

Thomas Umunnakwe Aguiyi-Ironsi was born into the family of Mazi Ezeugo Aguiyi in Ibeku, Umuahia, in the present-day Abia State. At the age of eight, he went to live with his elder sister, Anyamma, who was married to Theophilus Johnson, a Sierra Leonean diplomat working in Umuahia. Aguiyi-Ironsi subsequently took the last name of his brother-in-law as his first name, in admiration of Mr. Johnson for the father-figure role he played in his life.

Aguiyi-Ironsi had his primary and secondary school education in Umuahia and Kano, respectively. In 1942, at the age of 18, he joined the Nigerian Regiment of the West African Frontier Force (WAFF) as a private with the Seventh Battalion, against the wishes of his sister. He was promoted in 1946 to company sergeant major. In addition, he was sent on an officer training course at Staff College in Camberley, England, in 1946, while on June 12, 1949, after finishing his course at Camberley, he received a short-service commission as a Second Lieutenant in the Royal West African Frontier Force, with a subsequent retroactive promotion to Lieutenant, effective from the same date.

Aguiyi-Ironsi was granted a regular commission on May 16, 1953 (seniority from October 8, 1947), and was promoted to Captain with effect from the same date (seniority from October 8, 1951). Aguiyi-Ironsi was one of the officers who served as equerry for Queen Elizabeth II of the United Kingdom when she visited Nigeria in 1956, for which he was appointed a Member of the Royal Victorian Order (MVO). He was promoted to major on October 8, 1958.

In 1960, Aguiyi-Ironsi was made commandant of the Fifth Battalion in Kano, with the rank of lieutenant colonel. He later headed the Nigerian contingent force of the United Nations operation in the Congo. From 1961 to 1962, he served as the military attaché to the Nigerian High Commission in London, during which period he was promoted to the rank of Brigadier. During his tenure as military attaché, he attended courses at the Imperial Defence College (renamed the Royal College of Defence Studies in 1961), Seaford House, and Belgrave Square. He was appointed a Member of the Order of the British Empire, Military Division (MBE) in 1962.

In 1965, Aguiyi-Ironsi was promoted to the rank of major general. Major General C.B. Welby-Everard, the British-born General Officer Commanding (GOC) of the Nigerian Army, handed over his position to Major General Johnson Thomas Umnakwe Aguiyi-Ironsi that same year, making him the first indigenous Nigerian officer to lead the entire Nigerian Army.

In January 1966, a group of army officers, led by Major Chukwuma Nzeogwu, overthrew the central and regional governments of Nigeria, killed the Prime Minister, and tried to take control of the government in a failed coup d'état.

On January 17, 1966, Aguiyi-Ironsi was named Military Head of State, a position he held until July 29, 1966, when a group of Northern army officers revolted against his government, and killed him while he was on tour of the Western Region, along with his host, Francis Adekunle Fajuyi, Military Governor of the region.

18. Chukwuma Nzeọgwụ (February 26, 1937–July 29, 1967)

Patrick Chukwuma Kaduna Nzeọgwụ was a revolutionist who played a leading role in the first military coup d'état of January 15, 1966, which overthrew the First Nigerian Republic. Born in Kaduna to Igbo parents of Okpanam Town near Asaba in present-day Delta State, Nzeogwu attended Saint Joseph's Catholic Primary School in Kaduna for his elementary education, and for his secondary education, he attended Saint John's College in Kaduna.

In March 1957, Nzeọgwụ enlisted as an officer cadet in the Nigeria Regiment of the West African Frontier Force and proceeded on a six-month preliminary training course in Ghana. He completed his training in October 1957 and proceeded to the Royal Military Academy, Sandhurst, where he was commissioned as an infantry officer in 1959. Nzeogwu later underwent a platoon officer's course in Hythe and a platoon commander's course in Warminster. Max Siollun, a military historian, described Nzeogwu as a "devout Catholic, a teetotaler, a non-smoker, and despite being a bachelor, did not spend much time chasing women".

On his return to Nigeria in May 1960, Nzeọgwụ was posted to the 1st Battalion of Nigerian Army in Enugu, where Major Aguiyi-Ironsi was the second-in-command under a British officer. He was later posted to the 5th Battalion in Kaduna, where he became friends with Olusegun Obasanjo. His Hausa colleagues in the Nigerian Army gave him the name "Kaduna" because of his affinity with the town. After serving in the Congo in 1961, Nzeọgwụ was assigned as a training officer at the ArmyTraining Depot in Zaria for about six months, before getting posted to Lagos to head the military intelligence section at the Army Headquarters, where he was the first Nigerian officer.

As a military intelligence officer, Major Nzeọgwụ participated in the treasonable felony trial investigations of Obafemi Awolowo and other Action Group party members. According to Olusegun Obasanjo, "Chukwuma had some scathing remarks to make about (Nigeria's) national security, and about those who were being investigated. If he had his way, he said, his treatment of the whole case would have been different".

Nzeọgwụ reportedly antagonised some of his army colleagues in his capacity as a military intelligence officer and even clashed with the

Minister of State for the Army, Ibrahim Tako. Consequently, he was posted to the Nigerian Military Training College in Kaduna, where he became Chief Instructor.

In the early hours of January 15, 1966, Nzeogwu led a group of soldiers on a supposed military exercise, taking them to attack the official residence of the Premier of the Northern Region, Sir Ahmadu Bello, in a bloody coup that saw the murder of the Premiers of Northern and Western Regions. The Prime Minister (Abubakar Tafawa Balewa), a federal minister (Festus Okotie-Eboh), and some top army officers from the Northern and Western regions, who were also killed.

After waiting for an early morning radio announcement from Major Adewale Ademoyega in Lagos, which did not take place because of the failure of the coup in Lagos, Major Nzeogwu made a mid-afternoon announcement, declaring martial law in Northern Nigeria. Following the announcement and information that Nzeogwu was gathering forces to attack Lagos, which was a huge possibility at the time, the Commander of the Army, General Aguiyi Ironsi, sent emissaries led by Lt. Col. Conrad Nwawo, whom Nzeogwu deeply respected, to Kaduna to negotiate peace talks with him and a possible surrender. Nzeogwu set conditions, which Ironsi agreed to.

Nzeogwu was arrested on January 18, 1966, and detained in Kirikiri Maximum Security Prison, Lagos, contrary to agreements earlier reached between him and Ironsi. He was later transferred to Aba Prison, where he was released in March 1967 by the Governor of the Eastern Region, Colonel Chukwuemeka Odumegwu-Ojukwu.

On May 30, 1967, Ojukwu declared Biafra's independence from Nigeria, while the Nigerian federal government, on July 6, declared war on Biafra. On July 29, 1967, Nzeogwu, who had been promoted to the rank of Lt. Colonel in the Biafran Army, was trapped in an ambush near Nsukka while conducting a night reconnaissance operation against federal troops of the 21st Battalion under Captain Mohammed Inuwa Wushishi. He was killed in action. At the end of the Biafra War, the Nigerian Military Head of State, General Yakubu Gowon, ordered that Nzeogwu be buried at the military cemetery in Kaduna with full military honours.

19. Chukwuemeka Odumegwu-Ojukwu (November 4, 1933 – November 26, 2011)

Chukwuemeka Odumegwu-Ojukwu, born in Zungeru, in present-day Niger State, to Sir Louis Odumegwu Ojukwu, an Igbo businessman from Nnewi, Anambra State, and one of the richest men in Nigeria at the time, began his education career in Lagos. He served as the Military Governor of Eastern Region from January 1966 to May 1967 and leader of the Republic of Biafra from 1967 to January 1970. He was also active in politics from 1983 until 2011 when he died at the age of 78.

Chukwuemeka Odumegwu-Ojukwu started his secondary school education at CMS Grammar School, Lagos, in 1943, at the age of 10. He later transferred to King's College, Lagos, in 1944, where he was involved in a controversy leading to his brief imprisonment for assaulting a British teacher who put down a student strike action that he was part of. This event generated widespread coverage in local newspapers. At 13, his father sent him to the United Kingdom to continue his education, first at Epsom College and later at Lincoln College, Oxford University, where he earned a master's degree in history. He returned to Nigeria in 1956.

Ojukwu joined the civil service in eastern Nigeria as an administrative officer at Udi. In 1957, after two years of working with the colonial civil service and seeking to break away from his father's influence over his civil service career, he left and joined the military, initially enlisting as a non-commissioned officer (NCO) in Zaria.

Ojukwu's decision to enlist as an NCO was forced by his father's pulling of political strings with the then Governor-General of Nigeria, John Macpherson, to prevent him from getting an officer cadetship. However, after an incident in which Ojukwu corrected a drill sergeant's mispronunciation of a catchword, the British Depot Commander recommended him for an officer's commission.

From Zaria, Ojukwu proceeded first to the Royal West African Frontier Force Training School in Teshie, Ghana, and next to Eaton Hall, where he received his commission in March 1958 as a Second Lieutenant. He was one of the first and few university graduates to receive an army commission. He later attended the Infantry School in Warminster and the Small Arms School in Hythe.

Upon completion of further military training, Ojukwu was assigned to the Army's Fifth Battalion in Kaduna. At that time, the Nigerian Military Forces had 250 officers, and only 15 were Nigerians. There were 6,400 other ranks, of which 336 were British. After serving in the United

Nations' Peacekeeping Force in the Congo under Major General Johnson Thomas Umunnakwe Aguiyi-Ironsi, Ojukwu was promoted to the rank of Lieutenant Colonel in 1964 and posted to Kano, where he was in charge of the 5th Battalion of the Nigerian Army.

Lieutenant Colonel Chukwuemeka Odumegwu-Ojukwu was in Kano when Major Patrick Chukwuma Kaduna Nzeogwu announced and executed the bloody military coup in Kaduna on January 15, 1966. Ojukwu supported the forces loyal to the Supreme Commander of the Nigerian Armed Forces, Major-General Aguiyi-Ironsi.

On Monday, January 17, 1966, Ojukwu was appointed Military Governor of the Eastern Region by Ironsi, along with three other military officers: Lieutenat Colonels Hassan Usman Katsina (North), Francis Adekunle Fajuyi (West), and David Akpode Ejoor (Mid-West). They formed members of the Supreme Military Council, the highest ruling body of the regime, along with Brigadier B.A.O. Ogundipe, Chief of Staff, Supreme Headquarters; Lt. Col. Yakubu Gowon; Chief of Staff, Army Headquarters, Commodore J. E. A. Wey, Head of the Nigerian Navy; Lt. Col. George T. Kurubo; Head of the Air Force, and Col. Sittu Alao, with Ironsi as Chairman.

By May 29, 1966, an anti-Igbo pogrom started in the North, which presented problems for Ojukwu, as he did everything in his power to prevent reprisals and even encouraged people to return to the North as assurances for their safety had been given by his colleagues. But on July 29, 1966, a group of Northern soldiers staged a counter-coup against the Ironsi regime. General Aguiyi-Ironsi, who wason tour of the Western Region, was abducted along with his host, Colonel Fajuyi, and killed in Ibadan.

On acknowledging Ironsi's death, Ojukwu insisted that the military hierarchy should be preserved, and in that case, the most senior army officer after Ironsi was Brigadier Babafemi Ogundipe, who should take over, and not Colonel Gowon, who was the coup plotters' choice. But Ogundipe was unable to muster enough force to establish his authority, which made him to opt out, and later surfaced in London as

High Commissioner. It was Ojukwu's insistence that the most senior military officer after Ironsi should take over that led to a standoff between him and Yakubu Gowon and to the sequence of events that resulted in the Nigerian civil war.

After failing to mediate the crisis internally, in January 1967, the Nigerian military leaders went to Aburi, Ghana, for a peace conference hosted by Ghana's Head of State, General Joseph Ankrah. The implementation of the agreements reached at Aburi fell apart upon the leaders' return to Nigeria, and on May 30, 1967, as a result of this, Ojukwu declared Eastern Nigeria a sovereign state, to be known as Biafra.

On July 6, 1967, Gowon declared war and attacked Biafra. After two and a half years of fighting and starvation, a hole appeared in the Biafran front lines, which was exploited by the Nigerian military. As it became obvious that the war was lost, Ojukwu decided to leave the country to avoid assassination. On January 9, 1970, he handed over power to his second-in-command, Major General Philip Effiong, and left for Ivory Coast, where President Félix Houphouet-Boigny granted him political asylum.

On May 18, 1982, President Shehu Shagari granted Ojukwu a state pardon, which allowed him to return to Nigeria on June 18. Thereafter, he entered politics and joined the then ruling National Party of Nigeria (NPN). His attempt to go to the Senate was unsuccessful as he was defeated at the polls. Ojukwu also unsuccessfully contested the presidency in 2003 and 2007.

Odumegwu Ojukwu died in London on November 26, 2011, at the age of 78, and was buried on February 27, 2012, in his home town, Nnewi, with full military honours. Among the dignitaries that attended his burial were former Nigerian President, Goodluck Jonathan and former Ghanaian President, Jerry Rawlings.

20. Charles Dadi Onyeama (August 5, 1917 – September 5, 1999)

Charles Dadi Umeha Onyeama was the first Nigerian judge at the International Court of Justice in The Hague. He was also appointed to the Supreme Court of Nigeria. Charles Dadi Onyeama was the son of the great Onyeama of Eke. He first went to the Government School in Bonny and later to the King's College in Lagos, where he received his secondary school education. Dadi Onyeama also attended Achimota

College, Ghana; University College, London; and Brasenose College, Oxford. He became a member of Lincoln's Inn.

Charles Dadi Onyeama began his career as an assistant district officer in Lagos in 1944, and he later served on the Legislative Council from 1944 to 1946. After being appointed Chief Magistrate in 1952, he became a judge of the high court in 1957. Onyeama served as Justice of the Supreme Court of Nigeria from 1964 to 1967. His contemporaries on the Supreme Court included Sir Adetokunbo Ademola, Sir Lionel Brett, Sir Vahe Bairamian, Justice G.B.A. Coker, Justice M.O. Ajegbo, and Justice Chike Idigbe.

After a series of unpopular judgments by the International Court of Justice (ICJ) in 1966, African countries demanded greater representation amongst its judges. The seat dedicated to the Commonwealth and taken by an Australian judge was then taken by Onyeama after getting elected in November 1966, raising the number of African judges on the ICJ to two. Onyeama served from 1967 to 1976 and was succeeded by Taslim Olawale Elias. He was appointed as a judge for the 1971 Beagle Channel Arbitration. From 1982 to 1990, he served as a judge at the World Bank Administrative Tribunal.

21. Dick Tiger (August 14, 1929 – December 14, 1971)

Richard Ihetu, popularly known as "Dick Tiger", was a professional boxer who held the World Middleweight and World Light Heavyweight Championships. Tiger emigrated to Liverpool, England, to pursue his boxing career, and later to the United States. During the Nigeria-Biafra War, he served as a lieutenant in the Biafran Army, primarily training soldiers in hand-to-hand combat.

Tiger became a two-time undisputed world middleweight champion and helped keep boxing alive during the 1950s boxing industry recession. He won the world middleweight title when he beat Gene Fullmer in 1962 and the light heavyweight title in 1966, when he dethroned José Torres of Puerto Rico.

However, before these accomplishments, Tiger seemed condemned to poor management and a resulting lack of exposure. In 1957, using Liverpool as his fighting base, Dick Tiger was fighting on undercards for small purses when by fortune facing off against popular favourite Terry Downes at Shoreditch Town Hall, he walked away with a TKO after six heats. New management saw to it that certain "errors in his style" were corrected, and in another year, Tiger had taken 17 of 19 fights and won the British Middleweight title.

In 1959, handled by the independent Jersey Jones, Tiger came to America to face adversity in a whole new way. Jersey Jones, resisting the influences of Madison Square Garden, brokered deals for Tiger by himself, which, in the short run, cost them both. In an independent promotion in Edmonton, Alberta, Tiger's Empire belt was lost in a more-than questionable 15 round nod to local challenger, Wilf Greaves. The decision as rendered had first been called a draw.

Appalled, Jones demanded a recount of the cards, which boomeranged, showing the fight, dominated by Tiger, as a win for Greaves. Tiger, who was sincere and honourable in his dealings, often found this virtuous approach not reciprocated, particularly in North America.

A.J. Liebling who saw Tiger fight Henry Hank of Detroit in 1962, described Tiger's appearance as, "... a chest like an old-fashioned black office safe, dropping away to a slender waist, big thighs, and slender legs; he boxed classically, his arms tight against his sides at the beginning of a punch, his savagely methodical blows moving in short arcs and straight lines."

Such a description was similarly evoked, albeit in simpler terms, by Tiger's contemporaries. Gene Fullmer:

> Tiger was a rough guy. I went to Nigeria to fight him, and of course, I don't know what happened over there. He beat me. He beat me badly. My mother and father could have been judge and referee, and I couldn't have won a round.

Joey Giardello: "I thank Dick Tiger because Dick Tiger was a man and Dick Tiger gave (a title shot) to me. He didn't have to give it to me. He could have given it to somebody else."

An additional comment from Giardello, in the form of a sarcastic bon mot, showed contemporary respect for Tiger as a fellow battler. The pair fought four times in all, the last two of which resulted in them swapping the middleweight title. Every fight went the distance, meaning that in terms of time, Dick Tiger and Joey Giardello contended face-to-facefor two and a half hours.

Before one of these latter encounters, when asked by the press if Giardello, a classic boxer, planned to trade punches with Tiger,

Giardello squelched this with, "I wouldn't trade stamps with him." Numerous accounts of Tiger as both a man and a fighting man, describe a solid, decent, un-announced person.

Unsurprisingly, a very Western gimmick, the literal "power of the press", or perhaps of Madison Avenue, appears lost on him. Contender Joey Archer, a scientific middleweight of uncommon speed, launched a small space ad campaign directed at Tiger. The ads, using copy such as "I'm a middleweight, and I've licked every man I ever fought, including you", were employed to create a sensation and perhaps a groundswell toward securing Archer a title fight.

Tiger had already signed to fight Emile Griffith, and Archer admonished, "The Middleweight Champion should meet the best middleweight (not a welterweight)." Archer carried his cause to talk shows, even to the New York Daily News, and was photographed taunting an angry, caged tiger at the Bronx Zoo.

Whether or not this bombast had any negative impact on Dick Tiger's pride, history never found out after Emile Griffith won Tiger's middleweight belt, effectively making Tiger a non-player in the drama. Joey Archer shifted his attentions, and, from 1966 on, Tiger campaigned as a full-time light heavyweight.

After deciding to give Jose Torres the title, Tiger then defended his crown against Torres and Montanan Roger Rouse before coming up short against veteran Bob Foster of Albuquerque, New Mexico. The left hook Foster used to dethrone Tiger in an instant was rated among "The 10 deadliest punches of the last 25 years" in 1975.

The power in the one-punch knockout made such an impact upon Garden promoters, it was felt that a rematch would do poor business. This attitude forced Tiger to contend for the right to regain his crown, and saw him matched against up-and-comer Frankie DePaula, who was coming off five consecutive knockouts.

The fight to qualify against Foster was, for its first four rounds, a war that saw both men go down twice and was selected by Ring magazine as "Fight of the Year". Though Dick Tiger took the decision, having proven his mettle, ill treatment on the American side seemed to cling, as Frankie DePaula, the man he had defeated, was inexplicably given the chance at Bob Foster.

Dick Tiger travelled from Nigeria to Liverpool, Western England, and eventually the United States in the later parts of his career, making a big contribution to boxing. After retiring from boxing, Tiger worked as a guard at the Metropolitan Museum of Art in New York.

One day, he felt a strong pain in his back. Tested by doctors, he was diagnosed with liver cancer. He was banned by the Nigerian government because of his involvement in the Biafran movement; however, the ban was lifted immediately after news about his condition arrived in Nigeria. He died of liver cancer on December 14, 1971, in Aba, at the age of 42.

The Ring Magazine named him Fighter of the Year in 1962 and 1965, while the Boxing Writers Association of America (BWAA) named him Fighter of the Year in 1962 and 1966.

Tiger was inducted into the International Boxing Hall of Fame in 1991. In 1996, Tiger was voted as one of the best boxers of the 1960s, and later in 1998, he was put in the book of "the Best boxers of the 20th century". In 2002, Tiger was voted by The Ring magazine as the 31st greatest fighter of the last 80 years.

22. Alvan Ikoku (1900 – 1971)

Alvan Ikoku was born in 1900 in Amanagwu Arochukwu, in present-day Abia State. He was an educationist, statesman, activist, and politician. Ikoku was educated at the Arochukwu Government Primary School from 1915 to 1920. He attended Hope Waddell College, Calabar, where he was a student under James Emmanuel Aggrey and was mates with Francis Akanu Ibiam, former Governor of the Eastern Region, and Eyo Eyo Esua, the first indigenous Chief Electoral Commissioner in Nigeria.

In 1920, he received his first teaching appointment with the Presbyterian Church of Nigeria and Church of Scotland at Itigidi, Cross River State, and two years later became a senior tutor at St. Paul's Teachers' Training College, Awka, Anambra State. While teaching at Awka, Ikoku earned his University of London degree in Philosophy in 1928 through its external programme. In 1932, Ikoku established a co-educational secondary school in West Africa: the Aggrey Memorial Secondary School, located in Arochukwu and named after his mentor, James E.K. Aggrey, an eminent Ghanaian educationist.

In 1946, after several constitutional changes allowing more Nigerians in the legislative chambers, he was nominated to the Eastern

Nigeria House of Assembly and assigned to the Ministry of Education. In 1947, he became part of the Legislative Council in Lagos as one of three representatives of the Eastern Region. In 1962, he called for an 'Education Bill of Rights' for primary school education to be free for sixyears nationwide in Nigeria. This was later accepted by the Federal Military Government as from 1976, and today, free education to all primary school has been granted.

Honours for his contribution to education in Nigeria include, an honorary doctorate in law (1965) at a special convocation of the University of Ibadan, the establishment of the Alvan Ikoku Federal College of Education, Owerri, a major road named after him, the Alvan Ikoku Way, in Maitama, Abuja, and his commemoration on a bill of Nigerian currency, the Ten Naira note. He died on November 18, 1971.

23. Kenneth Dike (December 17, 1917 – October 26, 1983)

Kenneth Onwuka Dike an educationist and historian, was the first Nigerian University Vice Chancellor. In 1962, he was the Vice Chancellor of the University College, Ibadan, now, the University of Ibadan. During the Nigerian civil war, Dike moved to Harvard University. He was the founder of the "Ibadan School", which dominated the writing of the history of Nigeria until the 1970s. He is credited with "having played the leading role in creating a generation of African historians who could interpret their own history without being influenced by Eurocentric approaches."

Born in Awka, Anambra State, Kenneth Dike was educated in West Africa, England, and Scotland. He attended Fourah Bay College in Sierra Leone and also Durham University for his BSc, the University of Aberdeen for his MA, and King's College London for his PhD. During the 1960s, as a member of the University of Ibadan's History Department, he played a pioneering role in promoting African leadership in scholarly works published on Africa.

As the head of the organising committee for the First International Congress of Africanists in Ghana in 1963, Kenneth Dike sought to strengthen meticulous non-colonially focused African research and the publication of research in various languages, including indigenous and foreign, so as to introduce native speakers to history and for people to view African history through a common lens. He was the first director of the International School, Ibadan. In 1965, he was elected chairman of the Association of Commonwealth Universities. His publications were a watershed in African historiography.

With a PhD from London, Dike became the first African to complete Western historical professional training. At the University College of Ibadan, he became the first African professor of history and head of a history department. He founded the Nigerian National Archives, and helped in the founding of the Historical Society of Nigeria. His book, "Trade and Politics in the Niger Delta, 1830-1885", dealt with 19th century economics and politics in the Niger Delta. He focused on internal African factors; especially defensive measures undertaken by the delta societies against imperialist penetration. Dike helped create the Ibadan School of African History and promoted the use of oral evidence by African historians.

His publications include: Report on the Preservation and Administration of Historical Records in Nigeria (1953), Trade and Politics in the Nigeria Delta, 1930-1890 (1956), A Hundred Years of British Rule in Nigeria (1957), and The Origins of the Niger Missions (1958).

24. Chike Obi (April 17, 1921 – March 13, 2008)

Chike Obi was born in Onitsha, Anambra State, and educated in various parts of Nigeria before studying mathematics as an external student at the University of London. In 1950, he became the first Nigerian to receive a PhD in mathematics. Immediately after his first degree, he won a scholarship to do research at Pembroke College, Cambridge, followed by doctoral studies at the Massachusetts Institute of Technology, in Cambridge, Massachusetts, United States.

Chike Obi returned to Nigeria to lecture at the University of Ibadan, but soon diverted into politics, to help form the Dynamic Party of Nigeria, for which he served as its first Secretary-General. Throught he party, he stood as a candidate in a parliamentary election in Ibadan in 1951 but lost. The party later entered into alliances with the National Council of Nigeria and Cameroon and the Action Group. Obi was elected as part of the Nigerian delegation that negotiated the country's path to self-rule at two London conferences in 1957 and 1958.

After Nigeria's independence from Britain in 1960, Chike Obi was elected a legislator in the Eastern House of Assembly in 1960. During the NCNC crisis in the Eastern Region, Chike Obi refused to vacate his seat in the national legislature in Lagos, but the Speaker of the Eastern House of Assembly ordered that he be physically removed by security agents. This order was obeyed.

In 1962, Chike Obi and Chief Obafemi Awolowo, Leader of the Action Group, were arrested and charged with treason for plotting to overthrow the federal government. He was later released for "want of evidence."

When the Nigerian civil war broke out in 1967, Chike Obi sided with Biafra, and worked for the Biafran leader, Chukwuemeka Odumegwu Ojukwu. After the war, he returned to lecture at the University of Lagos, where he quickly rose to the position of professor. He later left Lagos to return to his root in Onitsha, to establish the Nanna Institute for Scientific Studies. He was a member of the National Revenue Mobilisation Commission for a short time in the 1970s.

Chike Obi had won the Sigvard Eklund Prize for original work in differential equations from the International Centre for Theoretical Physics. He was a university teacher until his retirement as an emeritus professor in 1985.

In 1997, Chike Obi claimed to be the third person to solve Fermat's Last Theorem after Andrew Wiles and Richard Taylor in 1994. He also claimed to have found an elementary proof to Fermat's Last Theorem. This work was carried out at his Nanna Institute for Scientific Studies in Onitsha and published in Algebras, Groups, and Geometries.

The African Mathematics Union suggests that Chike Obi was the first Nigerian to hold a doctorate in mathematics. His early research dealt mainly with the question of the existence of periodic solutions of non-linear ordinary differential equations. He used the perturbation technique successfully, and several of his publications have greatly aided in stimulating research interest in this subject around the world, becoming classics in the literature. Obi was the author of several books and journals on mathematics and Nigerian politics.

Chike Obi derided religion, ethnic extremism, and the culture of corruption pervading the Nigerian political class. He was a national newspaper columnist in the 1980s, writing under the title, "I speak For the People." He was a visiting professor at the University of Rhode Island, USA, the University of Jos, and the Chinese Academy of

Science. Obi was a recipient of the national honour of Commander of the Order of the Niger (CON) and a Fellow of the Nigerian Academy of Science. Chike Obi died in 2008.

25. Chinua Achebe (November 16, 1930 –March 21, 2013)

Albert Chinualumogu Achebe, novelist, poet, and critic, regarded as the most dominant figure in modern African literature, wrote his first novel and magnum opus, *Things Fall Apart*, in 1958, which occupies a pivotal place in African literature and remains the most widely studied, taught and read African novel.

Achebe sought to escape the colonial perspective that predominated African literature and draw from the traditions of the Igbo people, Christian influences, and the clash of Western and African values to create a uniquely African voice. His style relies heavily on the Igbo oral tradition, and combines straightforward narration with representations of folk stories, proverbs, and oratory.

Along with *Things Fall Apart*, *No Longer at Ease* (1960) and *Arrow of God* (1964) Achebe completes the so called "African Trilogy". Later novels include *A Man of the People* (1966) and *Anthills of the Savannah* (1987). In addition to his seminal novels, Achebe's oeuvre includes numerous shortstories, poems, essay collections, and children's books. Raised by his parents in the Igbo town of Ogidi, Anambra State, Achebe excelled at Government College Umuahia and won a scholarship to study medicine, but changed his studies to English literature at University College Ibadan. He became fascinated with world religions and traditional African cultures and began writing stories as a university student.

After graduation, he worked for the Nigerian Broadcasting Service (NBS) and soon moved to the metropolis of Lagos. He gained worldwide attention for his novel, *Things Fall Apart*, in the late 1950s, which exerted a significant influence on subsequent literature. Achebe wrote his novels in English and defended the use of English, a "language of colonisers," in African literature.

In 1975, his lecture "An Image of Africa: Racism in Conrad's Heart of Darkness" featured a criticism of Joseph Conrad as "a thoroughgoing racist". It was later published in The Massachusetts Review, amid controversy.

When Biafra was declared in 1967, Achebe became a supporter of the regime, and acted as ambassador for the people of the new nation. At the end of the civil war in 1970, he involved himself in political parties but soon became disillusioned by his frustration over the corruption and elitism he witnessed. He had a car crash that left him partially disabled.

Upon Achebe's return to the United States in 1990, he began his tenure at Bard College as the Charles P. Stevenson Professor of Languages and Literature. Until 2013 when he died, he served as the David and Marianna Fisher University Professor and Professor of African Studies at Brown University.

Achebe's works were widely analysed, with a massive body of scholarly work discussing them. Some of the themes he touched on are politics, history, culture, colonialism, as well as masculinity and femininity. To date, his total influence remains unmatched in African literature. His legacy is celebrated annually at the Chinua Achebe Literary Festival.

Despite his scholarly achievements and the global importance of his work, Achebe never received a Nobel Prize, which some observers viewed as unjust. In 1988, he was asked by a reporter how he felt about never winning a Nobel Prize. He replied,

> My position is that the Nobel Prize is important. But it is a European prize. It's not an African prize ... Literature is not a heavyweight championship. Nigerians may think, you know, this man has been knocked out. It's nothing to do with that.

Achebe had twice refused the Nigerian honour of Commander of the Federal Republic, in 2004 and 2011, saying:

> I have watched particularly the chaos in my own state of Anambra, where a small clique of renegades, openly boasting its connections in high places, seems determined to turn my homeland into a bankrupt and lawless fiefdom. I am appalled by the brazenness of this clique and the silence, if not connivance of the Presidency.

26. F.C. Ọgbalụ (July 20, 1927 - 1990)

Frederick Chidozie Ọgbalụ, popularly known as Mazi F.C. Ọgbalụ, was born to Michael Obiefuna Ọgbalụ and Elizabeth Nwamgbogo Ogbalu of Adagbe, Abagana, in Njikoka Local Government Area, Anambra State. Fred, as he was fondly called by his childhood friends, had his primary education at St. Peter's Central School, Abagana, where he obtained the First School Leaving Certificate with distinction in 1940. Early the next year, he proceeded to Dennis Memorial Grammar School (DMGS) Onitsha, where, in addition to his studies, he joined the Society for Promoting African Culture (SPAC). It was this society that gave him some stimulating glimpses of the significance and meaning of African culture, and particularly of Igbo culture. Fred later displayed a brilliant performance at the Senior Cambridge School Certificate Examination held in November and December, 1944, where he passed in Grade 1 with what was then known as an exemption from London Matriculation, and thereby passed at a sitting, a prescribed combination of subjects at the level required for direct admission into London University.

On leaving secondary school, he entered the Teachers' Training College at Awka, where he obtained the Higher Elementary Certificate in 1946. In 1953, Fred obtained the Nigerian Senior Teachers' Certificate in Geography and History, while the following year, 1954, he got a degree from the University of London in Economics as a private candidate.

After leaving the Teachers' Training College, Fred was posted to teach at Ubulukwu in present-day Delta State, later to his Alma Mater, DMGS, and much later to St Augustine's Grammar School (SAGS), Nkwelle, where in 1949, he and his friends and colleagues founded the Society for Promoting Igbo Language and Culture (SPILC). This society was to be a veritable instrument with which he was to register most of his achievements for the language and culture of the Igbo people for the rest of his life.

Ọgbalụ dubbed the "father" of Igbo language and culture, was a life long teacher and champion of his Igbo heritage. He taught Latin, Geography and Igbo at a number of schools, and took a great interest in the Igbo-related controversies of his time. These controversies revolved around efforts to standardise the writing and spelling of the Igbo language, and to improve its numeral system.

Thus, in 1948, while teaching at Dennis Memorial Grammar School, Onitsha, Ogbalụ wrote a newspaper article in *The Nigerian Spokesman*, attacking the colonial administration for its failure to encourage standardisation of the Igbo language, and forcefully arguing against a new "Adams-Ward" orthography being advocated by some linguists. This orthography, which he called "obnoxious," involved phonetic symbols that would inevitably have complicated the process of learning to read the language. Ogbalu's principal at Dennis Memorial Grammar School then advised him that instead of writing to the newspapers, he would do better to write and publish his own material in the Igbo language. Ogbalu took up the challenge, and by the following year he founded the Society for Promoting Igbo Language and Culture (SPILC). He was then only 22 years old.

The SPILC had lofty aims, such as promoting the study and knowledge of the Igbo language; sponsoring lectures, conferences, and teaching materials; encouraging young writers; and raising the consciousness of the Igbo people so that they would not lose sight of their cultural heritage. The SPILC seminars were influential in the establishment of a Department of Igbo Language and Linguistics at the University of Nigeria, Nsukka. Most importantly, they resulted in the eventual creation of the 1961 Onwu Commission, which devised orthography more acceptable than the Adams-Ward one.

Ogbalụ published a remarkable number of works that gathered and preserved Igbo oral literature during his all-too-brief life. From his prolific pen flowed many Igbo publications, ranging from novels to poetry books, folktales and fantasy books, textbooks, and journals. They includethe popular Mbediogu (1975), Nza Na Obu, Dimkpa Taa Akụ A hụ Ichere Ya (1972), Ebube Dike (1974), Obiefula, Ụwaezuoke (1976), Nmoo Nmoo, Igbo Mbụ (1-6), Ilu Igbo, Omenala Igbo (1974), Ndụ Ndi Igbo, Ọnụ Ọgụgụ Igbo (1981), Ọkọwa Okwu (Igbo Dictionary), Junior Omenala Igbo, Ayoro (Poem for) Ụmụaka, Abu Ụmụaka (1979), Junior Igbo Course, Igbo Institutions andCulture, Okwu Ntụhị (A Book of Igbo Riddles, 1973), Mbem and Egwu Igbo (1977), Edemede Igbo, The New Practical Igbo Grammar, School Certificate Igbo (1974), Ọnụ Ọgụgụ Igbo, Igbo Idioms (1966), Ụyọkọ Mbem Igbo (Anthology of Igbo Poems, 1984), Mbido Igbo Maka Ụmụaka Nta

Akara (1977), Akwụkwọ Ọgụgụ Igbo (1972). In all, he published about 100 books on Igbo.

However, Ọgbalụ was not the first person to write a book in Igbo. Other writers on Igbo language abound, such as Bishop Ajayi Crowther's first Igbo primer, a 17-page booklet containing the Igbo alphabet, words, phrases, and sentences, written in the Isuama dialect (used by emancipated slaves of Igbo origin who settled in Sierra Leone and Fernando Po in the 1800s). It was published in 1859. There was also J. C. Taylor's New Testament Bible written in the Onitsha dialect of Igbo.

Although Taylor, born in Sierra Leone to parents who were Igbo freed slaves, grew up speaking Igbo as his mother tongue, his translation never saw the light of day, and never got published because of the disagreement that arose between him and J. F. Schön, a German CMS (Church Missionary Society) missionary and language expert who felt that the dialect was not a universally accepted one in the then known Igbo world.

Also, there were Archdeacon Henry Johnson's 1871 Book of Common Prayer, Archdeacon Thomas J. Dennis-led Igbo Language Translation Committee's 1910 and 1913 publications, respectively, of Ije Nke Onye Kraịst, and the Igbo Union Version Bible, which later became enmeshed in controversy after being rejected by Onitsha Igbo speakers, etc.

In terms of contribution to the development of Igbo language, culture, and literature, however, Ogbalu towers above them all, not only by dint of his copious Igbo literary offerings but also by his 1949 founding of the Society for Promoting Igbo Language and Culture (SPILC), to hasten and re-invigorate the battle for Igbo language. He went to bed dreaming about the development of its language, literature, and culture, and he woke up the next morning still thinking about it. He walked as much as he ran, and he flew with the ideas he had about its development.

Before he and his SPILC stepped in to bring some order and sanity into the chaotic scene that was Igbo orthography and language development, any mathematical figure above 400 was given an amorphous name called *nnu kwuru nnu* (*nnu* being the name that Igbo called 400 in numeracy, and *nnu kwuru nnu*, the hundreds and figures above nnu). But by dint of meticulous linguistic research that saw members of the committee traversing the length and breadth of Igboland, they came up with Igbo names for figures beyond hundred, thousand, million, and even billion. And that was how we got, in Igbo numerology, figures like *narị* (hundred), *puku* (thousand), *njeri/ijeri* (million) and *nde* (billion). They even added, for good measure, words like *Mahadum* (university) and *ekwenti* (telephone) to the burgeoning Igbo vocabulary.

Mazi Ọgbalụ sponsored the publication of a number of Igbo periodicals at various stages of the enterprise to provide fora for discussing matters of interest, and outlets for budding writers in the language. They included: *Anyanwu* (The Sun, the first Igbo newspaper), *Onuọra* (The Voice of the People), *Igbo Ga-Adị* (Igbo Shall Live), *Odenigbo* (that which is famous in Igboland), and *Igbo* (The Journal of SPILC). It was in the course of the fight that he took the title, *Mazi*, in place of Mr. and was thereafter referred to as Mazi Ọgbalụ.

27. Ngozi Okonjo-Iweala (June 13, 1954 -)

Ngozi Okonjọ-Iweala, a Nigerian-American economist, fair-trade leader, environmental sustainability advocate, human welfare champion, sustainable finance maven, and global development expert, was the daughter of Professor Chukwuka Okonjo, the late Obi of Obahai Royal Family of Ogwashi-Ukwu in Delta State, but is married to Physician Ikemba Iweala of Umuahia, Abịa State.

Ngozi Okonjọ-Iweala is the present Director-General of the World Trade Organization (WTO). She is the first woman and first African to lead the World Trade Organisation as Director-General.

Ngozi Okonjọ-Iweala sits on the boards of several international organisations such as Danone, Standard Chartered Bank, Twitter, the Mandela Institute for Development Studies (MINDS), the Carnegie Endowment for International Peace, the Georgetown Institute for Women, Peace and Security, One Campaign, Global Alliance for Vaccines and Immunization (GAVI), the Rockefeller Foundation, Results for Development (R4D), African Risk Capacity (ARC) the Earthshot Prize, etc.

A distinguished fellow with the Africa Growth Initiative in their global economy and development programme, Ngozi Okonjo-Iweala is a commissioner emeritus and co-chair of Global Commission on the

Economy and Climate. At the World Bank, she had a 25-year career as a development economist, rising to become Managing Director for Operations from 2007 to 2011.

She was the first Nigerian woman to serve two terms as Finance Minister of Nigeria, and also as Minister for Foreign Affairs.

28. Holy Nweje: Story of an Igbo Saint (1919 – June 1962)

Hezekiah Okoro Nweje was an Anglican priest and a native of Onitsha, in Anambra State. He was nicknamed "Holy Nweje" because of the very humble, extreme righteous, easy-going, and humanitarian life he lived. He was tenaciously devoted to the things of God. Whatever gifts he received from the church he shepherded, he always shared with those in the vineyard, the poor, and the less privileged. He did not hoard them at the expense of the needy.

In his philosophy, he believed that wealth was about sharing what you have without hoarding it. When he was nominated for the position of the Anglican Bishop on the Niger, he declined and nominated someone he felt was more qualified.

Rev. Hezekiah Okoro Nweje was seen as an upright, spotless, and righteous man. It was all those outstanding qualities he possessed while alive that brought about the name "Holy Nweje," depicting how holy one could be. He believed that one's anger should not see the next moment. In May 1956, Onitsha and Obosi were tussling for a piece of land, Rev Nweje was called as a witness, and he told the judge that none of the towns owned the land, "*Anị bụ anị Chukwu,*" the land and thereof was of the Lord. That ended the land tussle.

He was always on the side of peace. Around April 1956, during the daytime, local thieves invaded his house in Onitsha and stole tubers of yam and fowl. He ran after them and told them to come and take more, citing hunger as the reason for their unconventional behaviour. What a man!

Growing up in Igbo land, if you are seen or perceived as an upright "Holy Nweje", do not feel ashamed or mocked. It tells well of you. Nweje Lane in Onitsha metropolis is a street named to immortalise him.

29. Cyprian Michael Iwene Tansi (September 1903 – January 20, 1964)

Cyprian Michael Iwene Tansi was a Catholic priest and monk, currently aspiring to sainthood, according to the order of the Catholic Church. Cyprian Michael Iwene Tansi was ordained priest on December 19, 1937, for the Archdiocese of Onitsha, and worked in the parishes of Nnewi, Dunukofia, Akpu/Ajalli and Aguleri.

Iwene Tansi was born on September 1903. His father was Tabansi from Igbezunu in Aguleri in the present-day Anambra State. Later, he named his firstborn son 'Iwe-egbune', shortened to Iwene, meaning 'let malice not kill'. His parents were poor farmers and they were not Christian. After the death of his first wife, Iwene's father married again. He and his second wife had four boys and one girl.

When Iwene was a young child, he became permanently blind in one eye as a result of a mud fight with other children. His father sent Iwene to Holy Trinity School in Onitsha, which was run by the Holy Ghost Fathers. Tabansi meant for his son to get a better education that would help lead their family out of poverty. Iwene was baptised on July 7, 1913, with the Christian name of Michael. At the school, Michael served as an altar boy and catechist. Upon graduating, he became a teacher, and worked as a teacher from 1919 to 1925. Later, he became headmaster at St. Joseph's school in Aguleri.

At that time, there was little enthusiasm for blacks becoming priests in Nigeria. The bishop was Irish, and most of the clergy were Europeans. Bishop Shanahan saw the native Igbo, even after conversion, as still steeped in paganism and said that it was going to be difficult to teach them to be proper priests. While Igbo could become priests, they were subject to strict discipline and were often expelled from seminary for relatively minor lapses. The priests who taught them were concerned that only the very best men should become priests.

Michael attended the seminary at Igbariam from 1925 to 1937. His family was appalled at his entrance to the seminary because they wanted him to go into business or something that would take them out of poverty, which was what his father had always planned. His family was poor and his family was impoverished and sorely needed his assistance, but he believed that God, the same God he had learnt about at the mission school his parents had sent him to as a child to obtain material benefits for the family, intended him to remain in the seminary, rather than do something else. There, he developed a particular devotion to the Sacred Heart of Jesus and to the Blessed Virgin Mary.

At that time in Nigeria, almost all priests were foreign missionaries. Few Africans were being ordained to the priesthood. The foreign missionaries were generally unwilling to live in the same poverty or conditions that the native-born Nigerians endured. As a result, if an area wanted a parish priest, the local people had to raise enough money so that the priest could live well. This included building a church and rectory and buying a car, scooter, or bicycle for the priest's use.

Michael was ordained a priest on December 19, 1937. When he became a parish priest, he lived a very austere life in comparison to the other priests around him. He built his own home using adobe, mud brick, or other traditional materials. He would sleep on any bed, even if it was uncomfortable. He would eat even poorer food than what the local people ate, surviving on tiny portions of yam. He sometimes had a motorbike provided to him, but he often preferred to use a bicycle or even just to walk. He was not deterred from doing his work by tropical rainstorms.

His lifestyle shocked the Nigerian Catholics, who were not accustomed to this kind of priest. He became extremely popular and loved among the four parishes that he served: Nnewi, Dunukọfịa, Akpụ/Ajallị, and his home town, Aguleri. He organised the community to help the poor and needy, and he personally would help people build their own homes or perform other projects. He was very good at building homes, and taught people new building techniques with adobe or mud brick that were copied and used by the whole community. He was remembered as always being very kind.

Father Michael Iwene Tansi also stood up against the oppression of women within the traditional culture and advised women to fight back against those who would rape or mistreat them. On one occasion, a female parishioner was attacked by a group of males, and she fought back against them. Fr Michael Tansi, who was nearby, rode his bike over to her and joined her in fighting until they fled. He then encouraged her to bring the assailants to court, which she did, winning the case against them and forcing them each to pay her four pounds; this case was a milestone in the establishment of women's rights in Nigeria.

Father Tansi was unyielding in confronting vice among his flock. He had a special interest in preparing young women for marriage. With the help of local nuns, the women were taught about Christian marriage and how to care for the children they would have. He would organise the community to place the bride-to-be in a special home where she would be looked after until she got married. He would not allow men to see their brides before they got married, and if the groom attempted to go there without Fr. Tansi's permission, he could be penalised.

He also organised a women's group that would enforce discipline on its members to avoid premarital sex and deter abortion. He was also a very strict disciplinarian with students who failed to work hard at the parish school, to the point of hiding near the school, waiting for the bell to ring, and then, when he saw students coming late, coming out of his hiding place and penalising them for coming late to school.

Iwene Tansi was also opposed to some aspects of the traditional pagan culture in Nigeria, especially the masquerades, who were believed to be spirits and used to punish innocent people attimes. The pagans had murdered his own mother after claiming that she was a witch who had caused mischief.

Father Tansi gave the community advice and teachings about the right way to live in a practical fashion. For example, there were many mango trees in his locale, and it was common for people to go to the trees and throw rocks at the fruit. In the process, they would knock down far more than they were going to eat, or knock down the unripe fruit along with the ripened fruit, thus denuding the tree before the season was over. Michael considered this very wasteful and told his parishioners to pluck each mango individually so that nothing was wasted and that they would not lack mangoes to eat later. He was also remembered as being a perfectionist, which sometimes caused resentment among those under him. Later, his experience as a novice monk would give him insight into his earlier strict methods.

While serving in his last parish, in his own hometown of Aguleri, from 1949 to 1950, Michael began to become attracted to the monastic life. At that time, there were no monasteries established in Nigeria, and the bishop was interested in the idea of sending some candidates to a monastery there who would become monks in Europe and later return to Nigeria to start up the first Nigerian monastery. Michael and others were selected for this project.

In 1950, which was a jubilee year in the Church, Father Michael was first sent to Rome to make the pilgrimage to the four major basilicas. He was then sent to Mount St. Bernard in England to join the Trappist monks there. He arrived on June 8, 1950.

At the monastery, he joined the novitiate and took his vows, taking the name Cyprian, after the Roman martyr. Fr. Cyprian worked in the refectory and bookbindery, as well as in the vegetable gardens and orchard. He used to say, "If you are going to be a Christian at all, you might as well live entirely for God".

Father Anselm Stark, who knew Fr Cyprian, recalled: "As a person, he was very ordinary, very humble, obviously a great man of deep prayer and dedication." He was sensitive to criticism, and his novice master was very hard on the new monk, and could always find things that were wrong with what he had done. This caused him much stress, and it was during this trying time that he realised that he had made some mistakes in Nigeria with the hard discipline and expectations he had placed on those under him.

Despite fears of being treated with racial prejudice, he was fully accepted by the other monks, perhaps with the exception of one South African monk, who seemed to look for things to find wrong in his work. The English winter was also hard on him.

He was commissioned to establish a monastery not in Nigeria but in neighbouring Cameroon, but ill health changed those plans. He did not believe that the Nigerian independence movement had been carried out properly. His health deteriorated, but he accepted his death with no complaint.

Before he died, he went to Leicester Royal Infirmary, and, when he was examined, the doctor came out of the examination and spoke with the monastery priest, Fr. James, saying: "Can you help me please, Father? This man must be in terrific pain, but he will only admit that he has 'a little pain.'" He died the same day as a result of arteriosclerosis and a ruptured aneurysm.

The date of his death was January 20, 1964. His body was buried at the monastery in England, but was later interred at the Cathedral Basilica of the Most Holy Trinity, Onitsha.

After being recommended by Cardinal Francis Arinze, who was inspired by Tansi as a boy, he was beatified by Pope John Paul II on March 22, 1998, becoming the first West African to be beatified. The Pope said on the occasion, "Blessed Cyprian Michael Tansi is a prime example of the fruits of holiness that have grown and matured in the Church in Nigeria since the Gospel was first preached in this land. He received the gift of faith through the efforts of the missionaries, and, taking the Christian way of life as his own, he made it truly African and Nigerian."

Cyprian Michael Iwene Tansi's wise words:

i. Count no one saved, until he is found in heaven" (Onye afuro n'enuigwe, si a guyi na ya) "Do not be imitating the whites in everything, strive hard to gain the Kingdom of God. The whites are already in heaven in this world, but you are suffering every want. Are you going to suffer also in the next world

ii. Life on earth could be compared to the journey of a young student who received a slip for a registered parcel, and he had to go to Lagos to claim this parcel. On the way he passed through many beautiful towns, towns with very attractive things in the shops. He started going from one shop to another, stretching his hands over the beautiful things he saw. He stopped so often in these big towns that he almost forgot what he was travelling for. It was after a long time that he ultimately reached Lagos, and when he went to claim the parcel he was told that the parcel had lain in the post for so long without him arriving to claim it that they had finally decided to send it back to the sender.

iii. God will give you double for what you give Him". "If you want to eat vultures, you may as well eat seven of them, so that when people call you a "vulture eater" you really deserve the name. If you want to become Catholic, live as a faithful Catholic so that when people see you, they know that you are Catholic. If you are going to be a Christian at all, you might as well live entirely for God.

iv. Whether you like it or not, saving your soul is your own business. If you are weak and fall by the wayside, we shall push you aside and tread on you as we march forward to meet God.

v. She is not 'Onye Bem' (a common Nigerian expression for wife, meaning 'person' in my place) but your wife, your better half, part of your own body. 'Onye' means a stranger, which your wife is not. You must recognise the worth and position of your wife and treat her as your partner and equal. Unless you do that, she is not a wife to you but a servant, and that is not what God wants a wife to be to the husband.

30. Francis Cardinal Arinze (November 1, 1932 -)

His Eminence Francis Cardinal Arinze was Prefect of the Congregation for Divine Worship and the Discipline of the Sacraments from 2002 to 2008. He has been Cardinal Bishop of Velletri-Segni since 2005. Arinze was one of the principal advisers to Pope John Paul II and was considered papabile before the 2005 papal conclave, which elected Pope Benedict XVI.

Arinze was born in Eziowelle, Anambra state, Nigeria. A convert from an African traditional religion, he was baptised on his ninth birthday (November 1, 1941) by Father Michael Tansi who was beatified by John Paul II in 1998. His parents later converted to Catholicism. At 15, Arinze entered All Hallows Seminary of Onitsha, from which he graduated and earned a philosophy degree in 1950. His father was initially opposed to his entering the seminary, but after seeing how much Francis enjoyed it, he encouraged him. Arinze stayed at All Hallows until 1953 to teach.

In 1955, he travelled to Rome to study theology at the Pontifical Urban University, where he eventually received a doctorate in sacred theology summa cum laude. On November 23, 1958, at the chapel of the university, Arinze was ordained to the priesthood by Gregorio Pietro Agagianian, pro-prefect of the Sacred Congregation for the Propagation of the Faith (Propaganda Fide).

After ordination, Father Arinze remained in Rome, earning a master's in theology in 1959 and a doctorate in 1960. His doctoral thesis on "Ibo Sacrifice as an Introduction to the Catechesis of Holy Mass" was the basis for his much-used reference work, "Sacrifice in Ibo Religion", published in 1970. From 1961 to 1962, Arinze was professor of liturgy, logic, and basic philosophy at Bigard Memorial Seminary, Enugu. From there, he was appointed regional secretary for Catholic education in Eastern Nigeria. He was later transferred to London, where he attended the Institute of Education and graduated in 1964.

Francis Arinze became the youngest Roman Catholic bishop in the world when he was consecrated on August 29, 1965, at the age of 32. He was appointed titular bishop of Fissiana and named coadjutor to the Archbishop of Onitsha. He attended the final session of the Second Vatican Council in that same year. He became Archbishop of Onitsha on June 26, 1967, and was the first African to head this diocese, succeeding Archbishop Charles Heerey, an Irish missionary.

The new archbishop did not have much time to settle into his office before the Nigeria-Biafra War broke out. The entire archdiocese was located in Biafran territory during the war. As a result of the war, Archbishop Arinze had to flee his city of Onitsha and live as a refugee, first in Adazi and subsequently in Amichi, for the three years of the war, which lasted from 1967 to 1970.

Despite his own refugee status, Archbishop Arinze worked tirelessly for refugees, displaced persons, the sick, and the hungry, offering support to priests and religious, and giving the faithful hope for the future. With the help of foreign missionaries, he supervised what one international relief worker called one of "the most effective and efficient distributions of relief materials" in history. He also took care to keep the Church separate from the ongoing political conflict, gaining the respect of all factions in the country.

Francis Arinze was still Archbishop of Onitsha when the war ended in 1970. As a part of Biafra, Onitsha and its inhabitants endured severe hardships throughout the three-year conflict. The people's homes and businesses were destroyed, and the already poor region was sinking deeper into poverty.

The end of the war did not mean an end to the challenges facing the young archbishop. The Nigerian government deported all foreign missionaries stationed in the archdiocese, leaving only the native clergy and religious, who were few in number. The government also confiscated the Catholic schools, most of which also served as churches or parish halls.

Impressed by Arinze's many accomplishments as the leader of an archdiocese with few resources, and his ability to work side by side with Muslims who represent a strong and not-to-be-ignored minority, Pope John Paul II in 1979 appointed Arinze pro-president of the Vatican's Secretariat for Non-Christians, later renamed the Pontifical Council for Interreligious Dialogue. Arinze continued as the ordinand of his archdiocese, and was elected unanimously as President of the Nigerian Bishops Conference in 1984.

A year later, the people of Onitsha organised a pilgrimage to Rome when they learned that Archbishop Arinze would be named a Cardinal at the Consistory of May 25, 1985. In the same year, he was awarded the chieftaincy title of the Ọchudọuwa of Eziowelle.

On April 8, 1985, Arinze resigned from his post in Onitsha, and the Pope named him a Cardinal-Deacon of San Giovanni della Pigna in the consistory held on May 25, 1985. He was raised to the rank of cardinal-priest in 1996. Two days following his elevation to Cardinal Deacon, Arinze was appointed President of the Pontifical Council for Interreligious Dialogue. He served in various related capacities, including President of the Special Assembly for Africa of the Synod of Bishops. He also received honours in this capacity.

On October 24, 1999, Cardinal Arinze received a gold medal lion from the International Council of Christians and Jews for his outstanding achievements in inter-faith relations. He travelled extensively and became a popular speaker in the United States. Arinze was a member of the Committee for the Great Jubilee of the Year 2000. In that capacity, he worked closely with individual bishops and priests throughout the world in preparation for the rare celebration of the Church. On October 1, 2002, Pope John Paul named him prefect of the Congregation for Divine Worship and the Discipline of the Sacraments.

When Pope John Paul II died on April 2, 2005, all major Vatican officials, including Arinze, automatically lost their positions. He was considered papabile, that is, a candidate for election to the papacy, at the papal conclave that followed, in which he was a cardinal elector. He returned to his post as prefect of the Congregation for Divine Worship when confirmed by the newly elected Pope Benedict XVI on April 21, 2005, and on April 25, Benedict named him Cardinal Bishop of Velletri-Segni.

On December 9, 2008, Benedict accepted Arinze's resignation as Prefect of the Congregation of Divine Worship. Arinze remained active, and in 2009 he gave the commencement address at the Augustine Institute in Denver. He actively catechises via Family land TV to the Americas, the Philippines, Africa, and Europe. He has produced over 1,700 television programmes with the Apostolate for Family Consecration. The programmes cover almost all of Pope John Paul II's encyclicals and apostolic letters, Vatican II, and many other topics.

In July 2009, he delivered a major speech promoting interreligious dialogue at the City Club of Cleveland. Moreover, he is also the author of several books along with a complete "Consecration and Truth Catechetical Program" for children and adults.

Appendix

I. Identity Crisis In Rivers State

The following are excerpts from the report of the Commission appointed by the colonial government to "Enquire into the fears of Minorities and the Means of allaying them" otherwise known as The Willink Commission Report of June 1958. Setting the records of our collective history straight

1. More than 98% of people who inhabit this area (the 'Igbo Plateau' of the Eastern Region) are Igbo and speak one language, though of course, with certain differences of dialect. There are nearly five million of them, and they are too many for the soil to support: they are vigorous and intelligent and have pushed outward in every direction, seeking a livelihood by trade or in service in the surrounding areas of the Eastern Region, the Western Region, and the North as well as outside Nigeria. They are no more popular with their neighbours than is usual in the case of energetic and expanding people whose neighbours have a more leisurely outlook on life.
2. Though there has been no great kingdom or indigenous culture in the Eastern Region, the coastal chiefs grew on their trade with the (European merchant) ships, and they adopted customs, clothing, and housing more advanced than those of the peoples of the interior on whom they had at first preyed for slaves. They came during the 19th century to regard the people of the interior as backward and ignorant, and it was therefore a blow to their pride, as well as to their pockets, when the Igbos began to push outwards into the surrounding fringe of the country and particularly into the Calabar area, to take up land, to grow rich, to own houses and lorries, and to occupy posts in public services and in the services of large trading firms.

   It was among the Igbos, formerly despised by the people of Calabar as a source of slaves and as a backward people of the interior, now feared and disliked as energetic and educated, that the first political party formed.
3. It is important to remember that of this (Ogoja) Province's 1,082,000 inhabitants, 723,000 are Igbos, almost entirely in Abakaliki and Afikpo (divisions), while the census classifies 350,000 as "other Nigerian tribes."
4. The Rivers Province...includes the two divisions of Brass and Degema, both overwhelmingly Ijaw, and the Ogoni Division. The former Rivers Division also includes over 300,000 Igbos, of whom 250,000 are in the Ahoada Division and 45,000 in Port Harcourt. Port Harcourt is a town of recent growth and of rapidly increasing importance; it is built on land that belonged originally to an outlying branch of the Igbo tribe, the Diobus, but is largely inhabited by the Igbos from the interior who have come to trade or seek employment....Of the total 747,000 in the

Rivers Province, 305,000 are Ndị-Igbo, 240,000 are Ijaws, and 156,000 are Ogonis.
5. The strip to the south of the Igbo block is physically divided by a block of Igbo territory, tipped by the important Igbo town of Port Harcourt, and tribally divided between the Ijaws and the Ogonis.
6. In the whole of this non-Igbo area, there is present in varying degrees some fear of being overrun, commercially and politically, by the Igbos... if Ahoada and Port Harcourt, which are really Igbo, are considered, the solid centre of the Igbo population, there are 54 seats for the Igbo area and 30 for COR (Calabar, Ogoja, and Rivers) in (Eastern Regional House of Assembly).

The Fears and Grievances of Minorities

7. It was suggested (by non-Igbo petitioners) that it was the deliberate object of the Igbo majority in the region to fill every post with Igbos (in public posts and services)... However, when we came to consider specific complaints about the composition of public bodies, we found them to be in many cases exaggerated or unreasonable.
8. The allegation was put forward by counsel (to petitioners) that the judiciary (when not European) was predominantly Igbo, with the implication that this caused fear among those who are not Igbos. But it was clearly stated in evidence by Dr. Udoma, the leader of UNIP, that no occasion could be adduced of the judiciary acting with partiality. The fact is that the legal profession is largely Ndị-Igbo and the reasons for this do not seem to be government action. It is therefore inevitable that there should be Igbo preponderance among Judges and magistrates. Further, it is the declared policy of the government that the judiciary should be federal, and this doesnot indicate a desire to control it. Again, the operation and composition of the Public Service Commission here, as in the West, appeared to us in no way open to reproach.
9. In the Police, which in this region alone is wholly Federal, the number of Igbos in the higher appointments is not out of proportion to the Igbos in the region. The force is now federally controlled, and although there are a large number of Igbos in the lower ranks, this is due to the fact that it has for long been a tradition among the Igbos to offer themselves for recruitment in this force in far greater numbers than any other tribe.
10. We noted that in five years, 1952–1957, from a total of 412 secondary scholarships, 216 were awarded to persons living in the COR areas, while the figures for post-secondary scholarships were 211 out of 623. The latter is about one-third, the former considerably in excess. It was suggested that scholarships awarded to non-Igbos were of an inferior kind and that the best scholarships went to Igbos, but we were unable to see that this claim held any validity. On the evidence before us, we

conclude that the allegations of discrimination in the matter of scholarships are unjustified.
11. It was further suggested that loans by the Eastern Regional Finance Corporation, the Eastern Region Development Board, and the Eastern Region Development Corporation were made with some degree of preference to Igbos. It did appear that most of the loans made by these bodies were to Igbos, but that is not to say that this was necessarily improper. Igbos constitute two-thirds of the population of the region and have a bigger share of financial and commercial responsibility than their numbers warrant.
12. That there should be modern street lights in Onitsha, and not Calabar was also quoted as an example of discrimination; however, it proved that the Onitsha Urban District Council had financed this measure from their own resources.
13. The question of land was repeatedly raised, it being resented by the Efiks and Ibibios that the Igbos should acquire any land at all in their territory while the methods by which it was obtained were also questioned. There is no doubt that on the Igbo Plateau there is insufficient land for the people and the Igbos are thrusting outwards where possible; they acquire land and use it either for cultivation or building. This is a matter that will require legislation sooner or later, and it will be delicate to handle, but the economic process is in itself healthy, and we had little sympathy with a witness who remarked that there is much undeveloped land in the district and he was anxious that it should not fall into the hands of the Igbos....We believe that governments in Nigeria should be careful not to try to protect minorities by introducing measures that would restrict development.
14. A group of miscellaneous grievances and charges against the Igbos from Calabar may be treated together; we were told that the Igbos did not observe local customs in the markets... We formed the impression that jealousy of the Igbos' successes in the markets was the main factor.

The Proposal for New States

15. The Ogoja State proposed to us would include the former Ogoja province, whose population of slightly more than one million, including more than 700,000 Ibos... The main intention would be separation from the central body of the Ibo population, but they will still be linked together with as a minority with their Igbo neighbours in Abakaliki and Afikpo. A majority of the evidence we heard from Ogoja was direct: they preferred the present situation to any association with Calabar, and that they were at least as afraid of domination by Efiks and Ibibios as by Igbos.
16. The (Calabar, Ogoja, and Rivers or COR) State proposed would consist of Calabar, Rivers, and Ogoja provinces, excluding the two Igbo

divisions of Abakaliki and Afikpo. The population of this area is 2,649,000, and the following would be the five largest tribes:
Ibibio 717,000
Annang 435,000
Igbo 428,000
Ijaw 251,000
Ogoni 156,000

As already explained, the small but important Efik tribe of 71,000 consists of the (COR) area is far from homogenous, and many of the other tribes expressed at least as much fear of the Efiks and Ibibiosas of the Igbo. It would leave the Igbos of the Igbo Plateau surrounded by a state whose sole purpose was to be hostile to themselves: the Igbos are an expanding people…

17. The area claimed for Rivers State consists of the whole of the Rivers Province, that is: the divisions of Brass, Degema, Ogoni, Port Harcourt, and Ahoada, together with the Western Ijaw Division from the Western Region, and two small sections in the Eastern Region from outside the Rivers Province, Opobo and Andoni being one, Ndoki the other.

18. Port Harcourt is an Igbo town, and it is growing rapidly, and the indigenous branch of the Igbos, who are the original inhabitants, are already outnumbered by Igbos from the hinterland.

19. The people of Ahoada, a division of which a pan runs down to meet Port Harcourt, appear atone time to have favoured the idea of a Rivers State, but have changed their views and before us expressed themselves as strongly against it. Comparatively few of them live in the low-lying swampy country of the coastal strip, and they have voted consistently for the NCNC. They said themselves that a main factor in their change of front had been the inclusion of the Western Ijaws in the proposed state. They claimed that if the Rivers State was to consist of the River Province only, the Igbos would have been the most numerous tribes within it: the inclusion of the Western Ijaw Division put them at a numerical disadvantage beside the Ijaws and they therefore preferred to stay out.

Whether or not this was a line of reasoning that really had a wide appeal, the fact remains that before us, they were opposed to the idea of the state. This is not surprising because their problems are different from those of the Ijaws.

20. To include, Ahoada and Port Harcourt within Rivers State, we believe would create a problem as acute as that with which we were currently dealing with and would be sharply resented by Ndị-Igbo of the central plateau.

This was Willinks Commission Report to Queen of England in 1958.

N/B: Ikwerre, Etche, Ekpeye, Opobo, Ibani (Bonny), Uratta, Ogba, Ndoki are all indigineous Igbo extraction in Rivers State (Rivers Igbos). Before Independence, there was no identity crisis among them.

II. How Igbo Women Used Petitions To Influence British Authorities During Colonial Rule

By Bright Alozie, West Virginia University

Selected petitions and written correspondence between Igbo women and British officials between 1892 and 1960 shed fresh light on how women navigated male-dominated colonial institutions and structures of the time. African women responded in varied and complex ways to the situations they found themselves in. This ranged from subtle to overt opposition, and in some cases, violent resistance.

One response was through petition writing, as women took to the pen to articulate their concerns. In my research, I examined several petitions written by Igbo women to British officials during the colonial period. I found that petition writing was part of the complex power politics between the women and the colonial state.

On June 5, 1885, Great Britain proclaimed Nigeria a colony. It declared a protectorate over territories on the coast between the British Protectorate of Lagos and both banks of the Rivers Niger and Benue (The London Gazette, June 5, 1885). Although treaties were signed with rulers by 1885, actual British control of northern and southern Nigeria was not attained until 1900. Colonial rule lasted until 1960 and was resisted in various forms. In Igboland, this included warfare, protests, tax evasion, and petition writing.

The petitions help us figure out why women asked the government for help and why the government either helped them or did not. Women opened up debates and dialogues using petitions. This offers insights into their relationships with indigenous men and with British officers.

My research shows that writing petitions gave women a voice and gave them chances to be more assertive and involved in their communities. In this sense, petitions served a political purpose and proved a powerful tool for the disenfranchised - a group that included more than just women.

The Petitions

The political context of the time was that women were not incorporated in colonial administration. Petition writing was therefore a means by which women could influence, resist, negotiate, and counteract policies within the colonial framework.

It also challenged the outmoded narrative of the passivity of women in the colonial power structure. They were actively involved as individuals or groups in shaping public policies in the colonial era. In Igboland, women regularly approached British officials with personal requests and complaints. The focus of their petitions was on socio-political and economic issues such as taxation, politics, policies, price control, cost of living, family issues, representation, marriages, and so on.

These excerpts are drawn from a pool of petitions that I have dubbed "voices on ink".

On September 12, 1928, Igbo women led by Madam Chinwe petitioned the Lieutenant Governor of the Southern Provinces over the frustrations that the colonial economy placed on them. (The British National Archives (TNA), FCO 141/13669/2. Petitions and Complaints: Madam Chinwe)'

In view of the fact that Aba women at present suffer significant hardships regarding the high cost of staples, could you consider fixing the prices of foodstuffs at certain fixed rates? (Aba Progressive Union – Petitions, 9/12/1928, National Archives, Enugu (NAE), Abadist 13/12/15. File No. 99/28)

On November 16, 1937, Mary Nna of Ohambele petitioned the Senior Resident, Owerri Province, concerning what she perceived to be an unfair judgement against her in the group native court of Ikwueke. She wrote:

> I respectfully submit that the annulment of the Native Court judgment by the Reviewing Officer is bad in law ... The defendant's evidence is a tissue of lies, and the defendant set up the defence as an after thought in order to frustrate the course of justice and bring to ridicule and contempt British justice and fair play. (Petition from Mary Nna of Ohambele, Aba Division, 12/11/1937, NAE, Abadist 9/1/95, File No. OW. 3041/5)

On September 7, 1940, Maria Olumo petitioned the Resident to help restore her ownership of a piece of land that she alleged the Chiefs of Umuezi had taken from her and unlawfully transferred to a European firm, the United Africa Company. (Abadist 14/1/31. File No. 31 Vol. XVII. Maria Olumo (F): Petitions and Complaints: General)

What the Petitions Tell Us

Petition writing demonstrates the "politics from below" which regularly featured resistance by women during the colonial era. Women, along with their male counterparts, took advantage of opportunities to seek redress and inform the government of their needs and complaints.

Petitioning was an avenue to interact with colonial authorities despite the social distance that separated ordinary subjects from the colonial ruling elite. Seeking redress through petitions was a powerful tool that helped bridge the gap between men and women in a rigidly patriarchal colonial system. Even though women understood and respected this distance, it didn't mean they had no power or voice.

Petition writing also offered a legal means to bridge the gap. It gave female subjects, who generally had no other direct contact with the authorities, a legal mechanism to press the government to fulfilits obligations.

Additionally, they demonstrate that women were not passive and voiceless subjects of the empire, as much of the colonial historiography would have made one believe. On the contrary, women understood their qualifications as petitioners and their rights even as they stood before an administration that was male dominated.

Petitioning enabled women to occupy (as much as possible) colonial spaces that were designed to be exclusively male. Since they occupied substantially diminished roles, Igbo women evolved their roles into a semblance of their precolonial expressions of political and socioeconomic power. By petitioning, they could be heard in the corridors of power that were otherwise unapproachable to them. Sometimes they managed to get the upper levels of the colonial government to address a manifest wrong.

Even when the administration did not resolve their problems, analysis of these sources reveals a pattern of interaction between the coloniser and the colonised, one that has not been recognised before. Indeed, a study of "female voices on ink" demonstrates the need to shift narratives and focus on neglected but unsung female heroes of the colonial period. We must recognise these women for what they were – contestants and agents of power in a male-dominated, British colonial society.

III. The Igbo Firsts

The Igbo, since their arrival on the Nigerian political scene, have made significant impacts on the polity, and have recorded a lot of historical feats as could be seen below.

(a) The first Black Vice Chancellor of the University of Ibadan was an Igbo, Professor Kenneth Dike. He was also the first Nigerian Professor of History.

(b) The first Vice Chancellor of the University of Lagos was an Igbo, Professor Eni Njoku. He was also the first Nigerian Professor of Botany

(c) The first black person to be appointed University Vice Chancellor in the United Kingdom is an Igbo, Professor Charles Egbu. He was Vice Chancellor of Leeds Trinity University.

(d) The first Nigerian Professor of Mathematics was an Igbo. Professor Chike Obi, the man who solved Fermat's Last Theorem. He was followed by another Igbo man, Professor James Ezeilo, Professor of Differential Calculus and the founder of the Ezeilo Constant.

(e) The first African Professor of Agriculture and first Nigerian Professor of Geophysics is an Igbo, Professor Cyril Agodi Onwumechili

(d) The first Nigerian Professor of Anatomy and Physiology is an Igbo, Professor Chike Edozien, the Obi of Asaba.

(e) The first Nigerian Professor of Physics was an Igbo, Professor Okoye, who became a Professor of Physics at the Massachusetts Institute of Technology, USA in 1960. He was followed by the likes of Professor Alexander Animalu who has been nominated for the Nobel Prize for Physics three times for his research in Intermediate Quantum Physics.

(f) The first Nigerian Professor of Nuclear Physics and Chemistry is an Igbo, Professor Frank Ndili who gained a Ph.D in his early '20s at

Cambridge University in Nuclear Physics and Chemistry in the early 1960s.
(g) The first Nigerian Professor of Statistics was an Igbo, Professor James Adichie
(h) The first Nigerian Professor of Medicine was an Igbo, Professor Herbert Kodilinye. He was appointed a Professor of Medicine at the University of London in 1952, and later became the Vice Chancellor of the University of Nigeria, Nsukka after the war.
(i) The first Nigerian Professor of Astronomy was an Igbo, Professor Ntukoju
(j) The first Nigerian Professor of Demography and Statistical Research into population studies was an Igbo, Professor Chukwuka Okonjo, the father of Dr, Ngozi Okonjo-Iweala.
(i) The first Nigerian PhD in Mechanical Engineering was an Igbo, Professor Gordian Ezekwe.
(j) The first Nigerian Professor of Philosophy was an Igbo, Professor G D Okafor, who became a Professor of Philosophy at the Amherst College USA in 1953.
(k) The first Nigerian Professor of Economics was an Igbo, Dr. Pius Okigbo, who became a visiting scholar and Professor of Economics at the University of London in 1954. He was also the first Nigerian Ph.D in Economics.
(l) The first Nigerian Professor of Theology and Theological Research was an Igbo, Professor Njoku who became the first Nigerian to earn a PhD in Theology from Queens University Belfast in Ireland. He was appointed a Professor of Theology at the University College Zambia in 1952.
(m) The first Nigerian and West African female Cardiothoracic Surgeon was an Igbo, Dr Ogadimma M. Ggbaja.
(n) The first Nigerian female writer to be published internationally was an Igbo, Flora Nwapa.
(o) The first black Canadian Justice Minister is an Igbo, Kaycee Madu
(p) The first female commercial pilot and the first woman to pilot an aircraft in Nigeria is an Igbo, Captain Chinyere Onyenuchea

IV. The Igbo Spirit

Peter Alexander Ashikiwe Adione Egom,

The legendary "Motor-Park Economist"

I am of Igbo stock from Ukala-Okpunor in Oshimili North LGA of Delta State. I am 61 years old and have, since late 1965, during my undergraduate days at Downing College, Cambridge, England, been fascinated by my people, the Igbo, and specifically by what makes them such a pulsating enigma of a people.

It was, indeed, a chance remark by the late and distinguished scholar in social anthropology at Cambridge, Professor Meyer Fortes, which set me on my lifelong journey of private inquiry into the ethno-spiritual makeup of the Igbo. My then larger-than-life and bountiful companion was my fellow undergraduate at the Cambridge University faculty for archaeology and anthropology, Mallam Ibrahim Tahir of BBC Bush House fame. We were having tea at a teashop just across Ibrahim's King's College on this particular autumn afternoon, as was our custom, when our professor of Social Anthropology, Meyer Fortes, walked in and sat with us for a chat. One thing led to another, and we soon found ourselves discussing ethno-types in Africa.

Professor Fortes had been one of the bright lights in Lord Bailey's team of Africanists that did the regular tome of Africa Survey for the British Foreign and Colonial Office. And Professor Fortes told us that, according to Lord Bailey, the Igbo, out of the legion of African ethnic groups they studied, were the least encumbered with any cultural baggage. In a manner of speaking, the Igbo come light and go light with the baggage of culture.

Of course, Professor Fortes assumed that Ibrahim and myself knew what Lord Bailey meant with the concept of cultural baggage and did not venture into any explanation of it. But as soon as he took his leave of us, Ibrahim and I fell into a very passionate but friendly discussion of this hazy concept. And, if my memory serves me right, we eventually let the matter be without agreeing on what the concept of cultural baggage stands for. But there was something that my mind could not let go of after this encounter. I had to know more about my people, the Igbo, who come light and go light with the baggage of culture.

My lecturer in Social Anthropology at Cambridge, Mr. G. I. Jones, an ex-colonial administrator in the Eastern Region of Nigeria, and an Igbophil of sorts, was on hand to give me advice on where to find materials on the Igbo. And what I could glean from the diverse tomes of Igbo historical and ethnographical that came my way was this. There was no love lost between the European slave dealers and colonialists and the Igbo, either on the continent of Africa or in the Diaspora. Igbo slaves were difficult to handle, prone to rebellion, and bad for the economy of the slave-owner. And the fear of the Igbo was, in a manner of speaking, the beginning of economic wisdom among European slave-owners and, later, colonialists.

The Igbo were troublemakers and troubleshooters in bondage, as one saw in Haiti in the rebellious years leading up to the overthrow of the French and the independence of the island in 1805, and in the Southern States of North America, where Igbo slaves jumped into the sea rather than face slavery! So, the Igbo were bad news as slaves. And in the restricted freedom of colonial Nigeria, as the colonialists saw to their continued irritation, the Igbo were uppity, difficult to convince, and difficult to lead. He was never really the darling of the mandarins at the British Foreign and Colonial Office at Whitehall, London!

But that is exactly what European predators thought of the Igbo! I was not satisfied with it. I wanted to know what made the Igbo uppity, difficult to convince, and difficult to lead in the restricted freedom of colonial Nigeria, and what made him a troublemaker and troubleshooter in the bondage of slavery abroad. I simply wanted to touch the Igbo spirit in order to better understand who I am. And the books I read then in England at the time could not point me in the right direction. And so, I shelved the project of my search for the essential attributes of the Igbo without knowing whether I would ever come back to it.

But, did I really shelve this project? Not at all. For what I did not realise at the time in Cambridge was that I had embarked on a lifelong journey of inquiry into my essential identity as a member of the Igbo stock, and that this project would not be put on hold until the day I died.. Indeed, my search for what makes the Igbo what he is my search for my true identity as a full-blooded Igbo. There is no way my mind could rest on the matter as soon as it had embarked upon its search. So, what I do now see, in retrospect, is that my mind has been, for nearly four decades now, trying to give a tangible structure to the Igbo spirit. And what I do give in this brief write-up is my status report on what I think makes the Igbo what he is: a man of vision, mission, adventure, integrity, and compassion. But, before I embark upon this brief ode to the Igbo spirit, let me fill in the reader with a few titbits about my life after going down from Cambridge in June 1966.

My flight back to Nigeria was scheduled for that blighting day of July 29, 1966, but had to be shelved until August 4, 1966. I made it to Lagos on that day and came to see a Nigeria that was calm on the surface but was doing unspeakable horror and mayhem to the Igbo in Lagos, at Ibadan, and all over Northern Nigeria. But I never felt that I was in danger and went about Lagos without any fear for my life. And in so doing, I came to catch an instructive glimpse into the mind of the Igbo.

The heavens were about to fall upon him, and even the ground he stood on was giving way under him. Yet he did not panic. He reacted with bone-chilling firmness and maturity. Kai, was I happy to be an Igbo? Except for the Roman Catholic Church, the Igbo had no friends at home or abroad. This is what I saw with my own eyes in Lagos from August 4, 1966, until July 18, 1967, when I was taken into a seven-month detention spell at Ikoyi and Kirikiri prisons and mercifully kept out of harm's way in the hands of my fellow countrymen. And after my release from detention on March 14, 1968, I bolted for Europe on April 18, 1968.

I spent the ensuing fourteen years in Denmark and Tanzania teaching social anthropology, reading and teaching economics, and doing research in economics. But in late 1982, nature and culture reached out to me in Denmark and brought me back to Nigeria for keeps. And when I returned to Nigeria twelve years after the end of Biafran hostilities on January 15, 1970, what I saw astounded me as much as it encouraged me. The Igbo, my people, were back into the mainstream of Nigerian sociopolitical and economic life as if nothing had occurred between 1966 and 1970. I was happy to be back in Nigeria, and I have no desire whatsoever to ever leave Nigeria again for anywhere else. Why so? Because the Igbo spirit is the future of Nigeria.

The Igbo spirit is not a conquering spirit, an imperial spirit, or an exploiting spirit. The Igbo spirit is an Afrocentric spirit, a competitive spirit, a liberating spirit, and a spirit that restores. In fact, the Igbo spirit is the quintessential Islamo-Christian spirit of the common good, as one finds in the holy books of the Quran and the Bible. Thus, the Igbo spirit thrives and lives by the democratic ethic of "one for all and all for one".

This is the liberating and restoring spirit that is about to encompass Nigeria and take her to great heights of material and social plenty and of individual freedom. And there is nothing anyone anywhere on this earth or in the heavens can do to stop this Igbo spirit from encompassing and elevating Nigerians and the black race as a whole. For the matter has long been settled in the highest heavens, the abode of God Almighty.

So, it is quite understandable that the Igbo must go through, as they are doing today, the harassment and chicanery of the sworn enemies of light and of the liberation and restoration of the black race. The Igbo spirit is the bearer of light, and where light comes, darkness must disappear. So, what we are experiencing in Nigeria today is the era of pitch-darkness, which must precede the dawn of freedom and plenty. In fact, what we are witnessing in Nigeria today, with the Igbo bearing the full brunt of it, are the thrashing death throes of an old and uncaring dinosaur of a Nigeria of the ungodly, where local slave dealers have unleashed, on behalf of their old European slave-dealing puppet masters, a culture of impunity and lawlessness on all Nigerians and especially on the Igbo. But it will not last. This is simply because the 21st century is the century of the African, and the Igbo are at the forefront of the war for the economic liberation and empowerment of the black race. This is what makes the Igbo spirit the ethical template of the future for the common good of all Nigerians and every black person.

Then what are the attributes of the Igbo spirit? One, it is God-fearing and God loving. Two, it is democratic to the core. And three, it is a private enterprise write large. The Igbo puts God Almighty at the centre of his sociopolitical and economic life, and this is what explains why he is so fiercely democratic and so competitively entrepreneurial but so passionately communal to the core.

So, the Igbo spirit is not about the ethnic subjugation of one group by the other. Rather, it is about the opening up equal vents of opportunity for the small, the medium, and the large, for the weak, the half-weak and the strong.

It was, indeed, this very stark and unmistakable difference between the Eurocentric spirit of oppression and enslavement that rules Nigeria today and the Afrocentric Igbo spirit of liberation and restoration that will rule Nigeria tomorrow that I had in mind when I wrote as follows on pages xviii and xix of the Preface to my book of 2002, "Globalization at the Crossroads: Capitalism or Communalism?"

"Consequently, the centre is extremely attractive to any budding ethnic politician in Nigeria. They are all ethnic politicians, after all. It is there in the centre that the financial and fiscal power of Nigeria is concentrated. So, every ethnic politician wants to get to the imperial centre at all costs. And when he eventually gets there, he wants to keep the imperial reins of Nigeria's financial and fiscal power within his ethnic bailiwick for all time and at all costs. It is an ethnic winner-take-all affair where only the ruthless and the idolatrous survive.

"However, we do want a Nigeria that has ample room for all of us. This Nigeria must deal deal with all of us equally and fairly, regardless of our physical size or the alleged numerical strength of our ethnic origins. The law shall require equal representation and participation for all of us. Thus, each and every one of us, individuals and groups, who belong to Nigeria must be allowed to use our native and achieved financial, human, and material resources for our own private good and for the common good..."

But the reigning Eurocentric spirit of oppression and enslavement in Nigeria today is the sworn enemy of democracy. This is so because it puts Mammon, instead of God Almighty, at the centre of the socioeconomic and political lives of Nigerian. This is the source and sustainer of the culture of impunity and lawlessness that pervades all levels of governance in Nigeria today, because the whole of the law is god-hating and god-baiting where Mammon is in charge. Fortunately, however, the Afrocentric Igbo spirit, which seeks to put God Almighty first in the thoughts, words, and deeds of the Nigerian, is, most certainly, around the corner to consign this Eurocentric spirit of the congenital blighter, the cowardly scourge of the Nigerian and the black race, back to the pit of hell where it belongs.

Therefore, the Igbo in Nigeria have nothing to fear but fear themselves. They should always keep in mind that to whom much is given, much is expected in return.. God Almighty has blessed them with the knowledge of the financial and industrial ways and means of turning sand into gold. It is their duty to open up and spread this knowledge among their ethnic neighbours in the near and far beyond Africa in order to forge an ever widening and concentric wave of financial solidarity among different ethnic groups in Nigeria and Africa, that will empower each African ethnic group to yield its best social and industrial products for the common good of all Africans and to the glory of God Almighty.

In fact, the true social message of the Igbo spirit for the Nigerian in particular and for the black race in general comes straight from the Catholic Social Teaching and more specifically from St. Paul's 2 Corinthians 8: 1315 and St. Peter's 1 Peter 4:10 as follows: Financial solidarity among Nigerians and Africans leads to the industrial subsidiaries of each Nigerian and each African. This is what the dividend of democracy is essentially about. It is the enabling environment for dreaming and seeing one's dreams come true in one's lifetime. And this social message that allows the zillion flowers of entrepreneurial excellence to bloom in Nigeria and in Africa as a whole is the essential social ethic of Islam as in Qur'an 16:90, al'adl walihsan. Hence, the Igbo spirit is the Islamo Christian ethic for the economic liberation and restoration of man in Africa and beyond.

Consequently, the Igbo in Nigeria and in the Diaspora should take heart and continue to put all before the throne of grace. For their past and current tormentors, both Eurocentric and local, they are just a passing storm in a God-baiting and God-taunting teacup. Uyagami!

. *Peter Alexander Ashikiwe Adione Egom wrote this article before he died on March 3, 2013 at the age of 70.*

V. Nso Ani Or Abomination In Igboland

Fadafranklin Mmor

1. Parents having sex with their children. Father for daughters, mother for sons.
2. Siblings having sex with each other, even nuclear and extended family members.
3. Marriage to a member of one's family.

4. Rape.
5. Murder...The community can ostracize or banish you.
6. Poisoning of one's food.
7. Suicide.
8. Having sex on a farmland or committing murder on a farmland.
9. Fighting with your parents.
10. Deliberately pushing down an old man or woman.
11. Seeing the nakedness of your parents or any elder and making mockery of it.
12. Stealing from a blind man or ridiculing handicapped people.
13. Love portion. Using it on any man or woman, for luck, seduction etc.
14. Having sex with a widow whose husband is yet to be buried or who is yet to remove hermourning clothes.
15. Having sex with a widower whose wife is yet to be buried or still mourning her child.
16. Stealing or swapping someone's child from her mother.
17. Beating up a pregnant woman.
18. Visiting witch doctors with the intent of killing one's neighbor or relation.
19. Taking a land that does not belong to you by force. It can end your life. Comfortably having children and staying with a man who is not traditionally and legallymarried to you.
20. Having sex with your mother, Father, sister and in-laws.
21. Having sex with your father's wife. Your step mum or step-father.
22. Maltreating of someone's children under your care.
23. Harvesting someone's crops that is not yours.
24. Having sex on someone's matrimonial bed.

VI. The Igbo Isiagu Symbol

By Anozie Wambu

Abstract

In this essay, I use "akwa isiagụ" as a metaphor to illustrate that Igbos have not done exactly well to preserve their language and culture. I posit that they have abandoned their unique cultural symbol, that they are now parading a symbol of foreign popular culture as their foremost emblem. But I also present perspectives that might ignite a quest for self-rediscovery.

Akwa isiagụ is the clothing fabric patterned with motifs showing fierce-looking lion's head and mane. Some designs show a less stern lion's head, with two or three cow horns besides it.

Since the last 50 to 60 years, Igbos have managed to portray this fabric design as their classic cultural emblem, in fact, as something of a totem. Igbo chiefs and nze and ọzọ title holders use it to make their ceremonial gears. At native marriage ceremonies and similar cultural events, isiagụ garments of different colours and styles grace the day. Igbo people feel a certain sense of pride when they dress in isiagụ attire. Even non-Igbos consider isiagụ as to be to Igbos what the tartan is to Scots, or the yarmulke is to Jews. Such is the impression, that when they are identifying with or participating at an Igbo traditional practice (eg taking an Igbo chieftaincy), they dress in isiagụ gear. Recent examples include President Buhari, Fayose, and Zuma.

But this is an imported, foreign popular culture. Neither the lion nor the lion icon have any significance in Igbo cultural foundations. Indeed, using the descriptor 'isiagụ' to refer to a lion's head motif is the wrong use of the word "agụ".

Incorrect Language

Agụ is not a lion in Igbo. Agụ is a leopard. Folks have written about this before, and I've discussed it in other forums on the subject. It is pitiful that it remains a source of confusion for many adult Igbos. There is just a little understanding of Igbo origins and the names of feline (cat) species. You hear all manner of names that contradict biogeography. Like, "agụ is lion, and ọdụmis a tiger". Or, "agụ is a lion, and a leopard is edi abalị". But let's clear this up.

Just as jaguars and cougars are found only in the Americas, tigers inhabit only Eurasia. They do not belong to the fauna (native animals) of sub-Saharan Africa. Because the ancient Igbos had never seen or heard of tigers, they had no indigenous name for them.

Edi or edi abalị is the African civet. One of the 38 viverridae species, it is slightly smaller than the leopard. A carnivore, no doubt, but it is timider, less agile, and far less specialised in opportunistic hunting. It has a broadly cat-like general appearance, but its muzzle is more pointed than that of a typical feline. Leopard has distinct camouflage spots that allow it to use forest canopies for cover, enhancing its ability to hunt by surprise, But the African civet typically has black and white spots.

The ancient Igbo were well acquainted with the Edi or edi abalị a nocturnal creature that sleeps for approximately 20 hours per day, which is why the Igbo still use "edi" as a metaphor to refer to a person who sleeps a lot. The leopard is bold, agile, versatile, and highly admired in Igbo cultural foundations. But edi is loathed and associated with negativity, because it smells and relies more on con and coy to lure its preys. That's also why in Igbo "edi aghụghọ" is a metaphor that refers to a deceptive person. Knowing the structure of the Igbo language will reveal that agụ is not lion. Many Igbo words were created from metaphorical use of existing words. To form names for creatures or objects, the Igbo often devised a two-word metaphor comparing what was sought to be named to another named object or creature. For example, ụlọ is house, and school is "ụlọ-akwụkwọ" (house for books), while hospital is "ụlọ ọgwụ" (house for medication).

Leopard - agụ – preys on mammals and has spots on its fur. That is why the wall gecko, which hunts insects and has spots, is referred to as an agụ ụlọ (ie. house leopard). And the crocodile, that preys on water creatures and has patches that resemble the leopard's spots, is called agụ iyi (leopard of the waters). Similarly, the palm genet, a small mammal that resembles the squirrel but, unlike the squirrel has spots on its fur, is called "agụ nkwụ". In contrast, the lion has no spots on its fur. The lion's fur is generally brown.

The leopard is an Igbo animal totem. Being about three times the size of a leopard, the lion is stronger and sometimes even preys on the leopard. The Igbo say "ọdụm na-egbu agụ". Despite this, the lion has no special recognition in Igbo cultural systems. Ancient Igbo likely did not even have any or much contact with lions as a specie. For whereas leopards inhabit in rainforests (although they are very adaptable and thrive in other vegetations), lions inhabit mainly in savannah or grasslands. Savannah vegetation does not exist (and likely never existed) in Igboland. Igboid areas sit generally in lowland rainforest.

A lion can occasionally stray into a rainforest or refuge there if persecuted in its usual habitat. It must have been in such circumstances that the Igbo came to know about the lion. Yet that was not enough to diminish their fascination for the leopard, a beast with which they had contended for thousands and thousands of years.

It should be noted that while leopards operate alone, lions are the most social of the cat species. Lions operate in close-knit social groups called "pride". Ethologists (scholars of animal behaviour) have observed that this sociality makes the lion a better communicator than other big cats. It means lions roar frequently and easily broadcast their presence and emotions. Conversely, a leopard's solitary lifestyle makes it less detectable and more perceptive and reactive to intrusion. For this reason, its senses of vision and hearing are sharper than those of a lion. Ancient Igbo witnessed this firsthand. They saw how a leopard, hiding stealthily among forestcanopies, would detect the slightest animal or human movement and chase and pounce savagely. In a forest environment, a lion has little chance to fight down the more agile leopard. A lion's size and weight render it less agile to climb high. But a leopard can climb to the top of an iroko tree in less than 10 seconds. Leopard is probably the only big mammal that can descend a tree head first. It uses its long tail to maintain perfect aerodynamic balance.

With a top average speed of about 80 km per hour, lion is faster than leopard. But it can only run for very short bursts and needs to be close to its prey before starting an attack. But the leopard can run for far longer stretches, at an average top speed of about 58 km per hour. A leopard can make a singleleap of over 6 m (20 ft) horizontally and can jump up to 3 m (9.8 ft) vertically. And it is a powerful swimmer. Although its vision is sharpest in the dark, it can be equally keen-eyed during the day.

Incredibly versatile, the leopard hunts on land, up on the trees and in water. On the trees, it can out manoeuvre specialised climbers and jumpers, including monkeys and baboons. Leopards have been observed leaping into the air, snatching a monkey with a bite, and regaining control of tree branches. That is, it successfully launches a mid-air strike from a tree top and lands back on the tree. It goes into rivers and streams, where it over-powers creatures like alligators and hauls them off the water, all the way up a tree.

A silent predator, when discreteness will give it an advantage, can be elusive. It has a pad of tissue in the flat of its claws that acts as a silencer when it walks. It can literally hide in plain sight. When it tucks itself in between the forks of tree branches, it just blends with the tree trunk. It can create optical illusions to deceive its prey, including humans. A leopard will coil its head and tail into its body and crouch flat on the ground, appearing like dry wood lying about. Very patient. If its target is a troop of animals, it can hold its cool and then attack the last of the troop from behind.

When persecuted by humans, a leopard is more likely to fight back than a lion. It does not target one out of a group. It will attack one person after another, reason the Igbo say "ofu agụ na-achụ mba" (a single leopard can sack a town).

For thousands of years, the Maasai people of Kenya have practised the art of emerging from hiding to scare lions away from their kill and take it home for meat. But a leopard will drag its kill in its mouth and climb a tree. It climbs a tree carrying, in its mouth, a carcass far heavier than its own size. For example, animals like bull, giraffe, and antelope. In those days, it would attack someone's goat or sheep and drag it in its mouth deep into the forest and up onto a tree.

The lion lacks these amazing abilities. In terms of general efficiency and productivity as jungle hunters, the leopard beats the lion by many miles! Indeed, scientists have determined that, pound for pound (i.e., adjusted for differences in size and weight), the leopard is the strongest of all the big cat species.

It was for these reasons that the ancient Igbo revered the leopard as their totem animal for strength, agility, boldness, and courage. And that is also why the Igbo language is littered with similes, metaphors, adages, and proverbs that use agụ to illustrate positive energy and abilities. Like "omekagụ", "agụnwa", etcetera. And it is for this reason that many Igbo families and communities proudly derived their names and sobriquets after agụ. Like "Ụmụagụ, Amagụ Dimagụ, Eziagụ, Duruagụ etc.

Today, as urban dwellers, we can look down on the leopard. But to the Igbo of those jungle days, a snarling leopard on the loose was literally nature's force unleashed. Every hamlet had a chant or cry that was used to alarm the community when a leopard was sighted. The chant in my own area was "ọ wụ agụ o!" (it is a leopard o!).

Social codes dictated that a person who heard the cry also repeat it, until the entire community was alerted. And until the leopard was killed or confirmed to have returned to the deep forests, the usual daily activities were suspended. Children and women would not go to the streams to fetch water. No one went to the farms nor led their sheep out to graze. Able bodied men were then organised into groups to track down the leopard. And think of it. Those men did not have guns. They went with spears, bows, and sticks. Combating the leopard in these situations was an act of extraordinary bravery and patriotism, risking one's life for the safety of the community. That explains why the person who eventually killed the leopard instantly became a hero and was given the honorific "Ogbu Agụ".

And eating leopard meat was a once-in-a-generation experience. Till today, the Igbo use the metaphor "ọ bụanụ agụ?" (is it a leopard meat?) to question the value of a highly priced or scarce commodity. Of course, the leopard skin was dried and kept by the leopard killer. He and his descendants would display it with pride for hundreds of years afterwards. And legend has it that reputable native doctors harvested the leopard's bile or gall and used it to prepare the most potent charms or medicines, which warriors drank to boost their bravery and ferocity during intertribal wars.

This elusive and powerful animal was so perplexing to the ancient Igbo that they even considered it a mysterious creature, a reason many Igbo dialects added the suffix "mystery" or "invisible" ("owo", "owu", "owuru" or "awolo") to its name. Many areas call it agụ owuru – ie, leopard of mystery, mysterious leopard, or the leopard that suddenly appears and disappears. Igbo metaphysics believed that some men acquired powers to transform into leopards. To assume the nature and characteristics of a leopard, even for a short period, was considered the attainment of a transcendental and superior state of being.

Indeed, in ancient Igbo cosmology, the entire universe was explained as a mystical leopard persona. The weather system and visible changes in the skies were said to be a leopard, the sky leopard. The thick clouds that formed in the sky before rainfall were its shimmering eyes just waking up from sleep. The movement of the tick clouds was the movement of the leopard in its marauding character. The leopard's flashing eyes were the lightning strikes that preceded thunder. The thunder was its voice, snarling in anger and ready to pounce. The heavy rains were its urine gushing with the force typical of its strength. And bright day was the sky leopard fully awake, with eyes wide open.

The Lion Symbol Is Not Originally Igbo

This portrayal of the lion as symbolic cultural icon of the Igbos is only recent. It is driven by the influence of modern media and foreign popular culture. We watch a lot of animal documentaries these days and read a lot of books that continue to inform us that the lion is the king of the beasts. True! But they don't tell us about the king of our forests.

Today in global popular culture (e.g., children's cartoons, films, etc.), we are taught to be like the lion. Throughout history and in many parts of the world, the lion image has been used in stories, artwork, coats of arms, logos, and advertisements to depict strength, ferocity, power, confidence, and success. The Bible and other major religious texts also contain lion symbolism. And so, the Igbos yielded–completely! We abandoned our equivalent animal totem and even had to distort our language as a result. Yet Igbo folklore is filled with stories that reference "agụ" as the king of animals. First-generation Igbo intellectuals had no doubt that agụ was leopard. And they were acutely aware of its significance in the Igbo culture and worldview.

In Onuora Nzekwu's classic novel *Eze Goes to School* (published 1963), the ravaging beast that held the people of Ohia hostage and which Eze's father killed but later died from the wound it inflicted on him was a leopard, not a lion. Anezi Okoro's 1966 novel *The Village School* featured an intriguing student. Ismael was popular amongst his mates because his father was a reputed hunter who killed a leopard and took the title "The Leopard Killer".

In 1950, Cyprian Ekwensi published a novel entitled *'The Leopard's Claw'*. Chinua Achebe later published a short story with the title "*How the Leopard Got Its Claws*". He narrated an Igbo folktale featuring a leopard as the king of the animals. Achebe's other book; 'Anthills of the Savanah, narrates the incident when the leopard, the king of the forest, was to kill the tortoise and how the tortoise scattered sand and grass. And in the *'Arrow of God'* he masterfully devised an English translation of a popular Igbo proverb, 'Agụ aghaghị ịmụ ihe yiri agụ" as "what the leopard sires cannot be different from the leopard". These men did not talk about the lion.

Chukwumeka Ike's novel "*The Bottled Leopard*" explores Igbo metaphysics in the context of interpersonal strife during primal times. It tells the story of how men acquired metaphysical powers and transformed into leopards to terrify their neighbours or attack their animals.

Wago, the protagonist of *'The Great Ponds'* (the second novel of Elechi Amadi's trilogy), was revered in the community because he killed a leopard. He was even hailed with the honorific "The Leopard Killer". What surprised the members of the community was that the brave Leopard Killer later committed suicide, something they deemed an act of cowardice.

Gabriel Okara, an Ijaw man, was educated at Government College Umuahia and worked in Enugu for many years. He wrote the famous poem 'The Drum and the Piano'. Romanticising primal African life, he used the imagery of a "leopard snarling about to leap and the hunters crouching with spears poised".

If you've read the works of the late great poet Christopher Okigbo, you will see repeated references to the leopard. In a manuscript drafting the poem 'Land of Our Birth' which he intended to be Biafra's anthem, Okigbo wrote of the Eastern Region's (mostly Igbos) resolve to found its own republic: "This leopard is now unchained".

The defunct Biafran Armed Forces published and circulated a periodic newsletter/bulletin to engage the masses. It was not for nothing that the brand name of that bulletin/newsletter was "The Leopard". Indeed, the coat of arms of that republic, which was the same used by the Eastern Region, proudly featured a charging leopard.

Stay True To Who You Are

Leopard skin ("akpụkpọ agụ") was the totemic body-covering material in Igbo cultural foundations. In this modern era, if any fabric should be an emblem of Igbo culture, it is leopard-skin fabrics. This lion symbol expresses nothing unique about the Igbo.

Totemic symbols embody and express the spirit, history, character, and worldview of a people: what they have been through on their road to civilisation, how they see themselves in the world, the standards and qualities they aspire to, collectively and as individuals.

It is not difficult to see parallels between the leopard's characteristics and the core Igbo character: There is the leopard's individualism – that Igbo man's tendency to take his own destiny in his hands. The leopard is vigilant and opportunistic. The Igbo are wired to identify and take advantage of changing dynamics. Think of the spirit of enterprise and consider the leopard's ability to perform feats that are out of proportion to its size. What about the leopard's versatility?

The Igbo excel in any enterprise they truly apply their energy to. And then there's adaptability. The Igbo have not only survived different challenging conditions but have thrived in different regions and environments. They have turned adversities into opportunities and made huge successes out of nothing.

No imperial influence has forced the Scots to abandon the tartan, or has centuries of persecution swayed the Jews to discard the yarmulke. The leopard was also the animal totem of the Zulus, that the proud people of South Africa remain proud of it. Why then did the Igbo falter?

Bibliography

Abanobi, Chika (2016), Onitsha Ado: A Short History Of Onitsha available from https://www.nairaland.com/2853991/hystory-onitsha-chika-abanobi
Achebe, Chinua (1983) *The Trouble With Nigeria* (Enugu: Fourth Dimension Publishing Co. Ltd.)
Achebe, C, (2012) *There Was a Country* (London, Penguin Books)
Achebe, Chinua (1994) *Things Fall Apart* (London, Heinemann)
Acholonu, C. (2005), *The Gram Code of African Adam – Stone Books and Cave Libraries, Reconstructing 450,000 Years of Africa's Lost Civilizations* (Abuja: Afa Publications).
Ade, Obayemi (1972) *The Yoruba and Edo-speaking Peoples and their Neighbours Before 1600* (Ibadan, Institute of African Studies).
Adegbulu, Femi (2011) 'From Warrant Chiefs to Ezeship: A Distortion of Traditional Institution in Igboland?' *Afro Asian Journal of Social Sciences*, Volume 2, No. 2.2 Quarter II.
Adibe, Tony (2009) Lejja, 'The World's Oldest Iron Smelting Site In Nigeria' *The Nation*, April 29.
Afigbo, A.E. (1981) *Ropes of Sand: Studies in Igbo History and Culture* (Ibadan: University Press)
Afigbo, A.E. (2000) *Igbo Genesis*, (Uturu: Abia State University Press Ltd.)
Afigbo, A.E. (1992) *Groundwork of Igbo History* (Lagos, Vista Books).
Afigbo, A.E. (1981) *The Age of Innocence*, (Owerri, Ahiajioku Lecture)
Ali, Vincent Egwu (2014), 'A Critical Survey of the Growth, Decline, and Sustainability of Traditional Pottery Practice among the Igbo of South Eastern Nigeria', *The Journal of Modern Craft*. 7 (2): 123–139.
Anambra State of Nigeria (1981), 'Traditional Rulers' Law 1981
Andah, B. W., Derefaka, A. A. (1983) '1981 field season at the palaeolithic site of Ugwuele-Uturu, a preliminary report', *Paper Presented at the 9th Congress of the Pan African Association for Prehistory and Related Studies*, Jos, Nigeria.
Aniakor, Chike C. (1996) 'Household Objects and the Philosophy of Igbo Social Space' in Arnoldi, Mary Jo; M Geary, Christrand and Hardin, Kris L (1996), *African Material Culture* (Bloomington, Indiana University Press)
Animalu AOE (2001) Ucheakonam: *A Way of Life in the Modern Scientific Age* (Owerri, Ahiajioku Lecture)
Animalu, AOE et al (2003, eds.) The South East Today: The way forward, (Nsukka: Ucheakonam Foundation Ltd.)
Anozie, F.N. (1979), 'Early Iron Technology in Igboland (Lejja and Umundu) in Perspectives on West Africa's Past' in *West African Journal of Archaeology* Vol 9, pp119-134
Anyanwu, U. (1999) 'The Igbo Yoruba- Relations and their Problems' in *Nsukka Journal of the Humanities* No. 10, (Enugu, Magnet Business Enterprises)
Aye, E. U. (2000), *The Efik People*, (Calabar, Glad Tidings Press).
Azikiwe, Nnamdi (1970) *My Odyssey*, (Ibadan, Spectrum Books Limited)
Basden, G.T. (1938) *Niger Ibos*, (London: Seeley Co.)
Biobaku, S.O. (1971) *Origin of the Yoruba* (Ibadan: University Press)

Bernis, J. (2017) 'No Relationship Between The Igbo and The Jews', *Daily Post* August 27)

Bondarenko, Dmitri; Roese, Peter (1999). 'Benin Prehistory. The Origin and Settling Down of the Edo', *Anthropos: International Review of Anthropology and Linguistics*. 1 January.

Booth, Thomas J. Chamberlain, Andrew T. and Pearson, Mike Parker (2015), 'Mummification In Bronze Age Britain', *Antiquity*, Volume 89, Issue 347, (October 2015), pp. 1155 – 1173. Available from https://www.cambridge.org/core/journals/antiquity/article/mummification-in-bronze-age-britain/738F5B39 B75741D162FD22E1B1586E73

Boston, J.S, (1960) 'Notes on Contact Between the Igala and the Igbo' *Journal of the Historical Society of Nigeria* vol.2, Vo.1,)

Buah, F.K. (1986) *A History of West Africa States AD 1000, Book One: The People* (London: Macmillan)

Chambers, D.B. (1913) *Enslaved Igbo And Ibibio In America* (Enugu: Jemezie Associates)

Chambers, D.B. (2005), *Murder at Montpelier: Igbo Africans in Virginia*, (Mississippi, University Press).

Chieftaincy Edict No. 8 of September 2, 1976, published in the Official Gazette No. 31, Volume 1 of 25th November 1976

Chike, Gabriel, Onyiuke, Michael, Obumselu Benedict (1968), *Massacre of Ndi-Igbo in 1966 : Report of the G.C.M. Onyiuke Tribunal of Inquiry* (Print Books)

Chikwendu, VC (1975), Afikpo Excavations (Unpublished Thesis).

Chinweizu (2005) 'The Reconstruction of Nigeria: Four Delusions on Our Strategic Horizon' The Guardian newspapers, (Friday, June 24)

Coleman, JS (1958) Nigeria: Background to Nationalism, (Berkeley and Los Angeles, University of California Press)

Crowder, Michael (1962) The Story of Nigeria, Igbo Primer popularly known as "Azu Ndu", approved by Government Education Department for infant classes of primary schools in the Igbo Provinces of then Eastern Nigeria. Available from https://wap.org.ng/read/false-history-of-benin-ancestry-of-anioma-ikwere-onicha/

Davidson, Basil (1970) *Old Africa Rediscovered* (London: Longman)

Dudley, BJ (1966) *Instability and Political Order: Politics and Crisis In Nigeria* (Ibadan, University of Ibadan Press

Ebighgbo, Chris (2002) *The Igbo Lost Worlds* (Enugu: Ezu Books Ltd).

Egharevba J. U (1960), A short History of Benin, (Ibadan, Ibadan University Press)

Ejiofor, LU (1989), 'Azikiwe and the Nigerian Civil War' in Olisa, MSO and Ikejiani, OM (eds.) (1989), Azikiwe and the African Revolution (Onitsha, African Fep Publishers Limited)

Eltis, David, Behrendt, Stephen D, Richardson, David, And Klein, Herbert S.(Eds.) (1999) The Transatlantic Slave Trade: A Database *On CD-ROM*. Available from, www.slaveryvoyages.org

Ekeh, Peter et al (1989) *Nigeria Since Independence: The First Twenty-Five Years. Volume V, Politics and Constitution* (Ibadan: Heinemann Books)

Eluwa, B.O.N, (2008) *Ado-na-Idu, History of Igbo Origin* (Owerri: De-Bonelsons Global Ltd).

Emeka, Lawrence (1999) 'The Challenges of Two Lost Industrial Civilizations in Enugu State' *Okanga* magazine, Enugu State Arts and Culture) April – June.

Equiano, Olaudah (2005), *The Interesting Narrative of the Life of Olaudah Equiano, or Gustavus Vassa, the African* (New York W.W. Norton & Company).

Eze, Dons (2008) *Africa in Turmoil* (Enugu: Linco Press).

Eze, Dons (2011) *Akama Ogwugwu Ebenebe* (Enugu: Linco Press)

Eze, Dons (2018) *Ezeagu Igbudu: The Land and Its People* (Enugu: Linco Press)

Fanon, Frantz (1966) *The Wretched of the Earth* (New York, Grove Press)

Fukuda, Yuji (1995) 'Groupism', *Human Studies*, No. 15.

Glyn Leonard (2009), *The Lower Niger and Its Tribes* (Charleston, South Carolina, Biblio Bazaar, LLC)

Gurdasani, D., Carstensen, T., Tekola-Ayele, F. *et al.* (2015), 'The African Genome Variation Project shapes Medical Genetics in Africa', *Nature*, 517, 327–332

Hartle, D.D. (1967) 'Archeology in Eastern Nigeria', *Nigerian Magazine* No. 93, June

Hrbek, Ivan; Fāsī, Muḥammad (1988), *Africa from the Seventh to the Eleventh Century*, (London: UNESCO).

Ibiwoye, Dotun (2014) 'Controversy over Igbo Origin: We have Proof that Umueri is the Cradle of Ndigbo', *Vanguard*, September 2

Idigo, M.C.M (1955) *The History of Aguleri* (Yaba-Lagos, Nicholas Printing and Publishing Co).

Ike, Obiora (2001) *Understanding Africa* (Enugu: CIDJAP Publications).

Ikime, O. (1980) *Ground Work of Nigerian History*, (Ibadan: Heinemann Educational Books).

Isichei, E, (1997), *A History of the Igbo People* (London, Macmillan)

Jannah, Imanuel (2014) 'History: How Igbos Came to Nigeria and Settled in the South-East', Available from: https://obindigbo.com.ng/2014/11/history-igbos-came-nigeria-settled-south-east/#:~:text=They%20traveled%20by%20water%20and, Omambala%20Rivers)%20was%20to%20be

Jean-Charles, Moise (2022), 'Home-Coming Mission To Enugu', *Vanguard*, January 22)

Jeffreys, MDW (2007) 'Ikenga: The Ibo Ram-headed God', *African Studies*, (online), January 19, available from https://www.tandfonline.com/doi/epdf/10.1080/ 000 20185408706926

Klein, Herbert S., and Jacob Klein (1999), *The Atlantic Slave Trade* (Cambridge, Cambridge University Press) pp. 103–139.

LeVine, R. (1971) 'Dreams and Deeds: Achievement Motivation in Nigeria' in Melson and Wolpe, (eds.) *Nigeria: Modernization and the Politics of Communalism* (Michigan State University Press, Quoted in H.N. Nwosu, (1977) Political Authority & the Nigerian Civil Service (Enugu: Fourth Dimension Publishers.

Lovejoy, Paul E.; Hogendorn, Jan S. (1993) Slow Death for Slavery: The Course of Abolition in Northern Nigeria 1897 – 1936 (Cambridge, Cambridge University Press)

Luckham, Robin (1971) The Nigerian Military (Cambridge: Cambridge University Press.

Madukasi, Francis Chuks (2018), 'Ozo Title: An Indigenous Institution In Traditional Religion That Upholds Patriarchy In Igbo Land SouthEastern Nigeria', *The International Journal of Social Sciences and Humanities Invention*, 5(5):4640-4652

Mazrui A (1999) 'From Slave Ship to Space Ship, *African Studies* Q. 2(4). Available from: http://asq.africa.ufl.edu/files/ASQ-Vol-2-Issue-4-Mazrui.pdf

Mbiti, JS (1969) *African Religions and Philosophy* (London, Heinemann Educational Books Ltd.)

Meek, C.K. (1937) *Law and Authority in a Nigerian Tribe* (London: Oxford University Press)

Meltzer, Milton. (1993) *Slavery: A World History*, (Cambridge, Massachusetts, United States, Da Capo Press).

Miners, NJ (1971) *The Nigerian Army 1956-1966* (London: Matheu & Co. Ltd)

Moyers, Bill (ed. 1989) *A World of Ideas* (New York, Doubleday)

Nair, K. K. (1972), *Politics and Society in South Eastern Nigeria 1841 – 1906: A study of Power, Diplomacy and Commerce in Old Calabar* (Evanston, North-Western University Press).

Neaher, Nancy C. (1981). 'An Interpretation of Igbo Carved Doors', *African Arts*, 15 (1) , pp . 49-55

Nnamani, C. (2001) *Ndi-Igb and The Challenge of Nation Building* (Enugu, Dawn Functions Production).

Nsukka Analyst (1994) 'Marginalization in the Nigerian Polity: A Diagnosis of the Igbo Problem and the National Question', *Nsukka Analyst*, Vol .I, No. I, December.

Nwaezeigwe, N.T. (2013) *The Politics of Igbo Origin and Culture: The Igbo-Ukwu and Nri*

Nwaezeigwe, N.T. (2007) *The Igbo and their Nri Neighbours*, (Enugu, Sana Press Ltd). Factors Reconsidered (Nsukka: Institute of African Studies)

Nwanna, C. (2011), 'Awka, the Land of Metal Smiths', *Awka: Nka na Uzu*, Vol.1 No.2

Nwosu, HN (1977) *Political Authority & The Nigerian Civil Service* (Enugu: Fourth Dimension Publishers)

Obasanjo, O (2017) 'Hard Talk', interview with the BBC, September 11, Available from: https://www.bbc.co.uk/programmes/n3ct2kl7

Ofonagoro, Walter (1982) "An Aspect of British Colonial Policy in Southern Nigeria: The Problems of Forced Labour and Slavery, 1895-1928" in B.I. Obiechere (ed), *Studies in Southeastern Nigerian History*, (London, Frank Cass).

Ogbonna, CA (2002) *Nigerian Peoples & Politics* (Enugu: SNAAP Press Ltd)

Oguejiofor, 'Anu, Igbos of Nigeria and Ancient Kemitians of Kemet (Egypt)' available from www.africaresource.com

Ogundiran, Akinwumi (June 2005). 'Four Millennia of Cultural History in Nigeria (ca. 2000 B.C.–A.D. 1900): Archaeological Perspectives', *Journal of World Prehistory*. 19 (2): 133–168. doi:10.1007/s10963- 006-9003-y.

Okeke, Igwebuike Romeo (1994) 'The Chieftaincy Institution and Government Recognized Traditional Rulers in Anambra State. Maiden Edition', Enugu, Media Forum.

Okonjo, IM (1974) *British Administration in Nigeria 1900-1950* (New York: Nok Publishers)

Okoye, M. (1981) Embattled Men, (Enugu: Fourth Dimension Publishers).
Okoye, Mokwugo (1979) A Letter to Dr. Nnamdi Azikiwe: A Dissent Remembered (Enugu: Fourth Dimension Publishing).
Okoye, Mokwugo (1984) Storms on the Niger (Enugu, Fourth Dimension Publishing).
Omeife Omeife (2021) 'The Biafra Story'; *Daily Star*, February 10
Onuoha, G. (2014), 'The Politics of "Hope" and "Despair": Generational Dimensions
  to Igbo Nationalism in Post-Civil War Nigeria', in *African Sociological Review* Vol.18 1.
Onwuejeogwu, MA (1981) 'Igbo civilization: Nri Kingdom and Hegemony', *Ethnographica*.
Onwuejeogwu, M.A. (1987) *Ahiajoku Lecture: Evolutionary Trends in the History of the Development of the Igbo Civilization in the Cultural Theatre of Igboland in Southern Nigeria* (Owerri, culture Division Imo State Ministry of Information and Culture).
Onwuejeogwu, M.A. (1981) *An Igbo Civilization: Nri Kingdom and Hegemony*,(London &Benin City Ethnographica and Ethiope)
Onwumechili, CA (2000) *Igbo Enwe Eze: The Igbo Have No Kings* (Owerri, Ahiajioku Lectures)
Onwuka, B (nd),. 'Biafra Zionist Movement', Available at www.biafrazionist movement. com.
Onwutalobi, Anthony-Claret. 'New Yam Festival - The Official Nnewi City Portal', available from. www.nnewi.info.
Ozoene, S. (2016) 'Nsude Pyramids: Black Africa's Lost Heritage' *Vanguard*, Nov. 11,
Ryder, A.F.C. (1969), *Benin and The Europeans*, (Longmans, London)
Schwarz, FAO, (1965) *The Tribe, the Nation or the Race, The Politics of Independence*, (Cambridge: MIT Press)
Shaw, Thurstan (ed. 1975) *Discovering Nigeria's Past* (Ibadan OUP)
Shaw, Thurstan (1968), 'Radiocarbon dating in Nigeria', *Journal of the Historical Society of Nigeria*, Vol. 4, No. 3 (December), pp. 453-465
Smith, Harold (1992) 'The Politics of Ignorance: Nigeria and the Cross-Street Hacks', *The Guardian* (London), March 12.
Stephen Behrendt (1999). 'Transatlantic Slave Trade', Africana: The Encyclopedia of the African and African American Experience (New York, Basic Civitas Books).
Talbot, P.S. (1926) Southern Nigeria Vols, I & II, (London: Oxford University Press.
Temples, P. (1959*),* Bantu Philosophy (Paris, Presence Africaine)
The Northern Region of Nigeria (1953), *Report on the Kano Disturbances, 16th, 17th, 18th, and 19th May, 1953,* (Kaduna: Government Printer, 1953)
Tony Adibe (2009) Lejja, The World's Oldest Iron Smelting Site In Nigeria (The Nation Newspapers, Lagos, April 29).
Uchechi Ogbonna (2021), 'Igbo History' (Igbos Since 3,000 BC). Available from https://web.facebook.com/groups/httpsyoutube.comchannelucwgna8mhaahno xhhxlpi/posts/Uchechi-Ogbonna-posted-in-IGBO-HISTORY-(IGBOS--SINCE-3000BC)/5930077707064114/?_rdc=1&_rdr
Udo, Edet A. (1983) Who are the Ibibio? (Onitsha, Africana-Feb Publishers Limited)

Ujumadu, Vincent (2014), 'Where Did The Igbo Originate From?" (Vanguard August 10).

Ukpong, Onoyom (2021), 'History of Efik', Available from https://m.facebook.com/Esanpeopleblog/posts/history-of-efikby-onoyom-ukpong-phdthe-efik-are-an-ethnic-group-settling-along-t/260714136059230/?locale=ms_MY

Umeh, J.A. (1999) *Igbo People-Their Origin and Culture Area*, (Enugu, Nigeria; Gostak Printing and Publishing Co. Ltd),

Uzoigwe, G.N. (2004) 'Evolution and Relevance of Autonomous Communities in Pre-colonial Igboland', *Journal of Third World Studies*, Spring.

Uzoigwe, GN (1974) *Britain and the Conquest of Africa* (New York: Nok Publishers International

Index

A

Aba Women's Riot, 28, 181, 295
Abakaliki, 74, 97, 105, 222, 343, 345, 346
Abia, 17, 18, 19, 85, 143, 144, 221, 241, 242, 244, 251, 256, 258, 310, 313, 323, 363
Abiku, 36
Abuetor, 18
Achebe, Chinua, 38, 40, 41, 42, 45, 71, 153, 162, 192, 205, 215, 238, 327, 328, 360, 363
Acholonu, Catherine, 92, 93, 100, 101, 363
Action Group, 183, 184, 185, 186, 187, 188, 189, 213, 227, 228, 229, 302, 306, 315, 325
Adegbenro, D.S, 186
Ado Kingdom, 88, 90
Afigbo, Adiele, 28, 86, 91, 92, 105, 106, 363
Afikpo, 19, 26, 74, 86, 102, 103, 104, 105, 106, 206, 311, 343, 345, 346, 364
African Archeology Network, 104
African Dashiki, 59
African Genome Variation Project, 103
African Great Lakes, 106
African Information Retrieval System, 159, 160
African Traditional Religions, 62
Agbor, 18, 19
Ahmadu Bello University, 190
Ai-Aroga community, 146
Akalogholi, 37
Akintola, S.L, 185, 186, 187, 188, 190, 214, 223, 305, 310
Akpanya, 151
Akwa Ibom, 17, 142, 143, 144, 145, 221

Ala Igbo Development Foundation, 245
Allan-Burns Commission, 185
Alyufsalam Rocks of Ilorin, 201
Ambassador plenipotentiaries, 42
Ambazonia, 17
Amhara, 161
Anaang, 143
Anambra, 17, 19, 28, 29, 30, 31, 65, 72, 73, 74, 75, 76, 77, 80, 85, 86, 96, 146, 147, 148, 151, 219, 221, 230, 241, 244, 248, 250, 256, 257, 303, 317, 323, 324, 327, 328, 333, 334, 339, 363, 366
Anambra State, 30, 31, 66, 74, 85, 219
Anglo-Saxon culture, 62
Ani/Ala, 36
Animalu, Alexander, 35, 39, 349, 363
Aniocha, 17, 148
Aniọcha, 16
Anozie, F.N, 56, 103, 105
Anyanwu, 36, 83, 101, 216, 332, 363
Arab, 85, 90, 193, 194, 266
Archaeology, 56
Arguim story, 114
Arinze, Francis, 337, 341
Ark of the Covenant, 71
Aro, 16, 24, 25, 74, 78, 152, 170
Arọ Oracle, 152, 153
Arochukwu, 12, 18, 23, 25, 144, 323
Asaba, 18, 177, 192, 196, 229, 305, 315, 349
ASHE foundation, 161
Atlantic Ocean, 85, 112, 113, 114, 121, 130, 154, 165
Attah Igala, 148
Autochthonous Igbo society, 80
Awolowo, Obafemi, 183, 184, 186, 187, 188, 193, 224, 228, 229, 302, 303, 315, 326
Azikiwe, Nnamdi, 132, 182, 184, 186, 188, 224, 225, 227, 229, 235, 239, 241, 298, 301, 304, 307, 309, 363

B

Baikie, W.B, 19, 86, 171
Balewa, Tafawa, 186, 188, 190, 214, 229, 302, 304, 316
Barbados, 112, 121, 126, 127, 289, 290
Basden, G.T., 70, 363
Beckless, Hillary, 127
Bello, Ahmadu, 175, 184, 228, 229, 282, 316
Bende, 19, 26, 251, 291, 293, 294
Benin City, 153, 156
Benue, 17, 18, 19, 69, 73, 88, 91, 106, 139, 144, 146, 147, 149, 156, 162, 165, 177, 179, 254, 347
Bernis, Rabbi Jonatan, 80
Biafra Independent Movement, 240
Biafra Zionist Movement, 240, 251, 252, 253, 264
Bight of Biafra, 17, 111, 121, 122, 123, 170
Bini Royal Dynasty, 26
Bini-Igbo relationship, 152
Biobaku, S.O., 89, 90, 363
Blassingame, John, 116
Blyden, Edward Wilmot, 66, 111, 282, 283, 284, 285
British African colonies, 165
British Broadcasting Corporation, 262
British Parliament, 115, 170, 171, 290
Bronze Age, 97
Buah, F.K., 81, 364

C

Cameroon, 17, 144, 145, 159, 165, 208, 304, 308, 310, 325, 337
Canaan, 84, 95, 96, 97, 98
Canon Sportif of Cameroun, 201
Cape Coast, 159
Cape Lopez, 17, 121
Caribbean economies, 113
Catholics, 16, 292, 335
Caucasian race, 82
Chimezie, Bright, 59
Chi-neke, 36
Chi-ukwu, 36, 101
Christian missionaries, 55, 65, 84, 116, 206, 207, 209
Christophe, Henry, 275, 276, 277, 278, 279
Chukwu Okike, 36
Chukwuma, Ali, 59, 304, 314, 315, 318
Church Missionary Society, 146, 280, 292, 331
Coca-Colasation" of the world, 62
Cole, Robert Wellesley, 111
Coleman, J.S., 205, 211, 364
Creole, 119, 126, 298
Cross River, 17, 18, 107, 140, 144, 145, 169, 221, 323
Cultural monism, 62

D

Dahomey, 85, 88, 91, 154, 167, 172, 177
Dan Fodio, Usman, 167
Dasuki Committee, 28
Delta, 12, 16, 17, 19, 74, 121, 122, 139, 141, 147, 148, 152, 161, 166, 169, 172, 173, 176, 241, 242, 244, 254, 305, 315, 325, 329, 332, 350
Delta State, 12, 16, 18, 19, 139, 148, 242, 315, 329, 332, 350
Dennis Memorial Grammar School, 206, 307, 329
Diaspora Igbo, 130
Dike, Kenneth Onwuka, 324, 325, 330, 349
Diobu, 74
Diop, Cheik Anta, 157
Dispersion era, 80
Dr Sir Warrior, 59
Dunbar Creek, 124

E

Earth Goddess, 36, 58, 101
East Africa, 27, 99, 158, 173
East Central State, 28, 200, 220, 221
Ebighgbo, Chris, 37, 64, 364
Eboes, 15, 123, 125, 279
Ebonyi, 17, 19, 85, 147, 221, 241, 242, 244, 311
Edo, 16, 17, 18, 52, 69, 74, 84, 88, 89, 92, 102, 106, 139, 140, 147, 154, 168, 176, 305, 363, 364
Efik, 16, 125, 140, 141, 142, 144, 145, 146, 166, 168, 236, 346, 363
Egerton, Walter, 178, 222
Egungun, 91, 155, 160
Egyptian Pyramids, 105
Ejeagha, Mike, 59
Eke Avurugo Community, 18
Eke Okpokri, 18
Ekpeye, 17, 19, 142, 347
Ekwensu, 37, 71
Ekwueme, Alex, 218, 230, 231, 242
Emeagwali, Phillip, 26
Enahoro, Anthony, 184, 213, 225
Enu kwudo ana kwudo, 23
Enugu, 17, 19, 30, 32, 64, 82, 83, 85, 86, 87, 89, 134, 146, 147, 148, 150, 152, 179, 181, 196, 197, 198, 199, 200, 201, 208, 221, 222, 241, 242, 244, 245, 248, 252, 253, 254, 257, 268, 291, 292, 296, 303, 304, 308, 309, 310, 311, 315, 339, 348, 360, 363, 364, 365, 366, 367, 368
Enugu Metropolis, 86
Equatorial Guinea, 17, 111
Equiano, Olaudah, 15, 72, 102, 121, 275
Eri Temple, 75
Etche, 17, 92, 142, 347
Ethiopia, 74, 76, 79, 162, 177
European colonialism, 40, 61, 87
European history, 131
Evil forest, 37
Eze, 21, 22, 24, 25, 26, 31, 36, 47, 74, 78, 87, 150, 151, 152, 153, 154, 160, 168, 224, 311, 359, 365

Ezeagu, 86, 87, 195, 292, 365

F

Fajuyi, Francis Adekunle, 191, 314, 318
Fanon, Frantz, 63, 181, 365
FernandoPo, 17
Fernando Po, 171, 331
G

Gabon, 17
Germany, 172, 173, 245, 250, 297
Ghana, 159, 177, 182, 187, 191, 210, 223, 245, 280, 289, 300, 315, 317, 319, 324
Glover, Sir John, 111, 174
Goldie, George Taubman, 171, 173, 174
Gospel., 64
Gowon, Yakubu, 191, 192, 195, 197, 199, 200, 215, 217, 218, 220, 221, 222, 313, 316, 318, 319
Green Eagles, 200
Guatemala, 117
Gwari, 161

H

Haiti, 112, 117, 121, 122, 126, 134, 171, 276, 277, 278, 279, 351
Haitian Revolution, 122, 275, 276
Hammadi, Nag, 93, 94, 101
Hausa, 28, 33, 61, 62, 69, 107, 108, 161, 166, 167, 174, 184, 185, 205, 206, 208, 209, 212, 213, 217, 218, 242, 298, 315
Hausa/Fulani, 28, 33, 61, 62, 184, 185, 218, 242
Herodotus, 82
Highlife music, 59
Hispaniola, 117
Honduras, 117
Hope Waddell College, Calabar, 323

Horton, James Africanus Beale, 235, 238, 279, 280, 281, 282
Human Genome Diversity Project, 159

I

Ibaji, 18
Ibiam, Francis Akanu, 235, 237, 239, 311, 312, 313, 323
Ibibio, 16, 140, 141, 143, 144, 145, 166, 168, 234, 293, 346, 364, 367
Ibos, 15, 16, 126, 127, 225, 345, 363
Idigo, M.C.M, 77, 365
Idoma, 16, 69, 88, 92, 106, 140, 146, 147, 161, 166, 212
Idu, 22, 25, 70, 84, 85, 88, 89, 90, 91, 154, 156, 157, 158, 365
Igala, 16, 69, 74, 76, 77, 78, 80, 88, 91, 102, 106, 140, 146, 147, 148, 149, 153, 157, 159, 160, 161, 364
Igalamela, 18
Igbanke/Igboakiri, 18
Igbira, 69, 85, 88
Igbo Apprenticeship System, 50
Igbo calendar, 52, 60
Igbo detractors, 11
Igbo Enwe Eze, 21, 22, 367
Igbo justice system, 40
Igbo Kola nut, 45
Igbo mythology, 56
Igbo National Assembly, 240
Igbo Question in Nigeria, 245
Igbo spirit, 112, 351, 352, 353, 354
Igbo State Union, 209, 234, 236, 237, 238, 239, 240, 241
Igboid, 15, 18, 107, 140, 142, 357
Igbo-Israeli apologists, 71
Igbo-Jewish historical connections, 76
Igboness, 12, 15, 61, 108, 151
Igbo-Ukwu, 76, 91, 156, 366
Igbu ichi, 44
Igede, 69
Ihetu, Richard, 320

Ijaw, 16, 52, 74, 88, 140, 141, 145, 161, 166, 169, 343, 346, 360
Ijebu-Ode, 89
Ika, 18, 19, 143
Ikeja Airport, 40
Ikenga, 51, 52, 53, 54, 55, 126, 157, 240
Ikoku, Alvan, 323, 324
Ikoli, Ernest, 182, 223
Ikwerre, 17, 19, 142, 347
Imo, 17, 19, 28, 30, 31, 85, 141, 142, 219, 221, 230, 241, 244, 249, 286, 295, 307, 367
Indigenisation Decree, 216
Indigenous People of Biafra, 240, 242, 251, 253, 255, 257, 264
Indigenous Peoples of Biafra) or MASSOB, 219
Indirect Rule, 27, 180, 293
International HapMap Project, 159
Iron Age, 97
Ironsi, Aguiyi, 190, 313, 316, 318
Isiagụ, 59
Isichei, Elizabeth, 86, 87, 365
Isichie, Elizabeth, 26
Isobo, 18
Isu, 22, 25, 107, 158
Ita, Eyo, 176, 182, 223, 227, 304, 308

Ị

Ịgba Boyi, 50
Ịmụ Ahịa, 50

J

Jamaica, 111, 117, 118, 120, 121, 122, 125, 127, 128, 274
Jean-Charles, Moise, 134
Jeffreys, M.D.W, 53, 157
Jewish ancestry of the Igbo, 70
Jones, G. I., 83, 222, 321, 351
Jubogha, Jubo, 143, 286

K

Kabbalah, 100
Kalabari, 140, 141, 142, 145, 206
Kalu, Paulson, 59
Kano, 85, 167, 175, 179, 185, 197, 201, 205, 214, 218, 219, 224, 248, 269, 270, 313, 314, 318, 367
Kanu, Nnamdi, 242, 253, 254, 255, 256, 257, 258
Kikuyu, 162
kindreds, 19
King Jaja of Opobo, 288
Kogi states, 17
Komo River, 17
Kyoto University, 159

L

Lagos Youth Movement, 182, 223
Lake Chad, 85, 166
live and let live, 23
Long Juju of Aruchukwu, 152
Louisiana, 122, 285
Lower Niger Valley, 79
Lugard, Lord Frederick, 27, 177, 178, 180

M

Macaulay, Herbert, 182, 183, 222, 223, 224, 225, 300, 301
Mafra, 17
Mandinka, 18
Maroon Village, 111
Marshariki Bantus, 162
Masquerades, 44
MASSOB, 240, 246, 247, 248, 249, 250, 251, 252, 254, 264
Mbarga, Prince Nico, 59
Mbari architecture, 58
Mediterranean Sea, 76, 79
Meek, C.K., 81, 366
Metal Age, 97, 104, 105
Methodist Boys' High School, Oron, 146
Middle Belt zone, 139
Middle East, 69, 70, 73, 84, 88, 99
Mighty Jets, 200
Montego Bay, 111
Movement for the Actualisation of the Sovereign State of Biafra, 219, 249, 264
Murtala/Obasanjo military regime, 221

N

Napoleonic Wars, 170
National African Company, 173, 174
National Council of Nigeria and the Cameroons, 182, 223, 300, 306
National Council of Nigerian Citizens, 182
National Union of Nigerian Students, 182
Native Courts, 26, 27, 28
Ndigbo, 15, 42, 133, 209, 240, 241, 242, 243, 244, 246, 253, 257, 258, 263
Ndokwa, 16, 18
Ndoni, 17, 19
New World, 114, 115, 117, 169, 275
New Yam Festival, 38, 48, 367
Niger-Congo, 15, 69, 99, 140, 147
Nigeria National Alliance, 188
Nigeria-Biafra war, 135, 197, 199, 217, 220, 221, 254, 263, 270
Nigerian Civil War, 12, 311, 312, 364
Nigerian National Democratic Party, 182, 186, 222
Nigerian Peoples Party, 230, 242
Nigerian Youth Movement, 182, 184, 223, 300
Nkrumah, Kwame, 132
Nnoli, Okwudiba, 191, 210, 212, 238
Nok hypothesis, 91, 156
Nollywood, 65, 112, 127
Northern and Southern Protectorates, 38, 178, 180

Northern People's Congress, 184, 227
Northern Protectorate, 174, 177, 178, 179
Nri, 16, 22, 23, 24, 25, 60, 69, 72, 74, 75, 76, 77, 78, 80, 96, 102, 126, 148, 154, 158, 168, 175, 366, 367
Nsude pyramids, 82, 83
Nsukka, 17, 19, 36, 74, 77, 81, 85, 86, 92, 97, 104, 105, 106, 149, 208, 217, 218, 222, 303, 312, 316, 330, 350, 363, 366
Nwa Boyi, 51
Nwaezeigwe, Nwankwo, 76, 78, 366
Nwajala, 18
Nwala, Timothy Uzodinma, 245
Nwa-nshi, 100
Nweje, Hezekiah Okoro, 333
Nyong River, 17
Nzeogwu, Patrick Chukwuma Kaduna, 315, 316, 318

O

Oba Kosoko, 171
Obama, Barack, 133, 135
Obatala, 91, 154, 155, 158, 160
Obatala group, 91, 154
Obi, Z. C, 19, 26, 31, 75, 143, 153, 162, 237, 291, 325, 326, 327, 332, 349
Obigbo, 17, 139
Obollo-Afor, 147
Obollo-Eke, 146, 147
Obosi,, 19
Oduduwa, 69, 88, 89, 91, 155, 156, 160, 161, 183, 224, 227, 239
Ogba, 17, 19, 142
Ogbalu, Frederick Chidozie, 328
Ogbanje, 36
Ogbaru, 19, 148
Ogbomosho, 89
Ogidi, 25, 85, 327
Ogoni, 16, 74, 293, 343, 346
Ogunwusi, Oba Adeyeye, 90, 162
Oguta, 23, 80, 141, 291
Ohafia, 19

Oil Rivers Irregulars, 174
Oji Awusa, 46
Ojike, Mbonu, 62, 237, 239, 306, 307, 308, 309
Ojukwu, Dim Chukwuemeka Odumegwu, 162, 192, 193, 194, 195, 198, 199, 231, 254, 265, 303, 310, 316, 317, 318, 319, 326
Okigbo, Pius, 241, 360
Okigwe, 26, 74, 86, 92, 103, 104, 105
Okonjo-Iweala, Ngozi, 332
Okorie-Egbe, Nnete, 293
Okoro, Ogbonnaya, 149
Okoye, Mokwugo, 71, 225, 367
Okpara, Michael, 220, 222, 241, 309, 310, 311
Okpogho, 87, 88
Old Testament, 28, 72, 97
Oliver De Coque, 59
Omeruah, Sampson Emeka, 65
Omuma, 17
Onicha-Olona, 26, 89
Onicha-Ugbo, 26, 89
Onicha-Ugwu, 89
Onisa-Agbede, 89
Onitsha, 12, 19, 23, 25, 26, 64, 80, 86, 89, 106, 148, 153, 154, 162, 179, 196, 206, 291, 292, 296, 299, 300, 303, 304, 307, 311, 325, 326, 329, 331, 333, 334, 337, 339, 340, 341, 345, 363, 364
Onu, Ogbonnaya, 230
Onwu, Simon, 176, 235, 296, 297, 330
Onwuejeogwu, Michael Angulu, 63, 77, 104, 105, 106, 367
Onwuka, Benjamin, 251, 253
Onwumechili, Cyril, 20, 207, 349, 367
Onye kwe, Chi ya ekwe, 38
Onyeama N'Eke, 176, 290, 292
Onyeama, Charles Dadi Umeha, 176, 224, 290, 291, 292, 296, 319, 320
Ooni of Ife, 79, 90, 155, 162, 291
Opobo, 17, 140, 142, 143, 172, 175, 180, 206, 286, 287, 288, 290, 293, 346, 347

Orizu, Abyssinia Akweke Nwafor, 237, 239, 301, 303, 304, 305, 308
Oru, 22, 25, 158, 161
Osadebay, Dennis Chukude, 235, 239, 305, 306
Osadebe, Osita, 59
Osekwenike, 18
Oshimili, 18, 350
Osu, 23, 111, 112
Owerri, 58, 64, 74, 179, 206, 295, 348, 363, 365, 367
Oyi, 148
Oyo, Oyo Orok, 85, 89, 154, 160, 161, 167, 168, 179, 199
Ozara, 18
Ozo title, 16
Ozoemena Nwa Nsugbe, 59

Ọ

Ọdanduli stream, 77
Ọmabala River, 74
Ọmabala Valley, 79
Ọzọ title, 20, 24, 42, 43, 54, 57, 291

P

Patois language, 111
Persia, 81
Pope John Paul II, 337, 339, 340, 341
Prefect of the Congregation for Divine Worship and the Discipline of the Sacraments, 339

Q

Quenites, 97

R

Reconstruction, Rehabilitation and Reconciliation, 215, 216
Reincarnation, 37
Richards' Constitution, 180, 302

River Niger, 16, 17, 25, 73, 89, 153, 154, 165, 167, 196, 242, 273
Rivers, 17, 19, 73, 74, 139, 142, 145, 146, 162, 174, 177, 179, 241, 242, 244, 286, 343, 344, 345, 346, 347
Royal African Company, 170
Royal Niger Company, 174, 175, 176, 177
Roye, Edward James, 111, 285, 286

S

Sahara Desert, 166
Sarduana of Sokoto, 175, 184, 228
Shaw, Flora, 56, 102, 103, 177, 367
Shuwa-Arabs, 166, 177
Sierra Leone, 19, 122, 171, 235, 274, 280, 281, 283, 284, 285, 297, 298, 324, 330, 331
Sklar, Richard L., 239
South Carolina, 122, 125
Southern Rhodesia, 177
St. Anne's Bay, 111
Stepp Pyramid of Saqqara in Egypt, 83
Stone Technology, 104
Supreme Deity, 36

T

Tansi, Cyprian Michael Iwene, 333, 334, 335, 336, 337, 338, 339
The Igbo Lost Worlds, 35, 364
Things Fall Apart, 35, 38, 41, 45, 71, 327, 363
Togo, 91, 154, 173, 247
Town Union, 32, 33
Trans-Atlantic slave trade, 63
True Whig Party, 285

U

Ubulie-Umueze, 18
Ukwu, Celestine, 26, 59, 148
Ukwuani, 18, 19, 89
Uli, 57, 58, 59, 197

Umuahia, 19, 74, 198, 206, 258, 293, 294, 310, 311, 313, 327, 332, 360
Umuezekaoha, 18
Umuoye, 18
Unification Decree No. 34, 190
United African Company, 173
United Nations Educational, Scientific, and Cultural Organisation, 62
United Progressive Grand Alliance, 188
United States of America, 35, 62, 63, 64, 112, 113, 116, 118, 121, 124, 125, 126, 129, 130, 132, 133, 134, 169, 170, 176, 244, 245, 265, 275, 297, 306
University of Frankfurt, 97
Urhobo-Isoko, 16
Uwazuruike, Ralph, 246, 247, 250, 254
Uyo province, 143

Ụ

Ụmụdiana, 77, 78
Ụmụnri, 76, 78

V

Voodoo, 62

W

Warrant Chiefs, 27, 28, 293, 294, 295, 363
Wawa, 19, 97, 291
West Africa, 18, 56, 59, 63, 73, 74, 81, 87, 97, 98, 100, 111, 113, 114, 115, 121, 157, 159, 170, 173, 177, 276, 280, 281, 282, 283, 285, 286, 287, 288, 290, 299, 304, 323, 324, 364
West African Frontier Force, 175, 313, 315, 317
West Indies, 63, 112, 113, 118, 119, 121, 123, 129, 130, 132, 143, 170, 273, 274, 282, 289, 290
Western Europe, 35, 62, 64
Wolof, 18
Women's August meeting, 49
World Igbo Congress, 133, 240, 244

Y

Yahweh, 94, 95
Yoruba, 18, 22, 26, 28, 33, 36, 37, 61, 62, 64, 69, 79, 88, 89, 90, 91, 92, 106, 107, 108, 140, 154, 155, 156, 157, 158, 159, 160, 161, 162, 166, 167, 168, 176, 183, 184, 185, 205, 207, 208, 209, 212, 214, 217, 218, 223, 224, 225, 231, 234, 236, 238, 291, 298, 300, 303, 363

Z

Zikist Movement, 224, 225, 226, 227, 301, 310
Zimbabwe, 177, 189

www.ingramcontent.com/pod-product-compliance
Lightning Source LLC
Chambersburg PA
CBHW050900240426
43673CB00049B/1944